DEDICATION

TO MY MOTHER, WHO COULD USE A DRINK FOR HAVING
BEEN BLESSED WITH ME.

-STEPHEN

Adult language is contained in this book and is
intended for consumers of legal age.

PRINTED IN AMERICA

Copyright © 1994, 1996, 1997, 1998, 2000   B.B.B. S.K.C.
2001, 2002, 2003, 2004, 2005
SEVENTH EDITION

1ST	PRINTING	JUNE	2004
2ND	PRINTING	SEPT.	2004
3RD	PRINTING	OCT.	2004
4TH	PRINTING	NOV.	2004
5TH	PRINTING	APRIL	2005
6TH	PRINTING	AUG.	2005

TABLE OF CONTENTS:

Bartending Commandments

I. If there is *any possible way* a piece of broken glass may have flown into your ice, stop making drinks, melt all of the ice and clean all areas that could be harboring glass fragments.

Clean from the highest elevation toward the floor. Check surrounding bar surface, fruit trays, bottle tops, mixers, glassware and speed racks for glass fragments.

It's better to be safe than sorry. Toss the garnishes if there is any question of their safety. Only after a thorough cleaning do you replace the old ice.

II. If someone has come into your establishment who has had too much to drink, *DO NOT GIVE THEM ANOTHER DRINK*. Show them the door. Give them coffee. Feed them. Call the cops. Do whatever you want, just, *DO NOT GIVE THEM ANOTHER DRINK!*

III. If somebody is not of legal drinking age, *DO NOT GIVE THEM AN ALCOHOLIC BEVERAGE.*

If you suspect someone is not the legal drinking age, and they cannot come up with a legal form of identification (Driver's license, passport, Military ID, etc.) *DO NOT GIVE THEM AN ALCO-HOLIC BEVERAGE.*

If 10 people swear on their mothers' graves, it doesn't matter. If someone says "I am this person's parent, and I said it is all right if they want a drink" the answer is "NO".

As a bartender at an establishment or a house party you can be charged criminally if you give alcohol to a minor.

YOU JUST OPENED THE MOST IMPORTANT
DRINK BOOK OF OUR TIME

THE BARTENDER'S BLACK BOOK™ – 7TH EDITION

A MESSAGE TO OUR READERS

What makes THE BARTENDER'S BLACK BOOK™ unique from all other recipe guides on the market is that the book is updated on a yearly basis. Look for Mr. Parker's "Vintage Guide" and "The World's Greatest Wine Values" to be updated at the same time.

At that time, the latest recipes and new sections will be added to THE BARTENDER'S BLACK BOOK™ in order to keep the book current. Thank you for purchasing this edition of THE BARTENDER'S BLACK BOOK™.

The Publisher

NOTES FOR THE AMATEUR BARTENDER

If you are a AMATEUR BARTENDER, Here are some things you need. Everything listed is relatively cheap, except for the blender.

Speed pourers - Plastic or metal. They are cheap and essential. Every bar uses them. Always save the caps, bottle stoppers and a few corks. Depending on how fast you empty bottles and how often bottles are used, I recommend that after a party or lost weekend, you take out speed pourers and replace the caps. This will help keep the flavor and integrity of the bottled goods. Plus, it will keep out fruit flies which like to kill themselves in available open bottles. After use, soak your speed pourers overnight in soda water or soapy water. Do not put pourers in bottles of expensive cognacs, rare malt scotches or other high-end liquids.

Mixing Glass - 16oz. You need a couple to start. Shaker glass is the proper name, but people refer to them as a Boston shaker or pint glasses. Very versatile, you will be mixing your Martinis and shooters in these. Heck, you can make coffee drinks and serve beer in them as well. As a matter of fact, if you are just getting your act together go buy a dozen.

Strainers - indispensable for Martinis and shots. Buy two. The smallest bar should have two. Then when you get good you can strain 2 drinks at the same time. You should be rinsing these off between different drinks

Shaker Tin - you need at least one of these to start. You need to shake almost 75% of the most popular drinks today, and you can't shake a White Russian and then shake up a Tom Collins without cleaning the shaker. So, more is better. In busy bars many bartenders will line up shaker tins, designating one for milk or cream based drinks, one for Sour Mix/Lime Juice drinks, one for Martinis, etc., etc. Here is a tip: Some large plastic cups fit over your mixing glass quite well. I bet you have some in your cupboard.

Bar Spoon - a good one is 12"-16" long (30.48 cm-40.64 cm) with or without a spiral handle with a teaspoon or smaller size bowl. You are going to need this to make Classic Martinis, and to float different ingredients on top of each other.

Bar rag - anything will do. Just have something absorbent at the ready in case of a tragic drink spill.

Measurer/Jigger - You are going to need this until you have a consistent, trained eye. You will be ruining mixed drinks and wasting your alcohol if you don't take heed. I have 20+ years drink pouring experience, and I still measure some of the more delicate recipes.

Corkscrew/bottle opener - You can get by with a waiter's corkscrew which will have a corkscrew, bottle opener and a knife, but if you can find a nice heavy bottle opener at a restaurant supply store, get it.

Glassware, Mixing Glasses, Martini Glasses, Snifters, Lowball, Highball, Beer Glasses Wine Glasses, Champagne Glasses , Irish Coffee Glasses, Collins, Margarita Glasses, etc., etc. - Know your crowd. If this is a bar in a hunting lodge in the woods and everyone who goes there drinks bourbon and bottled beer, then all you need are enough lowballs/rocks glasses to go around. If this is a small apartment where everyone is going to be drinking Martinis and champagne, then you will need those glasses plus the mixing glasses.

Here are a couple things to keep in mind while equipping your bar.
1. Mixing glasses (shakers) can be used for beer and can double as highballs as well.
2. Instead of white wine glasses and red wine glasses find a glass you like that is in-between the two (medium mouthed).

A sharp knife and a cutting board - You can probably get by using a nice steak knife to cut your garnishes, but you would be better off with a paring knife or a small utility knife. Cutting boards come either in wood or plastic. The plastic ones can go through the dishwasher.

Blender - Nothing can cool you down and impress a guest like a nice frozen drink. There are150 awesome frozen drink recipes in this book, most of which you will find in no other book. My only advice here is if you are going to go out and buy a blender, go to a place that supplies restaurants and get a heavy duty 2 speed. They tend to last a lot longer than the domesticated ones that they market to homeowners. Buy an extra jar, blades and gaskets, and keep it clean and it should last for decades.

NOTES FOR THE PROFESSIONAL BARTENDER

If you are a PROFESSIONAL BARTENDER, I am going to assume you know everything I was directing to the AMATEUR previous.

So what does the Professional Bartender need? Customers and good ones. Good customers are groomed from people who just happened to be lucky enough to have come in contact with you. They come in every shape, color, size, background, social status.

A trained monkey can make a drink, you have to do more. You have to make people feel at ease, feel welcomed, feel appreciated, feel like leaving you a big tip and feel like coming back to do it again. Some people you can never win over. I hate to say it, but there are some truly miserable people walking the earth, and they could sit at your bar. They have sat at mine.

Your "Act" is totally personal. Some people are unhappy behind the bar. Even if they paste on a smile it doesn't work, they are not the money makers. The money makers like people, and they like themselves. They have fun while they work, they rise to meet the craziness that is inherent to the business. They treat everyone with the respect they deserve; they even treat people with respect if they don't deserve it. In my days of bar management, I would value personality as much as experience when hiring. It is easier to train a nice person to bar tend than to train a bartender to be nice.

You need to show some interest in peoples lives and or business or lifestyles. Find out what they do and where they do it. Now, I know there are people who will not want to share any with you, but there are far more that would like to interact. I know sometimes you are so busy mixing drinks that you can't have a meal, smoke, have a drink of water, or scratch an itch. So how do you interact with your customers then? With few words, with facial expressions, with hand gestures. One key thing to be able to do is to get people to interact with each other. Time is a premium when it is busy. If you can spark interaction between a couple of people sitting alone at the bar, that does two things it engages two people that were strangers a minute ago, and it frees you up to do something else.

And one more thing. Every once in a while you need to hook up people who come in consistently to spend their money with a free drink or a free dessert or an appetizer. But, always check with the boss before doing this, unless you have the authority to make those decisions.

THINGS A BARTENDER NEEDS
TO HAVE FOR EACH SHIFT

Lighter: nothing makes you look as on the ball as having the flame at the right time.

Wine Key: Get a decent folding one with a screw and a knife.

Bottle Opener: Experienced bartenders carry a heavy bottle opener. You tend to have more broken bottle neck mishaps with crappy light gauge bottle openers. It's a leverage thing.

Mints: They are for you and your guests. When someone is going to meet someone, offer one. Or offer your coworkers one when getting yourself one.

Secret: I always keep sweet hard candy at the service bar/waitress station. First of all they will dig that you put them out for them, and if you get a kiss from them, it will be that much sweeter.

Cigar Cutter: You want one with two opposing blades; they keep an edge. If you see someone take out a cigar, you could place it in a short glass in front of them, or just state, "I've got a cutter if you want to use it," or "I'll cut that for you if you want."

Pens: For phone numbers, for writing on tabs/bills. You need at least two.

A Smile: Nobody wants to be greeted with a frown...silly.

A Joke: I always keep a joke for the men and a joke I could tell my mother committed to memory.

Sense of Humor: Everybody thinks they have a sense of humor. Make sure you have a good one and keep it with you at all times.

Knowledge: People are going to turn to you for all kinds of knowledge. You don't need to commit an encyclopedia to memory, but you should know a few things:

— You should know what times the local ball games start.
— You should know a place where a traveler can get a cheeseburger or a salad at 2 AM.
— You should know where someone could go to dance, or to hear jazz, or to play a game of pool.
— You should know the quickest way to the Hospital/Police Station/Airport.
— You should know where the cool kids hang or where the socially elite gather to cut loose.
— You should know where there might be a romantic spot where lovers could go for a stroll or to gaze into each other's eyes.

You are not just a bartender, you are a referee, you are the catalyst for a good time, you are the face and voice of your establishment, and of your city for that matter. People should be leaving your establishment saying, "What a great place. That bartender was the best."

And you should be friendly with bar staff at all the gin joints in the immediate area. Bartenders with good relationships borrow things from each other (booze, fruit, glasses); they send each other customers, as well as warn one another about possible trouble (drunken idiots, police raids, angry mobs).

BAR INSIGHT FOR CUSTOMERS

If you are a CUSTOMER here is some insight from a bartender. You have no idea what a bartender has to deal with.

Some nights are long. Some nights are crazy. Some nights you are still smiling when your head hits the pillow.

Here are some crazy things I have had to deal with in my career:

An owner would be drinking at my bar before I opened and was still drinking when I left eight hours later. I personally counted 46 beers that went down his throat in one evening. And he rarely tipped, and it was never copasetic when he did...

A disgruntled customer who I had shut off earlier in the night meeting me outside after a shift in a revving truck aimed in my direction.

Being asked very politely and timidly by an elderly woman if I would help her husband who seemed to be choking on his steak. I had to Heimlich him.

A Hugely Famous Rock Star whacked on drugs and smashed on booze telling me "This is the worst party I have ever been to; this place sucks," after I asked if he was having a good time.

A cop reaching over the bar, pouring himself a beer.

Watching a fellow bartender lean over an uncovered running blender wearing a tie, and watching him turn blue and horrified.

Wait staff walking behind the bar and pouring themselves drinks or walking out of the restaurant with a bottle of booze.

Being one of two bartenders who showed up to work on a five person shift.

I have personally put out seven trash can fires which other care-less bartenders started.

Working in a seasonal Yacht club that would have power outages every time you ran the
Blender and the kitchen fans at the same time, this would disable the cash register; kill the refrigerators, and all the lights.

A gentleman who would take all the waitresses to his house after closing and keep the girls up partying until daylight, often missing their shifts the next day... wait a minute... that was me.

Walk outs/ Chew and Screws. Who do you think pays for that?

PLEASE:

If you need our attention, eye contact and/or a simple slight hand gesture work best.

Realize we know who is next. Wait patiently until we can get to you.

Have your order ready (especially for groups) before we give you our attention. If I am finally ready to take your group's order, and you turn to ask your friends what they want, there is a good chance I will be gone when you turn back around.
Have your stuff ready, order all your drinks at once. A good bartender will remember 4-10 drinks.

Have your money ready. We don't want to waste our precious time watching you dust and check bills three times before you hand it to us. That makes everybody else who wants our attention wait.

And Tip, Please Tip. SEE Being a Good Tipper, Page 12

PLEASE DON'T:

Snap fingers, yell, jump up and down waving your arms like you are marooned and you see a rescue helicopter, or whistle (we may ignore you completely or just shut you off).

Shout out a drink order unless we have asked you what you want.

Shout out my name if I don't know who you are. My friends who visit me while I am working don't shout out my name unless there is an emergency.

Monopolize a bartender's time. Sometimes we are ringing in To Go orders, ringing in employee meals, doing the cash transactions for the whole restaurant, making the drinks for the whole restaurant, running a lottery machine, restocking everything from beer, fruit, glassware, wine, booze, silverware, to ice, sometimes we take the deliveries from the purveyors (up to 20 or more deliveries in a day). And we often do not get 5 minutes to sit down and eat during a 8-16 hour shift. That third time you sent me after condiments for that $3 cheeseburger just took up my bathroom break . . . you'll be waiting for your next beer buddy.

Being a Good Tipper

tip. noun. 1. An extra sum of money given to someone for services rendered; gratuity.

Just in case this is being viewed by someone unfamiliar with inner workings of the Restaurant/Hospitality industry, many people rely on tips for their livelihood. Many people -- including myself -- receive a wage below the minimum wage. That's right -- $2 or $3 something an hour. Our favorite customers leave us 20% on upwards of their entire bill or $2 or $20 every round. Some of the favorite tips I've received over my 20+ years in the business have been $50 for two drinks, the Benjamin handshake, a Rolling Stones ticket, a day boating, a pinball machine, chinese food, homemade brownies and phone numbers.

Bill	Tip	Bill	Tip	Bill	Tip	Bill	Tip
$20	$4	$60	$12	$100	$20	$300	$60
$30	$6	$70	$14	$125	$25	$400	$80
$40	$8	$80	$16	$150	$30	$500	$100
$50	$10	$90	$18	$200	$40	$1000	$200

This chart is to show you how to make a bartender or server happy. If two of more bartenders or servers waited on you, don't worry; they are probably pooling their tips.

Never give a tip designated for wait staff to a manager. Many times the wait staff never sees it, especially for weddings and private parties.

If you made special requests of your bartender or you want to make a friend, feel free to over tip!!!

If you are cheap, *please, please, please,* stay home and drink.

Bartenders remember good tippers and they remember bad tippers. Bad tippers can look forward to bad service, weak drinks, and being waited on when we get around to it. You could very well be taking up space that could be filled by a good tipper. If you are feeling as if your presence is unwanted, it very well might be so.

INTERNAL TIPPING

How tipping works between bartenders and fellow employees

Who is tipping the bartenders?

Besides the public asking you for drink and/or food, you may very well have 5-50 wait staff taking up a big percentage of your time during your shift. Maybe they are taking up all your time.

For alcoholic drinks alone you should be receiving 10% minimum of the waitresses tips or 5% of their gross drink sales. The more you do for them the more it should go up. Are you doing all the money transactions? Pouring sodas and tonics? Making cappuccinos? They should be taking care of you better. If you did not get them any drinks, or help them at all, you should not be taking any of the waitstaff's money.

Cocktail waitresses are usually tight with their bartenders. They generate a way better than average tip percentage compared to a waitress due to the situation. The cocktail waitress's people turn over quickly, and are looking for fast service. They are not looking for drawn out or elaborate eating.

The cocktail waitress's needs should be taken care of with the same urgency as your own bar customers. A good cocktail waitress will address your needs as if they were her own. If she is near the kitchen and sees food for the bar in the window, she will bring it up for you. She will restock the drinking straws and tell you when trouble is afoot. And you should be doing the same for her. She should be tipping you out 15% of her tips or more, but at the same time, you should be treating her like gold.

*If you are not being taken care of for your work by a waitstaff member, bring it to the managers' attention. They have every right to hand out walking papers to staff members who don't play by the rules. Honey, if you are not spreading the wealth to your support staff (bartenders, buspeople, food runners, etc.) get out of the industry. You don't belong here. Every time we see you walk into work, you make us sick.

Who is the bartender tipping?

Bar backs or bus people that help the bar specifically by doing things the bartender would otherwise have to do. Examples: cut fruit for garnishes, get ice, carry out needed product (beer, wine, juices), change syrup for sodas/tonics, running to the store to get you lottery tickets and cigarettes, running food, taking out the trash.

Food runners - some restaurants have a specific person running food to the tables and the bar. You need to take care of that person accordingly. A good gauge could be a dollar a trip, or 10% of the bars tips.

Maybe you didn't sell that much food, at least give that person a couple bucks.

Maybe they worked hard, poured your soup, cut your bread, and garnished the plates. Don't be shy; tip this person well and then buy them a drink.

Money can buy you popularity and loyalty around a restaurant. If you don't take care of your fellow employees monetarily, they wouldn't tell you if you were on fire.

Weights and Measures
Beer Kegs

Kegs	U.S. gallons	Liters	U.S. oz.	12 oz.	16 oz.
20 Liter	5.3 gallons	20 liters	678 oz.	56	42
1/6 Keg	5.5 gallons	20.8 liters	704 oz.	58	44
1/4 Keg	7.75 gallons	29.3 liters	992 oz.	82	62
30 Liter	7.94 gallons	30 liters	1016 oz.	84	63
50 Liter	13.2 gallons	50 liters	1690 oz.	140	105
1/2 Keg	15.5 gallons	58.6 liters	1984 oz.	165	124

Wine Bottles

Bottles	Liters	U. S. oz.
Miniature	100ml	3.4
Split	187ml	6.3
Half Bottle	375ml	12.7
500ml	500ml	16.9
750ml or Standard Bottle	750ml	25.4
1 Liter	1 Liter	33.8
Magnum	1.5 Liters	50.7
Double Magnum or Jeroboam (Sparkling)	3 Liters	101.5
Rehoboam or Jeroboam (Reds)	4.5 Liters	152.2
Methuselah or Imperial	6 Liters	202.9
Salmanazar	9 Liters	304.4
Balthazar	12 Liters	405.8
Nebuchadnezzar	15 Liters	507.3

Standard bottle = 4 glasses   Case (12 bottles) = 48 glasses
1.5 Liter bottle = 8 glasses   Case (6 bottles) = 48 glasses

Liquor and Liqueur Bottles

Bottles	Liters	U. S. oz.
Nips or Miniatures	20- 50ml	3/4 - 1 3/4
100ml	100ml	3.4
200ml	200ml	6.8
500ml	500ml	16.9
750ml	750ml	25.4
1 Liter	1 Liter	33.8
1.75 Liter	1.75 Liters	59.2

Metric Conversion for our International Imbibers

U. S. oz.	Liters
tsp	5ml
2 tsp	10ml
Tblsp	15ml
1/4 oz	7.5ml
1/2 oz	15ml
3/4 oz	22.5ml
1 oz	3cl
1 1/2oz	4.5cl
2oz	6cl
4oz	12cl

MIXING

Pouring:

    The best way to get some practice would be to find yourself an empty liquor bottle, say an empty 1 liter Bacardi or Canadian Club bottle. If you don't have one, ask your friendly neighborhood bartender to put one aside for you. Fill it up with water, leaving the neck empty. Now pop in one of your new pourers. Let's stand in front of a sink, bottle next to sink. Now grab the bottle by the neck like a ski pole or like you might choke a chicken, making sure the pourer is aimed in the general direction of the sink.

    Lift the bottle off the counter and in a quick wrist-snapping motion turn the bottle upside down. When you have this action down you can progress to pouring into a jigger/measurer, Count to yourself as you pour so you know how many counts are an ounce (3cl), two ounces (6cl). When you think you have this mastered, set up 5 or 6 different kinds of glasses and free pour using your count. Then measure what you poured in each glass for accuracy.

    When you have that figured out, then you can touch your booze. You might want to have a little party/gathering when you are at this stage just because, if you are drinking all the mistakes alone, you are going to hurt yourself......and please send drunken pictures to: Bartendersblackbook@hotmail.com

Shaking:

Every drink that needs to be shaken -- and many that don't have to be shaken -- start in a mixing glass (shaker, Boston shaker, Pint). Before we start, make sure your mixing cup (tin or plastic) fits over your mixing glass. If it does, great, fill the mixing glass with ice and then water. Take the mixing cup, place it over the filled mixing glass, hold the glass still with one hand and give the bottom of the mixing cup a gentle tap. That should be all you need to secure them together (it creates a little vacuum). Now try pulling them apart gently and repeat the process a few times to get the feel of them together and apart. If they get stuck you need to tap the tin on the side against a sturdy edge like on a bar (do this with the cup on the bottom and the glass on top).

The Shake:

You have your ingredients in the glass. You have secured the mixing cup to the glass. Now pick them up, one hand on the glass, one hand on the cup, and let's get a little shaking going on. The trick is getting a little rhythm going. Try up and down like a piston in an engine. Try horizontally in front of yourself, in and out. Practice and choose whichever you feel better with (your fingers are going to go numb if you practice with ice)....and always keep in mind, the longer you shake a drink the more diluted from the melting ice it will become.

Open Cup Shake:

This is the proper way to mix a Bloody Mary. You make your cocktail to specs, by the recipe, and you pour with a little vigor into a large mixing cup and gently pour it back into the mixing glass. And remember to put your celery in the glass before you empty the mixing cup; if you don't, you'll know why real soon.

MIXING continued

Floating, Layering:
To make floating drinks, layered drinks, pousse-café, one must pour the heaviest liqueurs or liquors first, then slowly pour the lighter ones on top over the back of a spoon. If you have time to make drinks ahead of time you can refrigerate, and the individual ingredients will separate themselves in an hour or so.

NOTE: For more elaborate information on layering drinks and a gravity chart that shows the weights of various liqueurs, see the special "Shooters, Floaters and Layered Drinks" section, beginning on page 176.

Frosting and Chilling Glasses:
To chill a glass, if time permits simply place glasses in refrigerator for 5 minutes. If you don't have 5 minutes fill the glasses with ice and water, and let sit for 30 seconds.

To frost, you are going to need a freezer. Place glasses in freezer for 5-10 minutes. Leave them in a glass rack if there is ample room, and ask the chef if it is all right before you do it. You don't want anybody tripping over your frosting glasses, especially the cooks...they have sharp knives.

And never, never, never, put glasses in your well ice to chill. One chip and you are screwed.

Heating glasses:
Nothing is worse than craving and ordering a hot drink and getting a lukewarm drink.

If it is convenient, you can microwave the glass prior to making the drink in it.

I suggest filling the glass with hot water and letting it sit for 30-40 seconds. You can heat 10 at a time this way if you want.....the reverse chill.

Stirring:
You will not find bartenders in any high traffic restaurant stopping to stir a drink mid-rush except a traditional Martini or a Manhattan. Drinks that need to be mixed hard are either shaken or blended. There is little need to do anymore than get the ingredients in the glass for many cocktails. Gin and Tonics, Cape Codders, Scotch and Soda, Screwdriver, Rum and Cola, none of these type of drinks need to be stirred. You put a straw in it or a sip stick, the correct garnish, and that is it. Traditional Martinis and Manhattans on the other hand need to be stirred.

Muddling:
Muddle means to mash, jumble or mix. A muddler is no more than a wooden handle with a flat perpendicular end. Let's say you are making an Old Fashioned. Place an empty short glass on a flat surface and place the cherry, orange, sugar and bitters that need to be muddled into the glass. Grab your muddler and mash the four ingredients together with 4 to 7 downward movements. In a pinch I have used spoons, little flashlights and a nip bottle.

Straining:

I'm going to assume you have a strainer in your arsenal. It should fit over your mixing glass snugly. Why don't you turn to page 170 and look at SECRET #1 MARTINIS. You can practice your straining while you are perfecting your Martini pour in that exercise. All there is to it is a steady, sharp twist of the wrist. Practice with water. Your goal is to strain out every last drop and have it all come to a nice level in your martini glass, not too high, and not too low.

Later on you should be able to strain two drinks at the same time.

Flaming:

Any fluid with an alcohol concentration of 87 proof or greater will ignite if exposed to a direct flame. Many liquors as well as liqueurs of lesser proof will ignite if heated first and then exposed to direct flame. Caution, people have been maimed drinking flaming shots. A restaurant that I used to go to got sued because some idiot missed his mouth with a flaming shot and burned himself.

I would never recommend serving or drinking things that are on fire.

GARNISHES

Wash fresh fruit and vegetables thoroughly. Many are grown in foreign soil and may have been exposed to harmful insecticides.

Bananas: Ripe yellow cross sections of bananas make a colorful and stylish garnish. Before peeling and adding fresh banana to a blended drink, cut a 1/2-3/4 inch cross section from the middle. Then cut from the center through the peel. This should make it fit nicely onto the rim of a glass.

Celery: Always wash celery thoroughly. Cut off the base as well as the tips of the leaves, so that there is no discoloration, just healthy light green celery. When making a drink calling for celery as a garnish, make sure you leave room to accommodate the stick of celery. Keep celery in ice water, in a refrigerator until needed.

Cherries: Red Maraschino cherries are essential for adult drinks, as well as children's drinks. After opening the jar be sure to refrigerate.

Cinnamon: Ground cinnamon as well as cinnamon sticks are used in many recipes. It is easy to overpower a drink with cinnamon. Use ground cinnamon sparingly. In drinks calling for cinnamon sticks, leave whole unless specified. Long sticks can make excellent stirrers.

Cocktail Shrimp: Shrimp make delicious exotic garnish for drinks such as a Bloody Mary or a Red Snapper. Cook them as if they were for a shrimp cocktail, removing the black vein in the back. If shrimp, after cooking and waiting to be used become slimy, throw them away.

Coffee Beans: Coffee Beans are a traditional garnish for Sambuca drinks. Three beans represent Health, Wealth and Happiness.

Cucumber: Cut either into spears or wheels, cucumbers are a great garnish instead of, or in addition to celery for a Virgin Mary and other drinks of that nature. Wash thoroughly. Peeling is optional.

Lemons: *Wedges.* Cut off the ends of a lemon, then cut down the middle from flat end to flat end making two halves. Make a 1/4 inch incision in the center of the halves against the grain, then cut 3 or 4 equal sized wedges from the half. The tiny incision was made so your wedge will fit snugly on rim of glass.
    Twists. Cut off the ends of a lemon, then make 4 long lengthwise cuts into the rind (Be careful not to cut into the meat of the lemon). Soak lemon in hot tap water for 5 minutes. Separate the rind from the meat, and cut the rind into long 1/4 inch strips. When a twist is called for a drink, it should be twisted over the drink, then rubbed around the lip of the glass.

Limes: *Wedges.* Cut off the ends of a lime, then cut down the middle from flat end to flat end making two halves. Make a 1/4 inch incision in the center of the halves against the grain. Cut 3 or 4 equal sized wedges from the half. The tiny incision was made so your wedge will fit snugly on the rim of a glass.
    Wheels. Cut off the ends. Cut 1/6th inch cross sections. Cut the rind to allow a place to sit on the glass.

Olives: Green olives (with or without pimentos) are essential for martinis. Refrigerate after opening a fresh container.

Onions: Cocktail onions are the distinguishing difference between a Martini and a Gibson. They can be found in most grocery stores. Refrigerate after opening.

Oranges: Cut the ends off an orange. Cut down the middle from flat end to flat end. Cut half wheels across the grain approximately 1/6th inch thick. A slight pull on the the ends will allow you to sit it on the rim of the glass.

Pineapples: *Sticks*. Cut off the top, bottom and sides, making a solid block of pineapple meat. Cut this into equal sized sticks.
Wedges. Cut off the top and bottom, then quarter the pineapple the long way. Cut off the pointed inner part of quarter. Slice straight down the new flat smooth edge about a 1/4 inch deep. Then cut into 1/2 inch wedges.

Salt (Kosher): Salt is primarily used to rim glasses by moistening the glass with either water or fruit juice from a cut piece of fruit (lemon, lime, orange) and dipping the glass into the salt (which should be laid out in a dish or any contained flat surface).

Shaved Almonds: Commonly found in a cook's arsenal, they make a very appealing decoration for drinks with traces of Almond Liqueurs (Amaretto, Crème de Nouyax). Sprinkle them on whipped cream or float them on a creamy drink's surface.

Shaved Chocolate: A favorite at fancy establishments is freshly shaved dark chocolate. Just buy a block of chocolate and introduce it to your friendly cheese grater, and you are in business.

Sprinkles or Jimmies: Pleasant to the eye as well as the palate, they do justice to hot coffee drinks and many frozen concoctions. They are available at most convenience stores.

Strawberries: Fresh ripe strawberries enhance any drink containing berries or strawberry liqueur. Wash berries thoroughly. Cut large ones in two; leave small ones whole. Simply push a berry onto the rim of a glass until it fits snugly.

Whipped Cream: You can use either fresh or canned. Whipped cream is expected to top many hot drinks. If fresh whipped cream is used, you may want to add 1/2 tsp of sugar to your drink due to the fact that processed whipped cream is sweetened.

RECIPES A-Z

"Always carry enough money for a hotel room and a nice bottle of champagne . . . just in case"
— *Stephen Kittredge Cunningham*

A BAT AND A BALL
Whiskey and Beer)
Fill shot glass with American
Whiskey
Serve with a draft or bottle of
American Beer.

A-BOMB
Fill glass with ice.
1/2 oz Vodka or Orange Vodka
1/2 oz Coffee Liqueur
1/2 oz Irish Cream
1/2 oz Orange Liqueur
Shake.
Strain into shot glass.

ABBY ROAD
Fill glass with ice.
1 oz Amaretto
1 oz Black Raspberry Liqueur
1 oz Coffee Liqueur
Stir.

ABBY ROAD COFFEE
1 oz Amaretto
1 oz Black Raspberry Liqueur
1 oz Coffee Liqueur
Fill with hot Black Coffee.
Top with Whipped Cream.
Drizzle with Chocolate Syrup.

ABC (floater)
1/2 oz Amaretto (bottom)
1/2 oz Irish Cream
1/2 oz Orange Liqueur or Cognac
(top)

ABSINTHE COCKTAIL
Fill glass with ice.
1 1/2 oz Absinthe
1 1/2 oz Water
Dash of Bitters
Dash of Sugar Syrup
Shake.
Strain into chilled glass.

ABSINTHE DRIP COCKTAIL
1 or 2 oz Absinthe
Place slotted spoon or strainer
Holding sugar cube over glass.
Drip cold water over sugar until
it melts into drink.

ABSOLUTELY FABULOUS
Fill glass with ice.
2 oz Vodka or Citrus Vodka
1 oz Cranberry Juice
Shake. Strain into chilled glass.
Top with 1oz Champagne
Garnish with a twist.

ACAPULCO
Fill glass with ice.
1 oz Brandy
1 oz Gin
Dash of Grenadine
Dash of Sour Mix
Dash of Orange Juice
Fill with Ginger Ale.
Garnish with Orange and Cherry.

ACAPULCO GOLD
Fill glass with ice.
1 oz Tequila
1 oz Amber Rum
1 oz Cream of Coconut
1 oz Pineapple Juice
1 oz Grapefruit Juice
Shake.

ADIOS MOTHER aka
CODE BLUE
Fill glass with ice.
1/2 oz Vodka or Citrus Vodka
    or Orange Vodka
1/2 oz Rum
1/2 oz Tequila
1/2 oz Gin
1/2 oz Blue Curacao
Fill with Sour Mix.
Shake.

ADULT HOT CHOCOLATE aka
PEPPERMINT KISS,
COCOANAPPS, SNUGGLER
2 oz Peppermint Schnapps
Fill with Hot Chocolate.
Stir.
Top with Whipped Cream.
Sprinkle with Shaved
Chocolate or Sprinkles.

AFTER EIGHT (floater)
1/2 oz Coffee Liqueur (bottom)
1/2 oz White Crème de Menthe
1/2 oz Irish Cream (top)

AFTER FIVE (floater)
1/2 oz Coffee Liqueur (bottom)
1/2 oz Irish Cream
1/2 oz Peppermint Schnapps (top)

AFTER FIVE COFFEE
1/2 oz Coffee Liqueur
1/2 oz Irish Cream
1/2 oz Peppermint Schnapps
Fill with hot Black Coffee.
Top with Whipped Cream.
Sprinkle with Shaved
Chocolate or Sprinkles.

AFTERBURNER
Fill glass with ice.
1 oz Peppered Vodka
1 oz Cinnamon Schnapps
1 oz Coffee Liqueur
Shake.
Strain into shot glass.

AFTERBURNER 2
Fill glass with ice.
1/2 oz 151-Proof Rum
1/2 oz Jägermeister
1/2 oz Coffee Liqueur
Stir.
Strain into chilled glass.

AFTER SEX
Fill glass with ice.
1 1/2oz Vodka or Banana Vodka
1/2 oz Banana Liqueur
Fill with Orange Juice
Shake.
Top 1/4oz Grenadine

AGENT 99 (floater)
3/4 oz Orange Liqueur (bottom)
3/4 oz Blue Curacao
3/4 oz Sambuca or Ouzo (top)

AGENT O.
Fill glass with ice.
1/2 oz Vodka or Orange Vodka
1/2 oz Orange Liqueur
Fill with Orange Juice.
Shake.
Garnish with Orange.

AGGRAVATION aka TEACHER'S PET
Fill glass with ice.
1 oz Scotch
1 oz Coffee Liqueur
Fill with Milk or Cream.
Shake.

AIR GUNNER
Fill glass with ice.
2 oz Vodka or Citrus Vodka
Dash of Blue Curacao
1 oz Sour Mix
Shake and Strain into chilled glass.

ALABAMA
Fill glass with ice.
1 1/2 oz Brandy
1/2 oz Triple Sec
Fill with Sour Mix.
Shake.

ALABAMA SLAMMER
Fill glass with ice.
3/4 oz Vodka or Orange Vodka
3/4 oz Southern Comfort
3/4 oz Amaretto
Dash of Sloe Gin or Grenadine
Fill with Orange Juice.
Shake.
Garnish with Orange.

ALABAMA SLAMMER 2
Fill glass with ice.
1 oz Vodka
1 oz Southern Comfort
Dash of Sloe Gin or Grenadine
Fill with Orange Juice.
Shake.
Garnish with Orange.

ALABAMA SLAMMER 3
Fill glass with ice.
1 oz Southern Comfort
1 oz Amaretto
Dash of Sloe Gin or Grenadine
Fill with Orange Juice.
Shake.
Garnish with Orange.

ALABAMA SLAMMER 4
Fill glass with ice.
1/2 oz Southern Comfort
1/2 oz Triple Sec
1/2 oz Galliano
1/2 oz Sloe Gin
Fill with Orange Juice.
Shake.
Garnish with Orange.

ALABAMA SLAMMER 5
Fill glass with ice.
1/2 oz Whiskey
1/2 oz Southern Comfort
1/2 oz Amaretto
1/2 oz Sloe Gin
Fill with Orange Juice.
Shake.
Garnish with Orange.

ALABAMA SLAMMER (frozen)
In Blender:
1/2 cup of Ice
1 oz Vodka or Orange Vodka
1 oz Southern Comfort
Dash of Sloe Gin or Grenadine
Scoop of Orange Sherbet
Blend until smooth.
If too thick add Orange Juice.
If too thin add ice or sherbet.
Garnish with Orange.

ALASKAN ICED TEA
Fill glass with ice.
1/2 oz Vodka or Citrus Vodka
1/2 oz Gin
1/2 oz Rum
2 oz Blue Curacao
2 oz Sour Mix
Fill with Lemon-Lime Soda.
Garnish with Lemon.

ALBATROSS (frozen)
In Blender:
1 cup of Ice
1 oz Gin or Lime Gin
1 oz Melon Liqueur
1 Egg White
1 oz Lime Juice
Blend until smooth.

ALEXANDER
Fill glass with ice.
1 oz Gin
1 oz White or Dark Crème de Cacao
Fill with Milk or Cream.
Shake.

ALEXANDER THE GREAT
Fill glass with ice.
1 1/2 oz Greek Brandy
1/2 oz Dark Crème de Cacao
2 oz Milk or Cream
Shake.
Strain into chilled glass.

ALEXANDER'S SISTER
Fill glass with ice.
1 oz Gin
1 oz Green Crème de Menthe
Fill with Milk or Cream.
Shake.

ALGONQUIN
Fill glass with ice.
1 1/2 oz Whiskey
1 oz Dry Vermouth
1 oz Pineapple Juice
Shake.
Strain into chilled glass.

ALICE IN WONDERLAND aka DALLAS ALICE
Fill glass with ice.
3/4 oz Tequila
3/4 oz Orange Liqueur
3/4 oz Coffee Liqueur
Shake.
Strain into shot glass.

ALIEN ORGASM
Fill glass with ice.
3/4 oz Amaretto
3/4 oz Melon Liqueur
3/4 oz Peach Schnapps
Fill with equal parts Orange
and Pineapple Juice.
Shake.

ALIEN SECRETION
Fill glass with ice.
3/4 oz Coconut Rum
3/4 oz Melon Liqueur
3/4 oz Vodka
Fill with Pineapple Juice.
Shake.
Garnish with Cherry.

Metric Measurement Conversion Chart on page 14

ALIEN URINE SAMPLE
Fill glass with ice.
1/2 oz Coconut Rum
1/2 oz Banana Liqueur
1/2 oz Peach Schnapps
1/2 oz Melon Liqueur
Fill with Sour Mix leaving 1/2 inch from top.
Shake.
Splash Soda Water.
Top with 1/2 oz Blue Curacao

ALMOND ENJOY
Fill glass with ice.
1 oz Amaretto
1 oz Dark Crème de Cacao
1 oz Cream of Coconut
Fill with Cream or Milk.
Shake.

ALMOND JOY
Fill glass with ice.
1 oz Coconut Rum
1/2 oz Dark Crème de Cacao
Fill with Milk or Cream.
Shake.

ALMOND KISS aka COCOETTO
2 oz Amaretto
Fill with Hot Chocolate.
Stir.
Top with Whipped Cream.
Place Chocolate Kiss on top
or Shaved Chocolate.

ALMOND MOCHA COFFEE
1 oz Amaretto
1 oz Crème de Cacao
Fill with hot Black Coffee.
Top with Whipped Cream.
Sprinkle with Shaved Almonds
and/or Shaved Chocolate.

AMARETTO SOUR
Fill glass with ice.
2 oz Amaretto
Fill with Sour Mix.
Shake.
Garnish with Orange and Cherry.

AMARIST
1 oz Amaretto
1 oz Orange Liqueur
Microwave for 10-15 seconds.

AMBER CLOUD
1 1/2 oz Cognac
1/2 oz Galliano
Microwave for 10 seconds.

AMBER MARTINI
Fill glass with ice.
3 1/2 oz Vodka or Vanilla Vodka
1/2 oz Amaretto
1/2 oz Hazelnut Liqueur
Stir.
Strain into chilled glass.

AMBROSIA
Fill glass with ice.
1 oz Brandy
1/4 oz Triple Sec
Fill with Champagne.

AMBUSH COFFEE
1 oz Irish Whiskey
1 oz Amaretto
Fill with hot Black Coffee.
Top with Whipped Cream.
Sprinkle with Shaved Almonds.
Dribble 4-5 drops of Green Crème de Menthe on top.

AMERICAN GRAFFITI
Fill glass with ice.
1/2 oz Light Rum
1/2 oz Dark Rum
1/2 oz Southern Comfort
1/2 oz Sloe Gin
Dash of Lime Juice
Fill with equal parts Sour Mix and Pineapple Juice.
Shake.
Garnish with Lime.

AMERICAN SOUR
Fill glass with ice.
2 oz Bourbon
Dash of Orange Curacao
or Triple Sec
Dash of Orange Juice
Fill with Sour Mix.
Shake.

AMERICAN SNAKEBITE
Fill glass 3/4 with Hard Cider.
Fill with Ale or Lager.
Add 1 or 2 oz Vodka.

AMIGO aka WHITE BULL
Fill glass with ice.
1 oz Tequila
3/4 oz Coffee Liqueur
Fill with Milk or Cream.
Shake.

AMORE-ADE
Fill glass with ice.
1 1/2 oz Amaretto
1/2 oz Triple Sec
Fill with Soda Water.
Stir.

ANGEL FACE
Fill glass with ice.
1 oz Gin
1/2 oz Apricot Brandy
1/2 oz Apple Brandy
Shake.
Strain into chilled glass.

ANGEL KISS (floater)
1 oz Dark Crème de Cacao (bottom)
1 oz Milk or Cream (top)

ANGEL WING (floater)
1 1/2 oz White Crème de Cacao (bottom)
1/2 oz Irish Cream (top)

ANGEL WING 2 (floater)
1 oz White Crème de Cacao (bottom)
1 oz Brandy
1/2 oz Milk or Light Cream (top)

ANGEL'S LIPS
Fill glass with ice.
1 1/2oz Benedictine
1/2 oz Irish Cream
Stir.

ANGEL'S TIT (floater)
1 oz Dark Crème de Cacao (bottom)
1 oz Milk or Cream (top)
Garnish with Cherry on toothpick
across top of glass.

ANKLE BREAKER
Fill glass with ice.
1 1/2 oz 151-Proof Rum
1 oz Cherry Brandy
1 oz Lime Juice
1 tsp Sugar Syrup
Shake.

ANNA'S BANANA (frozen)
In Blender:
1/2 cup of Ice
2 oz Vodka
1/2 fresh ripe Banana
1 tsp Honey
Dash of Lime Juice
Blend until smooth.
If too thick add fruit.
If too thin add ice.
Garnish with Banana.

ANTI-FREEZE
Fill glass with ice.
1 oz Vodka
1 oz Green Crème de Menthe or
Melon Liqueur
Shake.
Strain into shot glass.

ANTI-FREEZE 2
Fill glass with ice.
1 oz Mentholated Schnapps
1 oz Blue Curacao
Shake.
Strain into chilled glass.
Top with Lemon-Lime Soda.

ANTIQUAN KISS
Fill glass with ice.
1/2 oz Light Rum
1/2 oz Dark Rum
1/2 oz Apricot Brandy
1/2 oz Peach Schnapps
Dash of Cranberry Juice
Fill with Orange Juice.
Shake.

ANTIQUAN SMILE
Fill glass with ice.
1 1/2 oz Dark Rum
1/2 oz Banana Liqueur
Pinch of Powdered Sugar
Fill with Orange Juice.
Shake.
Garnish with Lime.

APHRODISIAC
Fill glass 3/4 with Stout (let settle).
Stir in (gently) a raw egg and
1 tsp Honey or 1/2 tsp. Sugar.

APOLLO COOLER
Fill glass with ice.
1 1/2 oz Metaxa
1/2 oz Lemon Juice
Shake.
Fill with Ginger Ale.

**APPENDECTOMY aka
APPENDICITIS**
Fill glass with ice.
1 oz Gin
1/2 oz Orange Liqueur
1 oz Sour Mix
Shake and Strain into chilled glass.

APPETIZER
4 oz Red Wine
Fill with Orange Juice.
Dash of Bitters (optional)

APPLE COOLER
Fill glass with ice.
1 oz Light Rum or Spiced Rum
1 oz Brandy
Fill with Apple Cider or Juice.
Shake.
Strain into chilled glass.
Float 1/2 oz Dark Rum on top.

APPLE JOLL-E RANCHER
Fill glass with ice.
1 1/2oz Vodka or Citrus Vodka
1/2 oz Sour Apple Schnapps
2 oz Sour Mix
Shake.
Fill with Lemon-Lime Soda.

APPLE MARGARITA (frozen)
In Blender:
1 cup of Ice
1 oz Tequila
1 oz Apple Brandy
2 tbsp Applesauce
1 oz Sour Mix
Blend until smooth.
If too thick add applesauce or Sour
Mix.
If too thin add ice.
Rim glass with Cinnamon and
Sugar.

APPLE MARTINI
Fill glass with ice.
4 oz Apple Vodka
Dash Dry Vermouth or Apple
Liqueur (optional)
Stir
Strain into chilled glass
Or pour contents (with ice)
Into short glass.
Garnish with apple slice.

APPLE PIE
Fill glass with ice.
1 1/2 oz Vodka or Apple Vodka
1/2 oz Apple Cider or Juice
Strain into chilled glass.
Sprinkle with Cinnamon.

APPLE PIE (floater)
3/4 oz Apple Brandy (bottom)
3/4 oz Cinnamon Schnapps
3/4 oz Irish Cream (top)

APPLE POLISHER
2 oz Southern Comfort
Fill with hot Apple Cider.
Garnish with Cinnamon Stick.

APRES SKI
Fill glass with ice.
1 oz Peppermint Schnapps
1 oz Coffee Liqueur
1 oz White Crème de Cacao
Shake.

APRES SKI 2
1 oz Brandy
1 oz Apple Brandy
Fill with Apple Cider.
Garnish with Cinnamon Stick.

APRICOT FRAPPE
Fill large stemmed glass (Red Wine glass, Champagne saucer) with crushed ice.
1 oz Brandy
1 oz Apricot Brandy

APRICOT SOUR
Fill glass with ice.
2 oz Apricot Brandy
Fill with Sour Mix.
Shake.
Garnish with Orange and Cherry.

APRIL IN PARIS
1 oz Orange Liqueur
Fill with Champagne.
Garnish with Orange Slice.

ARIZONA LEMONADE
Fill glass with ice.
2 oz Tequila
2 tsp Powdered Sugar
Fill with fresh Lemon Juice.
Shake until sugar dissolves.
Garnish with Lemon.

ARMORED CAR
Fill glass with ice.
2 oz Bourbon
Dash of Simple Syrup
1 oz Fresh Lemon Juice
Stir.
Strain into chilled glass.

ARNOLD PALMER
Fill glass with ice.
Fill glass 1/2 with Iced Tea.
Fill glass 1/2 with Lemonade.
Shake.

AROUND THE WORLD
Fill glass with ice.
1 1/2 oz Gin
1 1/2 oz Green Crème de Menthe
1 1/2 oz Pineapple Juice
Shake.

ARTIFICIAL INTELLIGENCE
Fill glass with ice.
1/2 oz Dark Rum
1/2 oz Light Rum
1/2 oz Coconut Rum
Dash of Lime Juice
3 oz Pineapple Juice
Shake.
Strain into chilled glass.
Float 1/2 oz Melon Liqueur on top.

ASIAN MARTINI
Fill glass with ice.
3 1/2 oz Vodka
1/2 oz Ginger Liqueur
Stir.
Strain into chilled glass
or pour contents (with ice)
Into short glass.
Garnish with Lemon Twist.

ASPEN COFFEE
3/4 oz Coffee Liqueur
or Orange Liqueur
3/4 oz Irish Cream
3/4 oz Hazelnut Liqueur
Fill with hot Black Coffee.
Top with Whipped Cream.
Sprinkle with Shaved
Chocolate.

ASPEN HUMMER
1 oz 151-Proof Rum
1 oz Coffee Liqueur
Fill with hot Black Coffee.
Top with Whipped Cream.

ASSASSIN (floater)
3/4 oz Banana Liqueur (bottom)
3/4 oz Blue Curacao
3/4 oz Orange Liqueur (top)

ASSISTED SUICIDE
Fill glass with ice.
2 oz Grain Alcohol
1 oz Jägermeister
Fill with Cola
Stir.

ATOMIC BODYSLAM
Fill glass with ice.
1/2 oz Vodka
1/2 oz Gin
1/2 oz Dark Rum
1/2 oz Blackberry Brandy
Fill with Orange Juice or
Grapefruit Juice.
Shake.

ATOMIC DOG
Fill glass with ice.
1 oz Light Rum
1 oz Coconut Rum
1/2 oz Melon Liqueur
tsp Lemon Juice
Fill with Pineapple Juice.
Shake
Top with dash of Dark Rum
and 151-proof Rum

ATOMIC WASTE
Fill glass with ice.
3/4 oz Vodka
3/4 oz Melon Liqueur
1/2 oz Peach Schnapps
1/2 oz Banana Liqueur
Fill with Milk.
Shake.
Strain into chilled glass.

AUGUST MOON
Fill glass with ice.
1 oz Amaretto
1 oz Triple Sec
1 oz Orange Juice
Shake.
Strain into chilled glass.

AUNT JEMIMA (floater)
1/2 oz Brandy (bottom)
1/2 oz White Crème de Cacao
1/2 oz Benedictine (top)

AUNT MARY
Fill glass with ice.
2 oz Rum
1 tsp Horseradish
3 dashes of Tabasco Sauce
3 dashes of Worcestershire Sauce
Dash of Lime Juice
3 dashes of Celery Salt
3 dashes of Pepper
1 oz Clam Juice (optional)
Dash of Sherry (optional)
1 tsp Dijon Mustard (optional)
Fill with Tomato Juice.
Pour from one glass to another
until mixed.
Garnish with Lemon and/or Lime,
Celery and/or Cucumber and/or
Cocktail Shrimp.

Metric Measurement Conversion Chart on page 14

AVALANCHE (floater)
1/2 oz Coffee Liqueur (bottom)
1/2 oz White Crème de Cacao
1/2 oz Southern Comfort (top)

B & B
1 oz Brandy
1 oz Benedictine
Stir gently.

B-12 (floater)
1 1/2 oz Irish Cream (bottom)
1/2 oz Orange Liqueur (top)

B-50 (floater)
1 1/2 oz Irish Cream (bottom)
1/2 oz Vodka (top)

B-51 aka CONCORD (floater)
1/2 oz Coffee Liqueur (bottom)
1/2 oz Irish Cream
1/2 oz 151-Proof Rum (top)

B-52 (floater)
1/2 oz Coffee Liqueur (bottom)
1/2 oz Irish Cream
1/2 oz Orange Liqueur (top)

B-52 (frozen)
In Blender:
1/2 cup of Ice
3/4 oz Coffee Liqueur
3/4 oz Irish Cream
3/4 oz Orange Liqueur
Scoop of Vanilla Ice Cream
Blend until smooth.
If too thick add Milk or Cream.
If too thin add ice or Ice Cream.
Garnish with Chocolate
shavings or Sprinkles.

B-52 (rocks)
Fill glass with ice.
1 oz Coffee Liqueur
1 oz Irish Cream
1 oz Orange Liqueur
Shake.

B-52 COFFEE
1/2 oz Coffee Liqueur
1/2 oz Irish Cream
1/2 oz Orange Liqueur
Fill with hot Black Coffee.
Top with Whipped Cream.
Garnish with Orange.

B-52 ON A MISSION (floater)
1/2 oz Coffee Liqueur (bottom)
1/2 oz Irish Cream
1/2 oz Orange Liqueur
1/2 oz 151-Proof Rum (top)

**B-52 WITH A MEXICAN
TAILGUNNER** (floater)
1/2 oz Coffee Liqueur (bottom)
1/2 oz Irish Cream
1/2 oz Orange Liqueur
1/4 oz Tequila (top)

B-52 WITH BOMBAY DOORS
(floater)
1/2 oz Coffee Liqueur (bottom)
1/2 oz Irish Cream
1/2 oz Orange Liqueur
1/2 oz Dry Gin (top)

B-53 (floater)
1/2 oz Coffee Liqueur (bottom)
1/2 oz Sambuca
1/2 oz Orange Liqueur (top)

B-54 aka DC-10 (floater)
1/2 oz Coffee Liqueur (bottom)
1/2 oz Irish Cream
1/2 oz Amaretto (top)

B-55 (floater)
1/2 oz Coffee Liqueur(bottom)
1/2 oz Irish Cream
1/2 oz Absinthe or Pastis(top)

B-57 (floater)
1/2 oz Coffee Liqueur (bottom)
1/2 oz Amaretto
1/2 oz Cognac or Brandy (top)

B. M. P.
Fill glass with ice.
1 3/4 oz Amber Rum
1/2 oz Light Rum
3 oz Pineapple Juice
1 oz Lime Juice
Dash of Bitters
Shake.
Strain into glass.

BABBIE'S SPECIAL
Fill glass with ice.
1 oz Gin
3/4 oz Apricot Brandy
Fill with Milk or Cream.
Shake.

BACARDI COCKTAIL
Fill glass with ice.
2 oz Rum
Dash of Grenadine
Fill with Sour Mix.
Shake.
Garnish with Orange and Cherry.

BACK IN BLACK
Fill glass with ice.
1 1/2 oz Tequila
1/2 oz Orange Liqueur
Fill with cola.
Garnish with Lime.

BAHAMA MAMA
Fill glass with ice.
1 oz Light Rum
1 oz Dark Rum
1 oz Amber Rum
2 oz Sour Mix
2 oz Orange Juice
2 oz Pineapple Juice
Shake.
Put dash of Grenadine in second
glass and fill with mixture.
Garnish with Orange and Cherry.

BAHAMA MAMA 2
Fill glass with ice.
1 oz Light Rum
1 oz Coconut Rum
1 oz Amaretto
Dash of Grenadine
Fill with equal parts Orange and
Pineapple Juice.

BAHAMA MAMA 3
Fill glass with ice.
1 oz Light Rum
Fill with Pineapple Juice leaving a
1/2 inch from the top.
Shake.
Top with 1/2 oz 151-Proof Rum and
1/2 oz Dark Rum.

Metric Measurement Conversion Chart on page 14

BAILEY'S AND COFFEE
2 oz Irish Cream
Fill with hot Black Coffee.
Top with Whipped Cream.

BAILEY'S COMET
Fill glass with ice.
1 1/2 oz Vodka
1/2 oz Irish Cream

BAILEY'S FIZZ
Fill glass with ice.
2 oz Irish Cream
Fill with Soda Water.

BAJA MARGARITA
Fill glass with ice.
1 1/2 oz Tequila
1/2 oz Banana Liqueur
Dash of Lime Juice
4 oz Sour Mix
Dash of Orange Juice (optional)
Shake.
Rub rim of second glass with Lime
and dip into kosher salt.
Pour contents (with ice) or
Strain into salted glass.
Garnish with Lime.

BALALAIKA
Fill glass with ice.
1 1/2 oz Vodka or Citrus Vodka
1/2 oz Triple Sec
2 oz Sour Mix
Shake.
Strain into chilled glass.
Garnish with Lime.

BALI HAI
Fill glass with ice.
1 oz Gin
1 oz Rum
Dash of Amaretto
Fill with Sour Mix leaving 1/2 inch
from top.
Shake.
Top with Champagne.

BALTIMORE ZOO
Fill glass with ice.
1/2 oz Vodka or Citrus Vodka
1/2 oz Gin
1/2 oz Rum
1/2 oz Triple Sec
1 oz Sour Mix
Dash Grenadine
Shake
Fill with equal parts Beer and Cola.
Garnish with a Cherry, Lime,
Lemon, and Orange

BAMBINI ARUBA
Fill glass with ice.
1 oz Vodka
1 oz Rum
1 oz Bourbon
Dash of Grenadine
Fill with equal parts Sour Mix,
Orange and Pineapple Juice.
Shake.
Garnish with Orange and Cherry.

BANANA BOAT
Fill glass with ice.
1 oz Coconut Rum
1 oz Banana Liqueur
2 oz Pineapple Juice
Shake.
Strain into chilled glass.

BANANA COLADA (frozen)
In Blender:
1/2 cup of Ice
2 oz Light Rum or Banana Rum
2 tbsp Cream of Coconut
1 whole peeled ripe Banana
1 tbsp Vanilla Ice Cream
Blend until smooth.
If too thick add more fruit.
If too thin add ice or Ice Cream.
Garnish with Banana.

BANANA COW (frozen)
In Blender:
1/2 cup of Ice
1 1/2 oz Dark Rum
1/2 oz Banana Liqueur
1/2 peeled ripe Banana
Scoop of Vanilla Ice Cream
Blend until smooth.
If too thick add Milk.
If too thin add ice or Ice Cream.
Garnish with Banana.

BANANA CREAM PIE (frozen)
In Blender:
1/2 cup of Ice
1 oz Vodka
1/2 oz Irish Cream
1/2 oz Banana Liqueur
1/2 peeled ripe Banana
Scoop of Vanilla Ice Cream
Blend until smooth.

BANANA CREAM PIE MARTINI
Fill glass with ice.
3 1/2 oz Vodka
Dash Banana Liqueur
Dash Irish Cream
Shake.
Strain into chilled glass.

BANANA DAIQUIRI (frozen)
In Blender:
1 cup of Ice
1 1/2 oz Rum or Banana Rum
1/2 oz Banana Liqueur
Dash of Lime Juice
1 whole peeled ripe Banana
Blend until smooth.
If too thick add more fruit.
If too thin add ice.
Garnish with Banana.

BANANA FROST (frozen)
In Blender:
1/2 cup of Ice
1 1/2 oz Amaretto
1/2 oz Banana Liqueur
Scoop of Banana
or Vanilla Ice Cream
1/2 peeled ripe Banana
Blend until smooth.
If too thick add Milk.
If too thin add ice or Ice Cream.
Garnish with Banana.

BANANA NUT BREAD
In Blender: 1/2 cup of ice
1 oz Vodka or Banana Vodka or
Vanilla Vodka
1/2 oz Hazelnut Liqueur
1/2 oz Banana Liqueur
1/4 cup chopped walnuts
1/2 peeled ripe banana
Scoop Vanilla Ice Cream
Blend until smooth.

Metric Measurement Conversion Chart on page 14

BANANA POPSICLE (frozen)
In Blender:
1/2 cup of Ice
1 oz Vodka
1 oz Banana Liqueur
1/2 scoop Orange Sherbet
1/2 scoop Vanilla Ice Cream
1/2 peeled ripe Banana
Blend until smooth.
If too thick add Orange Juice or Milk.
If too thin add ice or Ice Cream.

BANANA SANDWICH (floater)
1/2 oz Coffee Liqueur (bottom)
1/2 oz Banana Liqueur
1/2 oz Rum Cream (top)

BANANA SOMBRERO
Fill glass with ice.
2 oz Banana Liqueur
Fill with Milk or Cream.
Shake.

BANANA SPLIT
Fill glass with ice.
1 1/2 oz Vodka or Vanilla Vodka
1/2 oz Banana Liqueur
1/2 oz Strawberry Liqueur
1/2 oz Dark Crème de Cacao
Fill with Milk.
Shake.

BANANA SPLIT (frozen)
In Blender:
1/2 cup of Ice
1 oz Rum or Banana or Vanilla Rum
1 oz Coffee Liqueur
1 tbsp Cream of Coconut
1/2 peeled ripe Banana
Scoop of Vanilla Ice Cream
1 tbsp Chocolate Syrup
1/4 cup fresh or canned Pineapple
2 Maraschino Cherries (no stems)
Blend until smooth.
Top with Whipped Cream.
Garnish with Cherry.

BANANA SPLIT MARTINI
Fill glass with ice.
3 oz Vodka or Pineapple Vodka
1/2 oz Banana Liqueur
Dash Strawberry Liqueur
Dash White Crème de Cacao
Dash Grenadine
Shake.
Strain into a chilled glass.

BANANA STRAWBERRY DAIQUIRI (frozen)
In Blender:
1 cup of Ice
1 oz Rum
1/2 oz Banana Liqueur
1/2 oz Strawberry Liqueur
1/2 cup fresh or frozen Strawberries
1/2 peeled ripe Banana
Blend until smooth.
If too thick add fruit.
If too thin add ice.
Garnish with Banana and Strawberry.

BANGING THE CAPTAIN 3 WAYS ON THE COMFORTER
Fill glass with ice.
1 oz Spiced Rum
1 oz Southern Comfort
Fill with equal parts Orange, Pineapple and Cranberry Juice.
Shake.

BANSHEE aka CAPRI
Fill glass with ice.
1 oz Banana Liqueur
1/2 oz White Crème de Cacao
Fill with Milk or Cream.
Shake.

BANSHEE (frozen)
In Blender:
1/2 cup of Ice
1 oz Banana Liqueur
1/2 oz White Crème de Cacao
Scoop of Vanilla Ice Cream
1 whole peeled ripe Banana
Blend until smooth.
If too thick add Milk.
If too thin add ice or Ice Cream.
Garnish with Banana.

BARBADOS PUNCH
Fill glass with ice.
1 1/2 oz Spiced Rum
1/2 oz Triple Sec
Dash of Lime Juice
Fill with Pineapple Juice.
Shake.

BARBARELLA aka BARBELLS
Fill glass with ice.
2 oz Orange Liqueur
1 oz Sambuca
Shake.
Serve or strain into chilled glass.

BARBARY COAST
Fill glass with ice.
1/2 oz Rum or Spiced Rum
1/2 oz Gin
1/2 oz Scotch
1/2 oz White Crème de Cacao or White Crème de Menthe
Fill with Cola.
Shake.
Serve or strain into chilled glass.

BARRACUDA
Fill glass with ice.
1 oz Amber Rum
1 oz Light Rum
1/2 oz Galliano
Dash of Lime Juice
1/2 tsp Powdered Sugar
2 oz Pineapple Juice
Shake.
Top with Champagne.

BART SIMPSON
Fill glass with ice.
1/2 oz Vodka
1/2 oz Coconut Rum
1/2 oz Melon Liqueur
Shake.
Strain into chilled glass.

BARTMAN
Fill glass with ice.
1 oz Light Rum
1 oz Apple Brandy
Dash of Grenadine
Dash of Sour Mix
Fill with Orange Juice.
Shake.
Garnish with Orange and Cherry.

BAT BITE
Fill glass with ice.
2 oz Rum
Fill with Cranberry Juice.
Garnish with Lime.

Metric Measurement Conversion Chart on page 14

BAT OUT OF HELL
Fill glass with ice.
1 1/2 oz Rum or Citrus Rum
1/2 oz Blue Curacao
Fill with Red Energy Drink.

BATTERED BRUISED AND BLEEDING (floater)
3/4 oz Grenadine (bottom)
3/4 oz Melon Liqueur
3/4 oz Blue Curacao (top)

BAVARIAN COFFEE
1 oz Peppermint Schnapps
1 oz Coffee Liqueur
Fill with hot Black Coffee
Top with Whipped Cream.

BAY BREEZE aka HAWAIIAN SEA BREEZE, DOWNEASTER
Fill glass with ice.
2 oz Vodka
Fill with equal parts Cranberry and Pineapple Juice.
Garnish with Lime.

BAY CITY BOMBER
Fill glass with ice.
1/2 oz Vodka or Citrus Vodka
1/2 oz Gin
1/2 oz Tequila
1/2 oz Triple Sec
Fill with equal parts Sour Mix, Cranberry, Orange, and Pineapple Juice.
Shake.
Top with 1/2 oz 151-Proof Rum.

BAZOOKA
Fill glass with ice.
1 oz Southern Comfort
1 oz Banana Liqueur
Dash of Grenadine
Shake.
Strain into shot glass.
Top with Whipped Cream.

BAZOOKA JOE
Fill glass with ice.
3/4 oz Irish Cream
3/4 oz Banana Liqueur
3/4 oz Blue Curacao
Shake.
Strain into shot glass.

BBC
1 oz Brandy
1 oz Irish Cream
Fill with hot Black Coffee.
Top with Whipped Cream.

BEACH BLANKET BINGO
Fill glass with ice.
3 oz Grapefruit Juice
3 oz Cranberry Juice
Fill with Soda Water.
Garnish with Lime.

BEACH HUT MADNESS (floater)
1/2 oz Irish Cream (bottom)
1/2 oz Amaretto
1/2 oz Sambuca (top)

BEACHCOMBER
Fill glass with ice.
1 1/2 oz Rum or Citrus Rum
1/2 oz Triple Sec
Dash of Grenadine
Fill with Sour Mix.
Shake.

BEACON HILL BLIZZARD
Fill glass with ice.
1 oz Dark Rum
1 oz Coconut Rum
Fill with equal parts Cranberry and Grapefruit Juice.
Garnish with Lime.

BEAM ME UP SCOTTI
Fill glass with ice.
1 oz Vodka
1 oz Irish Cream
1 oz Banana Liqueur
Shake.
Strain into shot glass.

BEAM ME UP SCOTTI (floater)
1/2 oz Coffee Liqueur (bottom)
1/2 oz Banana Liqueur
1/2 oz Irish Cream (top)
Dash of Vodka or
Hazelnut Liqueur (optional).

BEARHUG (Floater)
1/2 oz Coffee Liqueur (bottom)
1/2 oz Sambuca
1/2 oz Orange Liqueur (top)

BEAUTIFUL THING
Fill glass with ice.
1 oz Peppermint Schnapps
1 oz Irish Cream
Stir.

BEE STING
Fill glass with ice.
1 oz Jägermeister
1 oz Bärenjäger

BEE'S KNEES
Fill glass with ice.
1 1/2 oz Rum
1 tsp of Honey
1 oz Sour Mix
Shake.
Strain into chilled glass.

BEER BUSTER
In chilled beer glass:
2 oz chilled 100-Proof Vodka
3 dashes of Tabasco Sauce
Fill with Beer.

BEETLE JUICE
Fill glass with ice.
1 oz Dark Crème de Cacao
1 oz White Crème de Cacao
1/2 oz Peppermint Schnapps
1/2 oz Coffee Liqueur
Fill with Milk or Cream.
Shake.

BELFAST BOMBER (floater)
1 oz Irish Cream (bottom)
1 oz Irish Whiskey (top)

BELLINI
In Blender:
1 fresh Peach (no pit or skin) or
1/2 cup canned Peaches (no juice)
Blend.
Pour pureed peach into glass.
Fill with cold Champagne.

BELLY BUTTON SHOT
Find an attractive desirable belly button (inny).
Ask permission to use it.
If yes, lay owner of belly button on their back (totally nude if possible).
Fill belly button with favorite straight liquor or liqueur (be careful not to spill any or you'll have to clean it up with a rag or your tongue).
Place lips over belly button and slurp out drink as loudly as possible. Take turns and repeat process until interests change.

BELMONT
Fill glass with ice.
1 1/2 oz Gin
1/2 oz Black Raspberry Liqueur
Fill with Milk or Cream.
Shake.

BEND ME OVER
Fill glass with ice.
1 oz Vodka
or 1/2 oz Vodka and 1/2 oz Whiskey
1 oz Amaretto
1 oz Sour Mix
Shake.
Strain into chilled glass.

BENT NAIL
Fill glass with ice.
1 1/2 oz Canadian Whiskey
1/2 oz Drambuie
Stir.

BERLIN WALL
Fill glass with ice.
1 1/2 oz Vodka or Vanilla Vodka
1/2 oz Irish Cream
Stir.

BERMUDA TRIANGLE
Fill glass with ice.
1 oz Spiced Rum
1 oz Peach Schnapps
Fill with Orange Juice.
Shake.

BERMUDA TRIANGLE 2
Fill glass with ice.
3 1/2 oz Vodka or Citrus Vodka
Dash of Peach Schnapps
Dash of Amaretto
Dash of Orange Liqueur
Dash of Banana Liqueur
Dash of Pineapple Juice
Dash of Cranberry Juice
Shake. Strain into a chilled glass.

BETSY ROSS
Fill glass with ice.
1 oz Brandy
1 oz Port
1/2 oz Triple Sec
Dash of Bitters
Stir.
Strain into chilled glass.

BETWEEN THE SHEETS
Fill glass with ice.
1 oz Rum or Citrus or Orange Rum
1 oz Cognac or Brandy
1 oz Triple Sec
Dash of Sour Mix
Shake.
Strain into chilled glass.

BEVERLY HILLBILLY (floater)
1 oz 100-Proof Cinnamon Schnapps (bottom)
1 oz Jägermeister (top)

BIBLE BELT
Fill glass with ice.
2 oz Bourbon
or Southern Comfort
1 oz Triple Sec
2 oz Lime Juice
2 oz Sour Mix
Shake.
Rim glass with Powdered Sugar.
Garnish with a Lemon.

BIG BAMBOO
Fill glass with ice.
2 oz 151-Proof Rum
1 oz Dark Rum
1/4 oz Triple Sec
2 oz Orange Juice
2 oz Pineapple Juice
1/2 oz Sugar Syrup
Dash of Bitters
Shake.
Strain into 3 or 4 shot glasses.

BIG DADDY
Fill glass with ice.
1/2 oz Vodka or Citrus Vodka
1/2 oz Rum or Citrus Rum
1/2 oz Tequila
1/2 oz Whiskey
Fill with Lemon-Lime Soda.
Garnish with Lime.

BIG KAHUNA
Fill glass with ice.
1 1/2 oz Gin
1/2 oz Triple Sec or Blue Curacao
1/2 oz Sweet Vermouth
2 oz Pineapple Juice
Shake.
Strain into chilled glass.

BIG TITTY ORGY
Fill glass with ice.
1 oz Grain Alcohol
1 oz Vodka or Orange Vodka
1 oz Strawberry Liqueur
Fill glass with Orange Juice.
Shake.

BIKINI
Fill glass with ice.
1 oz Vodka
1 oz Rum
tsp Sugar
1 oz Sour Mix
1 oz Milk or Cream
Shake.
Strain into chilled glass.

BIKINI LINE
Fill glass with ice.
3/4 oz Vodka
3/4 oz Coffee Liqueur
3/4 oz Raspberry Liqueur

BIKINI LINE (floater)
1/2 oz Strawberry Liqueur (bottom)
1/2 oz Orange Liqueur
1/2 oz Vodka (top)

Metric Measurement Conversion Chart on page 14

BILLIE HOLIDAY
Fill glass with ice.
2 oz Vodka
Dash of Grenadine
Fill with Ginger Ale
Garnish with Cherry.

BIMINI ICE-T
Fill glass with ice.
1/2 oz Vodka or Citrus Vodka
1/2 oz Gin or Lime Gin
1/2 oz Rum or Spiced Rum
1/2 oz Tequila
1/2 oz Blue Curacao
1 oz Sour Mix
1 oz Orange Juice
1 oz Pineapple Juice
Shake.
Top with Cola.
Garnish with Lemon.

BIRD OF PARADISE
Fill glass 3/4 full with ice.
Fill 3/4 with Champagne.
Fill with Pineapple Juice.
Dash of Grenadine

BISCUIT NECK
Fill glass with ice.
1/2 oz 101-proof Bourbon
1/2 oz Amaretto
1/2 oz Irish Cream
1/2 oz Hazelnut Liqueur
Shake.
Strain into shot glass.

BIT OF HONEY (frozen)
In Blender:
1/2 cup of Ice
1/2 oz Scotch
1 tbsp Honey
Scoop of Vanilla Ice Cream
Blend until smooth.
Float 1/2 oz of B&B on top.

BITCH FIGHT
Fill glass with ice.
1 oz Peach Schnapps
1 oz Orange Liqueur
Dash of Lime Juice
Fill with Cranberry Juice.
Shake.
Garnish with Lime.

BLACK AND BLUE MARTINI
(CAUTION: DRY usually means
less Vermouth than usual.
EXTRA DRY can mean even less
Vermouth than usual or no
Vermouth at all.)
2 oz Top Shelf Gin
2 oz Top Shelf Vodka
1/2 oz Dry Vermouth
Stir.
Strain into chilled glass or pour
contents (with ice) into short glass.
Garnish with Lemon Twist or
Olives or Cocktail Onions.

BLACK AND TAN
Fill glass 1/2 with Amber Ale.
Fill glass 1/2 with Stout.

BLACK BARRACUDA
Fill glass with ice.
1 oz Dark Rum
1/2 oz Banana Liqueur
1/2 oz Blackberry Brandy
Dash of Lime Juice
Dash of Grenadine
Fill with Orange Juice.
Shake.
Garnish with Lime and Orange.

BLACK CAT
Fill glass with ice.
1 oz Vodka
1 oz Cherry Liqueur
Fill glass with equal parts
Cranberry Juice and Cola.

BLACK COW
In glass:
Scoop of Vanilla Ice Cream
Fill with Root Beer.
Serve with straw and spoon.

BLACK COW 2
Fill glass with ice.
1 oz Vodka or Vandermint
1 oz Dark Crème de Cacao
Fill with Cream or Milk.
Shake.

BLACK DEATH
1 oz 12 year old Scotch
Fill with Stout.

BLACK DOG
Fill glass with ice.
2 oz Bourbon
1 oz Blackberry Brandy
Stir.

BLACK EYE
Fill glass with ice.
1 1/2 oz Vodka
1/2 oz Blackberry Brandy
Stir.

**BLACK-EYED SUSAN aka
KENTUCKY SCREWDRIVER,
YELLOW JACKET**
Fill glass with ice.
2 oz Bourbon
Fill with Orange Juice.

BLACK FOREST (floater)
1/2 oz Coffee Liqueur (bottom)
1/2 oz Black Raspberry Liqueur
1/2 oz Irish Cream
1/2 oz Vodka (top)

BLACK FOREST (frozen)
In Blender:
1/2 cup of Ice
3/4 oz Vodka
3/4 oz Coffee Liqueur
3/4 oz Black Raspberry Liqueur
Scoop of Chocolate Ice Cream
Blend until smooth.
If too thick add Milk.
If too thin add ice or Ice Cream.
Garnish with Shaved Chocolate or
Sprinkles.

BLACK HAWK
Fill glass with ice.
1 1/2 oz Whiskey
1 1/2 oz Sloe Gin
Stir.
Strain into chilled glass.
Garnish with Cherry.

B

BLACK ICED TEA
Fill glass with ice.
3/4 oz Dark Rum
3/4 oz Brandy
3/4 oz Triple Sec
1 oz Orange Juice
Fill with Cola.
Garnish with Orange.

BLACK JAMAICAN
Fill glass with ice.
1 1/2 oz Jamaican Rum
1/2 oz Coffee Liqueur
Stir.

BLACK LADY
Fill glass with ice.
2 oz Orange Liqueur
1/2 oz Coffee Liqueur
1/2 oz Brandy
Shake.
Strain into chilled glass.

BLACK MAGIC
Fill glass with ice.
1 1/2 oz Vodka
1 oz Coffee Liqueur
Dash of Sour Mix
Stir.
Garnish with Lemon Twist.

BLACK MAGIC 2
3/4 oz Amaretto
3/4 oz Irish Cream
3/4 oz Coffee Liqueur
Fill with Hot Chocolate.
Top with Whipped Cream.
Sprinkle with Shaved Chocolate.

BLACK MARTINI
Fill glass with ice.
3 1/2 oz Gin, Vodka or Rum
1/2 oz Blackberry Brandy
or Black Raspberry Liqueur
Stir.
Strain into chilled glass
or pour contents (with ice) into
short glass.
Garnish with Lemon Twist
or Black Olive.

BLACK PRINCE
1 oz Blackberry Brandy
Dash of Lime Juice
Fill with Champagne.

BLACK ROSE
Fill glass with ice.
2 oz Rum
1 tsp Sugar
Fill with cold Black Coffee.
Shake.

BLACK ROSE (frozen)
In Blender:
1 cup of Ice
1/2 oz Gold Tequila
1/2 oz Coffee Liqueur
1/2 oz Black Raspberry Liqueur
1/2 cup fresh or frozen
Strawberries
1/2 oz Cream or Milk
Blend until smooth.
If too thick add cream or milk.
If too thin add ice.

BLACK RUSSIAN
Fill glass with ice.
1 1/2 oz Vodka
1 oz Coffee Liqueur
Stir.

BLACK RUSSIAN (frozen)
In Blender:
1/2 cup of Ice
1 1/2 oz Vodka
1 oz Coffee Liqueur
Scoop of Chocolate Ice Cream
Blend until smooth.
If too thick add Milk or Cream.
If too thin add ice or Ice Cream.
Garnish with Chocolate Shavings
or Sprinkles.

BLACK SABBATH
Fill glass with ice.
3/4 oz Bourbon
3/4 oz Dark Rum
3/4 oz Jägermeister
Shake.
Strain into chilled glass.

BLACK SHEEP
Fill glass with ice.
1 oz Blackberry Brandy
1 oz Black Raspberry Liqueur
1/2 oz Lime Juice
Stir.
Strain into chilled glass.
Garnish with Lime.

BLACK STRIPE
2 oz Dark Rum
tsp Molasses or Honey
Twist Lemon over glass and drop
in.
Fill with Hot Water.
Garnish with Cinnamon Stick.
Stir.

BLACK TIE (floater)
1/2 oz Amaretto (bottom)
1/2 oz Drambuie
1/2 oz Scotch (top)

BLACK VELVET
Fill glass 1/2 with Champagne.
Fill glass 1/2 with Stout.

BLACK VELVETEEN
Fill glass 3/4 with Hard Cider.
Fill glass with Stout.

BLACK WATCH
Fill glass with ice.
1 1/2 oz Scotch
1/2 oz Coffee Liqueur
Stir.

BLACK WITCH
Fill glass with ice.
1 1/2 oz Amber Rum
1/4 oz Dark Rum
1/4 oz Apricot Brandy
1/2 oz Pineapple Juice
Shake.
Strain into chilled glass.

BLACKJACK
Fill glass with ice.
1 oz Brandy
1 oz Blackberry Brandy
1 oz Cream
Shake.
Serve or strain into chilled glass.

Metric Measurement Conversion Chart on page 14

BLAST
Fill glass with ice.
1 oz Rum or Citrus Rum
1 oz Brandy
Dash of Sour Mix
Fill with equal parts Orange and
Pineapple Juice.
Shake.

BLEACHER CREATURE
Fill glass with ice.
1/3 oz Vodka or Citrus Vodka
1/3 oz Tequila
1/3 oz Rum or Citrus Rum
1/3 oz Triple Sec
1/3 oz Melon Liqueur
1/3 oz Green Crème de Menthe
Fill with Sour Mix.
Shake.

BLIND MELON
Fill glass with ice.
1 oz Melon Liqueur
1/2 oz Vodka or Orange Vodka
1/2 oz Rum or Orange Rum
1/2 oz Triple Sec
Shake.
Strain into chilled glass.

BLINKER
Fill glass with ice.
2 oz Whiskey
Dash of Grenadine
Fill with Grapefruit Juice.
Shake.

BLIZZARD (frozen)
In Blender:
1/2 cup of Ice
1/2 oz Dark Rum
1/2 oz Brandy
1/2 oz Coffee Liqueur
1/2 oz Irish Cream
Scoop of Vanilla Ice Cream
Blend until smooth.

BLOOD AND SAND
Fill glass with ice.
1 oz Scotch
3/4 oz Cherry Brandy
1/2 oz Sweet Vermouth
1 oz Orange Juice
Stir.
Strain into chilled glass.

BLOOD CLOT
Fill shot glass with:
2 oz Southern Comfort
Drop shot glass into larger glass:
Filled 3/4 with Lemon-Lime Soda
And a dash of Grenadine

BLOOD CLOT (floater)
1 1/2 oz 151-Proof Rum
Dash of Grenadine
Float 1/4 oz Cream on top.

BLOOD ORANGE MARTINI
Fill glass with ice.
3 1/2 oz Orange Vodka or Vodka
Dash Orange Liqueur
Dash Campari
Dash Blood Orange Juice or
Orange Juice
Shake.
Strain into a chilled glass.

BLOODY BASTARD
Fill glass 1/2 with ale.
1 tsp Horseradish
Fill with Bloody Mary Mix.
Rub rim of second glass with Lime
and dip into Kosher Salt.
Pour drink into second glass.

BLOODY BRAIN
1 oz Strawberry Liqueur
Dash of Grenadine
1/2 oz Irish Cream

BLOODY BREW
1 1/2 oz Vodka or Peppered Vodka
2 oz Tomato Juice
Fill with Beer or Malt Liquor.
Dash of Salt

BLOODY BULL
Fill glass with ice.
2 oz Vodka or Peppered Vodka
1 oz Beef Bouillon
1 tsp Horseradish
3 dashes of Tabasco Sauce
3 dashes of Worcestershire Sauce
Dash of Lime Juice
3 dashes of Celery Salt
3 dashes of Pepper
1 oz Clam Juice (optional)
Dash of Sherry (optional)
Fill with Tomato Juice.
Pour from one glass to another
until mixed. Garnish with Lemon
and/or Lime, Celery and/or
Cucumber and/or Cocktail Shrimp.

BLOODY CAESAR
Fill glass with ice.
2 oz Vodka or Peppered Vodka
1 tsp Horseradish
3 dashes of Tabasco Sauce
3 dashes of Worcestershire Sauce
Dash of Lime Juice
3 dashes of Celery Salt
3 dashes of Pepper
Dash of Sherry (optional)
1 tsp Dijon Mustard (optional)
Fill with equal parts tomato and
Clam Juice.
Pour from one glass to another
until mixed. Garnish with Lemon
and/or Lime, Celery and/or
Cucumber and/or Cocktail Shrimp.

BLOODY HOLLY aka
DANISH MARY
Fill glass with ice.
2 oz Aquavit
1 tsp Horseradish
3 dashes of Tabasco Sauce
3 dashes of Worcestershire Sauce
Dash of Lime Juice
3 dashes of Celery Salt
3 dashes of Pepper
1 oz Clam Juice (optional)
Dash of Sherry (optional)
1 tsp Dijon Mustard (optional)
Fill with Tomato Juice.
Pour from one glass to another
until mixed. Garnish with Lemon
and/or Lime, Celery and/or
Cucumber and/or Cocktail Shrimp.

B

BLOODY JOSEPHINE
Fill glass with ice.
2 oz Scotch
1 tsp Horseradish
3 dashes of Tabasco Sauce
3 dashes of Worcestershire Sauce
Dash of Lime Juice
3 dashes of Celery Salt
3 dashes of Pepper
1 oz Clam Juice (optional)
Dash of Sherry (optional)
1 tsp Dijon Mustard (optional)
Fill with Tomato Juice.
Pour from one glass to another
until mixed. Garnish with Lemon
and/or Lime, Celery and/or
Cucumber and/or Cocktail Shrimp.

BLOODY MARIA
Fill glass with ice.
2 oz Tequila
1 tsp Horseradish
3 dashes of Tabasco Sauce
3 dashes of Worcestershire Sauce
Dash of Lime Juice
3 dashes of Celery Salt
3 dashes of Pepper
1 oz Clam Juice (optional)
Dash of Sherry (optional)
1 tsp Dijon Mustard (optional)
Fill with Tomato Juice.
Pour from one glass to another
until mixed. Garnish with Lemon
and/or Lime, Celery and/or
Cucumber and/or Cocktail Shrimp.

BLOODY MARISELA
Fill glass with ice.
2 oz Light Rum
1 tsp Horseradish
3 dashes of Tabasco Sauce
3 dashes of Worcestershire Sauce
Dash of Lime Juice
3 dashes of Celery Salt
3 dashes of Pepper
1 oz Clam Juice (optional)
Dash of Sherry (optional)
1 tsp Dijon Mustard (optional)
Fill with Tomato Juice.
Pour from one glass to another
until mixed. Garnish with Lemon
and/or Lime, Celery and/or
Cucumber and/or Cocktail Shrimp.

BLOODY MARU
Fill glass with ice.
3 oz Sake
1 tsp Wasabi
3 dashes of Hot Sauce
3 dashes Soy Sauce
Dash of Lime Juice
3 dashes of White Pepper.
1 oz Oyster Liqueur (juice) optional
Pinch dry Chinese Mustard (option-
al)
Fill with Tomato Juice.
Shake.
Garnish with Lemon and/or Lime,
Celery and/or Cucumber and/or
Cocktail Shrimp.

BLOODY MARY
Fill glass with ice.
2 oz Vodka or Peppered Vodka
1 tsp Horseradish
3 dashes of Tabasco Sauce
3 dashes of Worcestershire Sauce
Dash of Lime Juice
3 dashes of Celery Salt
3 dashes of Pepper
1 oz Clam Juice (optional)
Dash of Sherry (optional)
1 tsp Dijon Mustard (optional)
Fill with Tomato Juice.
Pour from one glass to another
until mixed. Garnish with Lemon
and/or Lime, Celery and/or
Cucumber and/or Cocktail Shrimp.

BLOODY MOLLY
Fill glass with ice.
2 oz Irish Whiskey
1 tsp Horseradish
3 dashes of Tabasco Sauce
3 dashes of Worcestershire Sauce
Dash of Lime Juice
3 dashes of Celery Salt
3 dashes of Pepper
1 oz Clam Juice (optional)
Fill with Tomato Juice.
Pour from one glass to
another until mixed.
Garnish with Lemon and/or Lime,
Celery and/or Cucumber and/or
Cocktail Shrimp.

BLOW JOB aka
PEARL NECKLACE (floater)
1/2 oz Cream (bottom)
1/2 oz White Crème de Cacao
1/2 oz Vodka (top)
Top with Whipped Cream.
Contents should mix slightly.
To drink, place hands behind back
and pick up using only mouth.

BLOW JOB 2 (floater)
3/4 oz Coffee Liqueur (bottom)
3/4 oz Orange Liqueur
3/4 oz Banana Liqueur (top)
Top with Whipped Cream.
To drink, place hands behind back
and pick up using only mouth.

BLOW JOB 3 (floater)
1 oz Irish Cream (bottom)
1 oz Orange Liqueur or
Butterscotch Schnapps (top)
Top with Whipped Cream.

BLUE BAYOU (frozen)
In Blender:
1 cup of Ice
1 1/2 oz Vodka
1/2 oz Blue Curacao
1/2 cup fresh or canned Pineapple
2 oz Grapefruit Juice
Blend until smooth.
If too thick add juice.
If too thin add ice.
Garnish with Pineapple.

BLUE BIJOU (frozen)
In Blender:
1 cup of Ice
1 1/4 oz Rum or Orange Rum
1 oz Blue Curacao
3 oz Orange Juice
3 oz Pineapple Juice
3 or 4 drops of Lime Juice
Blend on low speed for 3-5
seconds.

Metric Measurement Conversion Chart on page 14

BLUE CANARY
Fill glass with ice.
1 1/2 oz Gin
1/2 oz Blue Curacao
Fill with Grapefruit Juice.
Shake.

BLUE DAIQUIRI (frozen)
In Blender:
1 cup of ice.
1 1/2 oz Rum
1/2 oz Blue Curacao
Dash of Lime Juice
Dash of Sour Mix
1/2 tsp Sugar
Blend until smooth.
If too thick add Sour Mix.
If too thin add ice.

BLUE HAWAIIAN
Fill glass with ice.
1 oz Rum or Coconut Rum
or Orange Rum
1 oz Blue Curacao
1 oz Cream of Coconut
Fill with Pineapple Juice.
Shake.
Garnish with Pineapple.

BLUE HAWAIIAN 2
Fill glass with ice.
1 1/2 oz Vodka
1/2 oz Blue Curacao
Fill with equal parts Orange and
Pineapple Juice.
Shake.
Garnish with Pineapple.

BLUE KAMIKAZE aka
NUCLEAR KAMIKAZE
Fill glass with ice.
2 oz Vodka or Lime Vodka
1/2 oz Blue Curacao
Dash of Lime Juice
Shake.
Serve or strain into chilled glass.
Garnish with Lime.

BLUE LADY
Fill glass with ice.
1 1/2 oz Gin
1/4 oz Blue Curacao
1 oz Sour Mix
Stir.

BLUE LAGOON
Fill glass with ice.
1 1/2 oz Vodka or Citrus or
Pineapple Vodka
1/2 oz Blue Curacao
Fill with Pineapple Juice or
Lemonade
or Lemon-Lime Soda.
Shake.

BLUE LEMONADE
1 oz Citrus Vodka
1 oz Blue Curacao
Dash of Sour Mix
Dash of Lemon-Lime Soda
Stir.

BLUE MARGARITA
Fill glass with ice.
2 oz Tequila
1 oz Blue Curacao
Dash of Lime Juice
3 oz Sour Mix
Shake.
Rub rim of second glass with Lime
and dip rim into Kosher Salt. Either
pour contents (with ice) or strain
into salted glass.
Garnish with Lime.

BLUE MEANIE
Fill glass with ice.
1 1/2 oz Vodka or Tequila or Gin
1/2 oz Blue Curacao
2 oz Sour Mix
Shake.
Strain into shot glass.

BLUE SHARK
Fill glass with ice.
1 oz Vodka
1 oz Tequila
1/2 oz Blue Curacao
Shake.
Strain into chilled glass.

BLUE TAIL FLY
Fill glass with ice.
1 oz Blue Curacao
1 oz White Crème de Cacao
Fill with Milk or light Cream.
Shake.

BLUE VALIUM
Fill glass with ice.
2/3 oz 151-Proof Rum
3/4 oz Whiskey
3/4 oz Blue Curacao
Dash of Sour Mix
Shake.
Strain into chilled glass.
Dash of Lemon-Lime Soda

BLUEBERRY MARTINI
Fill glass with ice.
3 1/2oz Vodka
1/2oz Blueberry Schnapps
1 tsp Blueberry jelly or syrup
(optional)
Shake. Strain into a chilled glass.

BMW
Bloody Mary with a Beer back
Make Bloody Mary and serve
With Small (5 - 8 oz) glass of beer

BOARDWALK BREEZER
Fill glass with ice.
1 1/2 oz Dark Rum
1/2 oz Banana Liqueur
1/2 oz Lime Juice
Fill with Pineapple Juice.
Shake.
Top with dash of Grenadine.
Garnish with Orange and Cherry.

BOB MARLEY
Fill glass with ice.
1 oz Dark Rum
1 oz Tia Maria
Dash of Cream of Coconut
Dash of Milk or Cream
Dash of Pineapple Juice
Shake.
Strain into chilled glass.

Metric Measurement Conversion Chart on page 14

BOCCI BALL
Fill glass with ice.
1 1/2 oz Vodka
1/2 oz Amaretto
Fill with Orange Juice.
Splash with Soda Water.
Garnish with Orange.

BOCA WEST FOREST CAKE
In Blender,
2 oz Chocolate Chip Liqueur
1 oz Vanilla Liqueur
Splash of Grenadine
Fill with cream
Blend until smooth
Garnish with whipped cream and
cherry

BODY SHOT
Pour shot of Tequila.
Lick unclothed area of
favorite person.
Sprinkle dampened area with salt.
Place Lime in favorite
person's mouth.
Lick salted area. Drink shot.
Suck Lime from
favorite person's mouth.
Take turns.

BOG FOG aka
RUM MADRAS
Fill glass with ice.
2 oz Rum or Citrus Rum
Fill with equal parts Orange and
Cranberry Juice.
Garnish with Lime.

BOILERMAKER
Fill shot glass with Whiskey.
Fill chilled glass 3/4 with Beer.
Either drink shot and chase with
beer or drop shot glass into beer
and drink.

BOMB
Fill glass with ice.
1/2 oz Scotch
1/2 oz Bourbon
1/2 oz 151-Proof Rum
1/2 oz Dark Rum
Dash of Grenadine
Fill with equal parts Orange and
Pineapple Juice.
Shake.

BON BON
Fill glass with ice.
3/4 oz Irish Cream
3/4 oz Black Raspberry Liqueur
3/4 oz Truffles Liqueur
Shake.
Strain into chilled glass.

BOOMER
Fill glass with ice.
1 oz Tequila
1 oz Apricot Brandy
Fill glass with equal pts Orange Juice
And Sour Mix.
Shake.

BOOTLEGGER
Fill glass with ice.
3/4 oz Bourbon
3/4 oz Tequila
3/4 oz Southern Comfort
Shake
Strain into chilled glass.

BOP THE PRINCESS
Fill glass with ice.
2 oz Premium Whiskey
Fill with equal parts Cranberry
Juice and Lemon-Lime Soda.
Garnish with Cherry and Lemon.

BORDER CROSSING
2 oz Tequila
Dash of Lime Juice
Fill with Cola.

BOS'N MATE
Fill glass with ice.
1 oz Light Rum
1 oz Dark Rum
Dash of Triple Sec
Dash of Grenadine
Fill with equal parts Lime and
Pineapple Juice.
Garnish with Lime and Pineapple.

BOSOM CARESSER
1 1/2 oz Brandy
1/2 oz Curacao
Dash of Grenadine
1 Egg Yolk
Shake.

BOSS
Fill glass with ice.
3/4 oz Bourbon
1/2 oz Amaretto
Stir.

BOSSA NOVA
Fill glass with ice.
1 oz Galliano
1 oz Amber Rum
1/4 oz Apricot Brandy
Dash of Sour Mix
1/2 Egg White
Fill with Pineapple Juice.
Shake.
Garnish with Orange and Cherry.

BOSTON COCKTAIL
Fill glass with ice.
1 1/2 oz Gin
1 1/2 oz Apricot Brandy
Dash GrenadineShake.
Strain into a chilled glass.
Garnish with a lemon twist.

BOSTON COOLER
Fill glass with ice.
2 oz Rum or Citrus Rum
4 oz Sour Mix
Shake.
Fill with Soda Water.
Garnish with lemon wedge
or twist.

BOSTON GOLD
Fill glass with ice.
1 1/2oz Vodka or Citrus Vodka
1/2oz Banana Liqueur
Fill with Orange Juice.
Shake

BOSTON ICED TEA
Fill glass with ice.
1/2 oz Vodka
1/2 oz Gin
1/2 oz Rum
1/2 oz Coffee Liqueur
1/2 oz Amaretto or Orange Liqueur
2 oz Sour Mix
Fill with Cola.
Garnish with Lemon.

Metric Measurement Conversion Chart on page 14

BOSTON MASSACRE
Fill glass with ice.
Dash of Irish Cream
Dash of Orange Liqueur
Dash of Coffee Liqueur
Dash of Hazelnut Liqueur
Dash of Irish Whiskey
Dash of Amaretto
Dash of Dark Crème de Cacao
Fill with Cream.
Shake.

BOSTON MASSACRE (frozen)
In Blender:
1/2 cup of Ice
Dash of Irish Cream
Dash of Orange Liqueur
Dash of Coffee Liqueur
Dash of Hazelnut Liqueur
Dash of Irish Whiskey
Dash of Amaretto
Dash of Dark Crème de Cacao
Scoop of Vanilla Ice Cream
Blend until smooth.
If too thick add Milk or Cream.
If too thin add ice or Ice Cream.
Pour into glass. Insert straw in
glass against side and dribble
Grenadine into straw. It should run
down inside of glass and look like
dripping blood.

BOSTON SIDECAR
Fill glass with ice.
1 1/2 oz Brandy
1 1/2 oz Rum
1/2 oz Triple Sec
1/2 oz Lime Juice
Shake.
Strain into chilled glass.
Garnish with Lime or Cherry.

BOSTON TEA PARTY
Fill glass with ice.
1 oz Vodka
1 oz Amaretto
1 oz Coffee Liqueur
1 oz Orange Liqueur
2 oz Sour Mix
Shake.
Fill with Cola.

BOSTON TEA PARTY 2
Fill glass with ice.
1/2 oz Vodka
1/2 oz Gin
1/2 oz Rum
1/2 oz Tequila
1/2 oz Triple Sec
1/2 oz Scotch
Dash Dry Vermouth
Dash Sour Mix or Lime Juice
1 oz Orange Juice
Shake.
Top with Cola

BOTTOM LINE
Fill glass with ice.
2 oz Gin or Lime Gin
1/2 oz Lime Juice
Fill with Tonic Water.
Stir.
Garnish with Lime.

BOURBON MANHATTAN
Fill glass with ice.
2 oz Bourbon
Dash of Sweet Vermouth
Stir.
Strain into chilled glass or pour
contents (with ice) into short glass
and serve.
Garnish with Cherry.
CAUTION: SWEET means extra
Sweet Vermouth.
DRY can mean either use Dry
Vermouth instead of Sweet
Vermouth, or less Sweet Vermouth
than usual and garnish with a
Lemon Twist or Cherry.

BOURBON OLD FASHIONED
Muddle together in short glass:
stemless Maraschino Cherry,
Orange Slice,
1/2 tsp of Sugar, and
3 dashes of Bitters.
Fill glass with ice.
2 oz Bourbon
Dash of Soda Water
Stir.

BOURBON SATIN
Fill glass with ice.
1 1/2 oz Bourbon
1 oz White Crème de Cacao
2 oz Milk or Cream
Shake.
Strain into chilled glass.

BOX CAR
Fill glass with ice.
1 1/2 oz Rum or Orange Rum
1/2 oz Triple Sec
Fill with Sour Mix.
Shake.
Garnish with Orange and Cherry.

BRAHMA BULL
Fill glass with ice.
1 1/2 oz Gold Tequila
1/2 oz Coffee Liqueur
Stir.

BRAIN
1 oz Strawberry Liqueur
or Peach Schnapps
1/4 oz Grenadine
1/2 oz Irish Cream.
Put in drop by drop.

BRAIN (floater)
Fill glass with ice.
1 oz Coffee Liqueur (bottom)
1 oz Peach Schnapps
1 oz Irish Cream (top)

BRAIN ERASER
Fill glass with ice.
1 oz Vodka
1/2 oz Coffee Liqueur
1/2 oz Amaretto
Splash with Club Soda.
Supposed to be drunk in one shot
through a straw.

BRAIN TUMOR
Fill glass with ice.
2 oz Irish Cream
5 or 6 drops of Strawberry Liqueur

B

BRAIN WAVE (floater)
1 1/4 oz Irish Cream (bottom)
3/4 oz Vodka (top)
Place a drop of Grenadine into center of drink.

BRANDY ALEXANDER
Fill glass with ice.
1 1/2 oz Brandy
1/2 oz Dark Crème de Cacao
3 oz Cream or Milk
Shake.
Serve or strain into chilled glass.
Sprinkle Nutmeg on top.

BRANDY ALEXANDER (frozen)
In Blender:
1/2 cup of Ice
1 1/2 oz Brandy
1/2 oz Dark Crème de Cacao
Scoop of Vanilla Ice Cream
Blend until smooth.
If too thick add Milk or Cream.
If too thin add ice or Ice Cream.
Sprinkle Nutmeg on top.

BRANDY ALMOND MOCHA
1 oz Brandy
1 oz Amaretto
Fill with equal parts Hot
Chocolate and hot Coffee.
Stir.
Top with Whipped Cream.
Sprinkle with Shaved Almonds.

BRANDY GUMP
Fill glass with ice.
2 oz Brandy
Dash of Grenadine
Fill with Sour Mix.
Shake.
Serve or strain into chilled glass.
Garnish with Orange and Cherry.

BRANDY HUMMER (frozen)
In Blender:
1/2 cup of ice
1 oz Brandy
1 oz Coffee Liqueur
Scoop of Vanilla Ice Cream
Blend until smooth.
If too thick add Milk or Cream.
If too thin add ice or Ice Cream.

BRANDY MILK PUNCH
2 oz Brandy
1 tsp Sugar or Sugar Syrup
Fill with Milk or Cream.
Shake.

BRASS MONKEY
Fill glass with ice.
1 oz Vodka or Citrus Vodka
1 oz Rum or Citrus RUm
Fill with Orange Juice.
Garnish with Orange.

BRASS MONKEY 2
Fill glass _ with Malt Liqueur
Fill the remaining _ with Orange
Juice.
Often made in 40oz bottles.

BRAVE BULL
Fill glass with ice.
1 1/2 oz Tequila
1/2 oz Coffee Liqueur
Stir.
Strain into shot glass.

BRAVE COW
Fill glass with ice.
3 1/2 oz Gin
1/2 oz Coffee Liqueur
Stir.
Serve or strain into chilled glass.

BRAZILIAN COFFEE
3/4 oz Coffee Liqueur
3/4 oz Brandy
3/4 oz Orange Liqueur
Fill with hot Black Coffee.
Top with Whipped Cream.
Sprinkle Brown Sugar on top.

BRAZILIAN COFFEE 2
In Blender: Cup of ice
2 oz Cachaca or Pinga
Dash Cream
tsp Sugar
Double Espresso
or cup of drip coffee
Blend until smooth.
Top with Whipped Cream
Garnish with 3 coffee beans.

BRIGHTON PUNCH
Fill glass with ice.
3/4 oz Brandy
3/4 oz Benedictine
3/4 oz Bourbon
Fill with equal parts Sour Mix and
Orange Juice.
Shake.
Top with Soda Water.

BROKEN DOWN GOLF CART
Fill glass with ice.
1 oz Vodka or Melon Liqueur
1 oz Amaretto
1 oz Cranberry Juice
Shake.
Strain into shot glass.

BROKEN HEART
Fill glass with ice.
1 oz Vodka
1 oz Black Raspberry Liqueur
Dash of Grenadine
Fill with Orange Juice.
Shake.

BRONCO COCKTAIL
Fill glass with ice.
1 oz Orange Liqueur
2 oz Orange Soda
Fill with Champagne.
Garnish with Orange.

BROWN COW
Fill glass with ice.
2 oz Dark Crème de Cacao
Fill with Milk or Cream.
Shake.

BROWN DERBY
Fill glass with ice.
2 oz Vodka
Fill with Cola.

BROWN SQUIRREL
1 oz Amaretto
1 oz Dark Crème de Cacao
1 oz Cream or Milk
Shake.
Strain into chilled glass.

Metric Measurement Conversion Chart on page 14

BROWN SQUIRREL (frozen)
In Blender:
1/2 cup of Ice
1 oz Amaretto
3/4 oz Dark Crème de Cacao
Scoop of Vanilla Ice Cream
Dash of Milk
Blend until smooth.
If too thick add Milk.
If too thin add ice or Ice Cream.

**BRUT AND BOGS aka
CHAM CRAN CHAM,
SCARLET LETTER**
Fill glass 3/4 with ice.
Fill glass 3/4 with Champagne.
Dash of Black Raspberry Liqueur
Fill with Cranberry Juice.

B-STING
Fill glass with ice.
1 1/2 oz B&B
1/2 oz White Crème de Menthe

BUBBLE GUM
Fill glass with ice.
1 oz Vodka or Banana Vodka
(Note: If using Banana Vodka, don't
add the Banana Liqueur)
1 oz Southern Comfort
1 oz Banana Liqueur
Dash of Grenadine
1 oz Cream
Shake.
Strain into chilled glass.
Garnish with Bubble Gum Stick.

BUBBLE GUM 2
Fill glass with ice.
1 oz Melon Liqueur
1 oz Amaretto
or Crème de Nouyax
1 oz Milk or Cream
Dash of Grenadine (optional)
Shake.
Strain into chilled glass.
Garnish with Bubble Gum Stick.

BUCK
Fill glass with ice.
2 oz desired Liquor
Fill with Ginger Ale.
Garnish with Lemon.

BUCKAROO
Fill glass with ice.
2 oz Rum
Fill with Root Beer.

BUCKHEAD ROOT BEER
Fill glass with ice.
2 oz Jägermeister
Fill with Club Soda.
Garnish with Lime and Orange.

BUCKING BRONCO (floater)
1 oz Southern Comfort (bottom)
1 oz Tequila (top)

BUFFALO PISS
Fill glass with ice.
2 oz Tequila
Fill with equal parts Grapefruit
Juice and Lemon-Lime Soda.

BUFFALO SWEAT
2 oz Bourbon
Dash of Tabasco Sauce
Stir.

BUFFALO SWEAT 2
1 oz Tequila
1 oz 151-Proof Rum
Dash of Tabasco Sauce

BULL SHOT
1 oz Vodka or Peppered Vodka
1 oz Beef Bouillon
Dash of Worcestershire Sauce
Dash of Salt & Dash of Pepper

BULL'S MILK
Fill glass with ice.
1 1/2 oz Brandy
1/2 oz Dark Rum
1/2 tsp Sugar
Fill with Milk.
Shake.
Sprinkle with Cinnamon.

BULLDOG
Fill glass with ice.
1 oz Vodka or Rum
1 oz Coffee Liqueur
Fill with equal parts Cream & Cola.

BULLFROG aka KAMIKAZE
Fill glass with ice.
2 oz Vodka or Citrus Vodka
1/2 oz Triple Sec
Dash of Lime Juice
Shake.
Serve or strain into shot glass.
Garnish with a Lime.

BULLFROG 2
Fill glass with ice.
2 oz Vodka
Fill with equal parts Sour Mix and
Grapefruit Juice.

BUMBLE BEE
Fill glass with ice.
2 oz Tia Maria
Fill with Milk.
Shake.
Top with Peach Schnapps.

BUNGEE JUMPER
Fill glass with ice.
2 oz Irish Mist
Dash of Cream
Fill with Orange Juice.
Shake.
Top with Amaretto.

**BURNING BUSH aka
PRAIRIE FIRE**
2 oz Tequila
Add Tabasco Sauce until pink.

**BURNT ALMOND aka ROASTED
TOASTED ALMOND, ORGASM**
Fill glass with ice.
1 oz Vodka
1 oz Coffee Liqueur
1 oz Amaretto
Fill with Milk or Cream.
Shake.

BURNT ALMOND (frozen)
In Blender:
1/2 cup of Ice
1 oz Vodka
1 oz Coffee Liqueur
1 oz Amaretto
Scoop of Vanilla Ice Cream
Blend until smooth.
If too thick add Milk or Cream.
If too thin add ice or Ice Cream.

BURNTOUT BITCH
Fill glass with ice.
1/2 oz Vodka
1/2 oz Rum
1/2 oz Tequila
1/2 oz Triple Sec
Fill with Orange Juice.
Shake.

BUSH DIVER (floater)
3/4 oz Coffee Liqueur (bottom)
3/4 oz Irish Cream
3/4 oz Apple Brandy (top)

BUSHWACKER aka SHILLELAGH
Fill glass with ice.
1 oz Irish Whiskey or Irish Mist
1 oz Irish Cream
Stir.

BUSHWACKER 2
Fill glass with ice.
1 1/2 oz Dark Rum
1/2 oz Coffee Liqueur
1/2 oz Dark Crème de Cacao
1 oz Cream of Coconut
Fill with Cream or Milk.
Shake.

BUSTED CHERRY (floater)
1/2 oz Coffee Liqueur (bottom)
1/2 oz Cream
1/2 oz Cherry Brandy (top)

BUSTED RUBBER (floater)
1/2 oz Raspberry Liqueur
(bottom)
1/2 oz Irish Cream
1/2 oz Orange Liqueur (top)

BUTT MUNCH (frozen)
In Blender:
1/2 cup of ice
1 oz Brandy
1 oz Rum
1 oz Coffee
1 oz Chocolate Syrup
1 oz Milk
tsp Honey
Blend until smooth.
Top with Whipped Cream.
Sprinkle with Cinnamon.

BUTTAFINGER
Fill glass with ice.
1/2 oz Vodka or Vanilla Vodka
1 oz Cookies and Cream Liqueur
1 oz Butterscotch Schnapps
Fill with Cream or Milk.
Shake.

BUTTAFINGER 2
1/2 oz Vodka or Vanilla Vodka
1/2 oz Irish Cream
1/2 oz Coffee Liqueur
1/2 oz Butterscotch Schnapps
Dash of Milk or Cream
Shake. Strain into shot glass.

BUTTER BALL (floater)
1 1/2 oz Butterscotch Schnapps
(bottom)
1/2 oz Irish Cream or Orange
Liqueur (top)

BUTTER SHOT aka
BUTTERY NIPPLE (floater)
1 oz Butterscotch Schnapps (bottom)
1/2 oz Irish Cream
1/2 oz Vodka or Vanilla Vodka (top)

BUTTERNUT COFFEE
1 oz Amaretto or Hazelnut Liqueur
1 oz Butterscotch Schnapps
Fill with hot Black Coffee.
Top with Whipped Cream.
Drizzle with Butterscotch.

C & B
1 oz Cognac
1 oz Benedictine

CABLE CAR
Fill glass with ice.
1 1/2 oz Gin
1/2 oz Triple Sec
1/2 oz Lime Juice
Shake.
Strain into chilled glass.

CABLEGRAM
Fill glass with ice.
2 oz Whiskey
1/2 oz Sour Mix
1 tsp Sugar Syrup
Shake.
Fill glass with Ginger Ale.
Garnish with Lemon.

CACTUS BANGER aka
FREDDY FUDPUCKER
Fill glass with ice.
1 1/2 oz Tequila
Fill with Orange Juice.
Top with Galliano.
Garnish with Orange.

CACTUS JUICE
Fill glass with ice.
1 1/2 oz Tequila
1/2 oz Amaretto
Fill with Sour Mix.
Shake.

CADILLAC MARGARITA
Fill glass with ice.
1 1/2 oz Tequila
1/2 oz Cointreau
Dash of Lime Juice
3 oz Sour Mix
Shake.
Top with Dash of Grand Marnier.

CADIZ
Fill glass with ice.
3/4 oz Blackberry Brandy
3/4 oz Dry Sherry
1/2 oz Triple Sec
1/4 oz Cream
Shake.

CAFÉ AMORE
1 oz Cognac
1 oz Amaretto
Fill with hot Black Coffee.
Top with Whipped Cream.
Sprinkle with Shaved Almonds.

CAFE AU LAIT
Heat coffee cup, mug, specialty
glass
Pour simultaneously equal parts
Fresh Coffee (Dark Roasted)
and Scalding Steamed Milk.
You can leave a layer of froth on
top of the mix
Sprinkle with Chocolate shavings or
powder, or
Cinnamon and or Nutmeg.

Metric Measurement Conversion Chart on page 14

CAFÉ BARBADOS

1 1/2 oz Dark Rum
1/2 oz Coffee Liqueur
Fill with hot Black Coffee.
Top with Whipped Cream.
Sprinkle with Powdered Chocolate.

CAFE CARIBBEAN

1 oz Rum or Vanilla Rum
1 oz Amaretto
Fill with Hot Black Coffee.
Top with Whipped Cream.
Garnish with Shaved Almonds.

CAFÉ DIABLO

3/4 oz Cognac or Brandy
3/4 oz Sambuca
3/4 oz Orange Liqueur
Fill with hot Black Coffee.
Sprinkle with grated Orange Rind,
Allspice and Brown Sugar.
Garnish with Orange.

CAFÉ FOSTER

1 oz Dark Rum
3/4 oz Banana Liqueur
Fill with hot Black Coffee.
Top with Whipped Cream.
Garnish with Banana.

CAFÉ GATES

3/4 oz Coffee Liqueur
3/4 oz Orange Liqueur
3/4 oz Dark Crème de Cacao
Fill with hot Black Coffee.
Top with Whipped Cream.
Sprinkle with Shaved Chocolate or
Sprinkles.

CAFÉ GRANDE

3/4 oz Orange Liqueur
3/4 oz Dark Crème de Cacao
3/4 oz Coffee Liqueur
Fill with hot Black Coffee.
Top with Whipped Cream.
Garnish with Orange.

CAFÉ ITALIA

1 1/2 oz Tuaca
1 tsp Sugar or Sugar Syrup
Fill with hot Black Coffee.
Top with Whipped Cream.
Sprinkle with Cinnamon.

CAFÉ MAGIC

3/4 oz Amaretto
3/4 oz Irish Cream
3/4 oz Coffee Liqueur
Fill with hot Black Coffee.
Top with Whipped Cream.
Sprinkle with Shaved Chocolate.

CAFÉ MARSEILLES

3/4 oz Hazelnut Liqueur
3/4 oz Black Raspberry Liqueur
3/4 oz Coffee Liqueur
Fill with hot Black Coffee.
Top with Whipped Cream.

CAFE MOCHA

Heat cup, mug or specialty glass.
Fill 3/4 with Fresh Coffee or Espresso.
Gently stir in 2 Tblsp Chocolate syrup
or powdered Hot Chocolate mix.
Fill the rest of the way with
Steamed Milk or Whipped Cream.
Should have layer of frothy milk on
top.
Sprinkle with Chocolate shavings or
powder.
SEE: ICED CAFE MOCHA

CAFÉ ORLEANS

1 oz Coffee Liqueur
1 oz Praline Liqueur
Fill with hot Black Coffee.
Top with Whipped Cream.
Sprinkle with crushed Peanut
Brittle.

CAFÉ REGGAE

3/4 oz Dark Rum
3/4 oz Coffee Liqueur
3/4 oz Dark Crème de Cacao
Fill with hot Black Coffee.
Top with Whipped Cream.

CAFÉ ROYALE

2 oz Cognac or Brandy
Fill with hot Black Coffee.
Garnish with Lemon Twist.

CAFÉ THEATRE

1/2 oz Irish Cream
1/2 oz White Crème de Cacao
Fill with hot Black Coffee.
Dash of Hazelnut Liqueur
Dash of Dark Crème de Cacao
Top with Whipped Cream.

CAFÉ VENITZIO

3/4 oz Amaretto
3/4 oz Brandy
3/4 oz Galliano
Fill with hot Black Coffee.

CAFE YBOR

2oz Licor 43
Fill with hot black coffee.
Top with Whipped Cream.
Drizzle tsp 151-Proof Rum and
tsp Grenadine on top.
Garnish with Orange.

CAFÉ ZURICH

3/4 oz Anisette
3/4 oz Cognac
3/4 oz Amaretto
Fill with hot Black Coffee.
Top with Whipped Cream.
Drizzle with Honey.

CAFFE AMERICANO

This is just a Espresso with water
added to
cut the strong black Coffee.
Heat a coffee cup.
Make single Espresso in cup
Add equal amount of Hot water.

CAFFE LATTE

Heat coffee cup, mug, or specialty
glass.
1 shot Espresso
Fill with liquid Steamed Milk.

CAIPIRINHA

Place 2 Lime wedges and
tsp Sugar in glass and muddle.
Fill glass with ice.
Fill with Cachaca or Rum.
Stir.

CAJUN COFFEE

2 oz Praline Liqueur
Fill with hot Black Coffee.
Top with Whipped Cream.
Garnish with crushed Peanut
Brittle.

B

C

Metric Measurement Conversion Chart on page 14

CAJUN MARTINI aka CREOLE MARTINI
Fill glass with ice.
3 1/2 oz Peppered Vodka
1/2 oz Dry Vermouth
Stir.
Strain into chilled glass.
Garnish with a Jalapeno Pepper.

CALIFORNIA BREEZE aka MADRAS
Fill glass with ice.
2 oz Vodka or Citrus Vodka
Fill with equal parts Orange and Cranberry Juice.
Stir.
Garnish with Orange or Lime.

CALIFORNIA COOL AID
Fill glass with ice.
2 oz Rum
Fill with equal parts Orange Juice and Milk.
Shake.

CALIFORNIA COOLER
Fill glass with ice.
2 oz Vodka or Orange Vodka
Fill with equal parts Orange Juice And Soda Water.

CALIFORNIA DRIVER
Fill glass with ice.
2 oz Vodka or Grapefruit Vodka
Fill with equal parts Orange and Grapefruit Juice.

CALIFORNIA ICED TEA
Fill glass with ice.
1/2 oz Vodka or Grapefruit Vodka
1/2 oz Gin
1/2 oz Rum
1/2 oz Tequila
1/2 oz Triple Sec
2 oz Grapefruit Juice
Top with Cola.
Garnish with Lemon.

CALIFORNIA LEMONADE
Fill glass with ice.
1/2 oz Vodka
1/2 oz Gin
1/2 oz Brandy
2 oz Sour Mix
2 oz Orange Juice
Dash of Grenadine
Shake.
Garnish with a Lemon.

CALIFORNIA LEMONADE 2
Fill glass with ice.
2 oz Blended Whiskey
1 oz Sour Mix
Dash of Lime Juice
Dash of Grenadine
Fill with Soda Water.
Garnish with Orange and Cherry.

CALIFORNIA MOTHER
Fill glass with ice.
1 oz Brandy
1 oz Coffee Liqueur
Fill with equal parts Milk or Cream and Cola.

CALIFORNIA ROOT BEER
Fill glass with ice.
1 oz Coffee Liqueur
Fill with Soda Water.
Top with 1/2 oz Galliano.
Dash of Cola or Beer or Milk (optional).

CALYPSO COFFEE
1 oz Tia Maria
or Dark Crème de Cacao
1 oz Rum
Fill with hot Black Coffee.
Top with Whipped Cream.
Sprinkle with Shaved Chocolate.

CAMPARI AND SODA
Fill glass with ice.
2 oz Campari
Fill with Soda Water.
Garnish with Lemon or Lime.

CAMSHAFT
Fill glass with ice.
3/4 oz Irish Cream
3/4 oz Rootbeer Schnapps
3/4 oz Jägermeister
Shake.
Strain into shot glass.

CANADA COCKTAIL
Fill glass with ice.
1 1/2 oz Canadian Whiskey
1/2 oz Triple Sec
2 dashes of Bitters
1 tsp Sugar
Shake.
Strain into chilled glass.
Garnish with Orange.

CANADIAN BLACKBERRY FIZZ
1 1/2 oz Canadian Whiskey
1/2 oz Blackberry Brandy
2 oz Sour Mix
Shake.
Fill with Soda Water.

CANADIAN CIDER (frozen)
In Blender:
1/2 cup of Ice
1 oz Canadian Whiskey
1/2 oz Cinnamon Schnapps
3 oz Apple Cider
1/4 ripe Red Apple
Blend until smooth.

CANADIAN COFFEE
2 oz Yukon Jack
Fill with hot Black Coffee.
Top with Whipped Cream.
Dribble 5-6 drops of Crème de Nouyax on top.

CANCUN (frozen)
In Blender:
1/2 cup ice
3/4 oz Coffee Liqueur
3/4 oz Sambuca
3/4 oz Irish Cream
3 oz cold espresso
Scoop of Vanilla Ice Cream.
Blend until smooth.

CANDY APPLE
Fill glass with ice.
1 oz Apple Brandy
1 oz Cinnamon Schnapps
Fill with Cranberry Juice.
Stir.

Metric Measurement Conversion Chart on page 14

CANDY ASS
Fill glass with ice.
3/4 oz Black Raspberry Liqueur
3/4 oz Crème de Cacao
3/4 oz Irish Cream
Shake.

CANDY CANE
Fill glass with ice.
2 oz Peppermint Schnapps
Fill with Milk.
Shake.
Float 1/2 oz Cherry Brandy
on top.

CANDY CANE (floater)
1 1/2 oz Peppermint Schnapps
(bottom)
1/2 oz Crème de Nouyax (top)

CANYON QUAKE
Fill glass with ice.
1 oz Brandy
1 oz Irish Cream
Fill with Milk or Cream.
Shake.

CAPE CODDER
Fill glass with ice.
2 oz Vodka
Fill with Cranberry Juice.
Garnish with Lime.

CAPITAL PUNISHMENT
Fill glass with ice.
1 oz Bourbon
1 oz Amaretto
Stir.
Strain into shot glass.

CAPOEIRA (frozen)
In blender: 2 cups crushed ice
2 oz Cognac or Brandy
2 oz Creme de Cacao
2 oz Cream of Coconut
Blend until smooth.

CAPPUCCINO
Heat coffee cup, mug or specialty
glass by filling it with hot water and
letting it sit for 30 seconds.
Fill 1/3 with Espresso (1 shot)
1/3 liquid Steamed Milk.
1/3 foam Steamed Milk
Sprinkle with Chocolate shavings
or powder, or Cinnamon and or
Nutmeg.

CAPRI aka BANSHEE
Fill glass with ice.
1 oz Banana Liqueur
1/2 oz White Crème de Cacao
Fill with Milk or Cream.
Shake.

CAPTAIN MARINER
Fill glass with ice.
1 1/2 oz Spiced Rum
1/2 oz Orange Liqueur
Dash of Grenadine
Fill with Orange Juice.
Shake.
Garnish with Orange.

CARA SPOSA aka SEXY
Fill glass with ice.
1 oz Coffee Liqueur
1 oz Orange Liqueur
Fill with Milk or Cream.
Shake.
Garnish with Orange.

CARAMEL APPLE MARTINI
Fill glass with ice.
3 1/2 oz Vodka
Dash Apple Cider or Apple Juice
Shake
Dip rim of chilled glass in caramel
or
Drizzle onto inside of glass.
Strain into chilled glass.

CARIBBEAN CHAMPAGNE
1 oz Light Rum
1 oz Banana Liqueur
Stir.
Fill with Champagne.
Garnish with Banana and Cherry.

CARIBBEAN DREAM COFFEE
3/4 oz Dark Rum
3/4 oz Dark Crème de Cacao
3/4 oz Banana Liqueur
Fill with hot Black Coffee.
Garnish with Banana.

CARIBBEAN MADRAS
Fill glass with ice.
2 oz Dark Rum
Fill with equal parts Cranberry and
Orange Juice.

CARIBBEAN SCREW
Fill glass with ice.
3/4 oz Coconut Rum
3/4 oz Banana Liqueur
3/4 oz Peach Schnapps
Fill with equal parts Milk, Orange,
and Pineapple Juice.
Shake.

CARIBBEAN SCREW WITH A SUNBURN
Fill glass with ice.
3/4 oz Dark Rum
3/4 oz Coconut Rum
3/4 oz Light Rum
Dash of Grenadine
Fill with Orange Juice.
Shake.

CARIBBEAN SURFER
Fill glass with ice.
1 1/2 oz Coconut Rum
1/2 oz Banana Liqueur
Fill with Pineapple Juice.
Shake.
Garnish with a cherry.

CARIBOU SCREW
Fill glass with ice.
2 oz Yukon Jack or Bourbon
Fill with Orange Juice.

CARROLL COCKTAIL
Fill glass with ice.
1 1/2 oz Brandy
3/4 oz Sweet Vermouth
Stir.
Strain into chilled glass.

CARROT CAKE
Fill glass with ice.
1 oz Irish Cream
1 oz Coffee Liqueur
1 oz Butterscotch Schnapps
1/2 oz Cinnamon Schnapps
Shake. Strain into chilled glass.

Metric Measurement Conversion Chart on page 14

CARTEL BUSTER (floater)
1 oz Coffee Liqueur (bottom)
1 oz Orange Liqueur
1 oz Gold Tequila (top)

CASABLANCA
Fill glass with ice.
2 oz Rum
1 1/2 tsp Triple Sec
1 1/2 tsp Cherry Liqueur
 or Cherry Rum
1 1/2 oz Lime Juice
Shake.
Strain into chilled glass.

CASINO COFFEE
3/4 oz Amaretto
3/4 oz Brandy
3/4 oz Crème de Cacao
Fill with hot Black Coffee.
Top with Whipped Cream.
Sprinkle with Shaved Almonds.

CATALINA MARGARITA
Fill glass with ice.
1 1/2 oz Tequila
Dash Blue Curacao
Dash Peach Schnapps
Dash Lime Juice
3 oz. Sour Mix
Shake.

CATFISH
Fill glass with ice.
1 1/2 oz Rum
1/2 oz Triple Sec
Fill with Cola.
Garnish with Lime.

CELTIC COMRADE (floater)
1/2 oz Coffee Liqueur (bottom)
1/2 oz Irish Cream
1/2 oz Vodka
1/2 oz Drambuie (top)

CEMENT MIXER
Fill shot glass with Irish Cream.
Add dash of Lime Juice.
Let set 30 seconds.

CEREBRAL HEMORRHAGE (floater)
Fill glass with ice.
1 oz Coffee Liqueur (bottom)
1 oz Peach Schnapps
1 oz Irish Cream (top)
Add several drops of Grenadine.

CHAIN LIGHTNING
3 oz Gin
1/2 oz Triple Sec
1 oz Fresh Lemon Juice
Shake.
Serve or strain into chilled glass.
Garnish with Lemon.

**CHAM CRAN CHAM aka
BRUT AND BOGS,
SCARLET LETTER**
Fill glass 3/4 with ice.
Fill glass 3/4 with Champagne.
Dash of Black Raspberry Liqueur
Fill with Cranberry Juice.

CHAMBERED ROUND
In shot glass:
1 oz Grain Alcohol or Vodka
1 oz Tequila
Garnish with an Olive.

**CHAMPAGNE COCKTAIL aka
LONDON SPECIAL**
In a Champagne glass:
1/2 tsp Sugar or 1 Sugar Cube
2 dashes of Bitters
Fill with Champagne.
Garnish with Lemon or Orange Twist.

CHAMPAGNE SUPER NOVA
Fill glass with ice.
1/2 oz Vodka
1/2 oz Gin
1/2 oz Blue Curacao
Dash of Cranberry Juice
Dash of Sour Mix
Fill with Champagne.

CHANNEL
2 oz Blackberry Brandy
Fill with Beer.
Matt Olga

CHAOS
Fill glass with ice.
1/2 oz 151-Proof Rum
1/2 oz Gin
1/2 oz Sloe Gin
1/2 oz Orange Liqueur
1/2 oz Lime Juice
Shake.
Strain into chilled glass.

CHARLIE CHAPLIN
Fill glass with ice.
1 oz Apricot Brandy
1 oz Sloe Gin
1 oz Lemon or Lime Juice
Shake.
Strain into chilled glass.

CHARRO
Fill glass with ice.
1 oz Tequila
1 oz Coffee
1 oz Milk
Stir.
Strain into shot glass.

CHASTITY BELT (floater)
3/4 oz Coffee Liqueur (bottom)
3/4 oz Irish Cream
3/4 oz Hazelnut Liqueur
Top with 1/2 oz Milk (top)

CHEAP SHADES
Fill glass with ice.
1 oz Vodka or Pineapple Vodka
1/2 oz Peach Schnapps
1/2 oz Melon Liqueur
Dash of Sour Mix
Dash of Pineapple Juice
Fill with Lemon-Lime Soda.
Garnish with Pineapple.

CHEAP SUNGLASSES
Fill glass with ice.
2 oz Vodka or Citrus Vodka
Fill with equal parts Cranberry
Juice and Lemon-Lime Soda.
Garnish with Lime.

CHELSEA SIDECAR
Fill glass with ice.
3 1/2 oz Gin
1/2 oz Triple Sec
Fill with Sour Mix.
Shake.
Strain into chilled glass.
Garnish with Orange and Cherry.

CHERRY BLOSSOM
Fill glass with ice.
1 oz Rum or Brandy
1 oz Cherry Brandy
1 tsp Grenadine
1 tsp Lemon Juice
Shake.
Garnish with Cherry.

CHERRY BOMB aka EAT THE CHERRY
Place pitted, stemless Cherry in shot glass.
1 tsp Cherry Juice
Fill with Grain Alcohol or Vodka.

CHERRY BOMBS
Drain jar of Maraschino Cherries.
Fill with Vodka or Rum or Grain Alcohol.
Let sit for 7 days.

CHERRY BUS GIRL
Fill glass with ice.
1 oz Rum
Fill with cola.
Garnish with cherry.
Tip her well and offer
Her a ride home.

CHERRY COLA
Fill glass with ice.
1 1/2 oz Cherry Brandy
Fill with Cola.
Garnish with Cherry.

CHERRY COLA FROM HELL
In shot glass pour:
1 oz Grain Alcohol
Ignite
Drop into glass containing:
1 oz Cherry Brandy
Filled 3/4 with Cola.

CHERRY HOOKER
Fill glass with ice.
2 oz Cherry Brandy
Fill with Orange Juice.
Shake.
Garnish with Lime.

CHERRY LIFE-SAVOR
Fill glass with ice.
2 oz Amaretto
Fill with Cranberry Juice.

CHERRY MARTINI
Fill glass with ice.
3 1/2 oz Cherry Vodka or Vodka
1/2 oz Cherry Brandy
Dash Cherry Juice
Shake. Strain into a chilled glass.
Garnish with Cherry.

CHERRY PIE
Fill glass with ice.
1 oz Vodka,
    or Vanilla or Cherry Vodka
1/2 oz Brandy
1/2 oz Cherry Brandy
Stir.
Strain into chilled glass.

CHERRY SCREW
Fill glass with ice.
2 oz Cherry Brandy
Fill with Orange Juice.
Shake.
Garnish with Orange and Lime.

CHERRY TART
Fill glass with ice.
1 oz Bourbon
1 oz Cherry Brandy
1 oz Lemon Juice
tsp Sugar
Shake.
Strain into chilled glass.

C

CHI-CHI
Fill glass with ice.
1 1/2 oz Rum
1/2 oz Blackberry Brandy
Fill with Pineapple Juice.
Shake.
Garnish with Pineapple.

CHI-CHI (frozen)
In Blender:
1/2 cup of Ice
2 oz Vodka
1/2 oz Blue Curacao
1/2 oz Cream of Coconut
1/2 cup fresh or canned Pineapple
Scoop of Vanilla Ice Cream
Blend until smooth.
If too thick add juice.
If too thin add ice or Ice Cream.
Garnish with Pineapple.

CHICAGO
Fill glass with ice.
1 1/2 oz Brandy
Dash of Curacao or Triple Sec
Dash of Bitters
Shake.
Strain into glass rimmed with sugar.
Fill with Champagne.

CHICKEN SHOT
1 oz Vodka
1 oz Chicken Bouillon
Dash of Worcestershire Sauce
Dash of Salt
Dash of Pepper

CHILES FRITOS
Fill glass with ice.
2 oz Tequila
Dash of Lime Juice
Dash of Celery Salt
Dash of Tabasco Sauce
Dash of Worcestershire Sauce
Dash of Pepper
Dash of Grenadine
Dash of Orange Juice
Shake.
Garnish with 2 Chili Peppers.

CHINA BEACH
Fill glass with ice.
1 oz Vodka
1 oz Ginger Liqueur
Fill with Cranberry Juice.
Stir.

CHINA BLUE MARTINI
Fill glass with ice.
3 1/2 oz Gin or Orange Gin
Dash Ginger Liqueur
Dash Blue Curacao
Shake.
Garnish with Ginger Candy.

CHINESE COCKTAIL
Fill glass with ice.
1 1/2 oz Dark Rum
1 tsp Triple Sec
1 tsp Cherry Liqueur
1 tsp Grenadine
Dash of Bitters
Shake.
Strain into chilled glass.

CHINESE TORTURE (floater)
1 1/2 oz Ginger Liqueur (bottom)
1/2 oz 151-Proof Rum (top)
Ignite.

CHIQUITA
Fill glass with ice.
1/2 oz Banana Liqueur
1/2 oz Orange Liqueur or Triple Sec
Fill with equal parts Orange Juice
and Milk.
Shake.

CHOCOLATE BANANA FREEZE
(frozen)
In Blender:
1/2 cup of Ice
1 oz Vodka
1 oz Dark Crème de Cacao
1/2 oz Banana Liqueur
1 tbsp Chocolate Syrup
1/2 fresh peeled ripe Banana
Scoop of Chocolate Ice Cream
Blend until smooth.
If too thick add fruit or Milk.
If too thin add ice or Ice Cream.
Garnish with Banana.
Top with Whipped Cream.

CHOCOLATE CAKE
Fill glass with ice.
3/4 oz Citrus Vodka
3/4 Hazelnut Liqueur
Stir.
Strain into shot glass.
Garnish with sugar coated lemon.

CHOCOLATE CHAOS (frozen)
In Blender: 1/2 cup of ice.
1 1/2 oz Chocolate Vodka
1/2 oz Crème de Cacao
2 oz Chocolate Syrup
Scoop of Chocolate Ice Cream
Blend until smooth.
Top with Chocolate Whipped
Cream.
Garnish with Chocolate Graham
Cracker

CHOCOLATE CORVETTE
1 1/2 oz Dark Rum
1/2 oz Dark Creme de Cacao
Fill with hot chocolate.
Top with heavy cream.
Garnish with marshmallows or
powdered cocoa.

CHOCOLATE COLADA (frozen)
In Blender:
1/2 cup of Ice
2 oz Rum
2 tbsp Cream of Coconut
1 oz Chocolate Syrup
Dash of Milk or Cream
Blend until smooth.

CHOCOLATE COVERED BANANA
Fill glass with ice.
3 oz Banana Rum
1 oz White Crème de Cacao
Stir.
Strain into Martini Glass rimmed in
Chocolate then dipped in chopped
Walnuts.   -- Bill Bona

CHOCOLATE COVERED CHERRY
Fill glass with ice.
1/2 oz Coffee Liqueur
1/2 oz Amaretto
1/2 oz White Crème de Cacao
Shake.
Strain into chilled glass.
Add 1 drop of Grenadine.

CHOCOLATE COVERED CHERRY (frozen)
In Blender:
1/2 cup of Ice
1 1/2 oz Vodka or Cherry
           or Chocolate Vodka
1/2 oz Dark Crème de Cacao
Dash of Cherry Brandy
4 Maraschino Cherries (no stems)
Scoop of Chocolate Ice Cream
Blend until smooth.
If too thick add Milk.
If too thin add ice or Ice Cream.

CHOCOLATE KISS
1 1/2 oz Peppermint Schnapps
1/2 oz Coffee Liqueur
Fill with Hot Chocolate.
Top with Whipped Cream.
Sprinkle with Shaved Chocolate or
Sprinkles.

CHOCOLATE MARTINI
Fill glass with ice.
3 1/2 oz Vodka or Chocolate Vodka
1/2 oz Crème de Cacao or
Chocolate Liqueur
Dash of Orange Liqueur (optional)
Stir.
Strain into chilled glass or pour
contents (with ice) into short glass.
Garnish with Chocolate-covered
Cherry or any small Chocolate.

CHOCOLATE MESS (frozen)
In Blender:
1/2 cup of ice.
1 oz Crème de Cacao
1 oz Coffee Liqueur
1 oz Black Raspberry Liqueur
Tbsp Powdered Cacao
Scoop of Chocolate Ice Cream
Blend until smooth.
Top with Whipped Cream.
Drizzle Chocolate Syrup on top.

CHOCOLATE MINT MARTINI
Fill glass with ice.
3 oz Vodka or (Mint Vodka with no
Crème de Menthe,
or Chocolate Vodka with no Crème
de Cacao)
1/2 oz White Crème de Cacao
1/2 oz White Crème de Menthe
Shake.
Strain into a chilled glass.

Metric Measurement Conversion Chart on page 14

CHOCOLATE RATTLESNAKE
Fill glass with ice.
1 oz Coffee Liqueur
1 oz Irish Cream
1/2 oz Crème de Cacao
1/2 oz Peppermint Schnapps
Stir.
Strain into shot glass.

CHOCOLATE SQUIRREL
Fill glass with ice.
3/4 oz Amaretto
3/4 oz Hazelnut Liqueur
3/4 oz Dark Crème de Cacao
Fill with Milk.
Shake.
Serve or strain into chilled glass.

CHOCOLATE THUNDER
2 oz Vodka
Fill with Ovaltine.

CHRISTIAN'S COFFEE
1 oz Coffee Liqueur
1 oz Irish Cream
1 oz Amaretto
Fill with hot Black Coffee.
Top with Whipped Cream.

CHUPACABRA
Fill glass with ice.
1 oz Tequila
1 oz Jägermeister
Shake.
Strain into shot glass.

CINCINNATI
Fill glass with equal parts
Beer and Soda Water.

CLAM DIGGER
Fill glass with ice.
2 oz Vodka or Gin
Dash of Tabasco Sauce
Dash of Worcestershire Sauce
Dash of Lime Juice or Sour Mix
Dash of Salt
Dash of Pepper
Dash of Tomato Juice
2 oz Clam Juice
Shake.

CLAM SHOT
In shot glass.
1 small raw clam (should take up
less than _ of glass)
Drizzle or fill with equal parts Vodka
or Peppered Vodka
and Bloody Mary mix.

CLIMAX
Fill glass with ice.
1/2 oz Vodka or Vanilla Vodka
1/2 oz Triple Sec
1/2 oz Amaretto
1/2 oz White Crème de Cacao
1/2 oz Banana Liqueur
Fill with Milk or Cream.
Shake.

CLIMAX 2
Fill glass with ice.
1/2 oz Brandy
1/2 oz Coffee Liqueur
1/2 oz Amaretto
1/2 oz Triple Sec
Fill with Milk or Cream.
Shake.

CLOUDS OVER SCOTLAND
(floater)
1 1/2 oz Green Crème de Menthe
or Melon Liqueur
(bottom)
1/2 oz Irish Cream (top)

CLUSTER FUCK (frozen)
In Blender: 1/2cup ice.
1/2 oz Vodka or Vanilla Vodka
1/2 oz Coffee Liqueur
1/2 oz Butterscotch Liqueur
1/2 oz Orange Liqueur
1/2 oz Irish Cream
2 sandwich cookies
_ a peeled ripe banana
Scoop of vanilla ice cream
Blend until smooth.
Top with Whipped Cream.
Garnish with Cherry.

COBRA aka KAHLUA CLUB
Fill glass with ice.
2 oz Coffee Liqueur
Fill with Soda Water.
Garnish with Lime.

COBBLER
Fill glass with ice.
2 oz desired Liquor,
Liqueur or Wine
Dash fruit syrup or juice
1/2 tsp sugar (optional)
Stir.
Garnish with Mint and Fresh Fruit.

COCA
Fill glass with ice.
3/4 oz Vodka
3/4 oz Southern Comfort
3/4 oz Black Raspberry Liqueur
1 oz Orange Juice
1 oz Cranberry Juice
Shake.
Strain into chilled glass.

COCA 2 aka GRAPE CRUSH
Fill glass with ice.
1 1/2 oz Vodka
1/2 oz Black Raspberry Liqueur
Dash of Sour Mix
Shake.
Fill with Lemon-Lime Soda.

COCA LADY
Fill glass with ice.
1/2 oz Vodka
1/2 oz Rum
1/2 oz Coffee Liqueur
1/2 oz Amaretto or Irish Cream
Fill with Milk or Cream.
Shake.
Dash of Cola

COCO LOCO
Fill glass with ice.
1 oz Dark Rum
1 oz Light Rum
1/2 oz Vodka
1/2 oz Banana Liqueur
1/2 oz Pineapple Juice
1/2 oz Sugar Syrup
1/2 oz Cream of Coconut
Shake.
Strain into chilled glass.

C

COCOANAPPS aka
ADULT HOT CHOCOLATE,
PEPPERMINT KISS,
SNUGGLER
2 oz Peppermint Schnapps
Fill with Hot Chocolate.
Stir.
Top with Whipped Cream.
Sprinkle with Shaved
Chocolate or Sprinkles.

COCOETTO aka
ALMOND KISS
2 oz Amaretto
Fill with Hot Chocolate.
Stir.
Top with Whipped Cream.
Sprinkle with Shaved Almonds or
Chocolate.

COCOPUFF
1 oz Coffee Liqueur
1 oz Irish Cream
Fill with Hot Chocolate.
Stir.
Top with Whipped Cream.
Sprinkle with Shaved
Chocolate or Chocolate Syrup.

CODE BLUE aka
ADIOS MOTHER
Fill glass with ice.
1/2 oz Vodka
1/2 oz Gin
1/2 oz Rum
1/2 oz Tequila
1/2 oz Blue Curacao
Fill with Sour Mix.
Shake.

COFFEE ALEXANDER
1 oz Brandy
1 oz Dark Crème de Cacao
Fill with hot Black Coffee.
Top with Whipped Cream.
Sprinkle with Nutmeg.

COFFEE COLADA (frozen)
In Blender:
1/2 cup of Ice
2 oz Coffee Liqueur
1 oz Rum
2 tbsp Cream of Coconut
1/2 cup fresh or canned Pineapple
1 tbsp Vanilla Ice Cream
Blend until smooth.
If too thick add fruit or juice.
If too thin add ice or Ice Cream.

COFFEE SOMBRERO
Fill glass with ice.
2 oz Coffee Liqueur
Fill with Milk or Cream.
Shake.

COLLINS
Fill glass with ice.
2 oz desired Liquor or Liqueur
Fill with Sour Mix.
Shake.
Splash with Soda Water.
Garnish with Orange and Cherry.

COLORADO BULLDOG
Fill glass with ice.
1 oz Vodka
1 oz Coffee Liqueur
Fill with equal parts Milk or Cream
and Cola.
Shake.

COLORADO BULLDOG 2
Fill shot glass with
1 oz Coffee Liqueur
1 oz Irish Cream
Fill chilled glass 3/4 with Beer
Drop shot glass into beer glass.

COLORADO MF
Fill glass with ice.
1/2 oz 151-Proof Rum
1/2 oz Vodka
1/2 oz Dark Rum
1/2 oz Coffee Liqueur
1/2 oz Galliano
Fill with Milk or Cream.
Shake.
Top with Grenadine.

COLORADO MOTHER
Fill glass with ice.
3/4 oz Vodka
3/4 oz Coffee Liqueur
3/4 oz Tequila
Fill with Milk or Cream.
Shake.
Top with Galliano.

COLORADO MOTHER 2
Fill glass with ice.
1 oz Tequila
1 oz Coffee Liqueur
Fill with equal parts Milk or Cream
and Cola.

COMBUSTIBLE EDISON
Fill glass with ice.
1 oz Campari
1 oz Lemon Juice
Shake. Strain into chilled glass.
Heat 2 oz Brandy and Ignite.
Pour Brandy into drink.

COMFORTABLE FUZZY SCREW
AGAINST THE WALL
Fill glass with ice.
3/4 oz Southern Comfort
3/4 oz Peach Schnapps
3/4 oz Vodka
Fill with Orange Juice
Shake.
Top with 1/2 oz Galliano.

COMFORTABLE SCREW
Fill glass with ice.
1 oz Southern Comfort
1 oz Vodka
Fill with Orange Juice.

CONCORD aka B-51 (floater)
1/2 oz Coffee Liqueur (bottom)
1/2 oz Irish Cream
1/2 oz 151-Proof Rum (top)

CONCORDE
1 1/2 oz Cognac
Dash of Apple Juice or Pineapple
Juice
Fill with Champagne.

CONEY ISLAND
Fill glass with ice.
1 oz Peppermint Schnapps
1 oz Dark Crème de Cacao
Fill with Soda Water.
Stir.

COOKIE MONSTER (floater)
1/2 oz Coffee Liqueur (bottom)
1/2 oz Irish Cream
1/2 oz 100-Proof Peppermint
Schnapps (top)

Metric Measurement Conversion Chart on page 14

COOKIES AND CREAM aka OR-E-OH COOKIE (frozen)
In Blender:
1/2 cup of Ice
1 oz Vodka
3/4 oz Dark Crème de Cacao
2 Oreo Cookies
Scoop of Vanilla Ice Cream
Blend until smooth.
If too thick add Milk or Cream. If too thin add ice or Ice Cream.
Garnish with cookie.

COOL AID
Fill glass with ice.
3/4 oz Vodka
3/4 oz Melon Liqueur or Peach Schnapps
3/4 oz Amaretto
Fill with Cranberry Juice.
Shake.

COOL AID 2
Fill glass with ice.
1 oz Southern Comfort
1/2 oz Amaretto
1/2 oz Melon Liqueur
Dash of Orange Juice
Dash of Cranberry Juice
Fill with Lemon-Lime Soda.

COOL BREEZE
Fill glass with ice.
2 oz Vodka
Fill with equal parts Cranberry and Grapefruit Juice.
Top with Ginger Ale.
Garnish with Lime.

COOL RUN
Fill glass with ice.
1/2 oz Spiced Rum
1/2 oz Coconut Rum
1/2 oz Citrus Rum
1/2 oz Orange Rum
1 oz Cranberry Juice
Dash Lime Juice
Dash Grenadine
Fill with Pineapple Juice
Shake.
Top with splash 151-proof Rum

COPENHAGEN POUSSE-CAFÉ (floater)
1/2 oz Banana Liqueur (bottom)
1/2 oz Cherry Brandy
1/2 oz Cognac or Brandy (top)

COPPERHEAD
Fill glass with ice.
2 oz Vodka
Fill with Ginger Ale.
Garnish with Lime.

CORAL SEA (frozen)
In Blender:
1 cup of Ice
1 1/2 oz Rum
1/2 oz Triple Sec
1 Egg White
1/2 cup fresh or canned Pineapple
1 tsp Grenadine
Blend until smooth.
If too thick add juice or fruit.
If too thin add ice.
Garnish with Pineapple and Cherry.

CORKSCREW
Fill glass with ice.
1 oz Rum
1/2 oz Peach Schnapps
1/2 oz Dry Vermouth
Stir.
Strain into chilled glass.

CORPSE REVIVER
Fill glass with ice.
3/4 oz Apple Brandy
3/4 oz Cognac or Brandy
1/2 oz Sweet Vermouth
Stir.
Strain into chilled glass.

COSMIC SCREW
Fill glass with ice.
1 1/2 oz Vodka or Citrus Vodka
1/2 oz Triple Sec
Fill with Orange Juice leaving a half inch from the top.
Top with Cranberry Juice.
Garnish with Lime.

COSMOPOLITAN
Fill glass with ice.
3 1/2 oz Vodka or Citrus Vodka
Dash of Triple Sec
Dash of Lime Juice
Dash of Cranberry Juice
Shake.
Strain into chilled glass.
Garnish with Lime.

COSMOPOLITAN (South Beach)
Fill glass with ice.
3 1/2 oz Citrus Vodka
Dash of Black Raspberry Liqueur
Dash of Lime Juice
Dash of Cranberry Juice.
Shake
Strain into chilled glass.

COUGH DROP
Fill glass with ice.
1 oz Mentholated Schnapps
1 oz Blackberry Brandy
Stir.

COWBOY
Fill glass with ice.
2 oz Bourbon
Fill with Milk.
Shake.

CRAMP RELIEVER
1 oz Blackberry Brandy

CRANAPPLE COOLER
Fill glass with crushed ice.
1 oz Vodka or Rum
1 oz Apple Brandy
Fill with Cranberry Juice.
Stir.
Garnish with Lime.

CRAN-APPLE MARTINI
Fill glass with ice.
3 1/2 oz Vodka or Cranberry or Apple Vodka
1/2 oz Apple Brandy
Dash Cranberry Juice or 1 tsp Cranberry Sauce and a pinch of sugar.
Shake.
Strain into chilled glass.

C

CRANBERRY KAMIKAZE
Fill glass with ice.
3 1/2 oz Cranberry Vodka
1/2 oz Triple Sec
Dash Lime Juice
Shake.
Serve or strain into shot glass.
Garnish with Lime
If no Cranberry Vodka, just add
Cranberry juice to basic recipe.

CRANBERRY MARTINI
aka CRANTINI
Fill glass with ice.
3 1/2 oz Vodka
1/2 oz Cranberry Liqueur or
Cranberry Juice
Stir.
Strain into chilled glass.
Garnish with Dried Cranberries
raisins
(you can soak them in Vodka an
hour prior to mixing drink)

CRANES BEACH PUNCH
1 gallon Cherry Cool Aid
1 liter cheap Red Wine
1 500ml bottle of Vodka

CRANIUM MELTDOWN
Fill glass with ice.
1/2 oz 151-Proof Rum
1/2 oz Coconut Rum
1/2 oz Black Raspberry Liqueur
1/2 oz Pineapple Juice
Shake.
Strain into chilled glass.

CRANKIN' WANKER
Fill glass with ice.
3/4 oz Vodka
3/4 oz Southern Comfort
3/4 oz Drambuie
Fill with equal parts Orange and
Pineapple Juice.

CRANTINI
aka CRANBERRY MARTINI 2
Fill glass with ice
3 1/2 oz Cranberry Vodka
1/2 oz Orange Liqueur or
Crème de Cassis
Dash Fresh Lime Juice.
Shake.
Strain into chilled glass
Garnish with Fresh Cranberries or
Dried Cranberry raisins

CRAZY BROAD
Fill glass with ice.
1 oz Vodka
1 oz Amaretto
1 oz Southern Comfort
Fill with equal parts Cranberry
Juice and Ginger Ale.

CRAZY RED HEAD
Fill glass with ice.
1 oz Jägermeister
1 oz Peach Schnapps
Fill with Cranberry Juice.
Shake.

CREAM DREAM
1 1/2 oz Dark Crème de Cacao
1 oz Hazelnut Liqueur
Fill with Cream.
Shake.
Tom Lewis

CREAM SODA
Fill glass with ice.
2oz Vanilla Vodka or Spiced Rum
Fill with Ginger Ale.
Dash Cola (optional)

CREAMSICLE
Fill glass with ice.
1 oz Rum or Orange or Vanilla Rum
1/2 oz Triple Sec
1/2 oz Vanilla Liqueur
Fill with equal parts Orange Juice
and Cream.
Shake.

CREAMSICLE 2
Fill glass with ice.
1 oz Banana Liqueur
1 oz Triple Sec
Fill with equal parts Orange Juice
and Milk.
Shake.

CREAMSICLE (frozen)
In Blender:
1/2 cup ice
1 oz Rum
1/2 oz Triple Sec
1/2 oz Vanilla Liqueur
1/2 scoop Vanilla Ice Cream
1/2 scoop Orange Sherbet
Blend until smooth.
If too thick add Milk or Orange Juice.
If too thin add ice or Ice Cream or
sherbet.
Garnish with popsicle stick.

CREAMSICLE MARTINI
Fill glass with ice.
1 3/4 oz Vanilla Vodka
1 3/4 oz Orange Vodka
Dash Triple Sec
Dash Orange Juice.
Shake.
Strain into chilled glass.

CREAMY SEX ON THE BEACH
Fill glass with ice.
3/4 oz Vodka
3/4 oz Coconut Rum
3/4 oz Peach Schnapps
Dash Grenadine
Fill with Pineapple Juice.
Top with a dollop Whipped Cream.
Shake.
Garnish with Cherry and/or
Pineapple.

CREATURE FROM THE BLACK
LAGOON (floater)
1 oz Jägermeister (bottom)
1 oz Black Sambuca (top)

CREME BRULEE MARTINI
Fill glass with ice.
3 1/2 oz Vanilla Vodka
Dash Butterscotch Schnapps
Dash Irish Cream
Dash Black Raspberry Liqueur
Dash Cream
Shake.
Strain into a chilled glass.

CREOLE MARTINI aka
CAJUN MARTINI
Fill glass with ice.
2 oz Peppered Vodka
1/2 oz Dry Vermouth
Stir, then strain into chilled glass.
Serve with Jalapeno Peppers.

CRICKET
Fill glass with ice.
1 oz Rum
3/4 oz White Crème de Menthe
3/4 oz Dark Crème de Cacao
Fill with Milk or Cream.
Shake.
Serve or strain into chilled glass.

CRIPPLER
Fill glass with ice.
1 oz Grain Alcohol
1 oz 151-Proof Rum
Dash of Triple Sec
Shake. Strain into shot glass.

CROCODILE COOLER
Fill glass with ice.
1 oz Citrus Vodka or Citrus Rum
1 oz Melon Liqueur
Dash of Sour Mix
Fill with Lemon-Lime Soda.

CRUISE CONTROL
Fill glass with ice.
1 oz Rum
1/2 oz Apricot Brandy
1/2 oz Orange Liqueur or Triple Sec
1/2 oz Sour Mix
Shake.
Fill with Soda Water.
Garnish with Lemon and Orange.

CUBA LIBRE
Fill glass with ice.
2 oz Light Rum
Fill with Cola.
Garnish with Lime.

CUBAN PEACH
Fill glass with ice.
1 1/2 oz Light Rum
1 1/2 oz Peach Schnapps
1/2 oz Lime Juice
Dash of Sugar Syrup
Shake.
Strain into chilled glass.
Garnish with Mint Sprig.

CUDDLER
1 oz Irish Cream
3/4 oz Amaretto
Heat in microwave for 7-8 seconds.

CUM DROP
1 oz Coffee Liqueur
1 oz Irish Cream
1/2 oz Banana Liqueur
Mix with no ice and pour into
shot glass
Pour into shot glass.
Top with whipped cream.
Then microwave on high for
3-5 seconds.

CUPID'S POTION
Fill glass with ice.
1 1/2 oz Amaretto
1/2 oz Triple Sec
Dash of Grenadine
Fill with equal parts Orange Juice
and Sour Mix.
Shake.

CURE-ALL
Fill glass with ice.
1 oz Peppermint Schnapps
1/2 oz Blackberry Brandy
Stir.

CURLEY'S DELIGHT COFFEE
3/4 oz Irish Whiskey
3/4 oz Irish Cream
3/4 oz Orange Liqueur
Fill with hot Black Coffee.
Top with Whipped Cream.
Linda Graham

DC-3 (floater)
1/2 oz Sambuca (bottom)
1/2 oz Irish Cream
1/2 oz Crème de Cacao (top)

DC-9 (floater)
1/2 oz Coffee Liqueur (bottom)
1/2 oz Sambuca
1/2 oz Rum Cream Liqueur (top)

D.O.A.
3/4 oz Barenjager
3/4 oz Jägermeister
3/4 oz 100-proof Peppermint
Schnapps
Shake. Strain into shot glass.

DAIQUIRI
Fill glass with ice.
2 oz Rum
2 oz Lime Juice
Dash of Sour Mix
1/2 tsp Sugar
Shake.
Garnish with Lime.

DAIQUIRI (frozen)
In Blender:
1 cup of Ice
2 oz Rum
2 oz Lime Juice
Dash of Sour Mix
1/2 tsp Sugar
Blend until smooth.
Garnish with Lime.

DAISY
Fill glass with ice.
2 oz desired Liquor or Liqueur
1/2 tsp Powdered Sugar
1 tsp Raspberry Syrup
or Grenadine
Shake.
Strain into chilled glass.

DAISY CUTTER
In shot glass:
1/2 oz Blue Curacao (bottom)
1 oz Grain Alcohol or American-
made Vodka (top)
In a pint glass:
1/2 oz. Grenadine (bottom)
Fill (gently) 3/4 with
Lemon-Lime soda.
Drop shot into pint glass.

DALLAS ALICE aka
ALICE IN WONDERLAND
FIll glass with ice.
3/4 oz Tequila
3/4 oz Orange Liqueur
3/4 oz Coffee Liqueur
Shake.
Strain into shot glass.

DAMN-THE-WEATHER
Fill glass with ice.
1 oz Gin
1/2 oz Sweet Vermouth
1/4 oz Triple Sec
1/2 oz Orange Juice
Shake.
Garnish with Cherry.

Metric Measurement Conversion Chart on page 14

C
D

DANCE MACHINE
Fill glass with ice.
2 oz Tequila
Fill with equal parts Sparkling water
and Energy Drink.
Garnish with Lime.

DANGEROUS LIAISONS
Fill glass with ice.
2 oz Orange Liqueur
2 oz Coffee Liqueur
1 oz Sour Mix
Shake.
Strain into chilled glass.

DANISH MARY aka
BLOODY HOLLY
Fill glass with ice.
2 oz Aquavit
1 tsp Horseradish
3 dashes of Tabasco Sauce
3 dashes of Worcestershire Sauce
Dash of Lime Juice
3 dashes of Celery Salt
3 dashes of Pepper
1 oz Clam Juice (optional)
Dash of Sherry (optional)
1 tsp Dijon Mustard (optional)
Fill with Tomato Juice.
Pour from one glass to
another until mixed.
Garnish with Lemon and/or Lime,
Celery and/or Cucumber and/or
Cocktail Shrimp.

DARB
Fill glass with ice.
1 oz Gin
1 oz Dry Vermouth
1 oz Apricot Brandy
1/2 oz Sour Mix
1 tsp Sugar
Shake.
Strain into chilled glass.

DARK AND STORMY
Fill glass with ice.(optional)
2 oz Dark Rum
Fill with Ginger Beer.
Garnish with Lime.

DARK SECRET
Fill glass with ice.
1 1/4 oz Black Sambuca
Fill with Club Soda.
Stir.

DARK SIDE
Fill glass with ice.
1 1/2 oz Vodka
1 1/2 oz Brandy
1 oz Coffee Liqueur
1/2 oz White Crème de Menthe
Stir.

DARTH VADER
Fill glass with ice.
1/2 oz Vodka
1/2 oz Gin
1/2 oz Rum
1/2 oz Tequila
1/2 oz Triple Sec
1 oz Sour Mix
Top with 1/2 oz Jägermeister
Garnish with action figure.

DAY AT THE BEACH
Fill glass with ice.
1 oz Amaretto
1 oz Coconut Rum
Dash of Grenadine
Fill with Orange Juice.

DC-10 aka B-54 (floater)
1/2 oz Coffee Liqueur (bottom)
1/2 oz Irish Cream
1/2 oz Amaretto (top)

DE RIGUEUR
Fill glass with ice.
1 1/2 oz Whiskey
3/4 oz Grapefruit Juice
1 tsp Honey
Shake.
Strain into chilled glass.

DEAD NAZI aka
SCREAMING NAZI
Fill glass with ice.
1 oz Jägermeister
1 oz 100-Proof Peppermint
Schnapps
Stir.
Strain into chilled glass.

DEAD RAT
Fill glass with ice.
1 1/2 oz Scotch
1/2 oz Green Chartreuse
Shake. Strain into shot glass.

DEATH IN THE AFTERNOON
1 oz Pernod
9 oz Champagne

DEATH MINT
1 oz Green Chartreuse
1 oz 100-Proof Peppermint
Schnapps
Stir.

DEATH ROW
Fill glass with ice.
1/2 oz Vodka
1/2 oz Citrus Vodka
1/2 oz Orange Vodka
1/2 oz Orange Liqueur
1/2 oz Amaretto
1/2 oz Sloe Gin
Shake.
Fill with Lemon-Lime Soda

DEATHWISH
Fill glass with ice.
1/2 oz 151-Proof Rum
1/2 oz 100-Proof Bourbon
1/2 oz 100-Proof Peppermint
Schnapps
1/2 oz Grenadine
Shake.
Strain into chilled glass.

DEAUVILLE
Fill glass with ice.
1 1/2 oz Apple Brandy
1/2 oz Triple Sec
Dash of Grenadine
2 oz Sour Mix
Shake.
Strain into chilled glass.

DECEIVER
Fill glass with ice.
1 1/2 oz Tequila
1/2 oz Galliano
Stir.

DEEP DARK SECRET
Fill glass with ice.
1 1/2 oz Dark Rum
1/2 oz Light Rum
1/2 oz Coffee Liqueur
1/2 oz Cream or Milk
Shake. Strain into chilled glass.

DEEP SEA
Fill glass with ice.
1/2 oz Gin
1/2 oz Blue Curacao
1/2 oz Pineapple Juice
1/2 oz Lime Juice
1/2 oz Sugar Syrup
Shake.

DEEP THROAT (floater)
1 oz Coffee Liqueur (bottom)
1 oz Vodka or Orange Liqueur (top)
Top with Whipped Cream.
To drink, place hands behind back
and pick up using only mouth.

DELMONICO
Fill glass with ice.
2 oz Brandy
1/2 oz Sweet Vermouth
Dash of Bitters (optional)
Stir.
Strain into chilled glass or pour
contents (with ice) into short glass.
Garnish with Cherry.

DEMON MARY
Fill glass with ice.
2oz Vodka or Peppered Vodka
1 tsp Horseradish
3 dashes of Habenero Sauce
3 dashes Worcestershire Sauce
Dash Lime Juice
3 dashes Celery Salt
3 dashes pepper
1oz Clam Juice (optional)
Dash Sherry (optional)
tsp Dijon Mustard (optional)
Fill with Tomato Juice.
Shake.
Garnish with Lemon and/or Lime,
Celery and/or Cucumber and/or
Cocktail Shrimp.

DEPTH BOMB
Fill glass with ice.
1 1/2 oz Apple Brandy
1 1/2 oz Brandy
1/4 tsp Grenadine
1/4 tsp Sour Mix
Shake.
Strain into chilled glass.

DEPTH CHAMBER (floater)
In shot glass:
1/2 oz Amaretto (top)
1/2 oz Irish Cream
1/2 oz Coffee Liqueur (bottom)
Fill chilled glass with Beer leaving
1 inch from top.
Drop shot glass into beer glass.

DEPTH CHARGE
Fill shot glass with Whiskey
or Peppermint Schnapps
or Drambuie.
Fill chilled glass with Beer leaving 1
inch from top.
Drop shot glass into beer glass.

DESERT SUNRISE
Fill glass with ice.
2 oz Tequila
Dash of Sour Mix
Fill with Orange Juice.
Top with 1/2 oz Blue Curacao.

DESIGNER JEANS
Fill glass with ice.
1/2 oz Dark Rum
1/2 oz Irish Cream
1/2 oz Raspberry Schnapps
Shake.
Strain into chilled glass.

DEVIL'S PUNCH
Fill glass with ice.
2 oz Tequila
1 oz Orange Liqueur
1 oz Limoncello
1 oz Sour Mix
Dash Orange Juice
Shake.

DEVIL'S TAIL (frozen)
In Blender:
1/2 cup ice
1 1/2 oz Rum or Citrus Rum
1 oz Vodka
1/2 oz Apricot Brandy
1 oz Lime Juice
1/2 oz Grenadine
Blend 4-5 seconds.
Garnish with Lime.

DIABLO
Fill glass with ice.
1 1/2 oz Brandy
1/2 oz Triple Sec
1/2 oz Dry Vermouth
2 dashes of Bitters
Stir.
Strain into chilled glass.
Garnish with Lemon Twist.

DIAMOND FIZZ
Fill glass with ice.
1 1/2 oz Gin
Dash of Sour Mix
1 tsp Powdered Sugar
Shake.
Strain into chilled glass.
Fill with Champagne.

DIAMOND HEAD
Fill glass with ice.
1 1/2 oz Gin
1/2 oz Curacao or Triple Sec
2 oz Pineapple Juice
1 tsp Sweet Vermouth
Shake.
Strain into chilled glass.
Garnish with Pineapple.

DICKIE TOECHEESE (floater)
1 oz Blue Curacao (bottom)
1/2 oz Vodka (top)
Either float 1/2 oz Milk or Cream on
Top or squeeze lemon covered with
Bitters.

DIESEL
Fill glass 3/4 with hard Cider.
Fill glass with Ale or Lager.
Add 1 oz Creme de Cassis.

D

DIKI DIKI
Fill glass with ice.
1 1/2 oz Apple Brandy
3/4 oz Gin
1 oz Grapefruit Juice
Shake.
Strain into chilled glass.

DINGO
Fill glass with ice.
3/4 oz Rum
3/4 oz Amaretto
3/4 oz Southern Comfort
Dash of Grenadine
Fill with equal parts Sour Mix and
Orange Juice.
Shake.

**DIRE STRAITS aka
DIRTY M. F.**
Fill glass with ice.
1 1/2 oz Brandy
1/2 oz Coffee Liqueur
1/2 oz Galliano
1/2 oz Milk or Cream
Shake.

DIRTY ASHTRAY
Fill glass with ice.
1/2 oz Vodka
1/2 oz Gin
1/2 oz Rum
1/2 oz Tequila
1/2 oz Blue Curacao
Dash of Grenadine
Fill with equal parts Pineapple
Juice and Sour Mix.
Shake.
Garnish with Lemon.

DIRTY BANANA
Fill glass with ice.
1 oz Dark Creme de Cacao
1 oz Banana Liqueur
1 oz Cream or Milk
Shake.
Strain into chilled glass.

DIRTY BIRD
Fill glass with ice.
1 oz Vodka or Tequila
1 oz Coffee Liqueur
Fill with Milk or Cream.
Shake.

DIRTY DOG
Fill glass with ice.
2 oz Vodka or Gin
Fill with Grapefruit Juice.
2 or 3 dashes of bitters

DIRTY G. S.
Fill glass with ice.
1 oz Vodka
    or Coffee Vodka, and use no
    Coffee Liqueur
    or Peppermint Vodka and use
    no Mint Liqueur
1/2 oz Coffee Liqueur
1/2 oz Peppermint Schnapps or
Crème de Menthe
Fill with Milk or Cream.
Shake.

DIRTY HARRY
Fill glass with ice.
1 oz Orange Liqueur
1 oz Coffee Liqueur
Shake.
Strain into shot glass.

DIRTY MARTINI
(*CAUTION:* DRY usually means
Less Vermouth than usual.
EXTRA DRY can mean even less
Vermouth than usual or
No Vermouth at all.)
Fill glass with ice.
3 1/2 oz Gin or Vodka
1/2 oz Olive Juice
1/2 oz Dry Vermouth (optional)
Stir.
Strain into chilled glass
or pour contents (with ice)
Into short glass.
Garnish with Olives

DIRTY MARTINI 2
Place 2 olives into mixing glass
and mash.
Fill glass with ice.
3 1/2 oz Gin or Vodka
1/2 oz Dry Vermouth (optional)
Shake.
Strain into chilled glass.
Garnish with Olives

DIRTY MONKEY (frozen)
In Blender:
1/2 cup of Ice
3/4 oz Vodka
3/4 oz Coffee Liqueur
3/4 oz Banana Liqueur
1/2 scoop Vanilla Ice Cream
Blend until smooth.

**DIRTY MOTHER aka
SEPARATOR**
Fill glass with ice.
1 1/2 oz Brandy
3/4 oz Coffee Liqueur
1 oz Cream (optional)
Stir.

DIRTY MOTHER 2
Fill glass with ice.
3/4 oz Tequila
3/4 oz Vodka
3/4 oz Coffee Liqueur
Fill with Milk or Cream.
Shake.

DIRTY M. F. aka DIRE STRAITS
Fill glass with ice.
1 1/2 oz Brandy
1/2 oz Coffee Liqueur
1/2 oz Galliano
1/2 oz Milk or Cream
Shake.

DIRTY SILK PANTIES
Fill glass with ice.
3/4 oz Vodka
3/4 oz Peach Schnapps
Stir and Strain into chilled glass.
Top with 2 or 3 drops Grenadine.

DIRTY SOUR APPLE MARTINI
Place 1/4 diced skinless Granny
Smith Apple
in mixing glass and mash.
Fill glass with ice.
3 1/2 oz Vodka
1/2 oz Sour Apple Liqueur
Shake vigorously.
Strain into chilled glass.

DIRTY WATER MARTINI
Muddle or Mash an olive, onion
and a lemon twist, and place them
in a chilled glass.
In a mixing glass:
Muddle or Mash an olive, onion
and a lemon twist.
Fill with ice.
3 1/2oz of desired Gin or Vodka
Dash Dry Vermouth.
Shake. Strain into chilled glass.

DIRTY WHITE MOTHER
Fill glass with ice.
1 1/2 oz Brandy
1/2 oz Coffee Liqueur
Float Cream on top.

DIZZY BUDDHA
Fill glass with ice.
1/2 oz Vodka
1/2 oz Dark Rum
1/2 oz Coconut Rum
1/2 oz Southern Comfort
1/2 oz Amaretto
1/2 oz Coffee Liqueur
1/2 oz Melon Liqueur
1/2 oz Banana Liqueur
Dash of Grenadine
Fill with equal parts Orange,
And Pineapple Juice.
Shake.

DOCTOR'S ELIXIR
Fill glass with ice.
1 oz Mentholated Schnapps
1 oz Black Raspberry Liqueur
Stir.

DOG SLED
Fill glass with ice.
2 oz Canadian Whiskey
1 tsp Grenadine
1 tbsp Sour Mix
Fill with Orange Juice.
Shake.

DOG'S NOSE
2 oz Gin
Fill with Beer.

DOLI
Fill large mouth jar
with fresh pineapple rings.
Cover fruit with Vodka.
Seal jar and let steep
for 4 to 7 days.
If you refrigerate while steeping,
you can serve as is, or serve over
ice, or shake over ice and strain
into chilled glass.
(Fresh coconut, berries, melon and
citrus fruit work instead of or in
addition to)

DON JUAN
Fill glass with ice.
1 oz Tequila
1 oz Dark Rum
1 oz Pineapple Juice
1 oz Grapefruit Juice
Shake and strain into chilled glass.

DOUBLE CAPPUCCINO
Heat cup, mug, or specialty glass.
Fill 2/3 with Espresso
Fill the rest with Steamed Milk.
1/6 liquid - 1/6 foam
Sprinkle with Chocolate shavings
or powder, or Cinnamon and or
Nutmeg.

DOUBLE-D (D-D)
Fill glass with ice.
3/4 oz Brandy
3/4 oz Southern Comfort
3/4 oz Cherry Brandy
Dash of Sour Mix
Dash of Cranberry Juice
Shake.
Strain into chilled glass.

DOUBLE ESPRESSO
Heat coffee cup, mug, or specialty
glass.
The best way is to fill it with hot
water,
and let it sit for 30 seconds.
Fill with 2 servings of Espresso.

DOUBLE H aka THE HULK
Fill glass with ice.
1 oz Cognac
1 oz Hpnotiq
Stir.

DOUBLE MINT BJ
In Flute glass.
1 oz Coffee Liqueur
1 oz Peppermint Schnapps
Top with Whipped Cream
To drink, place hands behind back
And pick up using only mouth.

DOUBLE TROUBLE
4 oz Prune Juice
Fill with Beer.

DOWNEASTER aka
HAWAIIAN SEA BREEZE,
BAY BREEZE
Fill glass with ice.
2 oz Vodka
Fill with equal parts Cranberry and
Pineapple Juice.
Garnish with Lime.

DR. FUNK
Fill glass with ice.
1 1/2 oz Dark Rum
2 oz Sour Mix
2 oz Pineapple Juice
Dash of Grenadine
Shake.
Top with 1/2 oz Triple Sec.

DR. FUNK 2
Fill glass with ice.
1/2 oz Light Rum
1/2 oz Dark Rum
1/2 oz Galliano
1/2 oz Triple Sec
1/2 oz Sour Mix
Fill with equal parts Orange and
Pineapple Juice.
Shake.
Garnish with Orange and Cherry.
Float 1/2 oz Cherry Brandy
on top.

DR. J
1 oz Mentholated Schnapps
1 oz Jägermeister

DR. P.
1/2 oz Amaretto
1/2 oz Light Rum or Brandy
Fill with cold Beer.

Metric Measurement Conversion Chart on page 14

DR. P. 2
Fill glass with ice.
1 oz Spiced Rum
1 oz Amaretto
Fill with Cola.

DR. P. FROM HELL
In shot glass pour:
3/4 oz 151-Proof Rum
3/4 oz Amaretto
Ignite.
Drop into glass of Beer 3/4 filled.

DRAGOON
Fill glass with ice.
1/2 oz Coffee Liqueur
1/2 oz Irish Cream
1/2 oz Black Sambuca
Stir.

DREAM COCKTAIL
Fill glass with ice.
1 1/2 oz Brandy
1/2 oz Orange Liqueur or Triple Sec
1/2 tsp Anisette
Stir.
Strain into chilled glass.

DREAMSICLE
Fill glass with ice.
2 oz Amaretto or Licor 43
Fill with equal parts Milk or Cream
and Orange Juice.
Float 1/2 oz Galliano on top
(optional).

DROOLING PASSIONATE LADY
Fill glass with ice.
2 oz Vodka or Citrus Vodka
1 oz Triple Sec
Fill with Pineapple Juice.
Shake.

DRUNKEN WAITER
Fill glass with ice.
Fill with equal parts Red Wine and
cola.

DRY ARROYO
Fill glass with ice.
1 oz Black Raspberry Liqueur
1 oz Coffee Liqueur
1 oz Sour Mix
1 oz Orange Juice
Shake.
Strain into chilled glass.
Fill with Champagne.
Garnish with Orange Twist.

DRY MANHATTAN
(CAUTION: DRY can mean make
drink with Dry Vermouth or less
Sweet Vermouth than usual.)
Fill glass with ice.
2 oz Whiskey
1/2 oz Dry Vermouth
or 1/4 oz Sweet Vermouth
Stir.
Strain into chilled glass, or pour
contents (with ice) into short glass.
Garnish with Lemon Twist.

DRY MARTINI
(CAUTION: DRY means less
Dry Vermouth than usual.
EXTRA DRY means even less or
no Vermouth at all).
Fill glass with ice.
3 1/2 oz Gin or Vodka
1/4 oz Dry Vermouth
Stir.
Strain into chilled glass or pour
contents (with ice) into short glass.
Garnish with Lemon Twist or Olives
or Cocktail Onions.

DRY ROB ROY
Fill glass with ice.
2 oz Scotch
1/4 oz Dry Vermouth
Stir.
Strain into chilled glass, or pour
contents (with ice) into short glass.
Garnish with Lemon Twist.

DUBLIN COFFEE
3/4 oz Irish Whiskey
3/4 oz Irish Mist
3/4 oz Coffee Liqueur
Fill with hot Black Coffee.
Top with Whipped Cream.
Drizzle with Green Creme de
Menthe.

DUBLIN MILKSHAKE
Fill glass with ice.
1 1/2 oz Irish Cream
1/2 oz Irish Whiskey
Fill with Chocolate Milk or Milk
Shake. Strain into pint glass.

DUBONNET COCKTAIL
Fill glass with ice.
1 1/2 oz Gin or Vodka
3/4 oz Dubonnet Rouge
Stir.
Strain into chilled glass.
Garnish with Lemon Twist.

DUBONNET MANHATTAN
Fill glass with ice.
1 1/2 oz Whiskey
3/4 oz Dubonnet Rouge
Shake.
Strain into chilled glass.
Garnish with Cherry.

DUCHESS
Fill glass with ice.
1 oz Pernod
3/4 oz Sweet Vermouth
3/4 oz Dry Vermouth
Shake.
Strain into chilled glass or pour
contents (with ice) into short glass.
Garnish with Cherry.

DUCK FART (floater)
1/2 oz Coffee Liqueur (bottom)
1/2 oz Irish Cream
1/2 oz Blended Whiskey (top)

DUDE
Fill glass with ice.
2 oz Scotch
Dash of Grenadine
Stir.
Float 1/2 oz Sherry on top.

DUNDEE
Fill glass with ice.
1 oz Gin
1/2 oz Drambuie
1/2 oz Scotch
1/2 oz Sour Mix
Shake.
Garnish with Lemon Twist or
Cherry.

DUSTY ROAD (frozen)
In Blender:
1/2 cup of Ice
1 oz Irish Cream
1 oz Black Raspberry Liqueur
1/2 scoop of Vanilla Ice Cream
Blend until smooth.
If too thick add Milk or Cream.
If too thin add ice or Ice Cream.

DUSTY ROSE
Fill glass with ice.
1 oz Irish Cream
1 oz Black Raspberry Liqueur
Stir.
Serve or strain into chilled glass.

DUTCH COFFEE
2 oz Vandermint
Fill with hot Black Coffee.
Top with Whipped Cream.
Sprinkle with Chocolate
shavings or Sprinkles.

DUTCH PIRATE
Fill glass with ice.
1 1/2 oz Vodka
1 oz Vandermint
1/2 oz Dark Rum
Shake.
Strain into chilled glass.
Garnish with Orange.

DUTCH TREAT
2 oz Brandy
Fill with Hot Chocolate.
Top with Whipped Cream.
Sprinkle with Chocolate
shavings or Sprinkles.

DYING NAZI FROM HELL
Fill glass with ice.
1 oz Vodka
1 oz Irish Cream
1 oz Jägermeister
Strain into shot glass.

81 CAMARO (frozen)
In Blender: 1/2 cup ice
2 oz Vodka
Scoop Vanilla Ice Cream
Dash Cola
Dash Orange Soda
Blend until smooth.
If too thick add soda.
If too thin add ice or
Ice Cream.

E. T. (floater)
1/2 oz Irish Cream (bottom)
1 oz Melon Liqueur
1 oz Vodka (top)

EARTHQUAKE
Fill glass with ice.
3/4 oz Amaretto
3/4 oz Anisette
3/4 oz Southern Comfort
Stir. Strain into shot glass.

EAST INDIA
Fill glass with ice.
1 1/2 oz Brandy
1/2 oz Curacao or Triple Sec
1 oz Pineapple Juice
Dash of Bitters
Shake.
Strain into chilled glass.

EAST INDIAN
Fill glass with ice.
1 oz Brandy
1/2 oz Dark Rum
1/2 oz Triple Sec
Dash of Bitters
1 oz Pineapple Juice
Shake.
Strain into chilled glass.

EAST SIDE
Fill glass with ice.
3/4 oz Rum
3/4 oz Amaretto
3/4 oz Coconut Rum
Fill with Milk or Cream.
Shake.

EAT HOT DEATH
Fill glass with ice.
1 1/2 oz 151-Proof Rum
1/2 oz fresh Lemon Juice or Lime
Juice
Stir. Strain into shot glass.

EAT THE CHERRY aka
CHERRY BOMB
Place pitted, stemless Cherry in
shot glass.
1 tsp Cherry Juice
Fill with Grain Alcohol or Vodka.

ECLIPSE
Place Cherry or ripe Olive in chilled
Martini glass and cover with 1/4 oz
Grenadine.
Fill separate glass with ice.
2 oz Gin
1 1/2 oz Sloe Gin
Dash of Sour Mix
Shake.
Strain gently into second glass so
as not to disturb fruit or Grenadine.

ECLIPSE 2
Fill glass with ice.
2 oz Black Sambuca
Dash of Cream
Stir.
Strain into chilled glass.

ECSTASY
Fill glass with ice.
1 1/2 oz Vodka or Citrus Vodka
1/2 oz Black Raspberry Liqueur
1/2 oz Pineapple Juice
1/2 Cranberry Juice
Shake.
Strain into chilled glass.

EDEN
Fill glass with ice.
2 oz Vodka
Fill with Apple Juice.
Garnish with Cherry.

Metric Measurement Conversion Chart on page 14

EDEN ROC FIZZ
Fill glass with ice.
1 1/2 oz Whiskey
Dash of Pernod
Dash of Sugar Syrup
Dash of Sour Mix
1/2 Egg White
Shake.
Fill with Soda Water.

EDITH DAY
Fill glass with ice.
2 oz Gin
tsp Sugar
Fill with Grapefruit Juice.
Shake.

EGGHEAD (frozen)
In Blender:
1/2 cup of Ice
2 oz Vodka
1 Egg
Scoop of Orange Sherbet
Blend until smooth.

EGGNOG
Separate 12 Eggs.
Beat Yolks and 2 cups of Superfine
Sugar until thick.
Stir in 2 cups of Cognac or Brandy,
2 cups of Dark Rum,
2 cups of Cream, and
6 cups of Milk.
Refrigerate mixture.
When thoroughly chilled, beat the
Egg Whites until stiff.
Carefully fold them into mixture.
Garnish with Nutmeg.

EL CID
Fill glass with ice.
1 1/2 oz Tequila
1/2 oz Orgeat Syrup
1 oz Lime Juice
Shake.
Fill with Tonic Water.
Top with dash of Grenadine.
Garnish with Lime.

EL DIABLO
Fill glass with ice.
1 oz Tequila
1/2 oz Crème de Cassis
Dash of Lime Juice
Fill with Ginger Ale.

EL SALVADOR
Fill glass with ice.
1 1/2 oz Rum
3/4 oz Hazelnut Liqueur
Dash of Grenadine
1/2 oz Lime Juice
Shake.
Strain into chilled glass.

ELECTRIC COOL AID
Fill glass with ice.
1/2 oz Amaretto
1/2 oz Triple Sec
1/2 oz Southern Comfort
1/2 oz Melon Liqueur
1/2 oz Cherry Brandy
1/2 oz Sour Mix
1/2 oz Cranberry juice
Dash of Grenadine
Shake.
Strain into chilled glass.

ELECTRIC LEMONADE
Fill glass with ice.
1/2 oz Vodka or Citrus Vodka
1/2 oz Gin or Citrus Gin
1/2 oz Rum or Citrus Rum
1/2 oz Tequila
1/2 oz Triple Sec
Fill with Sour Mix.
Shake.
Top with Lemon-Lime Soda.

ELECTRIC WATERMELON
Fill glass with ice.
1/2 oz Vodka
1/2 oz Gin
1/2 oz Rum
1/2 oz Tequila
1/2 oz Triple Sec
1/2 oz Melon Liqueur
1 oz Orange Juice
1 oz Grenadine
Fill glass with Lemon-Lime Soda.
Shake.

ELMER FUDPUCKER
Fill glass with ice.
1 oz Vodka or Orange Vodka
1 oz Tequila
Fill with Orange Juice.
Top with Apricot Brandy.
Garnish with Orange.

ELVIRA
Fill glass with ice.
1 1/2 oz Vodka or Citrus Vodka
1/2 oz Blackberry Brandy
Fill with Sour Mix.
Shake.

ELYSEE PALACE
Fill glass with ice.
1 oz Cognac or Brandy
1/2 oz Black Raspberry Liqueur
Fill with Champagne.
Float 1/4 oz Black Raspberry
Liqueur on top.

EMBRYO (floater)
1 oz Coffee Liqueur (bottom)
1/4 oz Cream
1/2 oz 100-proof Vodka (top)

EMERALD FOREST
Fill glass with ice.
1 1/2 oz Gin
1/2 oz Green Crème de Menthe
Stir.

EMPIRE STATE SLAMMER
Fill glass with ice.
1 oz Canadian Whiskey
1/2 oz Sloe Gin
1/2 oz Banana Liqueur
2 oz Orange Juice
Shake.
Strain into chilled glass.

ENERGIZER (floater)
3/4 oz Benedictine (bottom)
3/4 oz Irish Cream
3/4 oz Orange Liqueur (top)

ENGAGEMENT MARTINI
Fill glass with ice.
3 1/2 oz Top Shelf Gin or Vodka
Dash Dry Vermouth
Stir.
Strain into a chilled glass.
Garnish with
Diamond Engagement ring.

ENGLISH SCREWDRIVER
Fill glass with ice.
2 oz Gin
Fill with Orange Juice.
Garnish with Orange.

ERIE CANAL
Fill glass with ice.
1 1/2 oz Irish Whiskey
1/2 oz Irish Mist
1/2 oz Irish Cream
Stir.

ESPRESSO CON PANNO
1 shot Espresso
Top with Whipped Cream
Sprinkle with shaved or powdered
chocolate

ESPRESSO MARTINI
Fill glass with ice.
3 1/2 oz Vanilla Vodka, Coffee
Vodka, or Vodka
2 oz Chilled Espresso
Dash Coffee Liqueur(optional)
Dash Irish Cream(optional)
Dash Hazelnut Liqueur(optional)
Dash Crème de Cacao(optional)
Shake. Strain into chilled glass

EVERGLADES SPECIAL
Fill glass with ice.
3/4 oz Rum
3/4 oz White Crème de Cacao
1/2 oz Coffee Liqueur
1 oz Cream or Milk
Shake.

EXPRESS
Fill glass with ice.
1 1/2 oz Orange Liqueur
1/2 oz Vodka
Shake.
Strain into chilled glass.
Garnish with Orange.

EYE-OPENER
Fill glass with ice.
1 oz Rum
1/3 oz Triple Sec
1/3 oz White Crème de Cacao
1/3 oz Pernod
1 tsp Sugar Syrup
or Powdered Sugar
1 Egg Yolk
Shake.
Serve or strain into chilled glass.

F-16 (floater)
1/2 oz Coffee Liqueur (bottom)
1/2 oz Irish Cream
1/2 oz Hazelnut Liqueur
or Rum (top)

F-52 (floater)
1/2 oz Coffee Liqueur (bottom)
1/2 oz Irish Cream
1/2 oz Hazelnut Liqueur (top)

F ME HARD
Fill glass with ice.
1/2 oz Vodka
1/2 oz Gin
1/2 oz Rum
1/2 oz Amaretto
1/2 oz Coconut Rum
1/2 oz Melon Liqueur
1/2 oz Peach Schnapps
1/2 oz Sloe Gin
Fill with Orange Juice.
Shake.

F. U.
Fill glass with ice.
2 oz Hazelnut Liqueur
Fill with Lemon-Lime Soda.

FACE ERASER
Fill glass with ice.
1 oz Vodka or Citrus Vodka
1 oz Coffee Liqueur
Fill with Lemon-Lime Soda.
Supposed to be drunk in one shot
through straw.

FACE ERASER 2
Fill glass with ice.
1 1/2 oz Vodka
1/2 oz Coffee Liqueur
1/2 oz Irish Cream
Fill with Soda Water.
Supposed to be drunk in one shot
through straw.

FAHRENHEIT 5
Coat inside of shot glass with hot
sauce.
1 oz Peppered Vodka
1 oz Cinnamon Schnapps

FAIR AND WARMER
Fill glass with ice.
1 1/2 oz Rum or Orange Rum
Dash of Triple Sec or Curacao
1/2 oz Sweet Vermouth
Shake.
Serve or strain into chilled glass.
Garnish with Lemon.

FAIRCHILD (floater)
1 oz Melon Liqueur (bottom)
1/2 oz Orange Juice
1/2 oz Irish Whiskey (top)

FALLEN ANGEL
Fill glass with ice.
2 oz Gin
Dash of White Crème de Menthe
Dash of Bitters
2 oz Sour Mix
Shake.
Serve or strain into chilled glass.
Garnish with Cherry.

FALLEN ANGEL MARTINI
Fill glass with ice.
1 oz Vanilla Vodka
1 oz Irish Cream
1 oz Hazelnut Liqueur
1 oz Chocolate Liqueur
Dash of Cream.
Shake. Strain into a chilled glass.

FANTASIO
Fill glass with ice.
1 1/2 oz Brandy
3/4 oz Dry Vermouth
1 tsp White Crème de Cacao
1 tsp Cherry Liqueur
Shake.
Serve or strain into chilled glass.

FARE-THEE-WELL
Fill glass with ice.
1 1/2 oz Gin
1 oz Dry Vermouth
1/2 oz Triple Sec or Curacao
2 dashes of Sweet Vermouth
Shake.
Strain into chilled glass.

E

F

Metric Measurement Conversion Chart on page 14

FASCINATION
Fill glass with ice.
1 1/2 oz Dark Rum
3/4 oz Orange Liqueur
1/2 tsp Sugar
1/2 Egg White
Fill with Sour Mix.
Shake.
Strain into chilled glass.

FAT CAT (frozen)
In Blender:
1/2 cup of Ice
3/4 oz Cognac
3/4 oz Galliano
3/4 oz White Creme de Cacao
Scoop of Vanilla Ice Cream
Blend until smooth.
If too thick add Milk.
If too thin add ice or Ice Cream.

FATHER SHERMAN
Fill glass with ice.
1 1/2 oz Brandy
1/2 oz Apricot Brandy
1 oz Orange Juice
Shake.
Strain into chilled glass.

FAVORITE
Fill glass with ice.
3/4 oz Gin
3/4 oz Apricot Brandy
3/4 oz Dry Vermouth
1/4 tsp Sour Mix
Shake.
Strain into chilled glass.

FEDORA
Fill glass with ice.
3/4 oz Dark Rum
3/4 oz Bourbon
3/4 oz Brandy
Dash of Triple Sec
1 oz Sour Mix
Shake.
Strain into chilled glass.
Garnish with Lemon.

F.E.D.X.
Fill glass with ice.
1 1/2 oz Amaretto
1 oz Black Raspberry Liqueur
2 oz Sour Mix
Shake.
Strain into chilled champagne
glass.
Fill with Champagne.
Garnish with Lemon Twist.

FERN GULLY
Fill glass with ice.
1 oz Dark Rum
1 oz Light Rum
1/2 oz Crème de Nouyax
or Amaretto
1 oz Orange Juice
1/2 oz Cream of Coconut
1/2 oz Lime Juice
Shake.
Garnish with Lime and Orange.

FERRARI
Fill glass with ice.
1 oz Amaretto
2 oz Dry Vermouth
Stir.
Garnish with Lemon Twist.

FESTERING SLOBOVIAN HUMMER
Fill glass with ice.
1/2 oz 151-Proof Rum
1/2 oz Galliano
1/2 oz Peppermint Schnapps
Shake.
Strain into shot glass.

FESTIVAL
Fill glass with ice.
3/4 oz Dark Crème de Cacao
1 oz Apricot Brandy
1 tsp Grenadine
3/4 oz Cream
Shake.

FIDEL'S MARTINI
Fill glass with ice.
3 1/2 oz Russian Vodka
1/2 oz Banana Liqueur
Stir.
Strain into chilled glass.
Garnish with Banana.

FIERY KISS
Rim shot glass with Honey.
Fill with Cinnamon Schnapps
Dash of Amaretto (optional)

FIERY REDHEAD
Fill glass with ice.
3 1/2 oz Peppered Vodka
Dash Lime Juice
Dash Grenadine
Shake Strain into a chilled glass.
Garnish with a cherry.

FIFTH AVENUE aka
LAYER CAKE (floater)
3/4 oz Dark Crème de Cacao (bottom)
3/4 oz Apricot Brandy
1/2 oz Milk (top)

FIFTY FIFTY (Martini)
Fill glass with ice.
1 1/2 oz Gin
1 1/2 oz Dry Vermouth
Stir.
Strain into chilled glass.
Garnish with Olive.

57 CHEVY
Fill glass with ice.
1 oz Vodka
1 oz White Crème de Cacao
Stir.

57 CHEVY 2
Fill glass with ice.
1/2 oz Vodka
1/2 oz Rum
1/2 oz Amaretto
1/2 oz Southern Comfort
1/2 oz Orange Liqueur
Fill with equal parts Pineapple
Juice and Sour Mix.
Shake.
Serve or strain into chilled glass.

57 T-BIRD
Fill glass with ice.
3/4 oz Rum or Vodka
or Southern Comfort
3/4 oz Amaretto
3/4 oz Orange Liqueur
Fill with equal parts Pineapple,
Cranberry and Orange Juice.
Shake.

57 T-BIRD
(with California Plates)
Fill glass with ice.
3/4 oz Rum or Vodka
or Southern Comfort
3/4 oz Amaretto
3/4 oz Orange Liqueur
Fill with Grapefruit Juice.
Shake.

57 T-BIRD
(with Florida Plates)
Fill glass with ice.
3/4 oz Rum or Vodka
or Southern Comfort
3/4 oz Amaretto
3/4 oz Orange Liqueur
Fill with Orange Juice.
Shake.

57 T-BIRD
(with Hawaiian Plates)
Fill glass with ice.
3/4 oz Rum or Vodka
or Southern Comfort
3/4 oz Amaretto
3/4 oz Orange Liqueur
Fill with Pineapple Juice.
Shake.

57 T-BIRD
(with Massachusetts Plates)
Fill glass with ice.
3/4 oz Rum or Vodka
or Southern Comfort
3/4 oz Amaretto
3/4 oz Orange Liqueur
Fill with Cranberry juice.
Shake.

FIJI FIZZ
Fill glass with ice.
1 1/2 oz Dark Rum
1/2 oz Bourbon
1 tsp Cherry Brandy
3 dashes of Orange Bitters
Shake.
Fill with Cola.
Garnish with Lime.

FILBY
Fill glass with ice.
2 oz Gin
3/4 oz Amaretto
1/2 oz Dry Vermouth
1/2 oz Campari
Stir.
Garnish with Orange.

FINE AND DANDY
Fill glass with ice.
1 1/2 oz Gin
3/4 oz Orange Liqueur or Triple Sec
3/4 oz Sour Mix
Dash of Bitters
Shake.
Strain into chilled glass.
Garnish with Cherry.

FIRE AND ICE (floater)
1 oz Tequila (bottom)
1 oz Peppermint Schnapps or
Crème de Menthe (top)

FIRE-IN-THE-HOLE
Fill shot glass with Ouzo or
Sambuca
Add 3-5 dashes of Tabasco Sauce.

FIREBALL
Fill shot glass with Cinnamon
Schnapps.
Add 4-5 drops of Tabasco Sauce.
Stir.

FIREBALL 2
Fill glass with ice.
1/2 oz Vodka or Peppered Vodka
1/2 oz Cinnamon Schnapps
1/2 oz Cherry Brandy
4-5 drops Tabasco Sauce
Stir.
Strain into shot glass.

FIREBIRD
Fill glass with ice.
2 oz Peppered Vodka
Fill with Cranberry Juice.
Stir.

FIRECRACKER
Fill glass with ice.
2 oz Spiced Rum
1/2 oz Sloe Gin or Grenadine
Fill with Orange Juice
Shake.
Float 1/2 oz 151-Proof Rum on top.
Garnish with Orange.

FIRECRACKER 2
Fill glass with ice.
1 1/2 oz Tequila or Vodka or
Whiskey
1/2 oz Black Raspberry Liqueur
Fill with Sour Mix.
Shake.

FIREFLY
Fill glass with ice.
2 oz Vodka or Citrus Vodka
Dash of Grenadine
Fill with Grapefruit Juice.
Shake.

FIRESTORM
Fill glass with ice.
3/4 oz Cinnamon Schnapps
3/4 oz Peppermint Schnapps
3/4 oz 151-Proof Rum
Shake. Strain into shot glass.

FISH HOUSE PUNCH
Dissolve 3/4 lb Sugar in
1 qt Spring Water (non-carbonated).
1 1/2 cups Lemon Juice
1/2 cup Peach Schnapps
1 qt Cognac
2 qt Dark Rum
Pour mixture into cold bowl
containing cake of ice.

FIZZ
Fill glass with ice.
2 oz desired Liquor or Liqueur
1 oz Lemon Juice or Sour Mix
1 tsp Powdered Sugar
Shake.
Strain into chilled glass.
Fill with Soda Water.

F

FJORD

Fill glass with ice.
1 oz Brandy
1/2 oz Aquavit
1 oz Orange Juice
1/2 oz Lime Juice
1 tsp Grenadine
Shake.
Strain into chilled glass.

FLAMING BLUE J.

Fill glass with ice.
1 oz Southern Comfort
1/2 oz Blue Curacao
1/2 oz Peppermint Schnapps
Strain into chilled glass.
Float 1/2 oz 151-Proof Rum on top.
Ignite.

FLAMING HOOKER (floater)

1 oz Coffee Liqueur (bottom)
1 oz Ouzo (top)
Ignite.

FLAMING LAMBORGHINI

In straight up glass (martini)
1/2 oz Grenadine (bottom)
1 oz Galliano
1 oz Sambuca
1/2 oz Green Chartreuse
Ignite.
Let burn for 10 seconds
then through straw drink quickly,
while someone pours in
1 oz Blue Curacao
1 oz Irish Cream

FLAMING LAMBORGHINI 2

In shot glass   1 oz Galliano
In another   1 oz Coffee Liqueur
In another   1 oz Blue Curacao
In another   1 oz Milk
In straight up glass (martini)
1 oz Sambuca
Ignite Sambuca, and pour shot
glasses into it.

FLAMING LAMBORGHINI 3

In shot glass float
1 oz Blue Curacao
1/2 oz Milk (top)
In straight up glass (martini) float
1/2 oz Coffee Liqueur
1/2 oz Amaretto
1/2 oz Vodka
1/2 oz Green Chartreuse (top)
Ignite Chartreuse and pour
contents of shot glass into it.

FLAMING NORIEGA (floater)

1/2 oz Strawberry Liqueur
(bottom)
1/2 oz Green Crème de Menthe
1/2 oz Sugar Syrup
1/2 oz 151-Proof Rum (top)
Ignite.

FLAMINGO

Fill glass with ice.
1 1/2 oz Gin
1/2 oz Apricot Brandy
1/2 oz Lime Juice
Dash of Grenadine
Shake.
Strain into chilled glass.

FLAMINGO 2

Fill glass with ice.
2 oz Rum or Vodka
Fill with equal parts Sour Mix,
Pineapple Juice and Orange Juice.
Add Grenadine while stirring until
desired pink color.

FLIM FLAM

Fill glass with ice.
1 1/2 oz Rum or Citrus Rum
3/4 oz Triple Sec
1/2 oz Sour Mix
1/2 oz Orange Juice
Shake.
Serve or strain into chilled glass.

FLIP

Fill glass with ice.
2 oz desired Liquor or Liqueur
1 raw egg
1 tsp Powdered Sugar
Shake.
Strain into glass.
Garnish with Nutmeg.

FLIRTINI

Fill glass with ice.
3 oz Vodka
1 oz Pineapple Juice
Shake.
Strain into chilled glass.
Top with Champagne.

FLIRTINI 2

Fill glass with ice.
3 1/2 oz Raspberry Vodka
1/2 oz Orange Liqueur
Dash Lime Juice
Dash Pineapple Juice
Dash Cranberry Juice
Shake.
In chilled martini glass, muddle 2 or
3 Raspberries.
Strain into chilled glass.
Top with Champagne.

FLORIDA

Fill glass with ice.
1/2 oz Gin
1/4 oz Kirschwasser
1/4 oz Triple Sec
2 oz Orange Juice
1/4 oz Sour Mix
Shake.
Serve or strain into chilled glass.
Garnish with Orange.

FLORIDA 2

Fill glass with ice.
1 1/2 oz Light Rum
1/2 oz Green Crème de Menthe
1/2 oz Sugar Syrup
or 1/2 tsp Sugar
1/2 oz Lime Juice
1/2 oz Pineapple Juice
Shake.
Strain into chilled glass.
Fill with Soda Water.
Garnish with mint sprig.

FLORIDA ICED TEA

Fill glass with ice.
1/2 oz Vodka
1/2 oz Gin
1/2 oz Rum
1/2 oz Tequila
1/2 oz Triple Sec
2 oz Orange Juice
Top with Cola.
Garnish with Orange.

Metric Measurement Conversion Chart on page 14

FLORIDA LOBSTER
Fill glass with ice.
1 1/2 oz Whiskey
1/2 oz Amaretto
Fill with Cranberry Juice.

FLORIDA PUNCH
Fill glass with ice.
1 1/2 oz Brandy
1/2 oz Dark Rum
Fill glass with equal parts Orange,
and Grapefruit Juice.
Shake.

FLORIDA SUNRISE
Fill glass with ice.
2 oz Rum
Fill with Orange Juice.
Pour 1/2 oz Grenadine down
Spoon to bottom of glass.
Garnish with orange.

FLUFFY DUCK
Fill glass with ice.
1 oz Vodka, Citrus Vodka,
 or Rum, or Citrus Rum
1 oz Advokaat
Dash cream
Shake.
Fill with Lemon-Lime Soda or
Fill with Orange Juice.
Shake,

FLUFFY DUCK 2
Fill glass with ice.
1 oz Gin or Orange Gin
1 oz Advokaat
Dash Orange Liqueur
Dash Orange Juice
Shake.
Top with Soda Water or
Lemon-Lime Soda.

**FLYING GRASSHOPPER aka
VODKA GRASSHOPPER**
Fill glass with ice.
1 oz Vodka
3/4 oz Green Crème de Menthe
3/4 oz White Crème de Cacao
Fill with Milk or Cream.
Shake.
Serve or strain into chilled glass.

FLYING GRASSHOPPER (frozen)
In Blender:
1/2 cup of Ice
1 oz Vodka
3/4 oz Green Crème de Menthe
3/4 oz White Crème de Cacao
Scoop of Vanilla Ice Cream
Blend until smooth.
If too thick add Milk or Cream. If
too thin add ice or Ice Cream.

FLYING KANGAROO (frozen)
In Blender:
1/2 cup of Ice
3/4 oz Vodka
3/4 oz Rum
3/4 oz Galliano
2 tbsp Vanilla Ice Cream
Blend until smooth.
If too thick add Milk or Cream.
If too thin add ice or Ice Cream.
Garnish with Pineapple and Cherry.

**FLYING MADRAS aka
RUSSIAN NIGHTS**
Fill glass with ice.
2 oz Vodka
2 oz Cranberry Juice
2 oz Orange Juice
Fill with Champagne.
Garnish with Orange.

FLYING SCOT
Fill glass with ice.
1 oz Scotch
1 oz Sweet Vermouth
1/4 oz Sugar Syrup
2-4 dashes of Bitters
Shake.

FOG CUTTER
Fill glass with ice.
1 oz Rum or Citrus Rum
1 oz Brandy
1 oz Gin
Dash of Crème de Nouyax
or Triple Sec
Dash of Sour Mix
Fill with equal parts Orange and
Pineapple Juice.
Top with 1/2 oz Sherry.
Shake.

FOG HORN
Fill glass with ice.
2 oz Gin
Fill with Ginger Ale or Ginger Beer.
Garnish with Lemon.

FORBIDDEN JUNGLE
Fill glass with ice.
1 1/2 oz Coconut Rum
1/2 oz Peach Schnapps
Dash of Lime Juice
Fill with Pineapple Juice.
Shake.

FORESTER
Fill glass with ice.
1 1/2 oz Bourbon
3/4 oz Cherry Liqueur
1 tsp Sour Mix
Shake.

FORTY AKA 40
This refers to a bottled 40oz
Malt Beverage.
Beer, Malt Liqueur

44 MAGNUM
Fill glass with ice.
1/2 oz Vodka or Citrus Vodka
1/2 oz Light Rum
1/2 oz Dark Rum
1/2 oz Triple Sec
Dash of Sour Mix
Dash of Pineapple Juice
Shake.
Fill with Lemon-Lime Soda.

FOUR HORSEMEN
Fill glass with ice.
1/2 oz Bourbon
1/2 oz Sambuca
1/2 oz Jägermeister
1/2 oz 100-proof Peppermint
Schnapps
Shake. Strain into shot glass.

F

Metric Measurement Conversion Chart on page 14

FOUR HORSEMEN 2
Fill glass with ice.
1/2 oz Tequila
1/2 oz 151-Proof Rum
1/2 oz 100-proof Peppermint
Schnapps
1/2 oz Jägermeister
Shake. Strain into shot glass.

FOUR HORSEMEN 3
Fill glass with ice.
1/2 oz Jim Beam
1/2 oz Jack Daniels
1/2 oz Johnnie Walker
1/2 oz Jose Cuervo
Stir. Strain into shot glass.

FOURTH OF JULY (floater)
3/4 oz Grenadine (bottom)
3/4 oz Blue Curacao
3/4 oz Rum or Vodka or Milk (top)

FOX RIVER
Fill glass with ice.
1 1/2 oz Whiskey
1/2 oz Dark Crème de Cacao
2 or 3 dashes of Bitters
Stir.
Serve or strain into chilled glass.
Garnish with Lemon Twist.

FOX TROT
Fill glass with ice.
1 1/2 oz Rum or Citrus Rum
1/2 oz Triple Sec
1 oz Lime Juice or Sour Mix
Shake.
Strain into chilled glass.

FOXY LADY
Fill glass with ice.
1 oz Amaretto
1 oz Dark Crème de Cacao
Fill with Cream or Milk.
Shake.

FOXHOUND
Fill glass with ice.
1 1/2 oz Brandy
1 tsp Kummel
Dash of Sour Mix
Dash of Cranberry Juice
Shake.
Garnish with a Lemon.

FRANKENBERRY
Fill glass with ice.
1 oz Currant Vodka
1 oz Black Raspberry Liqueur
Fill with equal parts Sour Mix
and Pineapple Juice.
Shake.
*Frankie Gaul, Hog's Breath
Saloon, Key West*

FRANKENJACK
Fill glass with ice.
1 oz Gin
1/2 oz Triple Sec
1/2 oz Apricot Brandy
1/2 oz Dry Vermouth
Shake.

FRAPPE
Fill large stemmed glass (Red Wine
glass, Champagne saucer) with
crushed ice.
Add 2 oz desired Liquor or Liqueur

FRAPPE aka MILKSHAKE
(frozen)
In Blender: 1/2 cup of ice.
1/2 cup of Milk
Scoop of Desired flavored ice
cream.
3 Tblsp Desired flavored Syrup or
1/2 cup Fresh or
thawed Frozen berries or fruit.
Tblsp Sugar (optional)
Blend until smooth.

**FREDDY FUDPUCKER aka
CACTUS BANGER**
Fill glass with ice.
1 1/2 oz Tequila
Fill with Orange Juice.
Top with Galliano.
Garnish with Orange.

FREDDY KRUGER (floater)
1 oz Sambuca (bottom)
1 oz Jägermeister
1 oz Vodka (top)

FREEDOM FIGHTER (floater)
1 1/2 oz Irish Whiskey (bottom)
1/2 oz Irish Cream (top)

FRENCH COFFEE
2 oz Orange Liqueur or Cognac
Fill with hot Black Coffee.
Top with Whipped Cream.
Garnish with Orange and
Cinnamon.

FRENCH CONNECTION
Fill glass with ice.
1 1/2 oz Cognac or Brandy
1/2 oz Amaretto
or Orange Liqueur
Stir.

FRENCH CONNECTION COFFEE
1 1/2 oz Cognac or Brandy
1/2 oz Amaretto
Fill with hot Black Coffee.
Top with Whipped Cream.
Sprinkle with Shaved Almonds.

FRENCH DRAGON
1 oz Brandy or Cognac
1 oz Green Chartreuse
Stir.

FRENCH DREAM
Fill glass with ice.
1 oz Irish Cream
1 oz Black Raspberry Liqueur
1 oz Coffee Liqueur
Stir.

FRENCH HOOKER
Fill glass with ice.
1 1/2 oz Vodka or Raspberry Vodka
1 1/2 oz Black Raspberry Liqueur
Dash Sour Mix
Shake.
Strain into chilled glass.

FRENCH ICED COFFEE (frozen)
In Blender:
1/2 cup of Ice
2 oz Cognac or Brandy
Scoop of Vanilla Ice Cream
1/2 cup of Iced Coffee
Blend until smooth.
If too thick add coffee or Milk.
If too thin add ice or Ice Cream.

Metric Measurement Conversion Chart on page 14

FRENCH KISS
In Snifter:
3/4 oz Brandy or Cognac
3/4 oz Benedictine
3/4 oz Orange Liqueur
Heat in microwave 5-7 sec on high.

FRENCH LIFT
Fill glass 1/2 with Champagne.
Dash of Grenadine
Fill with sparkling water.
Garnish with 3 or 4 blueberries.

FRENCH MARTINI
Fill glass with ice.
3 oz Vodka or Raspberry
  or Peach Vodka
1/2 oz Black Raspberry Liqueur
1/2 oz Peach Schnapps
Shake.
Strain into chilled glass.
Garnish with Cherry.

FRENCH MARTINI 2
Fill glass with ice.
3 1/2 oz Vodka or Pineapple
  or Raspberry Vodka
1/4 oz Black Raspberry Liqueur
Dash Pineapple Juice
Shake.
Strain into chilled glass.

FRENCH 95
Fill glass with ice.
1 1/2 oz Bourbon or Gin
1 oz Sour Mix
1 oz Orange Juice
Fill with Champagne.
Float 1/2 oz Brandy on top.
Garnish with Orange or Cherry.

FRENCH 75
Fill glass with ice.
1 1/2 oz Cognac or Brandy
or Gin
1 oz Lemon Juice or Sour Mix
1/2 oz Sugar Syrup
Shake.
Fill with Champagne.
Garnish with Lemon Twist.

FRENCH DREAM
Fill glass with ice.
1 oz Coffee Liqueur
1 oz Black Raspberry Liqueur
1 oz Irish Cream
Stir.

FRENCH SUMMER
Fill glass with ice.
1 oz Black Raspberry Liqueur
Fill with sparkling water
or Soda Water.
Garnish with Orange.

FRENCH TICKLER
Fill glass with ice.
1 oz Orange Liqueur
1 oz 100-proof Cinnamon
Schnapps
Stir.
Strain into shot glass.

FRIAR TUCK
Fill glass with ice.
2 oz Hazelnut Liqueur
2 oz Lemon Juice or Sour Mix
2 dashes of Grenadine
Shake.
Garnish with Orange and Cherry.

FRISCO SOUR
Fill glass with ice.
1 1/2 oz Whiskey
3/4 oz Benedictine
1/2 oz Lemon Juice or Sour Mix
1/2 oz Lime Juice
Shake.
Strain into chilled glass.
Garnish with Orange.

FROG-IN-A-BLENDER (frozen)
In Blender:
1 cup of Ice
2 oz Vodka
4 oz Cranberry Juice
2 Lime wheels
Blend 3-5 seconds.

FROSTBITE
Fill glass with ice.
1 1/2 oz Tequila
1/2 oz White Crème de Cacao
1/2 oz Blue Curacao
Fill with Cream.
Shake.

FROSTBITE (frozen)
In Blender:
1 cup of Ice
1 1/2 oz Yukon Jack
3/4 oz Peppermint Schnapps
2 oz Sour Mix
Blend until smooth.
If too thin add ice.
If too thick add Sour Mix.

FROSTED ROMANCE (frozen)
In Blender:
1/2 cup of Ice
1 oz Black Raspberry Liqueur
1 oz White Crème de Cacao
Scoop of Vanilla Ice Cream
Blend until smooth.
If too thick add Milk or liqueur.
If too thin add ice or Ice Cream.

FROZEN BIKINI (frozen)
In Blender:
1 cup of Ice
2 oz Vodka
1 oz Peach Schnapps
3 oz Peach Nectar
2 oz Orange Juice
Whole Peach (no pit, no skin)
Blend until smooth.
Pour into large glass.
Top with Champagne.

FROZEN CAPPUCCINO AKA FRAPPE CAPPUCCINO
In Blender 1/2cup of ice.
Either 2 Cappuccino or
2 Espresso and 1/2cup of Milk
Scoop Vanilla ice Cream.
Blend until smooth.

FRU FRU
Fill glass with ice.
1 oz Peach Schnapps
1 oz Banana Liqueur
Dash of Lime Juice
1 oz Pineapple Juice
Shake.
Strain into chilled glass.
Garnish with Lime.

FRUITBAR
Fill glass with ice.
1 oz Peach Schnapps
1 oz Dark Creme de Cacao
Stir.

F

Metric Measurement Conversion Chart on page 14

FRUTTI NUEB
Fill glass with ice.
1/2 oz Vodka
1/2 oz Coconut Rum
1/2 oz Melon Liqueur
1/2 oz Black Raspberry Liqueur
Fill with Cranberry Juice.
Shake.

FU MANCHU
Fill glass with ice.
1 1/2 oz Dark Rum
1/2 oz Triple Sec
1/2 oz White Crème de Menthe
1/2 oz Lime Juice
Dash of Sugar Syrup
or 1/4 tsp Sugar
Shake.
Strain into chilled glass.

FUBAR
Fill glass with ice.
1/2 oz Vodka
1/2 oz Gin
1/2 oz Rum
1/2 oz Tequila
Fill with Hard Cider

FUDGESICLE (frozen)
In Blender:
1/2 cup of Ice
1 1/2 oz Vodka or Chocolate Vodka
1/2 oz Dark Crème de Cacao
1 tbsp Chocolate Syrup
Scoop of Chocolate Ice Cream
Blend until smooth.
If too thick add Milk or Cream.
If too thin add ice or Ice Cream.
Garnish with a popsicle stick.

FUEL-INJECTION
Fill glass with ice
1 1/2 oz Brandy
1/2 oz Mentholated Schnapps
Shake.
Strain into chilled glass.

FULL MOON
Fill glass with ice.
1 oz Orange Liqueur
1 oz Amaretto
Stir.

FUNKY MONKEY (frozen)
In Blender:
1/2 cup of Ice
3/4 oz Rum or Banana Rum
3/4 oz White Crème de Cacao
3/4 oz Banana Liqueur
1/2 fresh ripe peeled Banana
Scoop of Vanilla Ice Cream
Blend until smooth.
If too thick add Milk or fruit.
If too thin add ice or Ice Cream.
Garnish with Banana.

FUZZY ASTRONAUT
Fill glass with ice.
1 1/2 oz Vodka
1/2 oz Peach Schnapps
Fill with Tang.

FUZZY BASTARD
Fill glass with ice.
1 oz Dark Rum
1/2 oz 151-Proof Rum
1/2 oz Triple Sec
Fill with equal parts Orange Juice
and Sour Mix.
Shake.
Float 1/2 oz Peach Schnapps on top.

FUZZY FRUIT
Fill glass with ice.
2 oz Peach Schnapps
Fill with Grapefruit Juice.
Stir.

FUZZY GUPPIE
Fill glass with ice.
1 1/2 oz Vodka
1/2 oz Peach Schnapps
1 oz White Wine
Fill with Ginger Ale.
Originally garnished with a fish.
(I don't condone killing an
innocent animal for garnishes.)

FUZZY KAMIKAZE
Fill glass with ice.
2 oz Vodka
2 oz Peach Schnapps
1 oz Lime Juice
Shake.
Serve or strain into chilled glass.
Garnish with Lime.

FUZZY MONKEY
Fill glass with ice.
1 oz Banana Liqueur
1 oz Peach Schnapps
Fill with Orange Juice.
Stir.
Garnish with Orange or Banana.

FUZZY MOTHER
1 1/2 oz Gold Tequila
Top with 1/4 oz 151-Proof Rum.
Ignite.

FUZZY NAVEL
Fill glass with ice.
1 oz Vodka or Peach Vodka
Note: If using Peach Vodka, use
less or no Peach Schnapps
1 oz Peach Schnapps or
2 oz Peach Schnapps
Fill with Orange Juice.
Garnish with Orange.

FUZZY NAVEL WITH LINT
Fill glass with ice.
1 oz Vodka
1 oz Peach Schnapps
Fill with Orange Juice.
Top with 1/2 oz Irish Cream or Milk.

G AND C
Fill glass with ice.
1 oz Galliano
1 oz Cognac

G-SPOT
Fill glass with ice.
1 oz Vodka or Citrus Vodka
1 oz Orange Liqueur
1 oz Cranberry Juice
Stir.
Strain into chilled glass.

G-STRING
Fill glass with ice.
1 1/2 oz Vodka or Vanilla Vodka
1/2 oz Dark Crème de Cacao
1/2 oz Cream or Milk
Shake. Strain into shot glass.

Metric Measurement Conversion Chart on page 14

GAELIC COFFEE
3/4 oz Irish Whiskey
3/4 oz Irish Cream
3/4 oz Crème de Cacao
Fill with hot Black Coffee.
Top with Whipped Cream.
Drizzle Green Crème de Menthe on top.

GALE FORCE
Fill glass with ice.
1 oz Gin
1/2 oz Gold Rum
1/4 oz 151-Proof Rum
Dash of Lime Juice
Fill with Orange Juice.
Shake.

GALE WARNING
Fill glass with ice.
2 oz Scotch
Fill with equal parts Cranberry and Pineapple Juice.

GANDY DANCER
Fill glass with ice.
1 oz Yukon Jack
1 oz Amaretto
1 oz Banana Liqueur
1 oz Pineapple Juice
Shake.
Strain into chilled glass.

GANG BANGER
Fill glass with ice.
1 oz Vodka
1 oz Tequila
1 oz Bourbon
Fill with Lemon-Lime soda

GANGRENE
Fill glass with ice.
1 oz Light Rum
1/2 oz Spiced Rum
1/2 oz Melon Liqueur
1/2 oz Blue Curacao
Fill with Sour Mix.
Shake.

GASOLINE (floater)
1 oz Southern Comfort (bottom)
1 oz Tequila (top)

GAUGIN or GAUGUIN (frozen)
In Blender:
1 cup of Ice
2 oz Rum
1 tsp Passion Fruit Syrup
1 tsp Lime Juice
1 tsp Lemon Juice
Blend until smooth.
Garnish with Cherry and Lemon Twist.

GEISS
1/2 fill Pint glass or Mug with Dark German Beer
2oz German Brandy
Fill with Cola.

GENOA
Fill glass with ice.
1 1/2 oz Vodka
3/4 oz Campari
Fill with Orange Juice.
Shake.
Garnish with Orange.

GENTLE BEN
Fill glass with ice.
3/4 oz Vodka
3/4 oz Gin
3/4 oz Rum
Fill with Orange Juice.
Shake.
Garnish with Orange.

GENTLE BULL
Fill glass with ice.
1 1/2 oz Tequila
3/4 oz Coffee Liqueur
Fill with Cream or Milk.
Shake.

GEORGIA PEACH
Fill glass with ice.
2 oz Peach Schnapps
Fill with Cranberry Juice.
Stir.

GERMAN LEG SPREADER
Fill glass with ice.
3/4 oz Jägermeister
3/4 oz Chocolate Liqueur
3/4 oz 100-proof Peppermint Schnapps
Shake. Strain into shot glass.

GET LAID
Fill glass with ice.
1 1/2 oz Vodka or Orange Vodka
1/2 oz Raspberry Liqueur
Dash of Cranberry Juice
Fill with Pineapple Juice.
Shake.

GHETTO BLASTER (floater)
1/2 oz Coffee Liqueur (bottom)
1/2 oz Brandy
1/2 oz Tequila
1/2 oz Bourbon (top)

GHOSTBUSTER
Fill glass with ice.
1 oz Peach Schnapps
1 oz Melon Liqueur
Shake.
Strain into chilled glass.
Add 3-5 drops of Irish Cream into center of drink.

GIBSON
(Caution: DRY usually means less Vermouth than usual.
EXTRA DRY can mean even less Vermouth than usual, or no Vermouth at all.)
Fill glass with ice.
3 1/2 oz Gin
1/2 oz Dry Vermouth
Stir.
Strain into chilled glass or pour contents (with ice) into short glass.
Garnish with Cocktail Onions.

GILLIGAN
Fill glass with ice.
3/4 oz Light Rum
3/4 oz Coconut Rum
3/4 oz Banana Liqueur
Fill with equal parts Pineapple and Orange Juice.
Shake.

F
G

Metric Measurement Conversion Chart on page 14

GILLIGAN'S ISLE
Fill glass with ice.
2 oz Rum or Mango Rum
Dash of Amaretto
Dash of Maraschino Cherry juice
Dash of Lime Juice
Dash of Grapefruit Juice
Stir.
Strain into chilled glasses.

GIMLET
Fill glass with ice.
3 1/2 oz Gin or Vodka
1/4 oz to 1 oz Lime Juice
Stir.
Strain into chilled glass or pour
contents (with ice) into short glass.
Garnish with Lime.

GIN AND TONIC
Fill glass with ice.
2 oz Gin
Fill with Tonic Water.
Garnish with Lime.

GIN BUCK
Fill glass with ice.
2 oz Gin
Fill with Ginger Ale.
Stir.
Garnish with Lemon.

GIN CASSIS
Fill glass with ice.
1 1/2 oz Gin
1/2 oz Crème de Cassis
1/2 oz Lemon Juice or Sour Mix
Shake.
Serve or strain into chilled glass.

GIN DAISY
Fill glass with ice.
2 oz Gin
1 tsp Sugar
1 tsp Raspberry Syrup
or Grenadine
1 oz Lemon Juice or Sour Mix
Shake.
Fill with Soda Water.
Garnish with Orange and Lemon.

GIN FIZZ
Fill glass with ice.
2 oz Gin
1/2 tsp Sugar
1 oz Sour Mix
Dash of Lime Juice
Shake.
Fill with Soda Water.
Garnish with Cherry.

GIN RICKEY
Fill glass with ice.
2 oz Gin
1 tbsp Lime Juice
Fill with Soda Water.
Garnish with Lime.

GINGERBREAD MAN
Fill glass with ice.
1 oz Cinnamon Schnapps
1 oz Irish Cream
1 oz Butterscotch Schnapps
Shake.
Strain into chilled glass.

GINGERBREAD MAN 2 (floater)
3/4 oz Coffee Liqueur (bottom)
3/4 oz Irish Cream
3/4 oz 100-proof Cinnamon
Schnapps (top)

GINGER MARTINI
Fill glass with ice.
3 1/2 oz Vodka or Ginger Vodka
1/2 oz Ginger Liqueur
Shake. Strain into chilled glass.
Garnish with lemon twist and
candied ginger.

GINGER SNAP
Fill glass with ice.
2 oz Ginger Brandy
Fill with Ginger Ale.

GINZA MARY
Fill glass with ice.
1 oz Sake
1 oz Vodka
1 tsp Wasabi or Horseradish
3 dashes of Hot Sauce
3 dashes Soy Sauce or
Worcestershire Sauce
Dash of Lime Juice
3 dashes of White Pepper
1 oz Oyster Liqueur (juice) optional
Pinch dry Japanese Mustard (optional)
Fill with Tomato Juice.
Shake.
Garnish with Lemon and/or Lime,
Celery and/or Cucumber and/or
Cocktail Shrimp.

G. S. COOKIE
Fill glass with ice.
1 oz Peppermint Schnapps or
Crème de Menthe
1 oz Coffee Liqueur
Fill with Milk or Cream.
Shake.

G. S. COOKIE (floater)
1/2 oz Coffee Liqueur (bottom)
1/2 oz Irish Cream
1/2 oz Peppermint Schnapps (top)

G. S. COOKIE (frozen)
In Blender:
1/2 cup of Ice
1 oz Coffee Liqueur
1 oz Peppermint Schnapps or
Crème de Menthe
Scoop of Vanilla Ice Cream
Blend until smooth.
If too thick add Milk or Cream.
If too thin add ice or Ice Cream.
Garnish with Chocolate Shavings
or Sprinkles or a Cookie.

GLAM TRASH
Fill glass with ice.
2 oz Cinnamon Schnapps
Dash of Grenadine
1 oz Beer
Stir. Strain into shot glass.

GLASS TOWER
Fill glass with ice.
1 oz Vodka
1 oz Light Rum
1/2 oz Triple Sec
1/2 oz Peach Schnapps
1/2 oz Sambuca
Fill with Lemon-Lime Soda.
Garnish with Lime.

GLENDA
In Champagne flute
1/2 oz Peach Schnapps
1/2 oz Orange Liqueur
Fill with Champagne.

Metric Measurement Conversion Chart on page 14

GLOOMLIFTER
Fill glass with ice.
1 1/2 oz Whiskey
1/2 oz Brandy
1/2 oz Raspberry Syrup
or Black Raspberry Liqueur
1 tsp Sugar
1/2 oz Lemon Juice or Sour Mix
1/2 Egg White
Shake.

GLUEWEIN
In a sauce pan:
5 oz Dry Red Wine
1 Cinnamon Stick (broken up)
2 whole Cloves
1 tsp Honey
Pinch of ground Nutmeg
Heat without boiling.
Pour into mug.
Garnish with Lemon Twist and
Orange.

GO GIRL
Fill glass with ice.
1 oz Vodka or Citrus Vodka
1 oz Black Raspberry Liqueur
Dash of Sour Mix
Shake.
Fill with Soda Water.

GO-GO JUICE
Fill glass with ice.
1/2 oz Vodka
1/2 oz Gin
1/2 oz Rum
1/2 oz Tequila
1/2 oz Blue Curacao
1/2 oz Orange Juice
1 oz Sour Mix
Shake.
Fill with Lemon-Lime Soda.
Garnish with Lemon.

GODCHILD
Fill glass with ice.
1 1/2 oz Vodka
1/2 oz Amaretto
Fill with Milk or Cream.
Shake.

GODCHILD 2
Fill glass with ice.
1 1/2 oz Brandy or Cognac
1/2 oz Amaretto

GODFATHER
Fill glass with ice.
1 1/2 oz Scotch
1/2 oz Amaretto
Stir.

GODMOTHER aka
TAWNY RUSSIAN
Fill glass with ice.
1 1/2 oz Vodka
1/2 oz Amaretto
Stir.

GOLDEN BULL
Fill glass with ice.
1 oz Southern Comfort
1 oz Amaretto
Fill with Orange Juice.
Shake.
Top with Lemon-Lime Soda.
Garnish with Lemon.

GOLDEN CADDIE (frozen)
In Blender:
1 cup of Ice (or 1/2 cup of Ice if
using Ice Cream)
2 oz White Crème de Cacao
1 oz Galliano
3 oz Cream or Milk or
1/2 scoop of Vanilla Ice Cream
Blend 5 seconds on low speed.
Strain and serve.

GOLDEN CADDIE WITH
DOUBLE BUMPERS (frozen)
In Blender:
Cup of ice (or 1/2 cup Ice Cream)
1/2 oz Galliano
1/2 oz White Crème de Cacao
1/2 oz Brandy
1/2 oz Benedictine
3 oz Cream or Milk or
1/2 scoop Vanilla Ice Cream
Blend 5 seconds on low speed.
Strain and serve.

GOLDEN CAPPUCCINO
1 1/2 oz Galliano
Fill with Espresso.
Top with Steamed Milk.
Garnish with Lemon Twist.

GOLDEN DAWN
Fill glass with ice.
1 oz Gin
1 oz Apricot Brandy
1 oz Orange Juice
Shake.
Strain into chilled glass.

GOLDEN DAY
Fill glass with ice.
1 1/2 oz Vodka
1/2 oz Galliano
Stir.

GOLDEN DAZE
Fill glass with ice.
1 1/2 oz Gin
1/2 oz Peach or Apricot Brandy
1 oz Orange Juice
Shake.
Strain into chilled glass.

GOLDEN DELICIOUS MARTINI
Fill glass with ice.
2 oz Vodka or Apple Vodka
1 oz Apple Brandy
Dash Goldschlager
Shake.
Strain into chilled glass.

GOLDEN DELICIOUS CIDER
2 oz. Goldschlager
Fill with hot cider.
Top with whipped cream.

GOLDEN DRAGON
Fill glass with ice.
1 1/2 oz Yellow Chartreuse
1 1/2 oz Brandy
Stir and Strain into chilled glass.
Garnish with Lemon Twist.

GOLDEN DREAM
Fill glass with ice.
1 oz Galliano
1/2 oz Triple Sec
Fill with equal parts Orange Juice
and Cream or Milk.
Shake.
Serve or strain and serve.
Garnish with Orange.

G

Metric Measurement Conversion Chart on page 14

GOLDEN DREAM
(with Double Bumpers)
Fill glass with ice.
1/2 oz Galliano
1/2 oz Triple Sec
1/2 oz Brandy
1/2 oz Benedictine
Fill with equal parts of Orange Juice
and Cream or Milk.
Shake.
Serve or strain into chilled glass.

GOLDEN FIZZ
Fill glass with ice.
2 oz Gin
1 Egg Yolk
1 1/2 oz Sour Mix
or Lemon Juice
1 tsp Powdered Sugar
Shake.
Fill with Soda Water.
Garnish with Lemon Wedge.

GOLDEN GATE
Fill glass with ice.
1 oz Rum
1/2 oz Gin
1/2 oz White Crème de Cacao
1 tsp 151-Proof Rum
1 tsp Falernum
1 oz Lemon Juice or Sour Mix
Shake.
Garnish with Orange.

GOLDEN MARGARITA
Fill glass with ice.
1 1/2 oz Gold Tequila
1/2 oz Grand Marnier
or Cointreau or Triple Sec
1/2 oz Lime Juice
3 oz Sour Mix
Dash of Orange Juice (optional)
Shake.
Rub rim of second glass with Lime
and dip in kosher salt.
Strain or pour contents (with ice)
into salted glass.
Garnish with Lime.

GOLDEN MARGARITA (frozen)
In Blender:
1 cup of Ice
1 1/2 oz Golden Tequila
1/2 oz Grand Marnier or Orange
Liqueur or Triple Sec
1/2 oz Lime Juice
3 oz Sour Mix
Dash of Orange Juice
(optional)
Blend until smooth.
If too thick add juice.
If too thin add ice.
Rub rim of second glass with Lime
and dip in kosher salt.
Strain or pour contents (with ice)
into salted glass.
Garnish with Lime.

GOLDEN NAIL
Fill glass with ice.
2 oz Drambuie
Fill with Grapefruit Juice.
Stir.

GOLDEN RUSSIAN
Fill glass with ice.
1 1/2 oz Vodka
1 oz Galliano
Stir.
Garnish with Lime.

GOLDEN SCREW aka
ITALIAN SCREW
Fill glass with ice.
2 oz Galliano
Fill with Orange Juice.
Shake.

GOLDEN SHOWERS
Uncork bottle of chilled Champagne
or Sparkling Wine.
Cover top with thumb and shake.
Face bottle in direction of unsus-
pecting friend.
Remove thumb.

GOLDEN TORPEDO
Fill glass with ice.
1 oz Amaretto
1 oz Galliano
Fill with Cream or Milk.
Shake.

GOLDRUSH
Fill glass with ice.
1 oz Gold Tequila
1 oz Goldschlager

GOLDRUSH 2
Fill glass with ice.
1 1/2 oz Gold Tequila
1/2 oz Orange Liqueur
1/2 oz Lime Juice
Rub rim of second glass with Lime
and dip into Kosher Salt.
Strain or pour contents (with ice)
into salted glass.

GOLF
Fill glass with ice.
2 1/2 oz Gin
3/4 oz Dry Vermouth
2 dashes of Bitters
Stir.
Strain into chilled glass.
Garnish with Olive.

THE GOLF BALL
Fill glass with ice.
3 oz Vodka
3 oz Champagne
Fill with Orange Juice.
Stir gently.

GOLPEADO aka TEQUILA POP-
PER aka TEQUILA BOOM BOOM
aka TEQUILAZO
In shot glass:
1 oz Tequila
1 oz Ginger Ale or Lemon-Lime
Soda
Cover glass with napkin and hand,
Then slam on bar top.
Drink while foaming.

GOOD AND PLENT-E
1 oz Ouzo or Anisette
1 oz Coffee Liqueur
or Blackberry Brandy

GOOD AND PLENT-E (frozen)
In Blender:
1/2 cup of Ice
1 oz Vodka
1 oz Coffee Liqueur
1/2 oz Anisette
Scoop of Vanilla Ice Cream
Blend until smooth.
If too thick add Milk or Cream.
If too thin add ice or Ice Cream.

GOOD FORTUNE
Fill glass with ice.
1 oz Ginger Liqueur
1 oz Irish Cream
Stir.

GOOD GOLLY COFFEE
1 1/2 oz Dark Rum
1/2 oz Galliano
Dash Crème de Cacao
Fill with Hot Black Coffee
Top with Whipped Cream

GOOD LIFE
Fill glass with ice.
3 1/2 oz Rum
1/2 oz Triple Sec
Dash Lime Juice
Dash Grenadine
Dash Orange Juice
Shake. Strain into chilled glass.
Garnish with Lime Orange and
Cherry.

GOOMBAY SMASH
Fill glass with ice.
1 oz Rum or Orange Rum
1/2 oz Banana Liqueur
1 tsp Cream of Coconut
Dash of Orange Juice
Fill with Pineapple Juice.
Shake.
Top with Dark Rum.

GORILLA
Fill glass with ice.
1 oz Dark Crème de Cacao
1 oz Banana Liqueur
Fill with Orange Juice.

GORILLA FART
Fill glass with ice.
3/4 oz 151-Proof Rum
3/4 oz Bourbon
3/4 oz Southern Comfort or Ouzo
Stir. Strain into shot glass.

GRADEAL SPECIAL
Fill glass with ice.
1 1/2 oz Gin or Rum
3/4 oz Rum or Gin
3/4 oz Apricot Brandy
1 tsp Sugar Syrup
Shake.
Strain into chilled glass.

GRAND ALLIANCE
1 oz Amaretto
Fill with Champagne.

GRAND AM
Fill glass with ice.
1 oz Orange Liqueur
1 oz Amaretto
Stir.

GRAND APPLE
Fill glass with ice.
1 oz Apple Brandy
1/2 oz Cognac or Brandy
1/2 oz Orange Liqueur
Stir.
Strain into chilled glass.
Garnish with Orange and Lemon
Twist.

GRAND GOLD MARGARITA
Fill glass with ice.
1 1/2 oz Gold Tequila
1/2 oz Grand Marnier
Dash Lime Juice
3 oz Sour Mix
Dash of Orange Juice (optional)
Shake.
Garnish with lime.

GRAND MIMOSA
Fill glass with ice.
Fill 3/4 with Champagne.
Dash of Orange Liqueur
Fill with Orange Juice.
Garnish with Orange.

GRAND OCCASION
Fill glass with ice.
1 1/2 oz Rum or Citrus Rum
1/2 oz Orange Liqueur
1/2 oz White Crème de Cacao
1/2 oz Lemon Juice or Sour Mix
Shake.
Strain into chilled glass.

GRAND PASSION
Fill glass with ice.
2 oz Gin
1 oz Passion Fruit Nectar
2 or 3 dashes of Bitters
Shake.
Serve or strain into chilled glass.

GRAND SLAM
Fill glass with ice.
1 1/2 oz Swedish Punch
3/4 oz Dry Vermouth
3/4 oz Sweet Vermouth
Stir.
Strain into chilled glass.

GRAPE APE
Fill glass with ice.
2 oz Vodka
Fill glass with equal parts
Grape Juice and Lemon-Lime
Soda.

GRAPE CRUSH aka COCA
Fill glass with ice.
1 1/2 oz Vodka or Citrus Vodka
1/2 oz Black Raspberry Liqueur
Dash of Sour Mix
Shake.
Fill with Lemon-Lime Soda.

GRAPE NEHI
Fill glass with ice.
1 1/2 oz Vodka or Citrus Vodka
1/2 oz Black Raspberry Liqueur
2 oz Sour Mix
Shake. Strain into chilled glass.

GRAPE SOUR BALL
Fill glass with ice.
1 oz Vodka
1 oz Blue Curacao
2 oz Sour Mix
Fill with Cranberry Juice.
Shake.
Strain into chilled glass.

GRASS SKIRT
Fill glass with ice.
1 1/2 oz Gin
1/2 oz Triple Sec
Dash of Grenadine
Fill with Pineapple Juice.
Shake.
Garnish with Cherry.

G

Metric Measurement Conversion Chart on page 14

GRASSHOPPER
Fill glass with ice.
1 oz White Crème de Cacao
1 oz Green Crème de Menthe
Fill with Milk or Cream.
Shake.
Serve or strain into chilled glass.

GRASSHOPPER (frozen)
In Blender:
1/2 cup of Ice
1 oz White Crème de Cacao
1 oz Green Crème de Menthe
Scoop of Vanilla Ice Cream
Blend until smooth.
If too thick add Milk or Cream. If
too thin add ice or Ice Cream.

GRAVEYARD
Fill glass with ice.
1/2 oz Vodka
1/2 oz Gin
1/2 oz 151-Proof Rum
1/2 oz Tequila
1/2 oz Triple Sec
1/2 oz Scotch
1/2 oz Bourbon
Fill with equal parts Beer and Stout.

GREAT SECRET
Fill glass with ice.
1 1/2 oz Gin
1/2 oz Lillet
Dash of Bitters
Shake.
Strain into chilled glass.
Garnish with Orange.

GRATEFUL D.
Fill glass with ice.
1/2 oz Vodka
1/2 oz Gin
1/2 oz Rum
1/2 oz Tequila
1/2 oz Triple Sec
1/2 oz Black Raspberry Liqueur
Fill with Sour Mix
Shake.
Jerry, We miss you!

GREEK COFFEE
1 oz Metaxa
1 oz Ouzo
Fill with hot Black Coffee.
Top with Whipped Cream.

GREEN APPLE
Fill glass with ice.
1 oz Apple Brandy
1 oz Melon Liqueur
1 oz Sour Mix
Stir.

GREEN DEMON
Fill glass with ice.
3/4 oz Vodka or Citrus Vodka
3/4 oz Rum or Citrus Rum
3/4 oz Melon Liqueur
Fill with Lemonade
Shake.

GREEN DRAGON
Fill glass with ice.
2 oz Vodka
1 oz Green Chartreuse
Shake.
Strain into chilled glass.

GREEN EYES
Fill glass with ice.
1 1/2 oz Vodka or Orange Vodka
1/2 oz Blue Curacao
Fill with Orange Juice.
Shake.

GREEN GOBLIN
5 oz Hard Cider
5 oz Lager
Float 1/2 oz Blue Curacao on top.

GREEN GODDESS
Fill glass with ice.
1 oz Vodka
1/2 oz Melon Liqueur
1/2 oz Cream of Coconut
Shake.

GREEN HORNET aka
IRISH STINGER
Fill glass with ice.
1 1/2 oz Brandy
1/2 oz Green Crème de Menthe
Stir.
Serve or strain into chilled glass.

GREEN KAMIKAZE
Fill glass with ice.
2 oz Vodka or Lime or Citrus Vodka
1/2 oz Melon Liqueur
1 oz Lime Juice
Shake.

GREEN LIZARD
Fill glass with ice.
1/2 oz 151-Proof Rum
1 oz Green Chartreuse
Shake and Strain into shot glass.

GREEN MEANY
Fill glass with ice.
1 oz Southern Comfort
1 oz Melon Liqueur
1 oz Pineapple Juice
Stir and Strain into shot glass.

THE GREEN MONSTER
1/2 oz Vodka
1/2 oz Southern Comfort
1/2 oz Melon Liqueur
1/2 oz Peach Schnapps
Dash Blue Curacao
Fill with equal parts Beer and Hard
Cider
Garnish with hot dog or peanuts
or popcorn — **Go Red Sox**

GREEN MOUNTAIN MELON
Fill glass with ice.
1 oz Vodka
1/2 oz Melon Liqueur
1 oz Lime Juice
Fill with Sour Mix.
Shake.
Garnish with Lime.

GREEN RUSSIAN
Fill glass with ice.
1 1/2 oz Vodka
1/2 oz Melon Liqueur
Stir.

GREEN RUSSIAN 2
Fill glass with ice.
1 1/2 oz Vodka
1/2 oz Melon Liqueur
Fill with Milk or Cream.
Shake.
Strain into chilled glass.

GREEN SNEAKERS
Fill glass with ice.
1 oz Vodka or Citrus Vodka
1/2 oz Melon Liqueur
1/2 oz Triple Sec
2 oz Orange Juice
Shake.
Serve or strain into chilled glass.

GREEN SPIDER
Fill glass with ice.
2 oz Vodka
1 oz Green Crème de Menthe
Stir.
Serve or strain into chilled glass.

GREYHOUND
Fill glass with ice.
2 oz Vodka or Gin
Fill with Grapefruit Juice.
Garnish with Lime.

GROG
2 oz Amber Rum
1 tsp Sugar
Dash of Lemon Juice
3 whole cloves
1 Cinnamon Stick
Fill with boiling water.
Stir.
Garnish with Lemon.

GROUND ZERO aka
MINT CONDITION
Fill glass with ice.
3/4 oz Vodka
1/2 oz Coffee Liqueur
3/4 oz Bourbon
3/4 oz Peppermint Schnapps
Shake.
Serve or strain into chilled glass.

GUANA GRABBER
Fill glass with ice.
3/4 oz Light Rum
3/4 oz Dark Rum
1 oz Coconut Rum
Dash of Grapefruit Juice
Dash of Grenadine
Fill with Pineapple Juice.
Shake.
Garnish with Cherry.

GUILLOTINE
Fill glass with ice.
3/4 oz Vodka or Peppered Vodka
3/4 oz Tequila
3/4 oz Mentholated Schnapps
Shake.
Strain into chilled glass.

GUMBY
Fill glass with ice.
1 oz Vodka or Citrus Vodka
1 oz Melon Liqueur
1 oz Sour Mix
Shake.
Fill with Lemon-Lime Soda.

GUMDROP
Fill glass with ice.
1 oz Amaretto or Anisette
1 oz Dark Crème de Cacao
Strain into chilled glass.

GUMMY BEAR
Fill glass with ice.
3/4 oz Southern Comfort
3/4 oz Amaretto
3/4 oz Melon Liqueur
Dash of Grenadine
Fill with equal parts Orange and
Pineapple Juice.
Shake.
Garnish with Candy.

GUMMY MARTINI
Fill glass with ice.
3 oz Orange Vodka or Vodka
Dash Peach Schnapps
Dash Melon Liqueur
Dash Sour Apple Schnapps
Shake.
Strain into chilled glass
Garnish with Gummi Candy (fish,
bears, octopus)

GUMMY WORM MARTINI
Fill glass with ice.
3 oz Orange Vodka
or Citrus Vodka
Dash Sour Apple Schnapps
Dash Pineapple Juice
Shake
Strain into chilled glass.
Garnish with Candy Worm.

GUN RUNNER COFFEE
1 oz Irish Whiskey
1/2 oz Irish Cream
1/2 oz Coffee Liqueur
Fill with hot Black Coffee.
Top with Whipped Cream.
Sprinkle with Brown Sugar.

GUN RUNNER ICED COFFEE
Fill glass with ice.
1 oz Irish Whiskey
1/2 oz Irish Cream
1/2 oz Coffee Liqueur
Fill with Iced Coffee.
Add sugar or sweetener to taste.

GYPSY
Fill glass with ice.
2 oz Vodka or Citrus Vodka
1/2 oz Benedictine
1 tsp Lemon Juice or Sour Mix
1 tsp Orange Juice
Shake.
Serve or strain into chilled glass.
Garnish with Orange.

HEETH BAR (frozen)
In Blender:
1/2 cup of Ice
1 1/2 oz Vodka
1 oz Dark Crème de Cacao
1 Toffee Bar
1/2 scoop of Vanilla Ice Cream
Blend until smooth.
If too thick add Milk or Cream.
If too thin add ice or Ice Cream.

H. D. RIDER
1 oz Bourbon
1 oz Tequila or Yukon Jack

HAIRY APE
Fill glass with ice.
1 oz Vodka
1 oz Banana Liqueur
Fill with Orange Juice.
Shake.

G
H

HAIRY BITCH
Fill glass with ice.
1 1/2 oz Rum
1/2 oz Triple Sec
Dash Grenadine (optional)
Fill with Pineapple Juice.
Shake.

HAIRY MARY
Fill glass with ice.
2 oz Grain Alcohol
Fill with Bloody Mary Mix.

HAIRY NAVEL
Fill glass with ice.
1 oz Vodka
1 oz Peach Schnapps
Fill glass with Orange Juice.
Garnish with Orange.

HAITIAN ASSISTANT
Fill glass with ice.
1 oz Amber Rum
1/2 oz Orange Liqueur
1/2 oz Jägermeister
1 oz Pineapple Juice
Shake. Strain into shot glass.

**HALLEY'S COMFORT aka
HALLEY'S COMET**
Fill glass with ice.
1 1/2 oz Southern Comfort
1 1/2 oz Peach Schnapps
Fill glass with Soda Water.

HAMMER aka MEXICAN SCREW
Fill glass with ice.
2 oz Tequila
Fill with Orange Juice.
Garnish with Orange.

HAMMER (floater)
1 1/2 oz Sambuca (bottom)
2 oz Brandy (top)

**HAMMERHEAD AKA, RED EYE,
KICK START, SHOT IN THE
DARK, SPEEDBALL**
In large coffee cup:
2 shots Espresso
Fill with Hot Black Coffee.

HAMMERHEAD
Fill glass with ice.
1 oz Amber Rum
1 oz Amaretto
1 oz Curacao
1 or 2 dashes of Southern Comfort
Strain into chilled glass.

HAMMERHEAD 2
Fill glass with ice.
1/2 oz Vodka
1/2 oz Light Rum
1/2 oz Spiced Rum
1/2 oz Coconut Rum
Fill with equal parts Pineapple and
Orange Juice.

HAND JOB (floater)
1 oz Peach Schnapps (bottom)
1/2 oz Soda Water
1/2 oz 151-Proof Rum (top)
Ignite.

HAND RELEASE (floater)
1/2 oz Jägermeister (bottom)
1/2 oz Peppermint Schnapps
1/2 oz 151-Proof Rum (top)

HANGOVER RELIEVER
1 B-Complex Vitamin.
Glass filled with Soda Water,
with 5-10 dashes of Bitters in it.

HAPPY FELLER
Fill glass with ice.
1 1/2 oz Vodka
1/2 oz Black Raspberry Liqueur
1/2 oz Orange Liqueur
Dash of Lime Juice
Strain into chilled glass.

HAPPY JACK
Fill glass with ice.
1 oz Bourbon
1 oz Apple Brandy
Stir.
Strain into chilled glass.

HAPPY SUMMER
Fill glass with ice.
1 1/2 oz Amber Rum
1 1/2 oz Melon Liqueur
Fill with Orange Juice.
Michael T. Duratti

HARBOR LIGHTS (floater)
1 oz Galliano (bottom)
1 oz Brandy (top)
Ignite.

HARBOR LIGHTS 2 (floater)
3/4 oz Coffee Liqueur (bottom)
3/4 oz Tequila
or Southern Comfort
3/4 oz 151-Proof Rum (top)
Ignite.

HARD CANDY
Fill glass with ice.
1 oz Melon Liqueur
1/2 oz White Crème de Menthe or
Peppermint Schnapps
2 oz Sour Mix
Shake. Strain into shot glass.

HARD NIPPLE (floater)
1 oz Irish Cream (bottom)
1 oz Peppermint Schnapps (top)

HARD ON (floater)
3/4 oz Coffee Liqueur (bottom)
3/4 oz Amaretto
3/4 oz Milk (top)

HARDCORE
Fill glass with ice.
1 oz Grain Alcohol
1 oz 151-Proof Rum
1/2 oz Amaretto
1/2 oz Triple Sec
Fill with Cola
Stir.

HARI KARI
Fill glass with ice.
1 1/2 oz Brandy
1/2 oz Triple Sec
1 oz Orange Juice
Shake.
Strain into chilled glass.

HARLEM COCKTAIL
Fill glass with ice.
1 1/2 oz Gin
1 tsp of Cherry Liqueur
1 oz Pineapple Juice
Shake.
Strain into chilled glass.
Garnish with Pineapple.

HARMONY
Fill glass with ice.
1 1/2 oz Ginger Liqueur
1/2 oz Peach Schnapps
Fill with Orange Juice.
Shake.
Garnish with Orange.

HARVARD
Fill glass with ice.
1 1/2 oz Brandy
3/4 oz Sweet Vermouth
1/4 oz Lemon Juice or Sour Mix
1 tsp Grenadine
Dash of Bitters
Shake.
Strain into chilled glass.

HARVEY WALLBANGER
Fill glass with ice.
1 1/2 oz Vodka
Fill with Orange Juice.
Top with 1/2 oz Galliano.
Garnish with Orange.

HARVEY WALLBANGER (frozen)
In Blender:
1/2 cup of Ice
1 1/2 oz Vodka
Dash of Orange Juice
1/2 scoop Orange Sherbet
Blend until smooth.
Top with 1/2 oz Galliano.

HASTA LA VISTA, BABY
Fill glass with ice.
1/2 oz Vodka
1/2 oz Tequila
1/2 oz Triple Sec
1/2 oz Peach Schnapps
1/2 oz Amaretto
1/2 oz B&B
Dash of Dry Vermouth
Dash of Lime Juice
Fill with equal parts of Orange and
Pineapple Juice.
Shake.

HAVANA
Fill glass with ice.
1 1/2 oz Amber Rum
1/2 oz Sherry
1 1/2 oz Sour Mix
Shake.
Strain into chilled glass.
Garnish with Orange.

HAWAIIAN
Fill glass with ice.
2 oz Gin
1/2 oz Triple Sec
1/2 oz Pineapple Juice
Shake.
Strain into chilled glass.

HAWAIIAN 2
Fill glass with ice.
1 oz Amaretto
1 oz Southern Comfort
Dash of Orange Juice
Dash of Pineapple Juice
Dash of Grenadine
Shake.
Strain into chilled glass.

HAWAIIAN 3
Fill glass with ice.
1 oz Vodka
1 oz Blended Whiskey
1/2 oz Amaretto
Dash of Grenadine
Fill with equal parts Orange Juice
and Pineapple Juice.
Shake.
Garnish with Cherry and Pineapple.

HAWAIIAN COCKTAIL
Fill glass 3/4 with ice.
Fill 3/4 with desired White Wine.
Dash of Pineapple Juice
Dash of Pink Grapefruit Juice

HAWAIIAN GARDEN'S SLING
Fill glass with ice.
1 oz Rum
1 oz Sloe Gin
Dash of Grenadine
Fill with Sour Mix.
Shake.

HAWAIIAN MARGARITA (frozen)
In Blender:
1 cup of Ice
1 1/2 oz Tequila
1/2 oz Triple Sec
2 oz fresh or frozen
Strawberries
2 oz fresh or canned
Pineapple
Dash of Sour Mix
Blend until smooth.

HAWAIIAN MIMOSA
Fill glass 3/4 with Champagne
Fill with Pineapple Juice

HAWAIIAN NIGHTS
Fill glass with ice.
2 oz Rum
Fill with Pineapple Juice.
Float 1/4 oz Cherry Brandy
on top.

HAWAIIAN PUNCHED
Fill glass with ice.
3/4 oz Vodka
3/4 oz Southern Comfort
3/4 oz Amaretto
Dash of Sloe Gin or Grenadine
Fill with Pineapple Juice.
Shake.
Garnish with Pineapple.

HAWAIIAN PUNCHED 2
Fill glass with ice.
1 oz Vodka
1 oz Melon Liqueur
1 oz Amaretto
Dash of Southern Comfort
Fill with Cranberry Juice.
Shake.

HAWAIIAN PUNCHED 3
Fill glass with ice.
1/2 oz Vodka
1/2 oz Southern Comfort
1/2 oz Triple Sec
1/2 oz Amaretto
Dash of Pineapple Juice
Dash of Sour Mix
Dash of Cranberry Juice
Dash of Grenadine
Shake.
Garnish with Cherry and Orange.

H

Metric Measurement Conversion Chart on page 14

HAWAIIAN SEA BREEZE aka BAY BREEZE, DOWNEASTER
Fill glass with ice.
2 oz Vodka
Fill with equal parts Pineapple and Cranberry Juice.
Garnish with Lime.

HEAD BANGER
Fill glass with ice.
1 oz 151-Proof Rum
1 oz Sambuca
Dash of Grenadine
Shake. Strain into shot glass.

HEAD ROOM (floater)
1/2 oz Banana Liqueur (bottom)
1/2 oz Melon Liqueur
1/2 oz Irish Cream (top)

HEAD WIND
Fill glass with ice.
1 oz Vodka
1 oz 151-Proof Rum
1 oz Dark Rum
1 oz Brandy
1/2 oz Blue Curacao
Fill with equal parts Orange and Pineapple Juice and Sour Mix.
Shake.
Garnish with Lime.

HEADHUNTER
Fill glass with ice.
2 oz Rum or Coconut Rum
1 oz Vodka
1 tbsp Cream of Coconut
Dash of Cream
1 oz Orange Juice
Fill with Pineapple Juice.
Shake.
Garnish with Pineapple.

HEADREST aka UPSIDE DOWN MARGARITA
Rest head on bar.
Have friend pour ingredients into mouth.
1 oz Tequila
1/2 oz Triple Sec
Dash of Lime Juice
Dash of Sour Mix
Dash of Orange Juice
Slosh around mouth.
Swallow!

HEART THROB
Fill glass with ice.
2 oz Amaretto
Fill with equal parts Orange and Cranberry Juice.
Shake.

HEARTBREAK
Fill glass with ice.
2 1/2 oz Blended Whiskey
Fill with Cranberry Juice
Top with 1/2 oz Brandy.

HEATHER COFFEE aka RUSTY NAIL COFFEE
1 oz Scotch
1 oz Drambuie
Fill with hot Black Coffee.
Top with Whipped Cream.
Sprinkle with Cinnamon.

HEATWAVE
Fill glass with ice.
1 oz Dark Rum
1/2 oz Peach Schnapps
Fill with Pineapple Juice.
Dash of Grenadine
Stir.
Garnish with Cherry and Pineapple.

HEAVENLY SEX
Fill glass with ice.
1 oz Spiced Rum
1 oz Amaretto
1 oz Chocolate Liqueur
Dash Grenadine
Shake. Strain into chilled glass.

HELLO NURSE
Fill glass with ice.
1 1/2 oz Vodka or Coconut Vodka
1/2 oz Amaretto
Tbsp Cream of Coconut
1 oz Milk or Cream
Shake.
Strain into chilled glass.

HENRY MORGAN'S GROG
Fill glass with ice.
1 1/2 oz Whiskey
1 oz Pernod
1/2 oz Dark Rum
1 oz Cream
Shake.
Sprinkle ground Nutmeg on top.

HIGH JAMAICAN WIND (floater)
Fill glass with ice.
1 1/2 oz Dark Rum (bottom)
1/2 oz Coffee Liqueur
1/2 oz Milk or Cream (top)

HIGH ROLLER aka PRINCE IGOR
Fill glass with ice.
1 1/2 oz Vodka or Orange Vodka
3/4 oz Orange Liqueur
Dash of Grenadine
Fill with Orange Juice.
Shake.
Garnish with Orange and Cherry.

HIGHBALL
Fill glass with ice.
2 oz Whiskey
Fill with Water or Soda Water or Ginger Ale.

HIGHLAND COFFEE
1 1/2 oz Scotch
1/2 oz B&B
Fill with hot Black Coffee.
Top with Whipped Cream.

HIGHLAND FLING
Fill glass with ice.
1 1/2 oz Scotch
1/2 oz Sweet Vermouth
2-3 dashes of Orange Bitters
Shake.
Strain into chilled glass.
Garnish with Olive.

HILLARY WALLBANGER
Fill glass with ice.
4 oz Dry White Wine
Fill with Orange Juice
Top with 1/2 oz Galliano.

Metric Measurement Conversion Chart on page 14

HIT-IT
Fill glass with ice.
1 oz Vodka
1/2 oz Triple Sec
1/2 oz Cherry Brandy
2 oz Orange Juice
2 oz Cranberry Juice
Shake.
Strain into chilled glass.

HOFFMAN HOUSE
Fill glass with ice.
1 1/2 oz Gin
1/2 oz Dry Vermouth
2-3 dashes of Orange Bitters
Stir.
Strain into chilled glass.
Garnish with Olive.

HOG SNORT
Fill glass with ice.
1 oz Coconut Rum
1 oz Blue Curacao
Dash of Sour Mix
Dash of Pineapple Juice
Shake.
Strain into shot glass.

HOGBACK GROWLER
1 oz 151-Proof Rum
1 oz Brandy

HOLE IN ONE (floater)
1 oz Melon Liqueur (bottom)
1 oz Apple Brandy (top)
Add one drop of Cream into center
of drink.

**HOLLYWOOD aka
RASPBERRY SMASH**
Fill glass with ice.
1 1/2 oz Vodka or Citrus Vodka
1/2 oz Black Raspberry Liqueur
Fill with Pineapple Juice.
Shake.
Garnish with Pineapple.

HOLLYWOOD 2
Fill glass with ice.
1 oz Vodka or Citrus Vodka
1/2 oz Black Raspberry Liqueur
1/2 oz Peach Schnapps
Fill with Pineapple Juice.
Shake.

HOLLYWOOD MARTINI
Fill glass with ice.
3 oz Vodka or Citrus Vodka
1/2 oz Black Raspberry Liqueur
Dash of Pineapple Juice
Shake.
Strain into chilled glass.

HOMECOMING
Fill glass with ice.
1 oz Amaretto
1 oz Irish Cream
Shake.
Strain into chilled glass or pour
contents (with ice) into short glass.

HONEY BEE
Fill glass with ice.
2 oz Rum
1/2 oz Honey
1/2 oz Lemon Juice or Sour Mix
Shake.
Strain into chilled glass.

HONEYDEW
Fill glass with ice.
1 1/2 oz Melon Liqueur
2 oz Sour Mix
1/2 tsp Sugar
Shake.
Fill with Champagne.

HONEYMOON
Fill glass with ice.
3/4 oz Apple Brandy
3/4 oz Benedictine
1 tsp Triple Sec or Curacao
1 oz Lemon Juice or Sour Mix
Shake.
Strain into chilled glass.

HONOLULU
Fill glass with ice.
3/4 oz Gin
3/4 oz Benedictine
3/4 oz Cherry Liqueur
Stir.
Strain into chilled glass.

HONOLULU (frozen)
In Blender:
1 cup of Ice
1 1/2 oz Rum
Dash of Grenadine
Dash of Sour Mix
1/2 cup of fresh or canned
Pineapple
Blend for 3-6 seconds on low
speed.

HOOPLA
Fill glass with ice.
3/4 oz Brandy
3/4 oz Orange Liqueur
3/4 oz Lillet
3/4 oz Lemon Juice
or Sour Mix
Shake.
Strain into chilled glass.
Garnish with Lemon Twist.

HOOT MAN
Fill glass with ice.
1 1/2 oz Scotch
3/4 oz Sweet Vermouth
1 tsp Benedictine
Stir.
Strain into chilled glass.
Garnish with Lemon Twist.

HOOTER
Fill glass with ice.
1 1/2 oz Vodka
1/2 oz Amaretto
Fill with Pineapple Juice.
Shake.

HOP-SKIP-AND-GO-NAKED
Fill glass with ice.
1 oz Vodka
1 oz Gin or Lime Gin or Citrus Vodka
Dash of Lime Juice
Fill with Orange Juice (leaving 1/2
inch from top)
Float Beer on top.

HOP TOAD
Fill glass with ice.
1 oz Rum
1 oz Apricot Brandy
1 oz Lime Juice
Stir.
Strain into chilled glass.

H

HORSE'S NECK
Fill glass with ice.
2 oz Whiskey
Fill with Ginger Ale.
Garnish with Lemon Twist.
(In the original recipe, a whole
lemon should be peeled in a
continuous spiral for garnish.)

HOT APPLE PIE
2 oz Tuaca
Fill with hot Apple Cider.
Top with Whipped Cream.
Garnish with Cinnamon Stick.

HOT APPLE PIE 2
Fill glass ice.
1 oz Vodka or Apple Vodka
1 oz Apple Brandy
2 oz Apple Juice
Shake.
Strain into chilled glass.
1 oz Lemon-Lime Soda
Sprinkle with Cinnamon.

HOT APPLE TODDY
2 oz Whiskey or Apple Brandy
1 tsp Honey or Sugar
Fill with hot Apple Cider.
Stir.
Garnish with Lemon, Cinnamon
Stick, and 2-3 whole Cloves.

HOT BUTTERED RUM
2 oz Dark Rum
1/2 oz Sugar Syrup
Pinch of Nutmeg
Fill with hot Water.
Garnish with Cinnamon Stick and
Pat of Butter.

HOT DOG
Fill glass with ice.
2 oz Peppered Vodka
Fill with Grapefruit Juice.

HOT DOG 2
Rub rim of glass with Lime and dip
one side of glass in Kosher Salt.
Fill glass with Beer.
Add 5-7 drops of Tabasco Sauce.

HOT MILK PUNCH
2 oz Bourbon
1/2 oz Sugar Syrup
or 1/2 tsp Sugar
Fill with hot Milk.
Stir.
Sprinkle with Nutmeg.

HOT NAIL
2 oz Scotch
1 oz Drambuie
Dash of Lemon Juice
Fill with boiling Water.
Garnish with Orange, Lemon, and
Cinnamon Stick.

HOT PANTS
Fill glass with ice.
1 1/2 oz Tequila
1/2 oz Peppermint Schnapps
Dash of Grenadine
1 oz Grapefruit Juice
Shake and pour contents (with ice)
into second glass rimmed with salt.

HOT PEPPERMINT PATTY
1 oz Peppermint Schnapps
1/2 oz Dark Crème de Cacao
1 tsp Crème de menthe
Fill with Hot Chocolate.
Top with Whipped Cream.
Sprinkle with Shaved Chocolate or
Sprinkles.

HOT RASPBERRY DREAM
1 oz Black Raspberry Liqueur
1 oz Dark Crème de Cacao
4-6 oz steamed Milk
Stir.

HOT SCOTCH
1 oz Scotch
1/4 oz Drambuie
1 oz Lemon Juice
1/2 tsp Sugar
2 oz hot Water
Stir.
Garnish with Lemon.

HOT SEX
1 oz Coffee Liqueur
1 oz Orange Liqueur
Microwave for 10-15 seconds.

HOT SHOT (floater)
In a shot glass:
1 oz Hot Coffee (bottom)
1 oz Favorite Liqueur
Top with Cream or Whipped Cream
(optional)

HOT TAMALE
Fill glass with ice.
1 1/2 oz Cinnamon Schnapps
1/2 oz Grenadine
Strain into shot glass.
Garnish with Hot Candy.

HOT TODDY
2 oz Whiskey or Rum or Brandy
1 tsp Honey or Sugar
Fill with boiling Water.
Stir.
Garnish with a Lemon,
Cinnamon Stick, and
2-3 whole Cloves.

HOT TUB
Fill glass with ice.
1 1/2 oz Vodka or Currant Vodka
1/2 oz Black Raspberry Liqueur
Dash of Sour Mix
Dash of Cranberry Juice
Shake.
Fill with Champagne.
Strain into chilled glass.

HOT YOUNG LADY
Fill glass with ice.
1/2 oz Cinnamon Schnapps
1/2 oz Peppermint Schnapps
1/2 oz Coffee Liqueur
1/2 oz Irish Cream
Shake. Strain into shot glass.

HOTEL CALIFORNIA (frozen)
In Blender:
1/2 cup of ice.
1 oz Tequila or Vodka
1 oz Apricot Brandy
Scoop Orange Sherbet
Blend until smooth.
Float 1/2 oz Grenadine on top.

Metric Measurement Conversion Chart on page 14

HOUND DOG
Fill glass with ice.
2 oz Rum
Fill with Grapefruit Juice.
Stir.

HOUNDSTOOTH
Fill glass with ice.
2 oz Vodka
1/2 oz White Crème de Cacao
1/2 oz Blackberry Brandy
Stir.
Serve or strain into chilled glass.

HUDSON BAY
Fill glass with ice.
1 oz Gin
1/2 oz Cherry Brandy
1 1/2 tsp Lime Juice
1 tsp Orange Juice
Shake and Strain into chilled glass.

HUETCHEN
Fill glass with ice.
2 oz Brandy
Fill with Cola.

THE HULK aka DOUBLE H
Fill glass with ice.
1 oz Cognac
1 oz Hypnotiq
Stir.

HUMMER (frozen)
In Blender:
1/2 cup of Ice
1 oz Dark Rum
1 oz Coffee Liqueur
Scoop of Vanilla Ice Cream
Blend until smooth.
If too thick add Milk or Cream.
If too thin add ice or Ice Cream.

HUNTER'S COCKTAIL
Fill glass with ice.
1 1/2 oz Whiskey
1/2 oz Cherry Brandy
Stir.
Garnish with Cherry.

HUNTRESS COCKTAIL
Fill glass with ice.
1 oz Bourbon
1 oz Cherry Liqueur
1 oz Cream or Milk
Dash of Triple Sec
Shake.
Strain into chilled glass.

HURRICANE
Fill glass with ice.
1 oz Light Rum
1 oz Amber Rum
1/2 oz Passion Fruit Syrup
1/2 oz Lime Juice
Shake.
Strain into chilled glass.
Garnish with Lime.

HURRICANE 2
Fill glass with ice.
1/2 oz Gin
1/2 oz Light Rum
1/2 oz Dark Rum
1/2 oz Amaretto
Dash of Grenadine
Fill with equal parts Pineapple,
Orange and Grapefruit Juice.
Shake.
Garnish with Orange, Lemon, Lime
and Cherry.

HUSSIE
Fill glass with ice.
1 oz Amaretto
1 oz Beer
1 oz Sour Mix
Shake. Strain into shot glass.

I FOR AN I aka
IRISH BROGUE
Fill glass with ice.
1 1/2 oz Irish Whiskey
1/2 oz Irish Mist
Stir.
Serve or strain into chilled glass.
Garnish with Lemon Twist.

ICE BALL (frozen)
In Blender:
Cup of ice
1 oz Gin
1 oz Sambuca
1 oz White Crème de Menthe
1 oz Milk or Cream
Blend until smooth.

ICE BOAT
Fill glass with ice.
1 1/2 oz Vodka
            or Peppermint Vodka
1 1/2 oz Peppermint Schnapps
Stir.
Strain into chilled glass.

ICE CREAM FLOAT
In pint glass or beer mug:
1 scoop of Ice Cream
Fill (gently) with stout, porter any
dark beer or Root Beer or Cola
Serve with straw and spoon.

ICE PICK
Fill glass with ice.
2 oz Vodka or Tequila
Fill with Iced Tea.
Flavor with sugar and/or lemon as
desired.
Garnish with Lemon.

ICEBERG
Fill glass with ice.
2 oz Vodka
1 tsp Pernod or Peppermint
Schnapps
Shake.
Strain into chilled glass.

ICED COFFEE MOCHA
Fill glass with ice.
2-3 Tblsp Chocolate Syrup
Fill with Ice Coffee.
Shake.

ICE CREAM COFFEE
aka COFFEE ALA MODE
Fill large coffee cup 3/4 with hot
black Coffee
Gently place small scoop of desired
ice cream on top.
Serve immediately with a spoon.
Optional toppings (whipped cream,
shaved chocolate,
chocolate syrup, shaved coconut,
crushed candy, etc.)

ICE CREAM SODA
In pint glass or beer mug:
2-4oz Syrup (Strawberry,choco-
late,raspberry,etc.)
add 1 - 4 scoop ice cream
Fill Gently with Soda Water

H
I

ICHBIEN
Fill glass with ice.
2 oz Apple Brandy
1/2 oz Curacao
1 Egg Yolk
2 oz Milk or Cream
Shake.
Strain into chilled glass.
Garnish with Nutmeg.

IDEAL
Fill glass with ice.
1 1/2 oz Gin
1/2 oz Dry or Sweet Vermouth
1 tbsp Grapefruit Juice
1 tsp Cherry Liqueur
Shake.
Strain into chilled glass.
Garnish with Cherry.

IGUANA
Fill glass with ice.
1/2 oz Vodka
1/2 oz Tequila
1/4 oz Coffee Liqueur
1 1/2 oz Sour Mix (optional)
Shake.
Strain into chilled glass.
Garnish with Lime.

IL MAGNIFICO aka
IL PARADISO (frozen)
In Blender:
1 cup of Ice
1 oz Tuaca
1 oz Curacao
1 oz Cream
Blend for 3 or 4 seconds on low speed.

INCIDER
Fill glass with ice.
2 oz Whiskey
Fill with Hard Cider
Stir.

INCOME TAX
Fill glass with ice.
2 oz Gin
Dash of Sweet Vermouth
Dash of Dry Vermouth
Dash of Orange Juice
Dash of Bitters
Shake.
Serve or strain into chilled glass.

INDIAN SUMMER
2 oz Apple Brandy
Pinch of Sugar
Pinch of Cinnamon
Fill with hot Apple Cider.
Stir.
Garnish with Cinnamon Stick.

INDIAN SUMMER 2
Fill glass with ice.
1 oz Vodka
1 oz Coffee Brandy
2 oz Pineapple Juice
Shake.
Strain into shot glass.

INDIAN SUMMER HUMMER
Fill glass with ice.
1 oz Dark Rum
1/2 oz Apricot Brandy
1/2 oz Black Raspberry Liqueur
Fill with Pineapple Juice.
Shake.

INFUSED VODKAS
Fruits, Vegetables, Herbs & Spices
Find a wide mouthed jar (with lid)
Place prepped ingredients in jar.
Examples: strawberries cleaned
and diced, vanilla beans split,
oranges, lemons peeled and diced,
habenero or jalapeno peppers
diced.
Cover with Premium Vodka.
Seal jar.
Let steep for 7-14 days.
You may open and stir after
3 or 4 days.
You can chill jar in refrigerator 12
hours prior to taste testing.
If you expect to keep longer than a
month, remove the fruit.

INK STREET
Fill glass with ice.
2 oz Whiskey
Fill with equal parts Orange Juice
and Sour Mix.
Shake.
Strain into chilled glass.
Garnish with Orange.

INTERNATIONAL INCIDENT
Fill glass with ice.
1/2 oz Vodka or Vanilla Vodka
1/2 oz Amaretto
1/2 oz Coffee Liqueur
1/2 oz Irish Cream
Shake. Strain into shot glass.

INTERNATIONAL STINGER
Fill glass with ice.
1 1/2 oz Metaxa
1/2 oz Galliano
Stir.
Serve or strain into chilled glass.

INVERTED NAIL (floater)
1 oz Drambuie (bottom)
1 oz Single Malt Scotch (top)

IRA COCKTAIL
1 1/2 oz Irish Whiskey
1 oz Irish Cream
Stir.

IRISH ANGEL
Fill glass with ice.
1 oz Irish Whiskey
1/2 oz Dark Crème de Cacao
1/2 oz White Crème de Menthe
Fill with Cream.
Shake.

IRISH BROGUE aka
I FOR AN I
Fill glass with ice.
1 1/2 oz Irish Whiskey
1/2 oz Irish Mist
Stir.
Serve or strain into chilled glass.
Garnish with Lemon Twist.

IRISH BUCK
Fill glass with ice.
2 oz Irish Whiskey
Fill with Ginger Ale.
Garnish with Lemon Twist.

IRISH CAR BOMB (floater)
Fill shot glass with
1 oz Irish Whiskey (bottom)
1 oz Irish Cream (top)
Drop shot glass into beer glass
3/4 filled with Stout.

Metric Measurement Conversion Chart on page 14

IRISH COFFEE
2 oz Irish Whiskey
1 tsp Sugar (optional)
Fill with hot Black Coffee.
Top with Whipped Cream.
Dribble 5-6 drops of Green Crème
de Menthe on top (optional).

IRISH COFFEE ROYALE
1 oz Irish Whiskey
1 oz Coffee Liqueur
1/2 tsp Sugar
Fill with hot Black Coffee.
Top with Whipped Cream.
Dribble 5-6 drops of Green Creme
De Menthe on top.

IRISH COW
In a saucepan:
4 oz Irish Cream
4 oz Milk
Warm on low heat
Pour into tempered glass.
Garnish with Nutmeg.

IRISH CREAM SODA
Fill glass with ice.
2 oz Irish Cream
Fill with Soda Water.

IRISH FIX
Fill glass with ice.
2 oz Irish Whiskey
1/2 oz Irish Mist
1 oz Pineapple Juice
1/2 oz Lemon Juice
or Sour Mix
1/2 tsp Sugar Syrup
Shake.
Garnish with Lemon.

IRISH FLAG (floater)
3/4 oz Green Crème de Menthe
(bottom)
3/4 oz Irish Cream
3/4 oz Orange Liqueur or Brandy
(top)

IRISH GENTLEMAN
1 oz Irish Whiskey
1 oz Irish Cream
Fill with hot Black Coffee.
Top with Whipped Cream.
Drizzle Green Crème de Menthe on
top.

IRISH HEADLOCK
1/2 oz Irish Whiskey
1/2 oz Irish Cream
1/2 oz Brandy
1/2 oz Amaretto
Shake.
Strain into chilled glass.

IRISH ICED COFFEE
Fill glass with ice.
2 oz Irish Whiskey
Fill with Iced Coffee.
Add Cream or Milk and sugar or
sweetener to taste.

IRISH ICED TEA
Fill glass with ice.
1/2 oz Vodka
1/2 oz Gin
1/2 oz Rum
1/2 oz Triple Sec
1/2 oz Melon Liqueur
Fill with Lemon-Lime Soda.

IRISH MAIDEN COFFEE
1 oz Irish Whiskey
1 oz Irish Cream
Fill with hot Black Coffee.
Top with Whipped Cream.
Dribble 1/2 oz Green Crème de
Menthe on top.

IRISH MAIDEN ICED COFFEE
Fill glass with ice.
1 oz Irish Whiskey
1 oz Irish Cream
Fill with Iced Coffee.
Sugar to taste.

IRISH MANHATTAN
(Caution: Sweet means use more
Sweet Vermouth than usual.
Dry can either mean make drink
with Dry Vermouth instead of
Sweet Vermouth or less Sweet
Vermouth than usual.
Perfect means use Sweet and Dry
Vermouth.)
Fill glass with ice.
2 oz Irish Whiskey
1/2 oz Sweet Vermouth
Stir.
Strain into chilled glass or pour
contents (with ice) into short glass.
Garnish with Cherry or Lemon Twist.

IRISH MARIA (floater)
1 oz Tia Maria (bottom)
1 oz Irish Cream (top)

IRISH MOCHA COOLER
Fill glass with ice.
2 oz Irish Whiskey
1 oz Dark Crème de Cacao
Fill with Iced Coffee.

IRISH MONEY COFFEE
1 oz Irish Whiskey
1/2 oz Dark Crème de Cacao
Fill with hot Black Coffee.
Top with Whipped Cream.

IRISH MONK
Fill glass with ice.
1 oz Irish Cream or Irish Whiskey
1 oz Hazelnut Liqueur
Stir.

IRISH MONK COFFEE
1 oz Irish Whiskey or Irish Cream
1 oz Hazelnut Liqueur
Fill with hot Black Coffee.
Top with Whipped Cream.

IRISH ROVER
Fill glass with ice.
1 oz Irish Whiskey
1 oz Irish Cream
1 oz Coffee Liqueur
Shake.

IRISH RUSSIAN
1 oz Vodka
1 oz Coffee Liqueur
Fill with Irish Stout.
Dash Cola (optional)

IRISH SKIPPER COFFEE
3/4 oz Irish Mist
3/4 oz Irish Cream
3/4 oz White Crème de Cacao
Fill with hot Black Coffee.
Top with Whipped Cream.

Metric Measurement Conversion Chart on page 14

IRISH SPRING
Fill glass with ice.
1 oz Irish Whiskey
1/2 oz Peach Schnapps
1 oz Orange Juice
1 oz Sour Mix
Shake.
Garnish with Orange and Cherry.

**IRISH STINGER aka
GREEN HORNET**
Fill glass with ice.
1 1/2 oz Brandy
1/2 oz Green Crème de Menthe
Stir.
Serve or strain into chilled glass.

IRON CROSS
Fill glass with ice.
1 oz Apricot Brandy
1 oz Peppermint Schnapps
Stir. Strain into shot glass.

ISRAELI COFFEE
2 oz Sabra Liqueur
Fill with hot Black Coffee.
Top with Whipped Cream.

ITALIAN COFFEE
2 oz Amaretto
Fill with hot Black Coffee.
Top with Whipped Cream.
Sprinkle with Shaved Almonds.

ITALIAN COFFEE 2
2 oz Galliano
Fill with hot Black Coffee.
Top with Whipped Cream.
Sprinkle with Cinnamon.

ITALIAN DELIGHT
Fill glass with ice.
1 oz Amaretto
1/2 oz Orange Juice
1 1/2 oz Cream
Shake.
Strain into chilled glass.
Garnish with Cherry.

ITALIAN ICED COFFEE
Fill glass with ice.
2 oz Amaretto or Galliano
Fill with Iced Coffee.
Add Cream or Milk and
sugar or sweetener to taste.

**ITALIAN SCREW aka
GOLDEN SCREW**
Fill glass with ice.
2 oz Galliano
Fill with Orange Juice.
Shake.

ITALIAN STALLION
Fill glass with ice.
1 1/2 oz Scotch
1/2 oz Galliano
Stir.

ITALIAN STALLION 2
Fill glass with ice.
1 1/2 oz Bourbon
1/2 oz Sweet Vermouth
1/2 oz Campari
Dash of Bitters
Stir.
Strain into chilled glass.
Garnish with Lemon Twist.

ITALIAN STINGER
Fill glass with ice.
1 1/2 oz Brandy
1/2 oz Galliano
Stir.
Serve or strain into chilled glass.

ITALIAN SUNRISE
Fill glass with ice.
2 oz Amaretto
Fill with Orange Juice.
Top with 1/2 oz Crème de Cassis.

ITALIAN SURFER
Fill glass with ice.
1 oz Coconut Rum
1 oz Amaretto
Fill with Pineapple Juice
Shake.
Top with splash of Cranberry Juice.

**ITALIAN SURFER WITH
A RUSSIAN ATTITUDE**
Fill glass with ice.
1 oz Vodka
1/2 oz Coconut Rum
1/2 oz Amaretto
Fill with Pineapple Juice.
Shake.
Top with splash of Cranberry Juice.

ITCHY BITCHY SMELLY NELLY
Fill glass with ice.
1 oz Coconut Rum
1 oz Melon Liqueur
Fill (leaving 1/2 inch from top) with
equal parts Sour Mix and Orange
Juice.
Shake.
Top with Lemon-Lime Soda.
*The Hogettes, Hog's Breath
Saloon, Key West*

IXTAPA
Fill glass with ice.
1 1/2 oz Coffee Liqueur
1/2 oz Tequila
Stir.
Strain into chilled glass.

J. OFF (floater)
1 1/2 oz Bourbon (bottom)
1/2 oz Irish Cream (top)

JACK FROST
Fill glass with ice.
1 oz Bourbon
1 oz Peppermint Schnapps
Stir.

JACK-IN-THE-BOX
Fill glass with ice.
1 1/2 oz Apple Brandy
1 oz Pineapple Juice
Dash of Lemon Juice
2-3 dashes of Bitters
Shake.
Strain into chilled glass.

JACK ROSE
Fill glass with ice.
2 oz Apple Brandy
Dash of Grenadine
Fill with Sour Mix.
Shake.
Garnish with Lemon.

JACKALOPE
Fill glass with ice.
3/4 oz Dark Rum
3/4 oz Coffee Liqueur
3/4 oz Amaretto
3 oz Pineapple Juice
Shake.
Strain into chilled glass.
Top with 1/2 oz Dark Crème de Cacao.

JACKARITA
Fill glass with ice.
1 1/2 oz Bourbon
1/2 oz Triple Sec
Dash of Lime Juice
3 oz Sour Mix
Dash of Orange Juice (optional)
Shake.
Serve or strain into chilled glass.

JACKHAMMER
Fill glass with ice.
1 1/2 oz Bourbon
1/2 oz Triple Sec
Fill with Sour Mix.
Shake.

JADE
Fill glass with ice.
1 1/2 oz Dark Rum
1/2 tsp Triple Sec or Curacao
1/2 tsp Green Crème de Menthe
Dash of Lime Juice
1 tsp of Powdered Sugar
or Sugar Syrup.
Shake.
Serve or strain into chilled glass.
Garnish with Lime.

JAEGER BOMB
Fill shot glass with
Jägermeister
Drop shot glass into large glass
That is filled æ with
Red Energy Drink

JAEGER MONSTER
Fill glass with ice.
1 oz Jägermeister
1/2 oz Amaretto
Dash of Grenadine
Fill with Orange Juice.
Shake.
Garnish with Orange.

JAEGER SALSA
Fill glass with ice.
2 oz Jägermeister
2 tsp Salsa
Fill with Bloody Mary Mix.
Shake.
Pour into glass with salted rim
(optional).
Garnish with Lemon and/or Lime
and Celery.

JAEGERITA
Fill glass with ice.
1/2 oz Jägermeister
1/2 oz Gold Tequila
1/2 oz Orange Liqueur
Dash of Lime Juice
Dash of Sour Mix
Shake.
Strain into chilled glass.

JAGUAR MILK (frozen)
In blender:
2 cups crushed ice
2 oz Vodka
2 oz White Creme de Cacao
2 oz Condensed Milk
Blend until smooth.

JAMAICA COOLER
Fill glass with ice.
2 oz Dark Rum
1/2 oz Lemon Juice or Sour Mix
2 dashes of Orange Bitters
1 tsp Sugar
Shake until sugar dissolves.
Fill with Lemon-Lime Soda.

JAMAICA ME CRAZY
Fill glass with ice.
1 1/2 oz Dark Rum
1/2 oz Coffee Liqueur
Fill with Pineapple Juice.
Shake.

JAMAICAN
Fill glass with ice.
1 oz Dark Rum
1 oz Coffee Liqueur
1 oz Lime Juice
Dash of Bitters
Fill with Lemon-Lime Soda.

JAMAICAN BOBSLED
Fill glass with ice.
1 1/2 oz Dark Rum
1/2 oz Butterscotch Schnapps
Fill with Root Beer.

JAMAICAN COFFEE
1 oz Tia Maria
1 oz Rum or Brandy
or 2 oz Tia Maria and no second
Liqueur
Fill with hot Black Coffee.
Top with Whipped Cream.
Sprinkle with Cinnamon.

JAMAICAN DELIGHT
Fill glass with ice.
1 oz Amber Rum
3/4 oz Apricot Brandy
3 oz Pineapple Juice
1/2 oz Lime Juice
1/2 oz Sugar Syrup
Shake.

JAMAICAN DUST
Fill glass with ice.
1 oz Dark Rum
1 oz Tia Maria
Fill with Pineapple Juice.
Shake.
Garnish with Lime.

JAMAICAN KISS
Fill glass with ice.
1 oz Amber Rum
1/2 oz Tia Maria
2 oz Milk
1/2 oz Sugar Syrup
Shake.

I

J

JAMAICAN MILK SHAKE (frozen)
In Blender:
1/2 cup of Ice
2 oz Bourbon
1 1/2 oz Dark Rum
Scoop of Vanilla Ice Cream
Dash of vanilla extract
Blend until smooth.
If too thick add Milk.
If too thin add ice or Ice Cream.

JAMAICAN MULE
Fill glass with ice.
1 oz Light Rum
1 oz Dark Rum
1/2 oz Amaretto
Fill with Ginger Beer.
Stir.

JAMAICAN PINE
Fill glass with ice.
2 oz Dark Rum
Fill with Pineapple Juice.
Garnish with Lime.

JAMAICAN TEN SPEED
Fill glass with ice.
1/2 oz Vodka or Citrus Vodka
1/2 oz Coconut Rum
1/2 oz Banana Liqueur
1/2 oz Melon Liqueur
1/2 oz Irish Cream
Shake. Strain into shot glass.

JAMAICAN WIND
Fill glass with ice.
1 1/2 oz Dark Rum
1/2 oz Coffee Liqueur
Stir.

JAMES BOND MARTINI
AKA VESPER
Fill glass with ice.
3 oz Gin
1 oz Vodka
1/2 oz Blond Lillet
Shake.
Strain into chilled glass.
Garnish with Lemon Twist.

JAPANESE FIZZ
Fill glass with ice.
2 oz Whiskey
3/4 oz Port
1/2 oz Lemon Juice
1 tsp Sugar Syrup
1 Egg White (optional)
Shake.
Fill glass with Soda Water.
Garnish with Pineapple and/or
Orange.

JAWBREAKER
Fill shot glass with
Cinnamon Schnapps
Add 4-5 drops of Tabasco Sauce.
Stir.

JAY WALKER
Fill glass with ice.
1 oz Rum or Citrus Rum
1/2 oz Triple Sec
Fill with Equal parts Sour Mix and
Pineapple Juice.
Shake.
Top with 1/2 oz 151-Proof Rum.

JELLO SHOTS (basic)
Make as instructed on box except:
Use 3/4 cup of boiling water
instead of 1 cup.
And replace the 1 cup of cold water
with 3/4 cup of desired Liquor or
Liqueur.
And pour mix into little platic cups
(look in party or restaurant supply
store).

JELLY BEAN
Fill glass with ice.
1 oz Anisette or Sambuca
1 oz Blackberry Brandy
Stir.

JELLY BEAN (floater)
1/2 oz Blackberry Brandy or
Grenadine (bottom)
1/2 oz Anisette or Sambuca
1/2 oz Southern Comfort (top)

JELLY DOUGHNUT
Fill glass with ice.
1 1/2 oz Irish Cream
1/2 oz Black Raspberry Liqueur
Stir.

JELLY FISH (floater)
1 1/2 oz White Crème de Cacao or
Crème de Menthe (bottom)
1/2 oz Irish Cream
1/2 oz Amaretto (top)
Place 2-3 drops of Grenadine in
center of glass.

JENNY WALLBANGER
Fill glass with ice.
1 1/2 oz Vodka
Fill with equal parts Orange Juice
and Milk or Cream.
Shake.
Top with 1/2 oz Galliano

JET FUEL
Fill glass with ice.
1/2 oz Vodka or Cinnamon Vodka
1/2 oz Jagermeister
1/2 oz 100-Proof Peppermint
Schnapps
1/2 oz 100-Proof Cinnamon
Schnapps
Strain into shot glass.

JEWEL
Fill glass with ice.
3/4 oz Gin
3/4 oz Sweet Vermouth
3/4 oz Green Chartreuse
1-3 dashes of Orange Bitters
Shake.
Serve or strain into chilled glass.
Garnish with a Lemon Twist.

JEWEL OF THE NILE
Fill glass with ice.
2 oz Gin
1/2 oz Green Chartreuse
1/2 oz Yellow Chartreuse
Stir.

JEZEBEL (floater)
1 1/2 oz Southern Comfort (bottom)
1/2 oz Irish Cream (top)

IGGY COCKFIGHTER
Fill glass with ice.
1/2 oz Rum
1/2 oz Gin
1/2 oz Tequila
Fill with equal parts Sour Mix
and Orange Juice.
Shake.

IZZ
Fill glass with ice.
1/2 oz Cognac
1/2 oz Irish Cream
1 oz Cream
Shake. Strain into shot glass.

JOCKEY CLUB
Fill glass with ice.
2 oz Gin
1/4 oz White Crème de Cacao
1/2 oz Lemon Juice
Dash of Bitters
Shake. Strain into chilled glass.

JOE COLLINS aka MIKE COLLINS, SCOTCH COLLINS
Fill glass with ice.
2 oz Scotch
Fill with Sour Mix.
Shake.
Dash of Soda Water
Garnish with Cherry and Orange.

JOHN COLLINS
Fill glass with ice.
2 oz Whiskey
Fill with Sour Mix.
Shake.
Dash of Soda Water
Garnish with Cherry and Orange.

JOHNNIE
Fill glass with ice.
1 1/2 oz Sloe Gin
3/4 oz Orange Liqueur or Triple
Sec or Curacao
1 tsp Anisette
Shake and Strain into chilled glass.

JOLL-E RANCHER
Fill glass with ice.
1 oz Vodka or Citrus Vodka
1/2 oz Amaretto
1/2 oz Melon Liqueur
Fill with equal parts Sour Mix and
Pineapple Juice.
Shake.

JOLL-E RANCHER 2
Fill glass with ice.
1 oz Vodka or Citrus Vodka
1/2 oz Apple Brandy
1/2 oz Peach Schnapps
Fill with Cranberry Juice.
Shake.

JOLL-E RANCHER 3
Fill glass with ice.
1 1/2 oz Southern Comfort
1/2 oz Melon Liqueur
Fill with Sour Mix.
Shake.

JOLLY ROGER
Fill glass with ice.
1 oz Rum
1 oz Drambuie
1/2 oz Lime Juice
Dash of Scotch
Shake.
Fill with Soda Water.

JOLLY ROGER 2
Fill glass with ice.
1 oz Dark Rum
1 oz Banana Liqueur
2 oz Lemon Juice
Shake.

JOSÉ WALLBANGER
Fill glass with ice.
1 1/2 oz Tequila
Fill with Orange Juice.
Top with 1/2 oz Galliano.

JUDGE, JR.
Fill glass with ice.
1 1/2 oz Gin
1 1/2 oz Rum
Dash of Grenadine
1/2 oz Lemon Juice
Shake.
Strain into chilled glass.

JUICY FRUIT
Fill glass with ice.
1 oz Vodka or Citrus Vodka
1/2 oz Peach Schnapps
1/2 oz Melon Liqueur
Fill with Pineapple Juice.
Shake.

JULIUS, ORANGE, STRAWBERRY, BLUEBERRY, MANGO, PEACH
In Blender: 1/2 cup of ice.
1 cup of desired fresh or frozen
fruit or 4 oz Orange Juice
Concentrate
2 oz Milk
tsp Vanilla Extract
2 Tblsp Sugar
Scoop of Vanilla ice cream
Blend until smooth.
If too thick add juice or water.
If too thin add ice or ice cream

JUMP ME
Fill glass with ice.
2 oz Dark Rum
3 dashes of Bitters
Fill with Pineapple Juice.
Squeeze 2 lime wedges over drink.
Stir.

JUMP STARTER
Fill glass with ice.
2 oz Dark Rum
Fill with Jolt Cola.
Stir.

JUMP UP AND KISS ME
Fill glass with ice.
1 1/2 oz Light Rum
1/2 oz Galliano
1/2 oz Apricot Brandy
1/2 Egg White
Dash of Sour Mix
Fill with equal parts Orange and
Pineapple Juice.
Shake.

JUMP UP AND KISS ME 2
Fill glass with ice.
1 1/2 oz Dark Rum
Dash of Bitters
1/2 oz Lime Juice
Fill with Pineapple Juice.
Shake.
Garnish with Pineapple and Lime.

J

Metric Measurement Conversion Chart on page 14

JUMPER CABLE aka SPEEDY
Fill glass with ice.
2 oz 151-Proof Rum
Fill with Jolt Cola
Stir.
Garnish with Lime.

JUNE BUG
Fill glass with ice.
3/4 oz Banana Liqueur
3/4 oz Melon Liqueur
3/4 oz Peach Schnapps
Fill with equal parts Pineapple
and Cranberry Juice.
Shake.

JUNGLE COFFEE
1/2 oz Brandy
1/2 oz Southern Comfort
1/2 oz Crème de Cacao
1/2 oz Banana Liqueur
Fill wth Hot Black Coffee
Top with Whipped Cream
Sprinkle with shaved chocolate.

JUNGLE JIM aka YELLOW RUSSIAN
Fill glass with ice.
1 oz Vodka or Banana Vodka
1 oz Banana Liqueur
Fill with Milk or Cream.
Shake.

JUNGLE JUICE
Fill a large bowl with prepared fresh
fruit, apricots,
cherries, oranges, bananas, man-
gos, cantaloupe,
strawberries, (take out pits and
seeds, peel if necessary)
Pour in Grain Alcohol until fruit is
swimming. Cover bowl
And refrigerate for 12-24 hours.
Also chill a gallon of
fruit punch and fill ice cube trays
with another gallon of punch.
Place special cubes, fruit with grain
alcohol and fruit punch in large
Punch Bowl or container.
*add a liter of Ginger Ale, Soda
Water or favorite carbonated
Beverage (optional)

JUPITER COCKTAIL
Fill glass with ice.
1 1/2 oz Gin
1/2 oz Dry Vermouth
1 tsp Parfait Amour
or Crème de Violette
1 tsp Orange Juice
Shake.
Strain into chilled glass.

KABUKI
Fill glass with ice.
1 1/2 oz Sake
1/2 oz Triple Sec
Dash of Lime Juice
1 oz Sour Mix
Shake.
Strain into chilled glass.

KAHLUA CLUB aka COBRA
Fill glass with ice.
2 oz Coffee Liqueur
Fill with Soda Water.
Garnish with Lime.

KAHLUA COFFEE aka MEXICAN COFFEE
2 oz Coffee Liqueur
Fill with hot Black Coffee
Top with Whipped Cream.
Sprinkle with Shaved
Chocolate or Sprinkles.

KAHLUA SOMBRERO
Fill glass with ice.
2 oz Coffee Liqueur
Fill with Milk or Cream.
Shake.

KAHLUA SOUR
Fill glass with ice.
2 oz Coffee Liqueur
Fill with Sour Mix.
Shake.
Garnish with Cherry and Orange.

KAHUNA
Fill glass with ice.
1/2 oz Dark Rum
1/2 oz Amber Rum
1/2 oz Spiced Rum
Dash Lime Juice
Fill with Pineapple Juice.
Shake.
Top with 151-Proof Rum.
Garnish with Cherry.

KAMA SUTRA
Fill glass with ice.
1 oz Cognac
1 oz Red Alize
1 oz Fresh Orange Juice
Shake.
Strain into a chilled glass.

KAMIKAZE aka BULLFROG
Fill glass with ice.
2 oz Vodka or Citrus Vodka
1/2 oz Triple Sec
Dash Lime Juice
Shake.
Serve or strain into shot glass.
Garnish with Lime.

KAPPA COLADA (frozen)
In Blender:
1/2 cup of Ice
2 oz Brandy
2 tbsp Cream of Coconut
1/2 cup of fresh or canned
Pineapple
1 tbsp Vanilla Ice Cream
Blend until smooth.
If too thick add fruit or juice.
If too thin add ice or Ice Cream.
Garnish with Pineapple and Cherry.

KATINKA
Fill glass with ice.
1 1/2 oz Vodka
1/2 oz Apricot Brandy
1/2 oz Lime Juice
Stir.
Strain into chilled glass.
Garnish with mint sprig.

KENTUCKY COCKTAIL
Fill glass with ice.
2 oz Bourbon
1 oz Pineapple Juice
Shake.
Strain into chilled glass.

Metric Measurement Conversion Chart on page 14

KENTUCKY COFFEE
2 oz Bourbon
1/2 tsp Sugar
Fill with hot Black Coffee.
Top with Whipped Cream
or float high-Proof Bourbon
on top and ignite.

KENTUCKY COLONEL
Fill glass with ice.
1 1/2 oz Bourbon
1/2 oz Benedictine
Stir.
Serve or strain into chilled glass.
Garnish with Lemon Twist.

KENTUCKY COOLER
Fill glass with ice.
1 1/2 oz Bourbon
1/2 oz Brandy
1 oz Sour Mix
2 tsp of Sugar Syrup
Shake.
Fill with Soda Water.
Float 1/4 oz Dark Rum on top.

KENTUCKY ORANGE BLOSSOM
Fill glass with ice.
1 1/2 oz Bourbon
1/2 oz Triple Sec
1 oz Orange Juice
Shake.
Garnish with Lemon.

KENTUCKY SCREWDRIVER
aka BLACK-EYED SUSAN, YELLOW JACKET
Fill glass with ice.
2 oz Bourbon
Fill with Orange Juice.

KENTUCKY SUNRISE
Fill glass with ice.
2 oz Bourbon
Fill with Orange Juice.
Pour 1/2 oz Grenadine down spoon
To bottom of glass.

KENTUCKY SWAMPWATER
Fill glass with ice.
2 oz Bourbon
1/2 oz Blue Curacao
Dash of Sour Mix
Fill with Orange Juice.

KENTUCKY WINDAGE
Fill glass with ice.
2 oz Bourbon
Dash of Lime Juice
Fill with Lemonade.
Shake.

KEOKE CAPPUCCINO
1/2 oz Coffee Liqueur
1/2 oz Cognac or Brandy
1/2 oz Dark Crème de Cacao
Fill with Espresso.
Top with Steamed Milk.
Sprinkle with Powdered Cacao.

KEOKE COFFEE
3/4 oz Coffee Liqueur
3/4 oz Cognac or Brandy
3/4 oz Dark Crème de Cacao
Fill with hot Black Coffee.
Top with Whipped Cream.
Sprinkle with Cinnamon.

KERRY COOLER
Fill glass with ice.
2 oz Irish Whiskey
1 1/2 oz Sherry
1 oz Orgeat Syrup
1 oz Lemon Juice or Sour Mix
Shake.
Fill with Soda Water.

KEY LARGO (frozen)
In Blender:
1/2 cup of Ice
2 oz Dark Rum
1 oz Cream of Coconut
Scoop of Orange Sherbet
Blend until smooth.
Garnish with Orange.

KEY LIME MARTINI
Fill glass with ice.
3 1/2 oz Vanilla Vodka
Dash Irish Cream (optional)
Dash of Cream (optional)
Tsp Sugar
1 oz Lime Juice.
Shake.
Strain into chilled glass.

KEY LIME PIE (frozen)
In Blender:
1 cup of Ice
2 oz Light Rum or Citrus Rum
3 tbsp frozen concentrated Limeade
Dash of Lime Juice
Blend until smooth.
Garnish with Lime and
a Graham Cracker.

KEY LIME SHOOTER
Fill glass with ice.
1 oz Rum or Vodka
1 oz Licor 43
Dash of Sour Mix
Dash of Cream
Dash of Orange Juice
Dash of Lime Juice
Shake.
Strain into chilled glass.

KEY WEST
Fill glass with ice.
1 oz Dark Rum
1/2 oz Banana Liqueur
1/2 oz Black Raspberry Liqueur
Fill with equal parts Sour Mix and
Orange Juice.
Shake.
Top with Soda Water.
Garnish with Cherry and Orange.

KGB
Fill glass with ice.
1 1/2 oz Gin
1/4 oz Kirschwasser
Dash of Apricot Brandy
Dash of Lemon Juice
Shake.
Strain into chilled glass.
Garnish with Lemon Twist.

KICK START, RED EYE, SHOT IN THE DARK, SPEEDBALL, HAMMERHEAD
In large coffee cup:
2 shots Espresso
Fill with Hot Black Coffee.

KILLER BEE (floater)
1 oz Bärenjägur (bottom)
1 oz Jägermeister (top)

J

K

KILLER COOL AID
Fill glass with ice.
1/4 oz Vodka
1/4 oz Gin
1/4 oz Rum
1/4 oz Black Raspberry Liqueur
Dash of Sour Mix
Fill with Cranberry Juice.

KILLER COOL AID (floater)
2 oz Cranberry Juice (bottom)
1/2 oz Amaretto
1/2 oz Peach Schnapps
1 oz Vodka (top)

KILLER WHALE
Fill glass with ice.
1 oz Vodka or Raspberry Vodka
1 oz Rum or Orange Rum
1/2 oz Black Raspberry Liqueur
1/2 oz Triple Sec
Fill with equal parts Cranberry
and Orange Juice.
Shake.
Top with Lemon-Lime Soda.

KING ALPHONSE (floater)
2 oz Coffee Liqueur (bottom)
1 oz Cream (top)

KING COBRA
Fill glass with ice.
1 oz Rum
1 oz Coffee Liqueur
Fill with Soda Water.
Garnish with Lime.

KING KONG COFFEE
3/4 oz Cognac or Brandy
3/4 oz Coffee Liqueur
3/4 oz Orange Liqueur
Fill with hot Black Coffee.
Top with Whipped Cream.
Garnish with Orange and
Cinnamon.

KING'S CUP
Fill glass with ice.
1 oz Galliano
1 oz Amaretto
Fill with Milk.
Shake.

KING'S PEG
Fill glass half full with ice.
2 oz Cognac or Brandy
Fill with Champagne.

KINGSTON COFFEE
1/2 oz Dark Rum
1/2 oz Coffee Liqueur
1/2 oz Irish Cream
1/2 oz Chocolate Syrup
Fill with hot Black Coffee.
Top with Whipped Cream.
Drizzle with Chocolate Syrup.

KIOLOA
Fill glass with ice.
1 oz Coffee Liqueur
1/2 oz Amber Rum
1 oz Cream
Shake.

KIR
1/2 oz Crème de Cassis
Fill with White Wine.
Garnish with Lemon Twist.

KIR ROYALE
1/2 oz Black Raspberry Liqueur
Fill with Champagne.
Garnish with Lemon Twist.

KISS
Fill glass with ice.
1 1/2 oz Vodka or Vanilla Vodka
1/2 oz Chocolate Liqueur
1/4 oz Cherry Liqueur
3/4 oz Cream or Milk
Shake.
Strain into chilled glass.

KISS IN THE DARK
Fill glass with ice.
3/4 oz Gin
3/4 oz Cherry Brandy
1/2 oz Dry Vermouth
Shake.
Strain into chilled glass.

KISS ME QUICK
Fill glass with ice.
2 oz Pernod
1/2 oz Curacao
3 dashes of Bitters
Stir.
Fill with Soda Water.

KISS THE BOYS GOODBYE
Fill glass with ice.
1 oz Sloe Gin
1 oz Brandy
1/4 oz Lemon Juice
1/2 Egg White
Shake.
Strain into chilled glass.

KIWI
Fill glass with ice.
1 oz Banana Liqueur
1 oz Strawberry Liqueur
Fill with Orange Juice.
Shake.

KIWI MARTINI
Mash (muddle) 1/2 small or
1/4 large skinned Kiwi
Fill glass with ice.
3 oz Vodka or Citrus Vodka
1/2 tsp Sugar
Shake.
Strain into chilled glass.

KLONDIKE COOLER
Fill glass with ice.
2 oz Whiskey
Dash of Orange Juice
Fill with Ginger Ale
or Soda Water.
Garnish with Lemon Twist or
Orange Twist.

KNICKERBOCKER
Fill glass with ice.
2 oz Gin
1/2 oz Dry Vermouth
1 tsp Sweet Vermouth
Stir.
Strain into chilled glass.

KOMANIWANALAYA
Fill glass with ice.
1/2 oz 151-Proof Rum
1/2 oz Amaretto
1 oz Pineapple Juice
1 oz Cranberry Juice
Shake.
Strain into chilled glass.
Top with 1/2 oz Dark Rum.

KOWLOON
Fill glass with ice.
1 oz Orange Liqueur
1 oz Coffee Liqueur
Fill with Orange Juice.
Shake.
Garnish with Orange.

KREMLIN COCKTAIL
Fill glass with ice.
1 oz Vodka
1 oz White Crème de Cacao
1 oz Cream
Shake.
Strain into chilled glass.

KRETCHMA
Fill glass with ice.
1 oz Vodka
1 oz White Crème de Cacao
Dash of Grenadine
1 tblsp Lemon Juice
Shake.
Strain into chilled glass.

KRUPNIK aka FIRE VODKA
In sauce pan on low heat:
6 oz Polish Vodka
4 Tblsp Honey
1 smashed Cinnamon Stick
6 whole cloves
Pinch Nutmeg
Stir periodically for 3-5 minutes.
Serves 2

KUNG FU
Fill glass with ice.
1 oz Jägermeister
1 oz Pisang Ambon
Fill with Cola.

KUWAITI COOLER
Fill glass with ice.
1 oz Melon Liqueur
1 oz Key Largo Schnapps
Dash of Sour Mix
Shake.
Strain into chilled glass.
Fill with Soda Water.

KYOTO
Fill glass with ice.
2 oz Gin or Orange Gin
1/2 oz Dry Vermouth
1/2 oz Melon Liqueur
or Apricot Brandy
1/2 oz Triple Sec
Dash of Lemon Juice (optional)
Shake.
Strain into chilled glass.

L. A. SUNRISE
Fill glass with ice.
1 1/2 oz Vodka or Citrus Vodka
1/2 oz Banana Liqueur
Fill with Equal parts Orange
and Pineapple Juice.
Shake.
Float 1/2 oz Dark Rum on top.

L.A.P.D.
Fill glass with ice.
1 oz Gold Tequila
1/2 oz Blue Curacao
1/4 oz Grenadine
Stir.
Strain into chilled glass.

L. S. D.
Fill glass with ice.
1 oz Scotch
1 oz Drambuie
1 oz Lemonade
Shake.
Strain into chilled glass.

LA BAMBA
Fill glass with ice.
1 1/2 oz Tequila
1/2 oz Orange Liqueur
Fill with equal parts Pineapple and
Orange Juice.
Shake.
Strain into chilled glass.
Top with Grenadine.

LA JOLLA
Fill glass with ice.
1 1/2 oz Brandy
1/2 oz Banana Liqueur
1 tsp Orange Juice
2 tsp Lemon Juice or Sour Mix
Shake.
Strain into chilled glass.

LA MOSCA
Either fill pony glass with Sambuca
or 3 oz Sambuca in Brandy snifter.
Add 3 Coffee Beans, for health
wealth and happiness.

LADIES
Fill glass with ice.
1 1/2 oz Whiskey
1 tsp Anisette
1/2 tsp Pernod
2 dashes of Bitters
Shake.
Strain into chilled glass.
Garnish with Pineapple.

LADY BE GOOD
Fill glass with ice.
1 1/2 oz Brandy
1/2 oz White Crème de Menthe
1/2 oz Sweet Vermouth
Shake.
Strain into chilled glass.

LADY BOY MARTINI
Fill glass with ice.
3 1/2 oz Gin
Dash Sloe Gin
Dash Black Raspberry Liqueur
Dash Grapefruit Juice
Shake.
Strain into chilled glass.
Garnish with 2 Raspberries.

LADY LUCK
Fill glass with ice.
3/4 oz Coconut Rum
3/4 oz Black Raspberry Liqueur
3/4 oz Banana Liqueur
Shake.
Strain into chilled glass.

LADYFINGER
Fill glass with ice.
1 oz Gin
1/2 oz Kirschwasser
1/2 oz Cherry Brandy
Shake.
Strain into chilled glass.

K

L

LAKE STREET LEMONADE
Fill glass with ice.
1 1/2 oz Vodka or Citrus Vodka
1/2 oz Amaretto
Fill with Lemonade.
Stir.
Garnish with Lemon.

LALLAH ROOKH
Fill glass with ice.
1 1/2 oz Rum or Vanilla Rum
3/4 oz Cognac or Brandy
1/2 oz Crème de Vanilla or Vanilla
Extract
1 tsp Sugar Syrup
Shake.
Top with Whipped Cream.

LAS BRISAS (frozen)
In Blender:
1/2 cup of Ice
1 oz Vodka or Vanilla Vodka
1 oz Coconut Rum
1/2 cup fresh or canned Pineapple
1/2 scoop Vanilla Ice Cream
Blend until smooth.

LASER BEAM
Fill glass with ice.
1 oz Bourbon
1 oz Southern Comfort
Fill with Cranberry Juice.
Stir.

LASER BEAM 2
Fill glass with ice.
1/2 oz Bourbon
1/2 oz Tequila
1/2 oz Amaretto
1/2 oz Triple Sec
Fill with Sour Mix.
Shake
Garnish with Lemon and Cherry.

LASER BEAM 3
Fill glass with ice.
1/2 oz Vodka
1/2 oz Southern Comfort
1/2 oz Melon Liqueur
1/2 oz Amaretto
1/2 oz Orange Liqueur
2 oz Sour Mix
Shake.
Fill with Lemon-Lime Soda.

LASKY
Fill glass with ice.
3/4 oz Gin
3/4 oz Swedish Punch
3/4 oz Grape Juice
Shake.
Serve or strain into chilled glass.

LATIN LOVER
Fill glass with ice.
1 1/2 oz Tequila
1/2 oz Amaretto
Stir.

LATTE
If you want to be a smart ass,
latte means milk.
Pour a glass of milk,
but they probably want a
CAFÉ LATTE

LAWHILL
Fill glass with ice.
1 1/2 oz Whiskey
1/2 oz Dry Vermouth
1/4 oz Pernod
1/4 oz Cherry Liqueur
1/2 oz Orange Juice
Dash of Bitters
Shake.
Strain into chilled glass.

LAYER CAKE aka
FIFTH AVENUE (floater)
3/4 oz Dark Crème de Cacao (bottom)
3/4 oz Apricot Brandy
1/2 oz Milk (top)

LATIN LOVER
Fill glass with ice.
1 1/2 oz Tequila
1/2 oz Amaretto
Stir.

LAUGHY TAFFY MARTINI
Fill glass with ice.
3 oz Vanilla Vodka
1/2 oz Banana Liqueur
1/2 oz White Crème de Cacao
Shake. Strain into chilled glass.
Garnish with candy.

LAVA LAMP MARTINI
Fill glass with ice
2 oz Citrus Vodka or Vodka
Stir. Strain into chilled glass
In Short glass or small bowl:
mix 1oz honey, and 1oz Raspberry
Schnapps
or Black Raspberry Liqueur, or
Blackberry Brandy.
Drizzle mixture into Vodka.

LEAF
Fill glass with ice.
1 oz Light Rum
1 oz Melon Liqueur
1 oz Cream
Shake.
Strain into chilled glass.

LEAP FROG
Fill glass with ice.
2 oz Gin
1/2 oz Lemon Juice
Fill with Ginger Ale.
Garnish with Lemon.

LEAP YEAR
Fill glass with ice.
2 oz Gin or Orange Gin
1/2 oz Orange Liqueur or Triple Sec
1/2 oz Sweet Vermouth
1 tsp Lemon Juice
Stir.
Strain into chilled glass.

LEAVE IT TO ME
Fill glass with ice.
1 oz Gin
1/2 oz Apricot Brandy
1/2 oz Dry Vermouth
1/4 oz Lemon Juice
1/4 oz Grenadine
Shake.
Strain into chilled glass.

LEAVING LAS VEGAS
Fill glass with ice.
1/2 oz Vodka
1/2 oz Gin
1/2 oz Rum
1/2 oz Triple Sec
1 tsp Sugar
Fill with Lemonade.
Shake.
Top with Splash of Lemon-Lime Soda.

LEBANESE COFFEE
1 oz Apricot Brandy
1 oz Coffee Liqueur
Fill with hot Black Coffee.
Top with Whipped Cream.

LEFT BANK
Fill glass with ice.
1 oz Irish Cream
1 oz Black Raspberry Liqueur
Stir.

LEFT-HANDED SCREWDRIVER
Fill glass with ice.
2 oz Gin or Orange Gin
Fill with Orange Juice.
Stir.
Garnish with Orange or Lime.

LEFT HOOK
Fill glass with ice.
1 oz Jagermeister
1 oz 100-proof Cinnamon Schnapps
Shake. Strain into shot glass.

LEG SPREADER
Fill glass with ice.
1 oz Galliano
1 oz Coffee Liqueur
Strain into chilled glass.

LEG SPREADER 2
Fill glass with ice.
1 oz Grain Alcohol
1 oz Black Raspberry Liqueur
Stir.

LEISURE SUIT
Fill glass with ice.
1 oz Banana Liqueur
1 oz Galliano
Fill with equal parts Orange, Cranberry and Pineapple Juice.

LEMONADE
2 tsp Sugar
2 oz Lemon Juice
Fill glass with ice.
Fill with Water.
Shake.

LEMON BOMB
Moisten inside of shot glass with Lemon Juice.
Coat inside of glass with Sugar.
Fill shot glass with chilled Grain Alcohol.

LEMON DROP
Moisten inside of shot glass with Lemon Juice.
Coat inside of glass with Sugar.
Fill shot glass with chilled Vodka.

LEMON DROP 2
Fill shot glass with Citrus Vodka.
Coat Lemon wedge with Sugar.

LEMON DROP MARTINI
Fill glass with ice.
3 1/2 oz Citrus Vodka
1/2 oz Orange Liqueur
1-2 oz Sour mix
Shake.
Strain into chilled glass.

LEMON FRAPPE
Fill large stemmed glass (Red Wine glass, Champagne saucer) with crushed ice.
1 oz Tuaca
1 oz Sour Mix

LEMON SLUSH (frozen)
In Blender:
1 cup of Ice
2 oz Vodka or Lemon or Citrus Vodka
3 tbsp Lemonade concentrate
Blend until smooth.

LEMONADE (modern)
Fill glass with ice.
1 1/2 oz Sloe Gin
1 1/2 oz Sherry
1 oz Sugar Syrup
or 1 tsp Powdered Sugar
2 oz Lemon Juice
Shake.
Top with Soda Water.

LEPRECHAUN
Fill glass with ice.
2 oz Irish Whiskey
Fill with Tonic Water.
Garnish with a Lemon Twist.

LEPRECHAUN 2
Fill glass with ice.
1 oz Vodka or Peach Vodka
1/2 oz Peach Schnapps
1/2 oz Blue Curacao
Fill with Orange Juice.

LESLIE
3 oz White Wine
3 oz Cranberry juice
3 oz Lemon-Lime Soda
Garnish with Lemon and Lime.

LETHAL INJECTION
Fill glass with ice.
1/2 oz Dark Rum
1/2 oz Spiced Rum
1/2 oz Coconut Rum
1/2 oz Amaretto
or Crème de Nouyax
1 oz Orange Juice
1 oz Pineapple Juice
Shake.
Strain into chilled glass.

LEWINSKY (floater)
1 1/2 oz Jägermeister (bottom)
1/2 oz Irish Cream (top)

LIBERTY COCKTAIL
Fill glass with ice.
1 1/2 oz Apple Brandy
3/4 oz Rum
1/4 tsp Sugar Syrup
Stir.
Strain into chilled glass.
Garnish with Cherry.

L

LICORICE STICK
Fill glass with ice.
1 1/2 oz Anisette
Fill with Milk or Cream.
Top with 1/2 oz Galliano.
Stir with Licorice Stick.

LICORICE WHIP (floater)
3/4 oz Coffee Liqueur (bottom)
3/4 oz Irish Cream
3/4 oz Ouzo (top)

LIEBFRAUMILCH
Fill glass with ice.
1 1/2 oz White Crème de Cacao
1 1/2 oz Cream or Milk
1/2 oz Lime Juice
Shake.
Strain into chilled glass.

LIFE LINE
Fill glass with ice.
1 oz Rum or Orange Rum
1/2 oz Brandy
1/2 oz Apricot Brandy
1/2 oz Triple Sec
1/2 oz Sweet Vermouth
1/2 oz Lemon juice
Shake.
Strain into chilled glass.

LIFE-SAVER (floater)
1 oz Banana Liqueur (bottom)
1 oz Blackberry Brandy (top)

LIFE-SAVOR
Fill glass with ice.
1/2 oz Triple Sec
1/2 oz Melon Liqueur
1/2 oz Coconut Rum
Fill with Orange Juice.
Shake.

LIFESAVER
Fill glass with ice.
1 1/2 oz Coconut Rum
1/2 oz Melon Liqueur
Fill with Pineapple Juice
Shake.

LIGHTHOUSE
Fill glass with ice.
1/2 oz Tequila
1/2 oz Coffee Liqueur
1/2 oz Peppermint Schnapps
Stir.
Strain into chilled glass.
Top with 1/2 oz 151-Proof Rum.

LILLET NOUYAX
Fill glass with ice.
1 1/2 oz Lillet Blanc
1/2 oz Gin
1 tsp Crème de Nouyax
Shake.
Strain into chilled glass.
Garnish with Orange Twist.

LIMBO
Fill glass with ice.
2 oz Rum or Orange Rum
1/2 oz Banana Liqueur
1 oz Orange Juice
Shake.
Strain into chilled glass.

LIMEADE
2 tsp Sugar
2 oz Lime Juice
Fill glass with ice.
Fill with Water.
Shake.

LIME RICKEY (no alcohol)
Fill glass with ice.
1oz Lime Juice
tsp sugar
Fill with Soda Water
Stir.

LIME RICKEY (adult)
Fill glass with ice.
1 1/2 oz Gin or Lime Gin
1/2 oz Lime Juice
Fill with Soda Water.
Stir.
Garnish with Lime.

LINSTEAD
Fill glass with ice.
1 1/2 oz Whiskey
Dash of Pernod
1 oz Pineapple Juice
Dash of Lemon Juice
3 dashes of Bitters (optional)
Shake.
Strain into chilled glass.

LION TAMER
Fill glass with ice.
3/4 oz Southern Comfort
1/4 oz Lime Juice
Stir.
Strain into chilled glass.

LIQUID ASPHALT (floater)
1 oz Black Sambuca (bottom)
1 oz Jägermeister (top)

LIQUID COCA
Fill glass with ice.
3/4 oz 151-Proof Rum
3/4 oz 100-Proof Peppermint
Schnapps
3/4 oz Jägermeister
Stir.
Strain into chilled glass.

LIQUID CRACK
Fill glass with ice.
1/2 oz 151-Proof Rum
1/2 oz 100-proof Peppermint
Schnapps
1/2 oz Jägermeister
1/2 oz Cinnamon Schnapps
Shake. Strain into chilled glass.

LIQUID PANTS REMOVER
Fill glass with ice.
1/2 oz Vodka
1/2 oz Dark Rum
1/2 oz Southern Comfort
1/2 oz Amaretto
1/2 oz Tequila
Fill with Cola.
Garnish with Cherry.

LIQUID VALIUM
Fill glass with ice.
1 oz Vodka
1/2 oz Peppermint Schnapps
Stir.

LITHIUM
Fill glass with ice.
2 oz Vodka
Tbsp Sugar
Fill with Milk.
Shake.

Metric Measurement Conversion Chart on page 14

LITTLE DEVIL
Fill glass with ice.
1 oz Gin
1 oz Rum
1/2 oz Triple Sec
1/2 oz Lemon Juice
or Sour Mix
Shake.
Strain into chilled glass.

LITTLE GREEN MEN
1 oz Sambuca
1 oz Melon Liqueur

LITTLE PRINCESS
Fill glass with ice.
1 1/2 oz Rum
1 1/2 oz Sweet Vermouth
Shake.
Strain into chilled glass.

LITTLE PURPLE MEN
1 oz Sambuca
1 oz Black Raspberry Liqueur

LOBOTOMY
Fill glass with ice.
1 oz Amaretto
1 oz Black Raspberry Liqueur
1 oz Pineapple Juice
Shake.
Strain into chilled glass.
Fill with Champagne.

LOCH NESS MONSTER aka NESI
(floater)
1/2 oz Melon Liqueur (bottom)
1/2 oz Irish Cream
1/2 oz Jägermeister (top)

LOLITA
Fill glass with ice.
1 1/2 oz Tequila
1/4 oz Lime Juice
1 tsp Honey
3-4 dashes of Bitters
Stir.

LOLLIPOP
Fill glass with ice.
3/4 oz Orange Liqueur
3/4 oz Kirschwasser
3/4 oz Green Chartreuse
Dash of Maraschino Liqueur
Shake.

LONDON SOUR
Fill glass with ice.
2 oz Scotch
Dash of Orange Curacao
or Triple Sec
Dash of Orange Juice
Fill with Sour Mix.
Shake.

LONDON SPECIAL aka CHAMPAGNE COCKTAIL
In a Champagne glass:
1/2 tsp Sugar or 1 Sugar Cube
2 dashes of Bitters
Fill with Champagne.
Garnish with Lemon or Orange Twist.

LONDON STINGER
Fill glass with ice.
1 1/2 oz Gin
1/2 oz White Crème de Menthe
Stir.
Serve or strain into chilled glass.

LONE TREE
Fill glass with ice.
3/4 oz Gin
3/4 oz Dry Vermouth
3/4 oz Sweet Vermouth
3 dashes of Orange Bitters
Stir.
Strain into chilled glass.
Garnish with Olive.

LONG BEACH ICED TEA
Fill glass with ice.
1/2 oz Vodka
1/2 oz Gin
1/2 oz Rum
1/2 oz Tequila
1/2 oz Triple Sec
1 oz Orange Juice
Fill with equal parts Sour Mix and
Cranberry Juice.
Shake.
Top with Cola (optional).
Garnish with Lemon.

LONG COMFORTABLE SCREW AGAINST THE WALL
Fill glass with ice.
3/4 oz Gin
3/4 oz Vodka
3/4 oz Southern Comfort
Fill with Orange Juice.
Shake.
Top with 1/2 oz Galliano

LONG HOT NIGHT
Fill glass with ice.
2 oz Bourbon
Fill with equal parts Pineapple and
Cranberry Juice.

LONG ISLAND ICED TEA
Fill glass with ice.
1/2 oz Vodka
1/2 oz Gin
1/2 oz Rum
1/2 oz Tequila
1/2 oz Triple Sec
1 oz Sour Mix
Shake.
Top with Cola.
Garnish with Lemon.

LONG ISLAND LEMONADE
Fill glass with ice.
1/2 oz Vodka
1/2 oz Gin
1/2 oz Rum
1/2 oz Tequila
1/2 oz Triple Sec
1 oz Sour Mix
Shake.
Top with Lemon-Lime Soda.
Garnish with Lemon.

LONG ISLAND MILKSHAKE
Fill glass with ice.
1/2 oz Vodka, Vanilla Vodka or
  Chocolate Vodka
1/2 oz Gin
1/2 oz Rum
1/2 oz Tequila
1/2 oz Triple Sec
1/2 oz Amaretto
1/2oz Crème de Cocao
Fill with Cream or Milk.
Shake.

L

LONG WILD SLOE COMFORTABLE FUZZY SCREW AGAINST THE WALL
Fill glass with ice.
1/2oz Gin
1/2oz Bourbon
1/2oz Sloe Gin
1/2oz Southern Comfort
1/2oz Peach Schnapps
Fill wth Orange Juice
Shake.
Top with 1/2 oz Galliano
Garnish with fake or actual phone number.

LONG SLOE COMFORTABLE FUZZY SCREW AGAINST THE WALL WITH A KISS
Fill glass with ice.
1/2 oz Gin
1/2 oz Sloe Gin
1/2 oz Southern Comfort
1/2 oz Peach Schnapps
Fill with Orange Juice.
Top with 1/2 oz Galliano.
Dash of Amaretto.

LONG SLOE COMFORTABLE FUZZY SCREW AGAINST THE WALL WITH SATIN PILLOWS THE HARD WAY
Fill glass with ice.
1/2 oz Gin
1/2 oz Sloe Gin
1/2 oz Southern Comfort
1/2 oz Peach Schnapps
Fill with Orange Juice
Shake.
Top with 1/2 oz Galliano
Dash of Frangelico
Dash of Whiskey

LOOK OUT BELOW
Fill glass with ice.
1 1/2 oz 151-Proof Rum
2 tsp Lime Juice
1 tsp Grenadine
Shake.

LOS ANGELES COCKTAIL
Fill glass with ice.
2 oz Whiskey
2-3 dashes of Sweet Vermouth
1/2 oz Lemon Juice
1 oz Sugar Syrup
1/2 raw Egg
Shake.

LOS ANGELES ICED TEA
Fill glass with ice.
1/2 oz Vodka
1/2 oz Gin
1/2 oz Rum
1/2 oz Tequila
1/2 oz Melon Liqueur
1 oz Sour Mix
Shake.
Fill with Lemon-Lime Soda.
Garnish with Lemon.

LOUDSPEAKER
Fill glass with ice.
1 oz Gin
1 oz Brandy
1/4 oz Orange Liqueur
1/2 oz Lemon Juice
Stir.
Strain into chilled glass.

LOUISIANA SHOOTER aka OYSTER SHOT
In shot glass:
1 raw Oyster
1-3 dashes of Hot Sauce
1/4 tsp Horseradish
Fill with Vodka or Peppered Vodka.

LOUNGE LIZARD
Fill glass with ice.
1 1/2 oz Dark Rum
1/2 oz Amaretto
Fill with Cola.
Stir.

LOVE
Fill glass with ice.
4 oz Sloe Gin
1 Egg White
1 oz Lemon Juice
1/2 oz Raspberry Syrup or Grenadine
Shake.
Strain into two chilled glass.

LOVE POTION (frozen)
In Blender:
1 cup of Ice
1 oz Rum or Citrus Rum
1 oz Banana Liqueur
1/2 oz Triple Sec
1 oz Orange Juice
1 oz Pineapple Juice
1/2 peeled ripe Banana
Blend 2-5 seconds on low speed.
Garnish with Orange, Pineapple and Banana.

LOVE POTION #9 (frozen)
In Blender:
1/2 cup of Ice
1 oz Vodka or Strawberry or Vanilla Vodka
1/2 oz White Crème de Cacao
1/2 cup fresh or frozen Strawberries
Scoop of Vanilla Ice Cream
Blend until smooth.
If too thick add berries or Milk.
If too thin add ice or Ice Cream.
Garnish with strawberry.

LOVE YOU LONG TIME
Fill glass with ice.
3 oz Citrus Vodka
1/2oz Black Raspberry Liqueur
1/2oz White Crème de Cacao
Shake. Strain into a chilled glass.

LUAU
Fill glass with ice.
1 oz Coconut Rum
1 oz Maui Schnapps
Fill with Pineapple Juice.
Shake.
Garnish with Pineapple and Cherry.

LUBE JOB
Fill glass with ice.
1 oz Vodka
1 oz Irish Cream
Stir.

LUGER
Fill glass with ice.
1 oz Brandy
1 oz Apple Brandy
Shake.
Strain into chilled glass.

Metric Measurement Conversion Chart on page 14

LYNCHBURG LEMONADE
Fill glass with ice.
2 oz Bourbon
1/2 oz Triple Sec
Dash of Sour Mix (optional)
Fill with Lemon-Lime Soda.

M-16 (floater)
1/2 oz Tia Maria (bottom)
1/2 oz Irish Cream
1/2 oz Cointreau (top)

MAC DADDY
Fill glass with ice.
1 1/2 oz Gin
1/2 oz Cherry Liqueur
Fill with Pineapple Juice.
Shake.

MACKENZIE GOLD
Fill glass with ice.
2 oz Yukon Jack
Fill with Grapefruit Juice.

MAD COW
Fill glass with ice.
1 oz 151-Proof Rum or Grain
Alcohol
1 oz Coffee Liqueur
1 oz Milk or Cream
Shake. Strain into shot glass.

MAD MAX
Fill glass with ice.
3 oz Champagne
Dash of Black Raspberry Liqueur
Fill with equal parts Cranberry and
Orange Juice.
Garnish with Orange.

MAD MONK
1 oz Hazelnut Liqueur
1 oz Peppermint Schnapps
Fill with equal parts Hot Chocolate
and hot Coffee.
Top with Whipped Cream.
Sprinkle with Shaved
Chocolate or Sprinkles.

MADEIRA COCKTAIL
Fill glass with ice.
1 1/2 oz Whiskey
1 1/2 oz Madeira
1 tsp Grenadine
Dash of Lemon Juice
Shake.
Garnish with Lemon.

MADRAS aka
CALIFORNIA BREEZE
Fill glass with ice.
2 oz Vodka or Citrus Vodka
or Orange Vodka
Fill with equal parts Orange and
Cranberry Juice.
Stir.
Garnish with Orange or Lime.

MADTOWN MILKSHAKE
In Blender:
1/2 cup of Ice
3/4 oz Irish Cream
3/4 oz Black Raspberry Liqueur
3/4 oz Hazelnut Liqueur
1/2 scoop Vanilla Ice Cream
Blend until smooth.
If too thick add Milk.
If too thin add ice or Ice Cream.

MAGGOT
Pour both liqueurs at the same time
on opposite sides of shot glass.
1 oz Irish Cream
1 oz Green Crème de Menthe

MAI TAI (frozen)
In Blender:
1 cup of Ice
1 oz Light Rum
1/2 oz Dark Rum
1/2 oz Apricot Brandy
1/2 cup of fresh or canned
Pineapple
Splash of Sour Mix
Splash Orange Juice
Blend for 3-4 seconds on low
speed.
Top with Dark Rum.
Garnish with Lime and Orange.

MAIDEN'S BLUSH
Fill glass with ice.
2 oz Gin
1 tsp Triple Sec or Curacao
1/2 tsp Lemon Juice
1/2 tsp Grenadine
Shake.
Strain into chilled glass.

MAIDEN'S DOWNFALL
Fill glass with ice.
1 oz Vodka
1 oz Rum
1 oz Lime Juice
Dash of Bitters
Fill with Grapefruit Juice.
Shake.

MAIDEN'S PRAYER
Fill glass with ice.
2 oz Gin
3/4 oz Triple Sec
1/2 oz Lemon Juice
Dash of Orange Juice
Shake.
Strain into chilled glass.

MAINBRACE
Fill glass with ice.
1 1/2 oz Gin
3/4 oz Triple Sec
1 oz Grape Juice
Shake.
Strain into chilled glass.

MAJOR TOM
Fill glass with ice.
1 oz Vodka or Cherry Vodka
1/2 oz Triple Sec
1/2 oz Cherry Brandy
Fill with Orange or Grapefruit Juice.

MALIBU DRIVER
Fill glass with ice.
3 oz Coconut Rum
Fill with Orange Juice.
Stir.
Garnish with Orange.

MALIBU SUNSET
Fill glass with ice.
2 oz Coconut Rum
Fill with Pineapple Juice.
Pour 1/2 oz Crème de Nouyax
down spoon to bottom of glass.
Garnish with Pineapple.

L

M

Metric Measurement Conversion Chart on page 14

MALIBU WAVE
Fill glass with ice.
1 oz Tequila
1/2 oz Triple Sec
1 tsp Blue Curacao
1 1/2 oz Sour Mix
Shake.
Garnish with Lime.

MAMIE TAYLOR
Fill glass with ice.
3 oz Scotch
1/2 oz Lime Juice
Fill with Ginger Ale.
Stir.
Garnish with Lemon.

MAN O'WAR
Fill glass with ice.
2 oz Bourbon
1 oz Orange Curacao
1/2 oz Sweet Vermouth
Dash of Lime Juice
Shake.
Strain into chilled glass.

MANGO MARTINI
Mash (muddle) 1/4 cup fresh
Mango, and
1/2 tsp Sugar together.
Fill glass with ice.
3 1/2 oz Vodka or Citrus Vodka
Shake.
Strain into chilled glass.

MANHASSET
Fill glass with ice.
1 1/2 oz Whiskey
1/4 oz Sweet Vermouth
1/4 oz Dry Vermouth
1 oz Lemon Juice
Shake.
Strain into chilled glass.
Garnish with Lemon Twist.

MANHATTAN
(*CAUTION:* DRY can mean either
make drink with Dry Vermouth or
less Sweet Vermouth than usual.
PERFECT means use equal
amounts of Sweet and Dry
Vermouth. SWEET means use
more Sweet Vermouth than usual.
NAKED means no Vermouth at all.)
Fill glass with ice.
2 oz Whiskey
1/2 oz Sweet Vermouth
2-4 dashes Bitters (optional)
Stir.
Strain into chilled glass or pour
contents (with ice) into short glass.
Garnish with Cherry or Lemon
Twist.

MAPLE LEAF
Fill glass with ice.
1 oz Canadian Whiskey
1/4 oz Lemon Juice
1 tsp Maple Syrup
Shake.
Strain into chilled glass.

MAPLE RUSSIAN
Fill glass with ice.
1 oz Vodka
1 oz Coffee Liqueur
1/2 oz Maple Syrup
Fill with Milk or Cream.
Shake.

MARCONI WIRELESS
Fill glass with ice.
1 1/2 oz Apple Brandy
1/2 oz Sweet Vermouth
2-3 dashes of Orange Bitters
Shake.
Strain into chilled glass.

MARGARITA (from Scratch)
2 tsp Sugar
2 oz Fresh Lime Juice
Fill glass with ice.
2 1/2 oz Tequila
1/2 oz Triple Sec
Shake.

MARGARITA
Fill glass with ice.
1 1/2 oz Tequila
1/2 oz Triple Sec
Dash of Lime Juice
3 oz Sour Mix
Dash of Orange Juice (optional)
Shake.
Rub rim of second glass with Lime
and dip into kosher salt.
Pour contents (with ice)
or strain into salted glass.
Garnish with Lime.

MARGARITA (frozen)
In Blender:
1 cup of Ice
1 1/2 oz Tequila
1/2 oz Triple Sec
1/2 oz Lime Juice
3 oz Sour Mix
Blend until smooth.
If too thick add juice.
If too thin add ice.
Rub rim of glass with Lime and dip
into Kosher Salt.
Pour contents into salted glass.

MARGARITA PRESIDENTE
Fill glass with ice.
1 1/2 oz Tequila
1/2 oz Triple Sec
Dash Brandy
Dash Lime Juice
Fill with Sour Mix
Shake.
Garnish with Lime.

MARIPOSA
Fill glass with ice.
2 1/2 oz Rum or Citrus Rum
1/2 oz Brandy
Dash Grenadine
Dash Lemon Juice
1oz Orange Juice
Shake. Strain into chilled glass.

MARLON BRANDO (floater)
Fill glass with ice.
1 1/2 oz Scotch (bottom)
1/2 oz Amaretto
1/4 oz of Cream (top)

MARMALADE
Fill glass with ice.
1 oz Benedictine
3/4 oz Curacao
Dash of Orange Juice
Fill with Tonic Water.
Stir.
Garnish with Orange.

MARTINEZ
Fill glass with ice.
1 1/2 oz Gin
2 oz Dry Vermouth
2 dashes of Maraschino Liqueur or
Triple Sec
2 dashes of Bitters
Shake.
Serve or strain into chilled glass.
Garnish with Cherry.

MARTINI
(*CAUTION:* DRY usually means
less Vermouth than usual.
EXTRA DRY can mean even less
Vermouth than usual or no
Vermouth at all.)
Fill glass with ice.
3 1/2 oz Gin or Vodka
1/2 oz Dry Vermouth
Stir.
Strain into chilled glass
or pour contents (with ice)
into short glass.
Garnish with Lemon Twist or Olives
or cocktail onions.

MARY GARDEN
Fill glass with ice.
1 1/2 oz Dubonnet
3/4 oz Dry Vermouth
Shake.
Strain into chilled glass.

MARY PICKFORD
Fill glass with ice.
1 1/2 oz Rum
3/4 oz Pineapple Juice
Dash of Grenadine
Shake.
Strain into chilled glass.

MASSACRE
Fill glass with ice.
1 1/2 oz Tequila
1/2 oz Campari
Fill with Ginger Ale.
Stir.

MATADOR
Fill glass with ice.
1 1/2 oz Tequila
1 1/2 oz Pineapple Juice
1/2 oz Lime Juice
1/2 tsp Sugar Syrup
Shake.
Strain into chilled glass.

MATTINI
Fill glass with ice.
2 oz Vanilla Vodka
Dash Coffee Liqueur
Dash Irish Cream
3 oz chilled espresso
Shake.
Strain into chilled glass.

MAURICE
Fill glass with ice.
2 oz Gin
1/2 oz Dry Vermouth
1/2 oz Sweet Vermouth
1/2 oz Orange Juice
Dash of Bitters
Shake.
Strain into chilled glass.

MAXIM
Fill glass with ice.
2 oz Gin
1 oz Dry Vermouth
Dash of White Crème de Cacao
Shake.
Strain into chilled glass.

MAXIM'S
In champagne flute
1 oz Brandy
1/2 oz Orange Liqueur
Dash of Orange Juice
Fill with Champagne.

MAXIM'S 2
In champagne flute
3/4 oz Orange Liqueur
3/4 oz Melon Liqueur
3/4 oz Banana Liqueur
Dash of Sour Mix
Shake.
Fill with Champagne.

MAXIM'S A LONDRES
Fill glass with ice.
1 1/2 oz Brandy
Dash of Orange Liqueur
Dash of Orange Juice
Shake.
Strain into chilled glass.
Fill with Champagne.
Garnish with Orange Twist.

MAY BLOSSOM FIZZ
Fill glass with ice.
2 oz Swedish Punch
2 oz Lemon Juice
Dash of Grenadine
Shake.
Fill with Soda Water.

McCLELLAND
Fill glass with ice.
1 1/2 oz Sloe Gin
3/4 oz Triple Sec or Curacao
2 dashes of Orange Bitters
Shake.
Strain into chilled glass.

ME SO HORNEY
1 oz Vodka or Cherry Vodka
1 oz Champagne
Fill with Hard Cider.

MEADOWLARK LEMON
Fill glass with ice.
1 1/2 oz Vodka
1/2 oz Orange Liqueur
1/2 oz Lemon Juice or Sour Mix
Stir.
Strain into chilled glass.
Garnish with Lemon.

MEDITERRANEAN COFFEE
1 1/2 oz Greek Brandy
1/2 oz Galliano
Fill with hot Black Coffee
Top with Whipped Cream.

MEISTER-BATION (frozen)
In Blender:
1 cup of Ice
1 1/2 oz Jägermeister
1/2 oz Banana Liqueur
1 tbsp Cream of Coconut
2 tbsp Vanilla Ice Cream
1/2 cup fresh or canned Pineapple
Blend until smooth.
Garnish with packaged condom.

M

Metric Measurement Conversion Chart on page 14

MELON BALL
Fill glass with ice.
1 oz Vodka
1 oz Melon Liqueur
Fill with Orange Juice.
Shake.
Garnish with Orange.

MELON BREEZE
Fill glass with ice.
1 oz Vodka
1 oz Melon Liqueur
Fill with equal parts Cranberry and
Pineapple Juice.
Shake.
Garnish with Pineapple and Cherry.

MELON COCKTAIL
Fill glass with ice.
2 oz Gin
1/2 oz Maraschino Liqueur
1/2 oz Lemon Juice
Shake.
Strain into chilled glass.
Garnish with Cherry.

MELON COLADA (frozen)
In Blender:
1 cup of Ice
1 oz Rum or Citrus Rum
1 oz Melon Liqueur
2 tbsp Cream of Coconut
1/2 cup fresh Honeydew melon or
fresh or canned Pineapple
1 tbsp Vanilla Ice Cream
Blend until smooth.
If too thick add juice or fruit.
If too thin add ice or Ice Cream.
Garnish with melon or Pineapple
and Cherry.

MELON GRIND
Fill glass with ice.
3/4 oz Vodka
3/4 oz Rum
3/4 oz Melon Liqueur
Fill with Pineapple Juice.
Shake.

MELON MARTINI
Fill glass with ice.
3 1/2 oz Vodka
1/2 oz Melon Liqueur
Dash Lime Juice (optional)
Shake.
Strain into chilled glass.

MELON ROYALE
1/2 oz Melon Liqueur
Fill with Champagne.

MELON SOMBRERO
Fill glass with ice.
2 oz Melon Liqueur
Fill with Milk or Cream.
Shake.

MELON SOUR
Fill glass with ice.
2 oz Melon Liqueur
Fill with Sour Mix.
Shake.
Garnish with Orange and Cherry.

MELON THUMPER
Fill glass with ice.
1 1/2 oz Vodka
1/2 oz Melon Liqueur
Dash Lime Juice
Fill with Sour Mix.
Shake.

MELTDOWN
1 oz Vodka or Peach Vodka
1/2 oz Peach Schnapps
Stir.

MEMPHIS BELLE
Fill glass with ice.
1 1/2 oz Brandy
3/4 oz Southern Comfort
1/2 oz Lemon Juice
3 dashes of Bitters
Shake.
Strain into chilled glass.

MENAGE a TROIS
Fill glass with ice.
3/4 oz Irish Cream
3/4 oz Black Raspberry Liqueur
3/4 oz Hazelnut Liqueur
Fill with Milk or Cream.
Shake.

MENAGE a TROIS 2
Fill glass with ice.
1 oz Dark Rum
1 oz Triple Sec
1 oz Milk or Cream
Shake. Strain into chilled glass.

MERRY WIDOW
Fill glass with ice.
1 1/4 oz Cherry Brandy
1 1/4 oz Maraschino Liqueur
Shake.
Strain into chilled glass.

METAL HELMET
Fill glass with ice.
1 1/4 oz Banana Liqueur
3/4 oz Vodka
Fill with Milk.
Shake.

METROPOLIS MARTINI
Fill glass with ice.
2 1/2 oz Vodka
    or Strawberry Vodka
1/2 oz Strawberry Liqueur
Stir.
Strain into chilled glass.
Top with 1 oz Champagne.
Garnish with Strawberry.

METROPOLITAN
Fill glass with ice.
3 1/2 oz Currant Vodka
1/2 oz Triple Sec
Dash Cranberry Juice
Dash Lime Juice (optional)
Shake.
Strain into chilled glass.

MEXICAN BLACKJACK
Fill glass with ice.
1/2 oz Tequila
1/2 oz Blended Whiskey
1/2 oz Bourbon
1/2 oz Triple Sec or Curacao
Shake.
Strain into chilled glass.

MEXICAN BOILERMAKER
Fill shot glass with Tequila
Fill chilled glass 3/4 with Beer.
Either drink shot and chase with
Beer or
Drop shot glass into Beer and
drink.

Metric Measurement Conversion Chart on page 14

MEXICAN CAPPUCCINO

1 1/2 oz Coffee Liqueur
Fill with espresso.
Top with steamed Milk.
Sprinkle with Powdered Sugar.

MEXICAN COFFEE

2 oz Coffee Liqueur
or 2 oz Tequila
Fill with hot Black Coffee.
Top with Whipped Cream.
Sprinkle with Shaved
Chocolate or Sprinkles.

MEXICAN COFFEE 2

1 oz Tequila
1 oz Coffee Liqueur
Fill with hot Black Coffee.
Top with Whipped Cream.
Sprinkle with Shaved
Chocolate or Sprinkles.

MEXICAN FLAG (floater)

1/2 oz Sloe Gin (bottom)
1/2 oz Vodka
1/2 oz Melon Liqueur (top)

MEXICAN JUMPING BEAN

Fill glass with ice.
3/4 oz Tequila
3/4 oz Coffee Liqueur
3/4 oz Anisette
Stir.

MEXICAN MISSILE

3/4 oz Tequila
3/4 oz Green Chartreuse
Dash of Tabasco Sauce

MEXICAN SCREW aka HAMMER

Fill glass with ice.
2 oz Tequila
Fill with Orange Juice.
Garnish with Orange.

MEXICAN SEABREEZE

Fill glass with ice.
2 oz Tequila
Fill with equal parts Cranberry and
Grapefruit Juice.
Garnish with Lime.

MEXICANO

Fill glass with ice.
2 oz Rum
1/2 oz Kummel
1 oz Orange Juice
3 dashes of Bitters
Shake.

MIAMI BEACH

Fill glass with ice.
2 oz Scotch
1 oz Dry Vermouth
1 oz Grapefruit Juice
Shake.
Strain into chilled glass.

MIAMI ICE

Fill glass with ice.
1/2 oz Vodka
1/2 oz Gin
1/2 oz Rum or Coconut Rum
1/2 oz Peach Schnapps
Dash of Cranberry Juice
Fill with Lemon-Lime Soda.

MIAMI MELON

Fill glass with ice.
1 oz Vodka
1 oz Melon Liqueur
Fill with Milk or Cream.
Shake.

MIAMI VICE

Fill glass with ice.
1 oz Rum
1/2 oz Blackberry Brandy
1/2 oz Banana Liqueur
Dash of Lime Juice
Dash of Grenadine
1 tbsp Cream De Coconut
Fill with Pineapple Juice.
Shake.
Garnish with Pineapple.

MICH

Fill glass with ice.
1 1/2 oz Gin
1/2 oz Sloe Gin
Dash of Lime Juice
Fill with equal parts Sour Mix and
Grapefruit Juice.
Shake.

MICK

Fill glass with ice.
1 1/2 oz Vodka
1/2 oz Banana Liqueur
2 oz Orange Juice
Shake.
Strain into chilled glass.

MIDNIGHT COWBOY

Fill glass with ice.
2 oz Bourbon
1 oz Dark Rum
1 oz Milk or Cream
Shake.
Strain into chilled glass.

MIDNIGHT DREAM

Fill glass with ice.
1 1/2 oz Vodka
    or Raspberry Vodka
1/2 oz Black Raspberry Liqueur
Dash of Cream
Fill with Cranberry Juice.
Shake.

MIDNIGHT MARTINI

Fill glass with ice.
3 1/2 oz Vodka or Coffee Vodka
1/4 oz Coffee Liqueur
or Coffee Brandy
Stir.
Strain into chilled glass or pour
contents (with ice) into shot glass.
Garnish with Lemon Twist.

MIDNIGHT SNOWSTORM

2 oz White Crème de Menthe
Fill with Hot Chocolate.
Stir.
Top with Whipped Cream.
Dribble 1/2 oz Green Crème de
Menthe on top.

MIDNIGHT SUN

Fill glass with ice.
2 1/2 oz Vodka or Citrus Vodka
1/2 oz Grenadine
Stir.
Strain into chilled glass.

M

MIDWAY RAT
Fill glass with ice.
1 oz Rum
1/2 oz Amaretto
1/2 oz Coffee Liqueur
Fill glass with Pineapple Juice.
Shake.
Garnish with Orange, Cherry and a
Black Licorice Whip.

MIKE COLLINS aka JOE COLLINS, SCOTCH COLLINS
Fill glass with ice.
2 oz Scotch
Fill with Sour Mix.
Shake.
Dash of Soda Water
Garnish with Orange and Cherry.

MIKE TYSON
Fill glass with ice.
1 oz Jägermeister
1 oz Coffee Liqueur
1 oz Anisette or Sambuca
Stir.

MILANO COFFEE
1 oz Rum
1 oz Amaretto
Fill with hot Black Coffee.
Top with Whipped Cream.
Garnish with Shaved Almonds.

MILK CHOCOLATE MARTINI
Fill glass with ice.
2 1/2 oz Vodka, Vanilla Vodka or
Chocolate Vodka
1/2 oz Chocolate Liqueur or Dark
Crème de Cacao
Dash Milk or Light Cream
Shake.

MILKSHAKE aka FRAPPE (frozen)
In Blender: 1/2 cup of ice.
1/2 cup of Milk
Scoop of Desired flavored ice
cream.
3 Tblsp Desired Flavored Syrup or
1/2 cup Fresh or
thawed Frozen berries or fruit.
Tblsp Sugar (optional)
Blend until smooth.

MILLIONAIRE
Fill glass with ice.
1 1/2 oz Bourbon
1/2 oz Pernod
1 tsp Curacao or Triple Sec
1 tsp Grenadine
1/2 Egg White
Shake.
Strain into chilled glass.

MILLIONAIRE'S COFFEE
1/2 oz Coffee Liqueur
1/2 oz Irish Cream
1/2 oz Orange Liqueur
1/2 oz Hazelnut Liqueur
Fill with hot Black Coffee.
Top with Whipped Cream.
Sprinkle with Shaved
Chocolate or Sprinkles.

MIMOSA
Fill glass 3/4 with ice (optional).
Fill 3/4 with Champagne.
Dash of Orange Liqueur
or Triple Sec (optional)
Fill with Orange Juice.
Garnish with Orange.

MIND ERASER
Fill glass with ice.
1 oz Vodka
1 oz Coffee Liqueur
Fill with Soda Water.
Garnish with a Lime.
Supposed to be drunk in one shot
through a straw.

MIND OBLITERATOR
Fill glass with ice.
1 oz Vodka
1 oz Coffee Liqueur
Fill with Champagne.
Supposed to be drunk in one shot
through a straw.

MINSTREL FRAPPE
Fill large stemmed glass (Red Wine
glass, Champagne saucer) with
crushed Ice.
1/2 oz Vodka
1/2 oz Coffee Liqueur
1/2 oz Brandy
1/2 oz White Crème de Menthe

MINT CHOCOLATE CHIP ICE CREAM
Fill glass with ice.
1/2 oz Vodka
1/2 oz Crème de Cacao
1/2 oz Peppermint Schnapps
1/2 oz Irish Cream
1/2 oz Coffee Liqueur
Fill with Milk or Cream.
Shake.

MINT CONDITION aka GROUND ZERO
Fill glass with ice.
3/4 oz Vodka
1/2 oz Coffee Liqueur
3/4 oz Bourbon
3/4 oz Peppermint Schnapps
Shake.
Serve or strain into chilled glass.

MINT JULEP
Muddle together in a glass:
10-20 Fresh Mint Leaves
1 tsp Sugar
2 tbsp Water
Fill with crushed Ice.
Fill 7/8 with Bourbon.
Float 1/2 oz Rum on top.
Garnish with 3 or 4 leaves.

MISSISSIPPI MUD
1/2 oz Coffee Liqueur
1/2 oz Hazelnut Liqueur
1/2 oz Triple Sec
1/2 oz Rum
Fill with hot Black Coffee.
Top with Whipped Cream.
Sprinkle with Shaved
Chocolate or Sprinkles.

MISSISSIPPI MULE
Fill glass with ice.
1 1/2 oz Gin
1 tsp Crème de Cassis
1 tsp Lemon Juice
Shake.
Garnish with Lemon.

MISSOURI MULE
Fill glass with ice.
2 oz Southern Comfort
Fill with Ginger Beer.
Stir.
Garnish with Lime.

Metric Measurement Conversion Chart on page 14

MIST
Is another way to say "On the rocks," but preferably with Shaved or crushed ice.

MOCHACCINO AKA MOCHA LATTE
Heat coffee cup, mug, or specialty glass.
1/3 Espresso
1/3 Liquid steamed Chocolate Milk
1/3 Foam steamed Chocolate Milk
Top with Whipped Cream.
Sprinkle with Chocolate shavings or powder.
DOUBLE MOCHACCINO (2/3 Espresso)

MO FO
Fill glass with ice.
1 1/2 oz Vodka
1/2 oz Peach Schnapps
Dash of Milk or Cream
Fill with Cranberry Juice.
Shake.

MOCHA BERRY FRAPPE (frozen)
In Blender:
1/2 cup of Ice
1 oz Coffee Liqueur
1 oz Black Raspberry Liqueur
1 oz Dark Crème de Cacao
Scoop of Vanilla Ice Cream
Blend until smooth.
If too thick add Milk or Cream.
If too thin add ice or Ice Cream.
Sprinkle with Shaved Chocolate or Sprinkles.

MOCHA MINT
Fill glass with ice.
3/4 oz Coffee Liqueur
or Coffee Brandy
3/4 oz White Crème de Menthe
3/4 oz White Crème de Cacao
Shake.
Strain into chilled glass.

MOCKINGBIRD
Fill glass with ice.
1 1/2 oz Tequila
1/2 oz White Crème de Menthe
1 oz Lime Juice
Shake.
Strain into chilled glass.

MODERN
Fill glass with ice.
1 1/2 oz Sloe Gin
3/4 oz Scotch
Dash of Pernod
Dash of Grenadine
Dash of Orange Bitters
Shake.

MODERN 2
Fill glass with ice.
3 oz Scotch
Dash of Dark Rum
Dash of Pernod
Dash of Lemon Juice
Dash of Orange Bitters
Shake.
Garnish with Cherry.

MOJITO
In short glass:
2 Lime Wedges
3-5 Mint sprigs
tsp Sugar
2-4 Dashes Bitters(optional)
Muddle.
Fill glass with ice.
2oz Light Rum
Dash Soda Water
Garnish with Lime and Mint.

MOJO
Fill glass with ice.
1 oz Rum
1 oz Cherry Brandy
3 oz Amber Beer or Ale
Fill with equal parts of Orange Juice, Pineapple Juice, Cola and Lemon-Lime Soda.

MOLL
Fill glass with ice.
1 oz Gin
1 oz Sloe Gin
1 oz Dry Vermouth
Dash of Orange Bitters
1/2 tsp Sugar (optional)
Shake.
Strain into chilled glass.

MOMOTARO
Fill glass with ice.
4 oz Sake
1/2 oz Peach Schnapps
Fill with Sour Mix.
Shake.

MON CHERIE
Fill glass with ice.
1 oz Cherry Brandy
1 oz White Crème de Cacao
1 oz of Milk or Cream.
Shake.

MONGA MONGA (frozen)
In Blender:
1 cup of Ice
1 1/2 oz Brandy
1 oz Dark Rum
1 oz Strawberry Liqueur
1 oz Lime Juice
1/2 cup fresh or frozen Strawberries
Blend until smooth.
If too thick add fruit.
If too thin add ice.
Garnish with Lime.

MONGOLIAN MOTHER
Fill glass with ice.
Dash of Vodka
Dash of Gin
Dash of Rum
Dash of Tequila
Dash of Triple Sec
Dash of Peach Schnapps
Dash of Amaretto
Dash of Sloe Gin
Dash of Southern Comfort
Dash of 151-Proof Rum
Dash of Grenadine
Fill with equal parts Cranberry and Orange Juice.
Shake.
Garnish with Orange, Lime, Lemon and Cherry.

M

Metric Measurement Conversion Chart on page 14

MONK SLIDE (floater)
1/2 oz Coffee Liqueur (top)
1/2 oz Irish Cream
1/2 oz Hazelnut Liqueur
(bottom)

MONK'S COFFEE
1 oz Benedictine
1 oz Orange Liqueur
Fill with hot Black Coffee.
Top with Whipped Cream.
Garnish with Orange.

MONKEY JUICE
Fill glass with ice.
1 1/2 oz Dark Rum
1/2 oz Irish Cream
1/2 oz Banana Liqueur
Stir.

MONKEY SPECIAL (frozen)
In Blender:
1 cup of Ice
1 oz Dark Rum
1 oz Light Rum
1/2 ripe peeled Banana
1/2 scoop Vanilla Ice Cream
Blend until smooth.
If too thick add Milk or Cream. If
too thin add ice or Ice Cream.
Sprinkle with Shaved Chocolate.

MONKEY WRENCH
Fill glass with ice.
2 oz Rum or Orange Rum
Fill with Grapefruit Juice.

MONKEY WRENCH 2
Fill glass with ice.
1 oz Vodka
1 oz Amaretto
1 oz Orange Juice
Strain into shot glass.

MONTANA
Fill glass with ice.
1 1/2 oz Brandy
1 oz Port
1/2 oz Dry Vermouth
Stir.

MONTE CARLO
Fill glass with ice.
1 1/2 oz Whiskey
1/2 oz Benedictine
3 dashes of Bitters
Shake.

MONTE CRISTO COFFEE
1 oz Coffee Liqueur
1 oz Orange Liqueur
Fill with hot Black Coffee.
Top with Whipped Cream.
Garnish with Orange.

MONTEGO BAY COFFEE
1/2 oz Dark Rum
1/2 oz Coffee Liqueur
Fill with hot Black Coffee.
Top with Whipped Cream.
Garnish with Banana.

MONTMARTE
Fill glass with ice.
2 oz Gin
1/2 oz Sweet Vermouth
1/2 oz Triple Sec
Stir.
Strain into chilled glass.

MONTREAL CLUB BOUNCER
Fill glass with ice.
1 1/2 oz Gin
1 oz Pernod

MOODY BLUE
Fill glass with ice.
3/4 oz Vodka or Orange Vodka
3/4 oz Peach Schnapps
3/4 oz Blue Curacao
Fill with Pineapple Juice.
Shake.

MOON CHASER (frozen)
In Blender:
1/2 cup of ice
3/4 oz Dark Rum
3/4 oz Coconut Rum
3/4 oz Amaretto
Scoop Orange Sherbet
Blend until smooth.

MOON RACKER
Fill glass with ice.
1 1/2 oz Tequila
1/2 oz Blue Curacao
Fill with Pineapple Juice
Shake.

MOONBEAM
Fill glass with ice.
1 oz Amaretto
1 oz White Crème de Cacao
Fill with Milk or Cream.

MOONLIGHT
Fill glass with ice.
2 oz Apple Brandy
1 oz Lemon Juice
1 tsp Powdered Sugar
or Sugar Syrup
Shake.
Splash of Soda Water (optional)
Garnish with Lemon Twist.

MOONPIE (frozen)
In Blender:
1 cup of Ice
1 oz Amber Rum
Dash of Peach Schnapps
Dash of Banana Liqueur
1/2 a ripe Banana
1/2 ripe peeled Peach
Dash of Orange Juice
Blend until smooth.
Garnish with Banana.

MOOSE MILK
In a large mixing bowl:
20 oz Dark Rum
10 oz Tia Maria
40 oz Milk
1/2 gallon Vanilla Ice Cream
Stir until smooth.
Serves 20 people.

MOOSEBERRY
Fill glass with ice.
1 oz Vodka or Raspberry Vodka
1 oz Amaretto
2 oz Cranberry Juice
2 oz Sour Mix
Shake.
Strain into chilled glass.
Top with 1/2 oz Orange Liqueur.

MORESQUE CAFE
3/4 oz Amaretto
3/4 oz Sambuca
3/4 oz Hazelnut Liqueur
Fill with hot Black Coffee
Top with Whipped Cream
Sprinkle with shaved chocolate.

MORNING
Fill glass with ice.
1 oz Brandy
1 oz Dry Vermouth
Dash of Triple Sec or Curacao
Dash of Maraschino Liqueur
Dash of Pernod
2 dashes of Orange Bitters
Stir.

MORNING GLORY
Fill glass with ice.
1 oz Scotch
1 oz Brandy
Dash of Pernod
2 dashes of Curacao
2 dashes of Bitters
Shake.
Top with Soda Water.
Stir with a spoon dipped in water
and coated with sugar.

MOSCOW MIMOSA
Fill glass with ice.
1/2 oz Vodka or Orange Vodka
Fill with equal parts Champagne
and Orange Juice.

MOSCOW MULE
Fill glass with ice.
2 oz Vodka
Fill with Ginger Beer.
Stir.
Garnish with Lime.

MOTHER LOVE
Fill glass with ice.
1 1/2 oz Canadian Whiskey
1/2 oz Peppermint Schnapps
Stir.

MOTHER SHERMAN
Fill glass with ice.
1 1/2 oz Apricot Brandy
1 oz Orange Juice
3-4 dashes of Orange Bitters
Shake.
Garnish with Orange.

MOULIN ROUGE
Fill glass with ice.
1 1/2 oz Sloe Gin
1/2 oz Sweet Vermouth
3 dashes of Bitters
Shake.
Strain into chilled glass.

MOULIN ROUGE 2
Fill glass with ice.
1 oz Cognac or Brandy
4-6 oz Orange Juice
Shake. Strain into chilled glass.
Top with 1oz Champagne.
Garnish with Orange.

MOUND BAR
2 oz Coconut Rum
Fill with Hot Chocolate.
Top with Whipped Cream.
Sprinkle with Shaved Chocolate.

MOUND BAR 2
Fill glass with ice.
3/4 oz Coconut Rum
3/4 oz Dark Crème de Cacao
3/4 oz Irish Cream
3/4 oz Milk or Cream
Shake.
Strain into chilled glass.

MOUNT FUJI
Fill glass with ice.
1 1/2 oz Gin
1/2 oz Lemon Juice
1/2 oz Heavy Cream
1 tsp Pineapple Juice
1 Egg White
3 dashes of Maraschino Liqueur
Shake.

MOUNT VESUVIUS
Fill glass with ice.
1 oz Coconut Rum
1 oz Triple Sec
Dash of Grenadine
Fill with Orange Juice.
Shake.
Top with 151-Proof Rum.

MOUNTAIN RED PUNCH
Fill glass with ice.
1/2 oz Amaretto
1/2 oz Brandy
1/2 oz Cherry Brandy
2 oz Ginger Ale
Fill with Red Wine.

MUDSLIDE
Fill glass with ice.
1 oz Coffee Liqueur
1 oz Irish Cream
1 oz Vodka
Shake.

MUDSLIDE 2
Fill glass with ice.
1 oz Vodka
1 oz Coffee Liqueur
1 oz Irish Cream
Fill with Milk or Cream.

MUDSLIDE (floater)
1/2 oz Coffee Liqueur (bottom)
1/2 oz Irish Cream
1/2 oz Vodka (top)

MUDSLIDE (frozen)
In Blender:
1/2 cup of Ice
1 oz Coffee Liqueur
1 oz Irish Cream
1 oz Vodka
Scoop of Vanilla Ice Cream
Blend until smooth.
If too thick add Milk or Cream.
If too thin add ice or Ice Cream.
Sprinkle with Shaved Chocolate or
Sprinkles.

MUDSLING
1/2 oz Coffee Liqueur
1/2 oz Irish Cream
1/2 oz Vodka
Fill with Hot Chocolate.
Top with Whipped Cream.
Sprinkle with Shaved Chocolate.

M

MUFF DIVER
Fill glass with ice.
1 oz Amaretto
1 oz White Crème de Cacao
Dash of Lime Juice or Lemon Juice
1 oz Milk or Cream
Shake. Strain into shot glass.

MULE SKINNER
1 1/2 oz Bourbon
1/2 oz Blackberry Brandy

MULE'S HIND LEG
Fill glass with ice.
3/4 oz Gin
3/4 oz Apple Brandy
3/4 oz Benedictine
3/4 oz Apricot Brandy
3/4 oz Maple Syrup
Shake.

MULLED CIDER
Place 2 smashed Cinnamon Sticks,
10 whole Cloves,
and 1 tsp Allspice Berries into
cheese cloth bag.
In saucepan on low heat, stir
together 1/2 gallon of Apple Cider,
and 1/2 cup Brown Sugar.
After sugar dissolves, place bag
containing spices in and keep heating for 5 minutes, then serve.
Garnish with Cinnamon Stick and
Dried Apple Ring.
(serves 10-15 people)

MULTIPLE ORGASM
Fill glass with ice.
1/2 oz Vodka
1/2 oz Coffee Liqueur
1/2 oz Amaretto
1/2 oz Irish Cream
1/2 oz Orange Liqueur
1 oz Milk
Shake
Strain into chilled glass.
Garnish with 2 or more Cherries.

MUSCLE BEACH
Fill glass with ice.
1 1/2 oz Vodka or Citrus Vodka
1/2 oz Triple Sec
Fill with Pink Lemonade.

MUTUAL ORGASM
Fill glass with ice.
3/4 oz Vodka
3/4 oz Amaretto
3/4 oz Crème de Cacao
1 oz Milk or Cream
Shake.
Strain into chilled glass.

NAKED G S (floater)
1 oz Chocolate Liqueur (bottom)
1 oz 100-proof Peppermint
Schnapps (top)

NAKED LADY
Fill glass with ice.
1 oz Rum
1 oz Apricot Brandy
Dash of Grenadine
1 oz Sour Mix
Shake.
Strain into chilled glass.

NAKED LADY 2
Fill glass with ice.
3/4 oz Vodka or Pineapple Vodka
3/4 oz Gin or Orange Gin
3/4 oz Brandy
1/2 oz Apricot Brandy
1/2 oz Blackberry Brandy
Fill with equal parts Orange
and Pineapple Juice.
Shake.
Top with tsp Grenadine.

NANTUCKET BREEZE
Fill glass with ice.
1 oz Vodka or Cranberry Vodka
1 oz Cranberry Liqueur
Fill with Grapefruit Juice.
Garnish with Lime.

NANTUCKET RED aka
POINSETTIA
Fill glass 3/4 with ice.
Fill 3/4 with Champagne.
Fill with Cranberry Juice.
Garnish with Lime.

NAPOLEON
Fill glass with ice.
1 oz Gin
1 oz Orange Liqueur
1 oz Dubonnet Rouge
Stir.
Strain into chilled glass.
Garnish with Orange Twist.

NARRAGANSETT
Fill glass with ice.
1 1/2 oz Bourbon
1 oz Sweet Vermouth
Dash of Anisette
Stir.
Garnish with Lemon Twist.

NASCAR DAD
In beer glass:
1 oz Bourbon Whiskey or
other American Made Liquor
1 oz Blackberry Brandy or
American Made Liqueur
Fill with American Made Beer.

NASTY GIRL
Fill glass with ice.
3/4 oz Dark Rum
1/4 oz Coconut Rum
1/4 oz Amaretto
1/4 oz Banana Liqueur
1/4 oz Peach Schnapps
Dash of Cranberry Juice
Dash of Pineapple Juice
Shake. Strain into shot glass.

NAUGHTY HULA PIE
Fill glass with ice.
1 oz Amaretto
1 oz Dark Crème de Cacao
Dash of Pineapple Juice
2 oz Cream or Milk
Shake.
Strain into chilled glass.

NAVY GROG
Fill glass with ice.
1 oz Light Rum
1 oz Dark Rum
1/2 oz Orange Juice
1/2 oz Guava Nectar
1/2 oz Pineapple Juice
1/2 oz Lime Juice
1/2 oz Orgeat Syrup
Shake.
Garnish with Lime and Mint Sprig.

NEGRONI
Fill glass with ice.
1 oz Gin
1 oz Campari
1 oz Dry or Sweet Vermouth
Stir.
Strain into chilled glass.
Garnish with Lemon Twist.

NELSON'S BLOOD
Fill glass with ice.
2 oz Pusser's Rum
Dash of Lime Juice.
Fill with Ginger Beer.

NELSON'S BLOOD 2
1 oz Tawny Port
Fill with Champagne.

NEON
Fill glass with ice.
1 oz Citrus Vodka or Currant Vodka
1/2 oz Melon Liqueur
1/2 oz Blue Curacao
Dash of Lime Juice.
Fill with Sour Mix.
Shake.

NERVOUS BREAKDOWN
Fill glass with ice.
1 1/2 oz Vodka or Raspberry Vodka
1/2 oz Black Raspberry Liqueur
Fill with Soda Water.
Top with splash of Cranberry Juice.
Garnish with Lime.

NESI aka LOCH NESS MONSTER
(floater)
1/2 oz Melon Liqueur (bottom)
1/2 oz Irish Cream
1/2 oz Jägermeister (top)

NETHERLAND
Fill glass with ice.
1 oz Brandy
1 oz Triple Sec
Dash of Orange Juice
Shake.
Serve or strain into chilled glass.

NEUTRON BOMB (floater)
1/2 oz Coffee Liqueur (bottom)
1/2 oz Irish Cream
1/2 oz Butterscotch Schnapps (top)

NEVINS
Fill glass with ice.
1 1/2 oz Bourbon
1 oz Apricot Brandy
1 oz Grapefruit Juice
1 tsp Lemon Juice
3 dashes of Bitters
Shake.

NEW WORLD
Fill glass with ice.
1 1/2 oz Whiskey
1/2 oz Lime Juice
1 tsp Grenadine
Shake.
Serve or strain into chilled glass.
Garnish with Lime.

NEW YORK COCKTAIL
Fill glass with ice.
1 1/2 oz Whiskey
1/2 oz Lime Juice
1 tsp Sugar Syrup or Powdered Sugar
Dash of Grenadine
Shake.
Garnish with Orange Twist.

NEW YORK SLAMMER
Fill glass with ice.
1 oz Blended Whiskey
1/2 oz Banana Liqueur
1/2 oz Sloe Gin
Fill with Orange Juice.
Shake.

NEW YORK SOUR
Fill glass with ice.
2 oz Whiskey
Fill with Sour Mix.
Shake.
Top with 1/2 oz Red Table Wine.
Garnish with Cherry and Lemon.

NEWBURY
Fill glass with ice.
1 1/2 oz Gin
1 1/2 oz Sweet Vermouth
3 dashes of Curacao
Stir.
Strain into chilled glass.
Garnish with Orange and Lemon Twist.

NIAGARA FALLS
Fill glass with ice.
1 1/2 oz Whiskey
1/2 oz Irish Mist
1/2 oz Heavy Cream
Shake.
Strain into chilled glass.

NIGHT TRAIN (frozen)
In Blender:
1/2 cup of Ice
1 oz Rum or Vanilla Rum
1/2 oz Cherry Brandy
1/2 oz White Crème de Cacao
1 oz Cream of Coconut
Dash of Pineapple Juice
Scoop of Vanilla Ice Cream
Blend until smooth.
Garnish with Cherry.

NIGHTINGALE
Fill glass with ice.
1 oz Banana Liqueur
1/2 oz Curacao
1 oz Cream
1/2 Egg White
Shake.
Strain into chilled glass.
Garnish with Cherry.

NIGHTMARE
Fill glass with ice.
1 oz Gin or Orange Gin
1 oz Dubonnet
1/2 oz Cherry Brandy
1 oz Orange Juice
Shake.
Strain into chilled glass.

Metric Measurement Conversion Chart on page 14

NINE-ONE-ONE or 911 aka 24 KARAT NIGHTMARE
1 oz 100-Proof Cinnamon Schnapps
1 oz 100-Proof Peppermint Schnapps

NINETEEN
Fill glass with ice.
2 oz Dry Vermouth
1/2 oz Gin
1/2 oz Kirschwasser
Dash of Pernod
1 tsp Sugar Syrup
Shake.
Strain into chilled glass.

NINETEEN PICK-ME-UP
Fill glass with ice.
1 1/2 oz Pernod
3/4 oz Gin
3 dashes of Sugar Syrup
3 dashes of Bitters
3 dashes of Orange Bitters
Shake.
Top with Soda Water.

NINJA (floater)
1/2 oz Dark Crème de Cacao (bottom)
1/2 oz Melon Liqueur
1/2 oz Hazelnut Liqueur (top)

NINJA TURTLE
Fill glass with ice.
1 1/2 oz Gin or Orange Gin
1/2 oz Blue Curacao
Fill with Orange Juice.
Stir.

NINJA TURTLE 2
Fill glass with ice.
1 oz Coconut Rum
1 oz Melon Liqueur
1 oz Pineapple Juice
Shake.
Strain into chilled glass.
Garnish with Cherry.

NINOTCHKA
Fill glass with ice.
3 oz Vodka or Vanilla
        or Chocolate Vodka
1/2 oz White Crème de Cacao
1 tsp Lemon Juice
Shake.
Serve or strain into chilled glass.

NO PROBLEM
Fill glass with ice.
1 oz Coconut Rum
1 oz Cherry Brandy
1 1/2 oz Apple Juice
1/2 oz Orange Juice
1/2 oz Lime Juice
1/2 oz Sugar Syrup
Shake.

NO TELL MOTEL
Fill glass with ice.
1 oz Bourbon
1 oz Mentholated Schnapps
Stir.
Strain into chilled glass.

NOCTURNAL
Fill glass with ice.
2 oz Bourbon
1 oz Dark Crème de Cacao
Fill with Cream or Milk.
Shake.

NORTHEAST SUICIDE
Mix 1 can of Orange Juice Concentrate with
1 liter of desired Liquor
(Vodka, Rum, Whiskey, Tequila, Gin)

NORTHERN LIGHTS
Fill glass with ice.
2 oz Yukon Jack
Dash of Peach Schnapps (optional)
Fill with equal parts of Orange and Cranberry Juice.
Stir.

NORTHERN LIGHTS 2
1 oz Yukon Jack
1 oz Orange Liqueur
Fill with hot Black Coffee.
Top with Whipped Cream and Rainbow Sprinkles.

NUCLEAR KAMIKAZE aka BLUE KAMIKAZE
Fill glass with ice.
2 oz Vodka or Lime Vodka
1/2 oz Blue Curacao
Dash of Lime Juice
Shake.
Serve or strain into chilled glass.
Garnish with Lime.

NUCLEAR MELTDOWN aka THREE MILE ISLAND
Fill glass with ice.
1/2 oz Vodka
1/2 oz Gin
1/2 oz Rum
1/2 oz Tequila
1/2 oz Triple Sec
Fill with Sour Mix
or Pineapple Juice.
Shake.
Top with 1/2 oz Melon Liqueur.

NUT AND HONEY (frozen)
In Blender:
1/2 cup of Ice
1 1/2 oz Vodka
1/2 oz Hazelnut Liqueur
1 tbsp Honey
Scoop of Vanilla Ice Cream
Blend until smooth.
If too thick add Milk.
If too thin add ice or Ice Cream.

NUTCRACKER
Fill glass with ice.
1 oz Vodka or Vanilla Vodka
1 oz Coffee Liqueur
1 oz Irish Cream
Shake.

NUTCRACKER 2
Fill glass with ice.
1 oz Vodka or Vanilla Vodka
1/2 oz Irish Cream
1/2 oz Amaretto
1/2 oz Hazelnut Liqueur
Shake.

NUTCRACKER (frozen)
In Blender:
1/2 cup of Ice
1 oz Vodka or Vanilla Vodka
1/2 oz Irish Cream
1/2 oz Amaretto
1/2 oz Hazelnut Liqueur
Scoop of Vanilla Ice Cream
Blend until smooth.
If too thick add Milk or Cream.
If too thin add ice or Ice Cream.

Metric Measurement Conversion Chart on page 14

NUTS AND BERRIES
Fill glass with ice.
3/4 oz Black Raspberry Liqueur
3/4 oz Hazelnut Liqueur
3/4 oz Coffee Liqueur
Fill with Cream.
Shake.

NUTS AND BERRIES 2
Fill glass with ice.
1/2 oz Vodka of Strawberry Vodka
1/2 oz Irish Cream
1/2 oz Black Raspberry Liqueur
1/2 oz Hazelnut Liqueur
Shake.
Strain into chilled glass.

NUTS AND CREAM
Fill glass with ice.
1 oz Amaretto
1 oz Hazelnut Liqueur
1 oz Cream
Shake.
Strain into chilled glass.

NUTTY BITCH
Fill glass with ice.
1 oz Vodka or Vanilla Vodka
1 oz Coffee Liqueur
1/2 oz Peppermint Schnapps
1/2 oz Irish Cream
Dash of Cola
Fill with Milk or Cream.
Shake.
Top with 1/2 oz Hazelnut Liqueur.

NUTTY CHINAMAN
Fill glass with ice.
1 oz Ginger Liqueur
1 oz Irish Cream
1 oz Hazelnut Liqueur
Stir.
Strain into chilled glass.

NUTTY COLADA (frozen)
In Blender:
1/2 cup of Ice
1 oz Amaretto
1 oz Rum
2 tbsp Cream of Coconut
1/2 cup fresh or canned Pineapple
1 tbsp Vanilla Ice Cream (optional)
Blend until smooth.
If too thick add fruit or juice.
If too thin add ice or Ice Cream.
Garnish with Pineapple, Cherry and
Shaved Almonds.

NUTTY IRISH COOLER
Fill glass with ice.
1 oz Irish Cream
1 oz Hazelnut Liqueur
Fill with Iced Coffee.
Shake.
Top with Whipped Cream.

NUTTY IRISHMAN
Fill glass with ice.
1 oz Irish Cream
1 oz Hazelnut Liqueur
Stir.

NUTTY IRISHMAN 2
Fill glass with ice.
1 oz Irish Whiskey
1 oz Hazelnut Liqueur
Fill with Milk or Cream.
Shake.

NUTTY IRISHMAN COFFEE
1 oz Irish Cream or Irish Whiskey
1 oz Hazelnut Liqueur
Fill with hot Black Coffee.
Top with Whipped Cream.
Sprinkle with Shaved Chocolate.

NUTTY JAMAICAN
Fill glass with ice.
1 oz Dark Rum
1 oz Hazelnut Liqueur
Stir.
Strain into chilled glass.

NUTTY RUSSIAN
Fill glass with ice.
1 oz Vodka
1 oz Hazelnut Liqueur
Fill with Milk or Cream.
Shake.

THE "O" MARTINI
Fill glass with ice.
2 oz Vodka
1 oz Coconut Rum
1 oz Banana Liqueur
Shake.
Strain into chilled glass.

007
Fill glass with ice.
3 1/2 oz Orange Vodka
Fill with equal parts Orange Juice
and Lemon-Lime Soda.
Stir.

OATMEAL COOKIE
Fill glass with ice.
1/2 oz Jägermeister
1/2 oz Cinnamon Schnapps
1/2 oz Irish Cream
1/2 oz Butterscotch Schnapps
Shake.
Strain into chilled glass.

OATMEAL COOKIE 2
Fill glass with ice.
3/4 oz Coffee Liqueur
3/4 oz Irish Cream
3/4 oz Cinnamon Schnapps
Dash of Milk or Cream
Shake.
Strain into chilled glass.

OCEAN VIEW SPECIAL
Fill glass with ice.
1 oz Vodka
1 oz Galliano
1 oz Green Crème de Menthe
Fill with Orange Juice.
Shake.

ODD McINTYRE
Fill glass with ice.
1 oz Brandy
1 oz Triple Sec
1 oz Lillet Blanc
1/2 oz Lemon Juice
Shake.
Strain into chilled glass.

OH, HENRY
Fill glass with ice.
1 1/2 oz Whiskey
1/4 oz Benedictine
3 oz Ginger Ale
Stir.
Garnish with Lemon.

N
O

Metric Measurement Conversion Chart on page 14

OIL SLICK
Fill glass with ice.
1 oz Vodka or Vanilla Vodka
1 oz White Crème de Cacao
1 oz Milk
Shake.
Float 1 oz Dark Rum on top.

OIL SLICK 2
1 oz Peppermint Schnapps
1/2 oz Blue Curacao
Stir.
Float 1/2 oz Jägermeister on top.

OLD FASHIONED
Muddle together in glass:
Stemless Maraschino Cherry,
Orange Slice, 1/2 tsp Sugar,
4-5 dashes of Bitters.
Fill glass with ice.
2 oz Whiskey
Splash with Soda Water.
Stir.

OLD GROANER
Fill glass with ice.
1 1/2 oz Whiskey
1/2 oz Amaretto
Stir.

OLD GROANER'S WIFE
Fill glass with ice.
1 1/2 oz Whiskey
1/2 oz Amaretto
Fill with Cream or Milk.
Shake.

OLIVER TWIST
Fill glass with ice.
3 1/2 oz Gin or Vodka
1/2 oz Dry Vermouth
Stir.
Strain into chilled glass or pour
contents (with ice) into shot glass.
Garnish with Lemon Twist & Olives.

OLYMPIC
Fill glass with ice.
1 oz Brandy
1 oz Curacao or Triple Sec
1 oz Orange Juice
Shake.

ONE SEVENTY
1 oz Brandy
Fill with Champagne.

110 IN THE SHADE
Fill shot glass with Tequila.
Fill glass 3/4 with beer.
Either drink shot and chase with
beer or drop shot glass into beer
and drink.

OOM PAUL
Fill glass with ice.
1 oz Apple Brandy
1 oz Dubonnet Rouge
3 dashes of Bitters
Shake.

OPEN GRAVE
Fill glass with ice.
1/2 oz 151-Proof Rum
1/2 oz Dark Rum
1/2 oz Vodka
1/2 oz Southern Comfort
1/2 oz Peach Schnapps
Fill with equal parts Sour Mix,
Orange, Grapefruit, Pineapple
and Cherry Juice.

OPENING
Fill glass with ice.
1 1/2 oz Whiskey
1 tsp Sweet Vermouth
1 tsp Grenadine
Stir.
Strain into chilled glass.

OPERA
Fill glass with ice.
2 oz Gin
1/2 oz Dubonnet
1/2 oz Maraschino Liqueur
Stir.
Strain into chilled glass.
Garnish with Orange Twist.

ORAL SEX ON THE BEACH
Fill glass with ice.
1 oz Vodka or Citrus Vodka
1/2 oz Black Raspberry Liqueur
1/2 oz Melon Liqueur
Fill with Orange Juice.
Shake.

ORANGE BLOSSOM
Fill glass with ice.
1 oz Gin or Orange Gin
1 oz Orange Juice
1/4 tsp Sugar Syrup
or Powdered Sugar
Shake.
Strain into chilled glass.
Garnish with Orange.

ORANGE BUCK
Fill glass with ice.
1 1/2 oz Gin or Orange Gin
1 oz Orange Juice
1 tbsp Lime Juice
Shake.
Strain into chilled glass.
Top with Ginger Ale.

ORANGE DROP
Moisten inside of shot glass with
Orange Juice, then coat inside of
glass with Sugar.
Fill shot glass with chilled Vodka.

ORANGE DROP 2
Fill shot glass with Orange Vodka
Coat Orange wedge with Sugar.

ORANGE FREEZE (frozen)
In Blender:
1/2 cup of Ice
2 oz Vodka or Orange Vodka
Scoop of Orange Sherbet
Dash of Orange Juice
Blend until smooth.
If too thick add orange juice.
If too thin add sherbet.

ORANGE JULIUS (frozen)
In Blender:
1/2 cup of Ice
1 1/2 oz Vodka or Vanilla,
        or Orange Vodka
1/2 oz Triple Sec or Curacao
1/2 Scoop of Orange Sherbet
1/2 Scoop of Vanilla Ice Cream
1 Egg White
Blend until smooth.
If too thick add orange juice.
If too thin add ice or sherbet.

ORANGE KRUSH
Fill glass with ice.
1 1/2 oz Vodka or Orange Vodka
1/2 oz Triple Sec
1 oz Orange Juice
1 oz Lemon-Lime Soda
Stir.
Serve or strain into short glass.

ORANGE MARGARITA (frozen)
In Blender:
1/2 cup of Ice
1 1/2 oz Tequila
1/2 oz Triple Sec
or Orange Liqueur
Dash of Lime Juice
Scoop of Orange Sherbet
Blend until smooth.
If too thick add juice.
If too thin add ice or sherbet.
Garnish with Orange and Lime.

ORANGE MARTINI
Fill glass with ice.
3 1/2 oz Orange Vodka or Vodka
Dash Triple Sec
tsp Marmalade
Shake.
Strain into chilled glass.
Garnish with Orange.

ORANGE OASIS
Fill glass with ice.
1 1/2 oz Gin or Orange Gin
1/2 oz Cherry Brandy
4 oz Orange Juice
Stir.
Top with Ginger Ale.

ORANGE WHIP
In Blender:
1/2 cup of Ice
1 Egg White
Scoop of Orange Sherbet
2 oz Orange Juice
Blend until smooth.
If too thick add juice.
If too thin add sherbet or ice.

OR-E-OH COOKIE aka
COOKIES AND CREAM (frozen)
In Blender:
1/2 cup of Ice
1 oz Vodka or Vanilla Vodka
3/4 oz Dark Crème de Cacao
2 cookies
Scoop of Vanilla Ice Cream
Blend until smooth.
If too thick add Milk or Cream.
If too thin add ice or Ice Cream.
Garnish with a cookie.

ORIENT EXPRESS
Fill glass with ice.
3/4 oz Ginger Liqueur
1 tsp Sugar
Fill with espresso.

ORIENTAL
Fill glass with ice.
1 oz Whiskey
1/2 oz Triple Sec
1/2 oz Sweet Vermouth
1/2 oz Lime Juice
Shake.
Strain into chilled glass.

ORGASM aka
BURNT ALMOND,
ROASTED TOASTED ALMOND
Fill glass with ice.
1 oz Vodka or Vanilla Vodka
1 oz Coffee Liqueur
1 oz Amaretto
Fill with Cream or Milk.
Shake.

ORGASM 2
Fill glass with ice.
1/2 oz Vodka or Vanilla Vodka
1/2 oz Triple Sec
1/2 oz Amaretto
1/2 oz White Crème de Cacao
1 oz Cream
Shake.
Serve or strain into short glass.

ORGASM 3
Fill glass with ice.
3/4 oz Coffee Liqueur
3/4 oz Amaretto
3/4 oz Irish Cream
Fill with equal parts Milk or Cream
and Soda Water.

ORSINI (frozen)
In Blender:
1/2 cup of Ice
1 1/2 oz Gin
1/2 oz Triple Sec
Dash of Sour Mix
Dash of Orange Juice
Scoop of Vanilla Ice Cream.
Blend until smooth.
If too thick add Milk or Cream. If
too thin add ice or Ice Cream.

OSTEND FIZZ
Fill glass with ice.
1 oz Kirschwasser
1 oz Crème de Cassis
Stir.
Top with Soda Water.
Garnish with Lemon Twist.

OTTER ROCKER
Fill glass with ice.
1 oz Rum or Mango Rum
1/2 oz Amaretto
1 oz Sour Mix
1 oz Mango Juice
Shake.
Top with 1/2 oz Dark Rum.

OUT OF THE BLUE
Fill glass with ice.
1/4 oz Vodka
1/4 oz Blue Curacao
1/4 oz Blueberry Schnapps
Dash of Sour Mix
Shake.
Top with Soda Water.

OUTRIGGER
Fill glass with ice.
1 oz Light Rum or Pineapple Rum
1/2 oz Amaretto
Fill with equal parts of Cranberry
and Pineapple Juice.
Top with Dark Rum.

OXBEND
Fill glass with ice.
1 oz Southern Comfort
1/2 oz Tequila
Dash of Grenadine
Fill with Orange Juice.
Stir.

O

Metric Measurement Conversion Chart on page 14

OYSTER SHOT aka LOUISIANA SHOOTER
In a shot glass:
1 raw oyster
1-3 dashes of Tabasco Sauce
1/4 tsp Horseradish
Fill with Vodka or Peppered Vodka.

OZARK MOUNTAIN PUNCH
Fill glass with ice.
1/2 oz Vodka
1/2 oz Gin
1/2 oz Tequila
1/2 oz Bourbon
Dash of Orgeat Syrup
Fill with Orange Juice.
Shake.
Top with 151-Proof Rum.

P. M. S.
Fill glass with ice.
3/4 oz Peach Schnapps
3/4 oz Coconut Rum
3/4 oz Russian Vodka
Stir and Strain into chilled glass.

PACIFIC PACIFIER
Fill glass with ice.
1 oz Orange Liqueur or Triple Sec
1/2 oz Banana Liqueur
1/2 oz Cream
Shake.

PADDY COCKTAIL
Fill glass with ice.
1 1/2 oz Irish Whiskey
3/4oz Sweet Vermouth
3 dashes of Bitters
Shake and Strain into chilled glass.

PAGO PAGO
Fill glass with ice.
1 1/2 oz Amber Rum
1/2 tsp White Crème de Cacao
1/2 tsp Green Chartreuse
1/2 oz Pineapple Juice
1/2 oz Lime Juice
Shake.

PAIN IN THE ASS (frozen)
In Blender:
1 cup of Ice
2 oz Rum or Citrus Rum
1/2 oz Banana Liqueur
1/2 oz Blackberry Brandy
Dash of Lime Juice
Dash of Grenadine
Dash of Cream of Coconut
1/2 cup fresh or canned Pineapple
Blend.

PAINT BALL
Fill glass with ice.
1/2 oz Southern Comfort
1/2 oz Triple Sec
1/2 oz Irish Cream
1/2 oz Banana Liqueur
1/2 oz Blue Curacao
Shake. Strain into shot glass.

PAIR OF JACKS (floater)
1 oz Yukon Jack (bottom)
1 oz Bourbon (top)

PAISLEY MARTINI
Fill glass with ice.
3 oz Gin
1/2 tsp Dry Vermouth
1/2 tsp Scotch
Shake.
Strain into chilled glass.

PALL MALL
Fill glass with ice.
1 oz Gin
1 oz Dry Vermouth
1 oz Sweet Vermouth
1 tsp White Crème de Menthe
2 dashes of Orange Bitters
Stir.

PALM BEACHER
Fill glass with ice.
1 1/2 oz Dark Rum
1/2 oz Amaretto
Fill with Orange Juice.
Shake.

PALMETTO
Fill glass with ice.
1 1/2 oz Rum
1 oz Sweet Vermouth
2 dashes of Bitters
Stir.
Serve or strain into chilled glass.
Garnish with Lemon Twist.

PAN GALACTIC GARGLE BLASTER
Fill glass with ice.
3/4 oz Vodka
3/4 oz Rum
3/4 oz Melon Liqueur
Dash of Sour Mix
Dash of Lime Juice
Shake.
Strain into chilled glass.
Fill with Lemon-Lime Soda.

PAN GALACTIC GARGLE BLASTER 2
Fill glass with ice.
1 1/2 oz Vodka
1/2 oz Triple Sec
Dash of Grenadine
4 oz Pineapple Juice
Shake
Strain into chilled glass.
Fill with Lemon-Lime Soda.

PAN GALACTIC GARGLE BLASTER 3
Fill glass with ice.
1 1/2 oz Vodka
1/2 oz Blue Curacao
4 oz Champagne
Stir (gently).
Strain into chilled glass.
Garnish with bitters-soaked
sugar cube
and a cocktail onion.

PANABRAITOR
Fill glass with ice.
1 oz Southern Comfort
1/2 oz Black Raspberry Liqueur
1/2 oz Triple Sec
Fill with equal parts Sour Mix and
Orange Juice.
Shake.

PANAMA
Fill glass with ice.
1 oz Dark Rum or Brandy
3/4 oz White Crème de Cacao
3/4 oz Cream
Shake.
Serve or strain into chilled glass.
Garnish with Nutmeg.

Metric Measurement Conversion Chart on page 14

PANAMA JACK
Fill glass with ice.
2 oz Yukon Jack
Fill with equal parts Pineapple and
Cranberry Juice.

PANAMA RED
Fill glass with ice.
1 1/2 oz Gold Tequila
1/2 oz Triple Sec
Dash of Grenadine
Dash of Sour Mix
Shake.
Strain into chilled glass.

PANCHO VILLA
Fill glass with ice.
1 oz Rum
1 oz Gin
1 oz Apricot Brandy
1 tsp Cherry Brandy
1 tsp Pineapple Juice
Shake.

PANDA BEAR (frozen)
In Blender:
1/2 cup of Ice
1 oz Amaretto
1/2 oz White Crème de Cacao
1/2 oz White Crème de Menthe
Scoop of Vanilla Ice Cream
2-3 dashes of vanilla extract
Blend until smooth.
If too thick add Milk or Cream.
If too thin add ice or Ice Cream.
Dribble Chocolate Syrup on the
inside of glass before pouring in
drink.

PANTHER
Fill glass with ice.
2 oz Tequila
2 oz Sour Mix
Shake.

PANTOMIME
Fill glass with ice.
1 1/2 oz Dry Vermouth
3 drops of Orgeat Syrup
Dash of Grenadine
1/2 an Egg White
Shake.
Strain into chilled glass.

PANTY BURNER
Fill glass with ice.
3/4 oz Amaretto
3/4 oz Hazelnut Liqueur
3/4 oz Coffee Liqueur
Shake. Strain into shot glass.

PANTY DROPPER
Fill glass with ice.
1 oz Vodka
1 oz Coffee Liqueur
1 oz Sloe Gin
Fill with Milk.
Shake.
Garnish with Cherry.

PARADISE
Fill glass with ice.
1 oz Gin
1 oz Apricot Brandy
1 oz Orange Juice
Stir.
Strain into chilled glass.

PARADISE PUNCH
Fill glass with ice.
1 oz Amber Rum
1 oz Dark Rum
1 oz Sour Mix
1 oz Cream of Coconut
1 oz Cream or Milk
Shake.

PARALYZER
Fill glass with ice.
1 1/2 oz Vodka or Tequila (or both)
1/2 oz Coffee Liqueur
2 oz Milk or Cream (optional)
Shake (if using Milk or Cream)
Fill with Cola or Root beer.

PARANOIA
Fill glass with ice.
1 oz Coconut Rum
1 oz Amaretto
Fill with equal parts Orange and
Pineapple Juice.
Shake.
Garnish with Pineapple or Orange.

PARFAIT
In Blender:
1/2 cup of Ice
2 oz Desired Liqueur
Scoop of Vanilla Ice Cream
Blend until smooth.
If too thick add Liqueur or Milk.
If too thin add ice or Ice Cream.

**PARIS MATCH aka
PARIS IS BURNING**
1 oz Cognac or Brandy
1 oz Black Raspberry Liqueur
Heat in microwave 10-15 seconds.

PARISIAN
Fill glass with ice.
1 oz Gin
1 oz Dry Vermouth
1 oz Crème de Cassis
Stir.
Strain into chilled glass.

PARISIAN BLONDE
Fill glass with ice.
1 oz Dark Rum
1 oz Triple Sec or Curacao
1 oz Cream
Shake.
Strain into chilled glass.

PARISIAN FRAPPE
Fill large stemmed glass (Red Wine
glass, Champagne saucer) with
crushed ice.
3/4 oz Dark Rum
3/4 oz Orange Liqueur
3/4 oz Cream

PARK AVENUE
Fill glass with ice.
1 1/2 oz Gin
1/2 oz Sweet Vermouth
1 oz Pineapple Juice
2-3 drops of Curacao (optional)
Stir.
Strain into chilled glass.

PARROT HEAD
Fill glass with ice.
1 1/2 oz Spiced Rum
1/2 oz Black Raspberry Liqueur
Fill with Pineapple Juice.
Shake.

O
P

PASSION MARTINI
Fill glass with ice.
3 1/2oz Vodka or Citrus Vodka
1/2oz Passion Fruit Liqueur
Dash of Cranberry Juice (optional)
Shake. Strain into chilled glass.
Dash of Champagne (optional)

PASSIONATE POINT
Fill glass with ice.
3/4 oz Amber Rum
3/4 oz Peach Schnapps
3/4 oz Orange Liqueur
2 oz Orange Juice
2 oz Cranberry Juice
Shake.
Strain into chilled glass.

PASSIONATE SCREW
Fill glass with ice.
1 oz Vodka or Citrus Vodka
1 oz Coconut Rum
1 oz Black Raspberry Liqueur
Dash of Grenadine
Fill with equal parts Orange and
Pineapple Juice.
Shake.
Garnish with Cherry and Orange or
Pineapple.

PEACH ALEXANDER (frozen)
In Blender:
1/2 cup of Ice
1 oz Peach Schnapps
1/2 oz White Crème de Cacao
1/2 fresh or canned Peach
1 1/2 oz Cream
or 1/2 scoop Vanilla Ice Cream
Blend until smooth.
If too thick add juice or Milk.
If too thin add ice or Ice Cream.

PEACH BLASTER
Fill glass with ice
2 oz Peach Schnapps
Fill with Cranberry Juice.
Stir.

PEACH BLOW FIZZ
Fill glass with ice.
2 oz Gin
1 oz Cream
1 tsp Sugar Syrup
or Powdered Sugar
1 oz Lemon Juice
1/4 fresh ripe Peach (mashed with
no skin or pit)
Shake.
Top with Soda Water.

PEACH BREEZE
Fill glass with ice.
1 oz Vodka or Peach Vodka
1 oz Peach Schnapps
Fill with equal parts Cranberry and
Grapefruit Juice.
Shake.

PEACH BUCK
Fill glass with ice.
1 1/2 oz Vodka or Peach Vodka
1/2 oz Peach Schnapps
1/2 oz Lemon Juice
Shake.
Top with Ginger Ale.
Garnish with peach.

PEACH BULLDOG
Fill glass with ice.
1 oz Vodka or Peach Vodka
1 oz Peach Schnapps
Fill with Cranberry Juice.
Stir.

PEACH COBBLER
1 oz Rum or Vanilla Rum
1 oz Peach Schnapps
Dash of Cinnamon Schnapps
Fill with hot Apple Cider.
Stir.
Top with Whipped Cream.

PEACH COLADA (frozen)
In Blender:
1/2 cup of Ice
2 oz Light Rum or Coconut Rum
2 tbsp Cream of Coconut
1 cup of fresh or canned Peaches
1 tbsp Vanilla Ice Cream (optional)
Blend until smooth.
If too thick add fruit or juice.
If too thin add ice or Ice Cream.
Garnish with Peach and Cherry.

PEACH DAIQUIRI (frozen)
In Blender:
1 cup of Ice
1 oz Rum
1 oz Peach Schnapps
1/2 cup of fresh or canned Peaches
Dash of Lime Juice
Blend until smooth.

PEACH FUZZ
Fill glass with ice.
2 oz Peach Schnapps
Fill with equal parts Milk and
Cranberry Juice.
Shake.
Serve or strain into chilled glass.

PEACH MARGARITA(frozen}
In Blender:1cup ice
1 1/2oz Tequila
1/4oz Triple Sec
1/4oz Peach Schnapps
1/4oz Lime Juice
1 skinned pitted fresh medium
peach,
or equivalent canned.
Blend until smooth.

PEACH MARTINI
Muddle 1/4 sweet fresh Peach in
mixing glass.
Fill glass with ice.
3 1/2 oz Peach Vodka or Vodka
1/2 oz Peach Schnapps
Dash Peach Nectar (optional)
Shake.
Strain into chilled glass.

PEACH MIMOSA
Fill glass with ice.
Fill 3/4 with Champagne.
Splash of Peach Schnapps
Fill with Orange Juice.
Garnish with Orange.

PEACH VELVET (frozen)
In Blender:
1/2 cup of Ice.
1 1/2 oz Peach Schnapps
1/2 oz White Crème de Cacao
1 scoop of Vanilla Ice Cream
1/2 fresh or canned Peach
Blend until smooth.

Metric Measurement Conversion Chart on page 14

PEACHES AND CREAM
Fill glass with ice.
1 oz Irish Cream
1 oz Peach Schnapps
Splash of Cream
Shake.
Top with Soda Water.

PEACHES AND CREAM MARTINI
Fill glass with ice.
2 oz Vodka or Peach Vodka
1/2 oz Peach Schnapps
1/2 oz Irish Cream
Shake and Strain into chilled glass.

PEANUT BUTTER AND JELLY
Fill glass with ice.
1 oz Hazelnut Liqueur
1 oz Black Raspberry Liqueur
Shake. Strain into shot glass.
Garnish with 3 or 4 peanuts.

PEANUT BUTTER AND JELLY
(frozen)
In Blender:
1/2 cup of Ice
1 oz Black Raspberry Liqueur
1 oz Hazelnut Liqueur
Dash of Irish Cream
3 tbsp Cocktail Peanuts
3 tbsp Grape Jelly
Scoop of Vanilla Ice Cream.
Blend until smooth.
If too thick add Milk.
If too thin add ice or Ice Cream.

PEAR MARTINI
Fill glass with ice.
3 1/2 oz Vodka or Pear Vodka
1/2 oz Pear Brandy
Dash Pear Nectar
Shake.
Strain into chilled glass.

PEARL DIVER
Fill glass with ice.
1 1/2 oz Vodka
1/2 oz Orange Juice
Strain into chilled glass.
Dash of Grenadine
Splash of Lemon-Lime Soda
Garnish with stemless Cherry.

PEARL DIVER 2
Fill glass with ice.
1 1/2oz Coconut Rum
1/4oz Blue Curacao
Dash Pineapple Juice.
Shake. Strain into chilled glass.
Garnish with Yogurt covered raisins

PEARL HARBOR
Fill glass with ice.
1 oz Vodka or Pineapple Vodka
1 oz Melon Liqueur
Fill with Pineapple Juice.
Shake.
Garnish with Cherry and Pineapple.

PEARL HARBOR (frozen)
In Blender:
1/2 cup of Ice
1 oz Vodka or Pineapple Vodka
1 oz Melon Liqueur
1/2 cup of fresh or canned
Pineapple
Scoop of Vanilla Ice Cream
Blend until smooth.
If too thick add fruit or juice.
If too thin add ice or Ice Cream.
Garnish with Cherry and Pineapple.

PEARL NECKLACE aka
BLOW JOB (floater)
1/2 oz Cream (bottom)
1/2 oz White Crème de Cacao
1/2 oz Vodka or Vanilla Vodka (top)
Contents should mix slightly.
To drink, place hands behind back
and pick up using only mouth.

PECKERHEAD
Fill glass with ice.
1 oz Yukon Jack or Southern
Comfort
1 oz Amaretto
1 oz Pineapple Juice
Shake.
Strain into chilled glass.

PEDRO COLLINS
Fill glass with ice.
2 oz Rum or Citrus Rum
Fill with Sour Mix.
Shake.
Splash of Soda Water
Garnish with Orange and Cherry.

PEGU CLUB
Fill glass with ice.
1 1/2 oz Gin
3/4 oz Orange Curacao
1 tsp Lime Juice
Dash of Bitters
Dash of Orange Bitters
Shake.
Strain into chilled glass.

PENDENNIS CLUB
Fill glass with ice.
1 1/2 oz Gin
3/4 oz Apricot Brandy
1/2 oz Lime Juice
1 tsp Sugar Syrup
3 dashes of Peychaud's Bitters
Shake.
Strain into chilled glass.

PENSACOLA (frozen)
In Blender:
1 cup of Ice
1 1/2 oz Rum or Mango Rum
1/2 oz Guava Nectar
1/2 oz Orange Juice
1/2 oz Lemon Juice
Blend until smooth.
If too thick add juice.
If too thin add ice.

PEPPER MARTINI
Fill glass with ice.
3 1/2 oz Peppered Vodka
1/2 oz Dry Vermouth
Stir.
Strain into chilled glass or pour
contents (with ice) into short glass.
Garnish with a Jalapeno Pepper.

PEPPERMINT KISS aka
**SNUGGLER, COCOANAPPS,
ADULT HOT CHOCOLATE**
2 oz Peppermint Schnapps
Fill with Hot Chocolate.
Top with Whipped Cream.
Sprinkle with Shaved
Chocolate or Sprinkles.

PEPPERMINT PATTIE
Fill glass with ice.
1 oz White Crème de Cacao or
Dark Crème de Cacao
1 oz White Crème de Menthe
Stir.

P

Metric Measurement Conversion Chart on page 14

PEPPERMINT PATTY
Fill glass with ice.
1 oz Peppermint Schnapps
1 oz Dark Crème de Cacao
2 oz Cream
Shake.

PEPPERMINT STINGER
Fill glass with ice.
1 1/2 oz Brandy
1/2 oz Peppermint Schnapps
Stir.
Serve or strain into chilled glass.

PERFECT MANHATTAN
Fill glass with ice.
2 oz Whiskey
1/4 oz Dry Vermouth
1/4 oz Sweet Vermouth
Stir.
Strain into chilled glass or pour
contents (with ice) into short glass.
Garnish with Cherry or Lemon
Twist.

PERNOD COCKTAIL
Fill glass with ice.
2 oz Pernod
3 dashes of Bitters
3 dashes of Sugar Syrup
1/2 oz Water
Stir.
Serve or strain into chilled glass.

PERNOD FLIP
Fill glass with ice.
1 oz Pernod
1/2 oz Orange Liqueur or Triple Sec
1/2 oz Lemon Juice
1 1/2 tsp Sugar Syrup
1 Egg
Shake.

PERNOD FLIP (frozen)
In Blender:
1 cup of Ice
1 1/2 oz Pernod
1 oz Heavy Cream
1/2 oz Sugar Syrup
or Orgeat Syrup
1 Egg
Blend until smooth.
Garnish with Nutmeg.

PERNOD FRAPPE
Fill glass with ice.
1 1/2 oz Pernod
1/2 oz Anisette
3 dashes of Bitters
Shake.
Strain into chilled glass.

PERSUADER
Fill glass with ice.
1 oz Brandy
1 oz Amaretto
Fill glass with Orange Juice.
Shake.

PETRIFIER
Fill glass with ice.
2 oz Vodka
2 oz Gin
2 oz Cognac
2 oz Triple Sec
3 dashes of Bitters
Dash of Grenadine
Shake.
Strain into chilled glass.
Fill with Ginger Ale.
Garnish with Orange and Cherry.

PEZ
Fill glass with ice.
1 oz Spiced Rum
1 oz Black Raspberry Liqueur
1 oz Sour Mix
Shake. Strain into shot glass.

PHOEBE SNOW
Fill glass with ice.
1 1/2 oz Cognac or Brandy
1 1/2 oz Dubonnet Rouge
2 dashes of Bitters
Stir.
Serve or strain into chilled glass.
Garnish with Lemon Twist.

PICKLED BRAIN (floater)
3/4 oz Irish Cream (bottom)
3/4 oz Vodka
1/2 oz Green Crème de Menthe
(top)

PICON FIZZ
Fill glass with ice.
1 1/2 oz Amer Picon
1/4 oz Grenadine
3 oz Soda Water
Float 1/2 oz Cognac or Brandy on top.

PICON ORANGE
Fill glass with ice.
2 oz Amer Picon
2 oz Orange Juice
Shake.
Fill with Soda Water.
Garnish with Orange.

PICON SOUR
Fill glass with ice.
1 1/2 oz Amer Picon
1 oz Sour Mix or Lemon Juice
1/2 tsp Powdered Sugar
or Sugar Syrup
Shake.
Strain into chilled glass.

PIERRE COLLINS
Fill glass with ice.
2 oz Cognac or Brandy
Fill with Sour Mix
Shake.
Splash with Lemon-Lime Soda.
Garnish with Orange and Cherry.

PILE DRIVER
Fill glass with ice.
2 oz Vodka
Fill with prune juice.
Stir.

PILOT BOAT
Fill glass with ice.
1 1/2 oz Dark Rum
1 oz Banana Liqueur
1 1/2 oz Sour Mix
Dash of Lime Juice
Shake.
Strain into chilled glass.

PIMLICO SPECIAL
Fill glass with ice.
1 1/2 oz Brandy
1/2 oz Amaretto
1/2 oz White Crème de Cacao
Shake.
Strain into chilled glass.

PIMM'S CUP
Fill glass with ice.
2 oz Pimm's Cup No. 1
Dash Sour Mix (optional)
Fill w/Ginger Ale or Lemon-Lime Soda.
Stir.
Garnish with Lemon and/or Cucumber.

PIÑA
Fill glass with ice.
1 1/2 oz Tequila
3 oz Pineapple Juice
1 oz Lime Juice
1 tsp Honey or Sugar Syrup
Shake.
Garnish with Lime.

PIÑA COLADA (frozen)
In Blender:
1/2 cup of Ice
2 oz Light Rum
2 tbsp Cream of Coconut
1/2 cup fresh or canned Pineapple
1 tbsp Vanilla Ice Cream (optional)
Blend until smooth.
If too thick add fruit or juice.
If too thin add ice or Ice Cream.
Garnish with Pineapple and Cherry.

PIÑATA
Fill glass with ice.
1 1/2 oz Tequila
1 oz Banana Liqueur
1 oz Lime Juice
Shake.
Serve or strain into chilled glass.

PINEAPPLE BOMB
Fill glass with ice.
1 1/2 oz Rum or Pineapple Rum
1/2 oz Amaretto
Fill with Pineapple Juice.
Shake.

PINEAPPLE BOMBER
Fill glass with ice.
1 oz Spiced Rum
1 oz Southern Comfort
1 oz Amaretto
Fill with Pineapple Juice.
Shake.

PINEAPPLE BOMBER 2
Fill glass with ice.
1 oz Yukon Jack
1 oz Amaretto
Fill with Pineapple Juice.
Shake.

PINEAPPLE COSMOPOLITAN
Fill glass with ice.
3 1/2 oz Citrus Vodka or Pineapple Vodka
Dash Triple Sec
Dash Pineapple Juice
Dash Lime Juice
Shake. Strain into chilled glass.

PINEAPPLE DAIQUIRI (frozen)
In Blender:
1/2 cup of Ice
1 2 oz Rum or Pineapple Rum
1/2 oz Lime Juice
1/2 cup of fresh or canned Pineapple
Blend until Smooth.
If too thick add juice.
If too thin add ice.

PINEAPPLE MARGARITA (frozen)
In Blender:
1 cup of ice
2 oz Tequila
1/2 oz Lime Juice
3/4 cup Fresh or canned Pineapple (with juice)
Blend until smooth. If too thick add juice.
If too thin add ice.
Garnish with Pineapple.

PINEAPPLE MARTINI
Fill glass with ice.
2 tbsp Crushed Pineapple
3 oz Vodka or Gin
Dash Simple Syrup or pinch Sugar
Shake.
Strain into chilled glass.

PINEAPPLE PASSION
Fill glass with ice.
1 1/2 oz Rum or Pineapple Rum
1 oz Orange Curacao
2 oz Pineapple Juice
1 oz Passion Fruit Juice
Shake.

PINK ALMOND
Fill glass with ice.
1 oz Whiskey
1/2 oz Crème de Nouyax
1/2 oz Amaretto
1/2 oz Kirschwasser
1/2 oz Lemon Juice
Shake.
Garnish with Lemon.

PINK CADDIE
Fill glass with ice.
1 1/2 oz Tequila
1/2 oz Triple Sec
Fill with equal parts Sour Mix and Cranberry Juice.
Shake.

PINK FLOYD (frozen)
In Blender:
1/2 cup of Ice
1 oz Vodka
1 oz Sloe Gin
1/2 cup fresh or canned Pineapple
Blend until smooth.
Top with Soda Water.
Garnish with Pineapple.

PINK GATOR
Fill glass with ice.
1 oz Light Rum
1 oz Amber Rum
1/2 oz Grenadine
Dash of Sour Mix
Fill with equal parts Orange and Pineapple Juice.

PINK GIN
Fill glass with ice.
3 1/2 oz Gin
2 dashes of Bitters
Stir.
Serve or strain into chilled glass.

PINK HOTEL
Fill glass with ice.
1 oz Vodka
1/2 oz Crème de Noyaux
Shake. Strain into short glass.
Dash of Ginger Ale
Fill with Beer.

P

Metric Measurement Conversion Chart on page 14

PINK LADY
Fill glass with ice.
1 1/2 oz Gin
1 1/2 oz Cream
1 tsp Grenadine
Shake.
Strain into chilled glass.

PINK LEMONADE
Fill glass with ice.
1 1/2 oz Vodka or Rum
1 oz Cranberry Juice
2 oz Sour Mix
Shake.
Fill with Lemon-Lime Soda.
Garnish with Lemon.

PINK LEMONADE 2
Fill glass with ice.
2 oz Citrus Vodka
Dash of Grenadine
Shake.
Strain into chilled glass.

PINK LEMONADE MARTINI
3 1/2 oz Citrus Vodka
1/2 oz Lemoncello
Dash Sour Mix
Dash Cranberry Juice
Shake.
Strain into chilled glass.

PINK MISSILE
Fill glass with ice.
1 1/2 oz Vodka or Grapefruit Vodka
1/2 oz Black Raspberry Liqueur
Dash of Grenadine
Dash of Cranberry Juice
Fill with equal parts Grapefruit
Juice and Ginger Ale.
Stir.

PINK PANTHER
Fill glass with ice.
3/4 oz Gin
3/4 oz Dry Vermouth
1/2 oz Crème de Cassis
1/2 oz Orange Juice
1/2 oz Egg White
Shake.
Strain into chilled glass.

PINK PANTY PULLDOWN
Fill glass with ice.
2 oz Grain Alcohol
Fill with Pink Lemonade
Garnish with Lemon.

PINK PARADISE
Fill glass with ice.
1 oz Coconut Rum
1 oz Amaretto
2 oz Pineapple Juice
Fill with Cranberry Juice.
Stir.

PINK PUSSYCAT
Fill glass with ice.
1 1/2 oz Gin or Vodka
1/2 oz Grenadine
Fill with Pineapple or Grapefruit Juice.
Shake.

PINK ROSE
Fill glass with ice.
1 1/2 oz Gin
1 tsp Lemon Juice
1 tsp Heavy Cream
1 Egg White
3 dashes of Grenadine
Shake.
Strain into chilled glass.

PINK SLIP
1 oz Coconut Rum
1 oz Cranberry juice
Fill with Champagne.

PINK SNAPPER
Fill glass with ice.
1 1/2oz Whiskey
1/2oz Peach Schnapps
Dash Cranberry Juice.
Shake. Strain into shot glass.

PINK SQUIRREL
Fill glass with ice.
1 oz Crème de Nouyax.
1 oz White Crème de Cacao
1 oz Cream or Milk
Shake.
Strain into chilled glass.

PINK VERANDA
Fill glass with ice.
1 oz Amber Rum
1/2 oz Dark Rum
1 1/2 oz Cranberry Juice
1/2 oz Lime Juice
1 tsp Sugar
1/2 Egg White
Shake.

PINK WHISKERS
Fill glass with ice.
1 oz Apricot Brandy
1/2 oz Dry Vermouth
1 oz Orange Juice
1 tsp Grenadine
3 dashes of White Crème de
Menthe
Shake.
Float 1 oz Port on top.

PISCO PUNCH
Fill glass with ice.
3 oz Brandy
1 tsp Lime Juice
1 tsp Pineapple Juice
2 oz cold Water (optional)
Stir.
Garnish with Pineapple.

PISCO SOUR
Fill glass with ice.
2 oz Brandy
1 oz Sour Mix
1/2 Egg White
Dash of Lime Juice
Shake.
Strain into chilled glass.
2-3 dashes of Bitters

PITBULL ON CRACK
Fill glass with ice.
3/4 oz Tequila
3/4 oz Jägermeister
3/4 oz 100-proof Peppermint
Schnapps
Shake. Strain into shot glass.

PIXIE STICK
Fill glass with ice.
1 oz Gin or Vodka
1 oz Melon Liqueur
Fill with Lemon-Lime Soda.

PIXIE STICK 2
Fill glass with ice.
1 oz Southern Comfort
1 oz Blackberry Brandy
Fill with Lemonade.
Shake.

LAID
Fill glass with ice.
1 1/2 oz Gin
1/2 oz Peach Schnapps
Fill with Ginger Ale.
Stir.

LANTER'S PUNCH
Fill glass with ice.
1 1/2 oz Light Rum
Dash of Grenadine
Fill with equal parts Sour Mix and
either Orange or Pineapple Juice.
Shake.
Top with 1/2 oz Dark Rum.
Garnish with Orange and Cherry.

LANTER'S PUNCH 2
Fill glass with ice.
1 oz Dark Rum
1 oz Amber Rum
Dash of Brandy
Dash of Sweet Vermouth
Dash of Bitters
1 tsp of Cherry Juice
or Grenadine
Fill with equal parts Sour Mix and
Pineapple Juice.
Shake.

PLATINUM BLOND
Fill glass with ice.
1 1/2 oz Rum or Orange Rum
3/4 oz Orange Liqueur or Curacao
or Triple Sec
Fill with Milk or Cream.
Shake.

PLAYBOY COOLER
Fill glass with ice.
1 oz Rum
1 oz Coffee Liqueur
Dash of Lime Juice
Fill with Pineapple Juice.
Shake.
Dash of Cola.

PLAZA
Fill glass with ice.
3/4 oz Gin
3/4 oz Dry Vermouth
3/4 oz Sweet Vermouth
1 tbsp Pineapple Juice (optional)
Shake.
Strain into chilled glass.

PLEASURE DOME (floater)
3/4 oz Brandy (bottom)
3/4 oz White Crème de Cacao
3/4 oz Benedictine (top)

**POINSETTIA aka
NANTUCKET RED**
Fill glass 3/4 with ice.
Fill 3/4 with Champagne.
Fill with Cranberry Juice.
Garnish with Lime.

POINT (floater)
3/4 oz Drambuie (bottom)
3/4 oz White Crème de Menthe
3/4 oz Irish Cream (top)

POKER
Fill glass with ice.
1 1/2 oz Amber Rum
1 oz Dry Vermouth
Stir.
Strain into chilled glass.
Garnish with Orange Twist.

POLISH BUTTERFLY
1 oz Grain Alcohol
1 oz Blue Curacao
Dash of Grenadine

POLLYANNA
Fill glass with ice.
3 1/2 oz Gin
1/4 oz Sweet Vermouth
1/4 oz Grenadine
Shake.
Strain into chilled glass.

POLLY'S SPECIAL
Fill glass with ice.
1 1/2 oz Scotch
1/2 oz Triple Sec
1/2 oz Grapefruit Juice
Shake.

POLO
Fill glass with ice.
3 1/2 oz Gin or Orange Rum
1 tbsp Orange Juice
1 tbsp Lemon or Grapefruit Juice
Stir.
Serve or strain into chilled glass.

POLYNESIAN
Fill glass with ice.
1 1/2 oz Vodka or Cherry Vodka
3/4 oz Cherry Brandy
3/4 oz Lime Juice
Shake.
Rub rim of second glass with Lime
and dip rim in Powdered Sugar.
Strain into second glass.

POMEGRANATE MARTINI
Fill glass with ice
3 1/2 oz Vodka or Citrus Vodka
1/2 tsp sugar
Dash Triple Sec (optional)
Dash Lime Juice (optional)
1 oz Pomegranate Juice
Shake. Strain into chilled glass.

POND SCUM
Fill glass with ice.
2 oz Vodka or Currant Vodka
Fill with Soda Water.
Float 1/4oz Irish Cream on top.

POOP DECK
Fill glass with ice.
1 oz Blackberry Brandy
1/2 oz Brandy
1/2 oz Port
Shake.
Strain into chilled glass.

PONTIAC
Fill glass with ice.
2 oz Amaretto
Fill with Soda Water.

POP-SICLE
Fill glass with ice.
2 oz Amaretto
Fill with equal parts Cream
and Orange Juice.
Shake.

POP-SICLE 2
Fill glass with ice.
1 1/2 oz Southern Comfort
1/2 oz Amaretto
Dash of Grenadine
1 oz Orange Juice
Fill with Lemon-Lime Soda.

P

Metric Measurement Conversion Chart on page 14

POP-SICLE 3
Fill glass with ice.
1 1/2 oz Vodka or Orange Vodka
1/2 oz Triple Sec
Dash of Milk or Cream
Fill with Orange Juice.
Shake.

POPPER
In shot glass:
1 oz Desired Liqueur or Liquor
1 oz Ginger Ale
or Lemon-Lime Soda
Cover glass with napkin and hand,
then slam on bar top.
Drink while foaming.

PORCH CLIMBER
Fill glass with ice.
1 oz Rum or Cherry Vodka
1/2 oz Apricot Brandy
1/2 oz Cherry Brandy
Fill with Sour Mix.
Shake.

PORT IN A STORM
Fill glass with ice.
1 oz Brandy or Cognac
2 oz Port
Fill with Red Wine
Strain.
Garnish with mint sprig.

PORT AND STARBOARD (floater)
1 oz Green Crème de Menthe
(bottom)
Grenadine (top)

PORT ANTONIO
Fill glass with ice.
1 oz Amber Rum
1/2 oz Dark Rum
1/2 oz Lime Juice
1/2 oz Tia Maria
1 tsp Falernum
Shake.
Garnish with Lime.

PORT PELICAN
Fill glass with ice.
1 oz Rum or Banana Vodka
1/2 oz Banana Liqueur
1/2 oz Galliano
Fill with Orange Juice.
Shake.

PORT SANGAREE
Fill glass with ice.
2 oz Port
1/2 tsp Powdered Sugar
1 oz Water
Fill with Soda Water.
Stir.
Float 1 tsp Brandy on top (optional).

POUSSE CAFÉ
A glass of liqueurs arranged
in layers.

POUSSE CAFÉ (floater)
Layer ingredients in order and in
equal amounts.
1/4 oz Grenadine (bottom)
1/4 oz Coffee Liqueur
1/4 oz White Crème de Cacao
1/4 oz Blue Curacao
1/4 oz Galliano
1/4 oz Green Chartreuse
1/4 oz Brandy (top)

PRADO
Fill glass with ice.
1 1/2 oz Tequila
1/2 oz Maraschino Liqueur
3/4 oz Lime Juice
1/2 Egg White
1 tsp Grenadine
Shake.
Garnish with Cherry.

PRAIRIE CHICKEN
In shot glass:
1 oz Tequila
1 raw egg yolk
2-10 dashes of Tabasco.

PRAIRIE FIRE aka
BURNING BUSH
2 oz Tequila
Add Tabasco Sauce until pink.

PRAIRIE OYSTER
1 oz Brandy or Whiskey
1 unbroken Egg Yolk
Dash of Wine Vinegar
Dash of Tabasco Sauce
1 tsp Worcestershire Sauce
2 oz Tomato Juice
Pinch of Salt
Stir gently.

PREAKNESS
Fill glass with ice.
1 1/2 oz Whiskey
1/4 oz Benedictine
1/4 oz Sweet Vermouth
Dash of Bitters
Stir.
Strain into chilled glass.
Garnish with Lemon Twist.

PRESIDENTE
Fill glass with ice.
1 1/2 oz Rum
1/2 oz Dry Vermouth
1/2 oz Curacao
Dash of Grenadine
Shake.
Serve or strain into chilled glass.
Garnish with Lemon Twist.

PRESS
Fill glass with ice.
2 oz Whiskey
Fill with equal parts Ginger Ale and
Soda Water.

PRIMAL SCREAM
Fill glass with ice.
1 oz Tequila or Grain Alcohol
1 oz Coffee Liqueur
Fill with Soda Water.

PRINCE EDWARD
Fill glass with ice.
1 1/2 oz Scotch
1/2 oz Lillet Blanc
1/4 oz Drambuie
Shake.
Serve or strain into chilled glass.
Garnish with Orange.

PRINCE IGOR aka
HIGH ROLLER
Fill glass with ice.
1 1/2 oz Vodka or Orange Vodka
3/4 oz Orange Liqueur
Dash of Grenadine
Fill with Orange Juice.
Shake.
Garnish with Orange and Cherry.

Metric Measurement Conversion Chart on page 14

PRINCE OF WALES
Fill glass with ice.
1 oz Brandy
1 oz Madeira
or any sweet Red Wine
1/4 oz Curacao
3 dashes of Bitters
Shake.
Strain into wine glass.
Fill with Champagne.
Garnish with Orange.

PRINCE'S SMILE
Fill glass with ice.
3 1/2 oz Gin
1/2 oz Apricot Brandy
1/2 oz Apple Brandy
1/4 oz Lemon Juice
Shake.
Strain into chilled glass.

PRINCESS MARY'S PRIDE
Fill glass with ice.
1 1/2 oz Apple Brandy
3/4 oz Dubonnet Rouge
1/2 oz Dry Vermouth
Shake.
Strain into chilled glass.

PRINCETON
Fill glass with ice.
1 1/2 oz Gin
3/4 oz Port
3 dashes of Orange Bitters
Shake.
Strain into chilled glass.
Garnish with Lemon Twist.

PRISON BITCH
Fill glass with ice.
1 1/2 oz Vodka or Citrus Vodka
1/2 oz Triple Sec
1/2 oz Amaretto
Fill with equal parts Orange
and Cranberry Juice.
Shake.

PROFESSOR AND MARYANN
Fill glass with ice.
1 1/2 oz Vodka
1/2 oz Apricot Brandy
Dash of Lime Juice
Fill with Soda Water.
Stir.
Garnish with Lime.

PROVINCETOWN
Fill glass with ice.
2 oz Vodka or Cranberry,
     or Grapefruit Vodka
2 oz Cranberry Juice
2 oz Grapefruit Juice
Strain into chilled glass.
Fill with Soda Water.
Garnish with Lemon wedge.

PTERODACTYL
Fill glass with ice.
1/2 oz Vodka or Citrus Vodka
1/2 oz Rum or Citrus Rum
1/2 oz Triple Sec
1/2 oz Amaretto
1/2 oz Southern Comfort
Dash of Grenadine
Fill with Orange Juice.
Shake.
Garnish with Orange.

PUCCINI
Fill glass with ice.
1 1/2 oz Vodka
1 oz Melon Liqueur
1/2 oz Tuaca
Fill with Orange Juice.
Shake.

PUERTO RICAN SCREW
Fill glass with ice.
2 oz Rum or Orange Rum
Fill with Orange Juice.

PUFF
Fill glass with ice.
2 oz Desired Liquor or Liqueur
2 oz Milk
Fill with Soda Water.

PUMPKIN PIE (floater)
1/2 oz Coffee Liqueur (bottom)
1/2 oz Irish Cream
1/2 oz Cinnamon Schnapps (top)

PUNT E MES NEGRONI
Fill glass with ice.
1/2 oz Gin or Vodka
1/2 oz Punt e Mes
1/2 oz Sweet Vermouth
Shake.
Strain into chilled glass.
Garnish with Orange Twist.

PURPLE ALASKAN
Fill glass with ice.
1/2 oz Bourbon
1/2 oz Southern Comfort
1/2 oz Amaretto
1/2 oz Black Raspberry Liqueur
1/2 oz Orange Juice
Shake. Strain into shot glass.

PURPLE ARMADILLO
Fill glass with ice.
1 1/2 oz Rum or Citrus Rum
1/2 oz Blue Curacao
Fill with equal parts Sour Mix and
Cranberry Juice.
Shake.
Top with Lemon-Lime Soda.

PURPLE BUNNY
Fill glass with ice.
1 oz Cherry Brandy
1/2 oz White Crème de Cacao
1 oz Cream or Milk
Shake.
Strain into chilled glass.

PURPLE DREAM
Fill glass with ice.
1 oz Black Raspberry Liqueur
1 oz White Crème de Cacao
Fill with Milk or Cream.
Shake.

PURPLE ELASTIC THUNDER
Fill glass with ice.
1/2 oz Vodka or Raspberry Vodka
1/2 oz Whiskey
1/2 oz Amaretto
1/2 oz Southern Comfort
1/2 oz Black Raspberry Liqueur
Dash Cranberry Juice
Dash Pineapple Juice
Shake.
Strain into chilled glass.

P

Metric Measurement Conversion Chart on page 14

PURPLE FLIRT
Fill glass with ice.
1 1/2 oz Amber Rum
1/2 oz Blue Curacao
Dash of Pineapple Juice
Dash of Cranberry Juice
Dash of Sour Mix
Dash of Grenadine
Shake.
Strain into chilled glass.

PURPLE HAZE
Fill glass with ice.
1 1/2 oz Vodka or Raspberry Vodka
1/2 oz Black Raspberry Liqueur
Fill with equal parts Sour Mix,
Cranberry, and Pineapple Juice.
Shake.

PURPLE HAZE 2
Fill glass with ice.
1 oz Vodka or Raspberry Vodka
1 oz Black Raspberry Liqueur
1 oz Cranberry Juice
Stir.
Strain into chilled glass.

PURPLE HEATHER
Fill glass with ice.
1 1/2 oz Scotch
1/2 oz Crème de Cassis
Fill with Soda Water.

PURPLE HELMETED WARRIOR
Fill glass with ice.
1/2 oz Gin
1/2 oz Southern Comfort
1/2 oz Peach Schnapps
1/2 oz Blue Curacao
Dash of Grenadine
Dash of Lime Juice
Shake. Strain into shot glass.

PURPLE HOOTER or
PURPLE KAMIKAZE,
RASPBERRY GIMLET
Fill glass with ice.
2 oz Vodka or Citrus Vodka
1/2 oz Black Raspberry Liqueur
1/2 oz Lime Juice
Stir.
Strain into shot glass.

PURPLE JESUS
1 oz Canadian Whiskey
1 oz Blackberry Brandy
1 oz Peppermint Schnapps
Dash of Tabasco
Stir.

PURPLE MARGARITA
Fill glass with ice.
1 oz Tequila
1/2 oz Sloe Gin
1/2 oz Blue Curacao
Dash of Lime Juice
3 oz Sour Mix
Shake.

PURPLE MARTINI
Fill glass with ice.
3 1/2 oz Vodka or Raspberry Vodka
Dash Black Raspberry Liqueur
Dash Blue Curacao
Dash Sloe Gin
Shake.
Strain into chilled glass.

PURPLE MATADOR
Fill glass with ice.
1 1/2 oz Amaretto
1 oz Black Raspberry Liqueur
1/2 oz Pineapple Juice
Shake.
Strain into chilled glass.

PURPLE NASTY
1/2 oz Crème de Cassis
Fill with equal parts Hard Cider and Ale.

PURPLE NIPPLE (floater)
1/2 oz Black Raspberry Liqueur
(bottom)
1/2 oz Irish Cream (top)

PURPLE PASSION aka
TRANSFUSION
Fill glass with ice.
2 oz Vodka
Fill with equal parts Grape Juice
and Ginger Ale or Soda Water.

PURPLE PASSION 2
Fill glass with ice.
2 oz Vodka
Fill with Grape Cool Aid.

PURPLE RAIN
Fill glass with ice.
1/2 oz Vodka
1/2 oz Gin
1/2 oz Rum
1/2 oz Tequila
1/2 oz Triple Sec
Fill with Sour Mix.
Shake.
Top with Black Raspberry Liqueur.
Garnish with Lime.

PURPLE RAIN 2
Fill glass with ice.
1 1/2 oz Vodka
1/2 oz Blue Curacao
1 oz Cranberry Juice
Stir.
Strain into chilled glass.

PURPLE RUSSIAN
Fill glass with ice.
1 1/2 oz Vodka or Raspberry Vodka
1/2 oz Black Raspberry Liqueur
Stir.

PURPLE THUNDER
Fill glass with ice.
1 oz Light Rum
1 oz Amber Rum
1/2 oz Blue Curacao
Fill with equal parts Grape and
Cranberry Juice.
Shake.
Strain into chilled glass.
Fill with Soda Water.

PUSSER'S PAINKILLER
Shake without ice.
2 oz Pusser's Rum
1 oz Cream of Coconut
1 oz Orange Juice
4 oz Pineapple Juice
Pour over ice.
Garnish with a pinch of
Cinnamon and Nutmeg.

PUSSY GALORE (floater)
1/2 oz Banana Liqueur
(bottom)
1 oz White Crème de Cacao
1/2 oz Irish Cream (top)

PUSSY SUPREME
Fill glass with ice.
1 oz Irish Cream
1 oz Orange Liqueur
2 oz Cream
Shake.
Strain into chilled glass.

QUAALUDE
Fill glass with ice.
1/2 oz Vodka or Vanilla Vodka
1/2 oz Coffee Liqueur
1/2 oz Hazelnut Liqueur
1/2 oz Dark Crème de Cacao
1/2 oz Orange Liqueur
Fill with Milk or Cream.
Shake.

QUAALUDE 2
Fill glass with ice.
1 oz Southern Comfort
1 oz Bourbon
Splash of Orange Juice
Fill with Pineapple Juice.
Shake

QUAKER CITY COOLER
Fill glass with ice.
1 oz Vodka or Vanilla Vodka
3 oz Chablis
1/2 oz Sugar Syrup
1/2 oz Lemon Juice
3 dashes of Vanilla Extract
Stir.
Top with 1/4 oz Grenadine.

QUARTER DECK
Fill glass with ice.
1 1/2 oz Rum
1/3 oz Sherry
1 tsp Lime Juice
Shake.
Serve or strain into chilled glass.

QUEBEC
Fill glass with ice.
1 1/2 oz Canadian Whiskey
1/2 oz Amer Picon
1/2 oz Maraschino Liqueur
1/2 oz Dry Vermouth
Shake.
Strain into chilled glass.

QUEEN
Muddle 1/2 cup Pineapple in glass.
Fill glass with ice.
1 1/2 oz Gin
1/2 oz Dry Vermouth
Stir.
Strain into chilled glass.

QUEEN ELIZABETH
Fill glass with ice.
1 oz Gin
1/2 oz Orange Liqueur
1/2 oz Lemon Juice
1 tsp Pernod
Stir.
Strain into chilled glass.

QUEEN ELIZABETH WINE
Fill glass with ice.
1 1/2 oz Benedictine
3/4 oz Dry Vermouth
3/4 oz Lemon Juice
Shake.
Strain into chilled glass.

QUELLE VIE
Fill glass with ice.
1 1/2 oz Brandy
3/4 oz Kummel
Stir.
Strain into chilled glass.

QUICK F (floater)
3/4 oz Coffee Liqueur (bottom)
3/4 oz Melon Liqueur
3/4 oz Irish Cream (top)

QUICKIE
Fill glass with ice.
1 oz Bourbon
1 oz Rum or Orange Rum
1/4 oz Triple Sec
Stir.
Strain into chilled glass.

QUIET NUN
Fill glass with ice.
1 oz Benedictine
1 oz Tripe Sec
1 oz Cream or Milk
Shake.
Strain into chilled glass.

R AND V
Fill glass with ice.
2 oz Vodka or Citrus Vodka
Fill with Energy Drink.

R. ROGERS
Fill glass with ice.
Fill with Cola.
Dash of Grenadine
Garnish with Cherry.

R. ROYCE
Fill glass with ice.
1 1/2 oz Gin
1/2 oz Dry Vermouth
1/2 oz Sweet Vermouth
Stir.
Strain into chilled glass.

RACQUET CLUB
Fill glass with ice.
1 1/2 oz Gin
3/4 oz Dry Vermouth
Dash of Bitters
Stir.
Strain into chilled glass.

RADIOACTIVE ICED TEA
Fill glass with ice.
1/2 oz Vodka
1/2 oz Gin
1/2 oz Rum
1/2 oz Coconut Rum
1/2 oz Tequila
1/2 oz Triple Sec
1/2 oz Melon Liqueur
1 oz Sour Mix
Top with Cola.
Garnish with Lemon.

P

Q

R

RAGNAR
Fill glass with ice.
2 oz Citrus Vodka or Currant Vodka
Squeeze in tsp fresh Lime Juice.
Fill with Lemonade or Lemon-Lime Soda.
Stir.

RAIN MAN
Fill glass with ice.
1 oz 151-Proof Rum
1 oz Melon Liqueur
Fill with Orange Juice.
Shake.

RAINBOW (floater)
1/2 oz Dark Crème de Cacao
(bottom)
1/2 oz Crème de Violette
1/2 oz Yellow Chartreuse
1/2 oz Maraschino Liqueur
1/2 oz Benedictine
1/2 oz Green Chartreuse
1/2 oz Cognac (top)

RAINBOW 2 (floater)
1/2 oz Crème de Nouyax
(bottom)
1/2 oz Melon Liqueur
1/2 oz White Crème de Cacao (top)

RAINFOREST (frozen)
In Blender:
1 cup of Ice
1 oz Dark Rum
1 oz Melon Liqueur
1 tbsp Cream of Coconut
1 oz Passion Fruit Liqueur
Blend until smooth.

RAMOS FIZZ
Fill glass with ice.
1 1/2 oz Gin or Orange Gin
1/2 oz Cream
1 1/2 oz Sour Mix
1 Egg White
1 tsp Triple Sec or Curacao
or Orange Juice
Shake.
Strain into chilled glass.
Fill with Soda Water.

RANCH VALENCIA RUM PUNCH
Fill glass with ice.
1 oz Light Rum
1 oz Amber Rum
2 dashes of Bitters
Fill with equal parts Orange and
Pineapple Juice.
Shake.
Strain into glass.
Float 1/2 oz Dark Rum on top.
Garnish with Orange and/or
Pineapple.

RASBARETTA (frozen)
In Blender:
1/2 cup of Ice
1 oz Raspberry Liqueur
1 oz Amaretto
Scoop of Vanilla Ice Cream
Blend until smooth.
If too thick add liqueur or Milk. If
too thin add ice or Ice Cream.

RASPBERRY BELLINI
In Blender: 1/2 cup fresh or frozen
Raspberries.
Blend.
Pour the pureed berries into glass.
Fill with Champagne.

RASPBERRY BERET
Fill glass with ice.
1 oz Vodka or Raspberry Vodka
1 oz Black Raspberry Liqueur
Dash of Milk or Cream
Shake.
Strain into shot glass.
Top with Soda Water.

RASPBERRY CHEESECAKE
(frozen)
In Blender:
1/2 cup ice
1 1/2 oz Vanilla Vodka or Vodka
1/2 oz Black Raspberry Liqueur
2 tsp Raspberry Jam
2 Tblsp Cream Cheese
Blend until smooth.
Garnish with Graham Cracker.

RASPBERRY COLADA (frozen)
In Blender:
1/2 cup of Ice
1 oz Rum or Raspberry Rum
1 oz Black Raspberry Liqueur
2 tbsp Cream of Coconut
1/2 cup fresh or frozen Raspberries
1 tbsp Vanilla Ice Cream (optional)
Blend until smooth.

RASPBERRY COSMOPOLITAN
Fill glass with ice.
3 1/2 oz Raspberry Vodka
Dash Black Raspberry Liqueur
Dash of Lime Juice
Dash of Cranberry Juice
Shake. Strain into chilled glass.
Garnish with Lime.

RASPBERRY DAIQUIRI
(frozen)
In Blender:
1 cup of Ice
1 1/2 oz Rum or Raspberry Rum
3/4 oz Raspberry Liqueur
Dash of Lime Juice
1/2 cup of fresh or frozen
Raspberries
or 2 tbsp Raspberry Jam
Blend until smooth.
If too thick add berries.
If too thin add ice.
Garnish with Lime.

RASPBERRY GIMLET aka
PURPLE HOOTER, PURPLE
KAMIKAZE
Fill glass with ice.
2 oz Vodka or Raspberry Vodka
1/2 oz Black Raspberry Liqueur
1/2 oz Lime Juice
Stir.
Strain into shot glass.

RASPBERRY KISS
Fill glass with ice.
1 oz Black Raspberry Liqueur
1 oz Dark Crème de Cacao
1 oz Milk or Cream
Shake.
Strain into chilled glass.

RASPBERRY LIME RICKEY (adult)
Fill glass with ice.
1 1/2 oz Vodka or Gin or Rum or
Whiskey
1/2 oz Black Raspberry Liqueur
Dash of Lime Juice
Fill with Soda Water
Garnish with Lime.

Metric Measurement Conversion Chart on page 14

RASPBERRY MARGARITA
(frozen)
In Blender:
1/2 cup of Ice
1 1/2 oz Tequila
1/2 oz Black Raspberry Liqueur
1/2 cup fresh or frozen
Raspberries or 2 tbsp of Raspberry
Jam
Dash of Lime Juice
Blend until smooth.
If too thick add juice or alcohol.
If too thin add ice.
Garnish with Lime.

RASPBERRY MARTINI
Fill glass with ice.
3 1/2 oz Raspberry Vodka or Vodka
Dash Triple Sec
tsp Raspberry Jam
Shake.
Strain into chilled glass.
Garnish with lemon twist.

RASPBERRY SHERBET
Fill glass with ice.
1 1/2 oz Vodka
1/2 oz Black Raspberry Liqueur
Dash of Grenadine
Dash of Orange Juice
Dash of Lime Juice
Fill with Sour Mix.
Shake.
Nick G. Zeroulias

RASPBERRY SMASH aka HOLLYWOOD
Fill glass with ice.
1 1/2 oz Vodka or Raspberry Vodka
1/2 oz Black Raspberry Liqueur
Fill with Pineapple Juice.
Garnish with Pineapple.
Shake.

RASPBERRY SOMBRERO
Fill glass with ice.
2 oz Black Raspberry Liqueur
Fill with Milk or Cream.
Shake.

RASPBERRY THUMPER
Fill glass with ice.
1 1/2 oz Vodka or Raspberry Vodka
1/2 oz Black Raspberry Liqueur
Dash Lime
Fill with Sour Mix.
Shake.

RASPBERRY TORTE
Fill glass with ice.
1 oz Vodka or Raspberry Vodka
1 oz Black Raspberry Liqueur
Stir.

RASTA MAN (floater)
1/2 oz Coffee Liqueur (bottom)
1/2 oz Myer's Rum Cream
1/2 oz Chocolate Liqueur (top)

RATTLER
Fill glass with ice.
1 1/2 oz Tequila
1/2 oz Triple Sec
Fill with Grapefruit Juice.
Garnish with Lime.

RATTLESNAKE
Fill glass with ice.
1 1/2 oz of Whiskey
1/2 Egg White
1/4 tsp Pernod
1 tsp Powdered Sugar
or Sugar Syrup
1 tsp Lemon Juice
Shake.

RATTLESNAKE 2
Fill glass with ice.
1 1/2 oz Southern Comfort
or Yukon Jack
1/2 oz Blackberry Brandy
1/4 oz Sugar Syrup
Stir.

RATTLESNAKE 3
Fill glass with ice.
1/2 oz Coffee Liqueur
1/2 oz Irish Cream
1/2 oz Peppermint Schnapps
Stir.
Strain into chilled glass.

RAZORBACK HOGCALLER
Fill glass with ice.
1 oz 151- Proof Rum
1 oz Green Chartreuse
Strain into chilled glass.

REAR BUSTER
Fill glass with ice.
1 oz Tequila
1 oz Coffee Liqueur
Fill with Cranberry Juice.
Shake.

REAR ENTRY
2 oz Vodka or Chocolate Vodka
Fill with Chocolate Yoo Hoo.

REBEL RUSSIAN
Fill glass with ice.
1 oz Southern Comfort
1 oz Coffee Liqueur
Fill with Milk or Cream.
Shake.

REBEL YELL
Fill glass with ice.
1 1/2 oz Bourbon
1/2 oz Triple Sec
1 oz Lime Juice
Shake. Strain into shot glass.

RED APPLE
Fill glass with ice.
1 oz Vodka or Apple Vodka
1 oz Apple Vodka
1/2 oz Lemon Juice
3-4 dashes of Grenadine
Shake.
Serve or strain into chilled glass.

RED BARON
Fill glass with ice.
2 oz Gin
Dash of Grenadine
Fill with equal parts Sour Mix
and Orange Juice.
Shake.

RED BEER
2 oz Tomato Juice
Fill with Beer.
Add Salt to taste.

R

RED BEER SHOOTER
In shot glass:
Dash of Tabasco
Dash of Tomato Juice
Fill with Beer.

RED CLOUD
Fill glass with ice.
1 1/2 oz Gin
1/2 oz Apricot Liqueur
1/2 oz Lemon Juice
1 tsp Grenadine
Dash of Bitters
Shake.
Strain into chilled glass.

RED DEATH
Fill glass with ice.
1/2 oz Vodka
1/2 oz Southern Comfort
1/2 oz Amaretto
1/2 oz Triple Sec
1/2 oz Sloe Gin
1/2 oz Lime Juice
Fill with Orange Juice.
Shake.

RED DEATH 2
Fill glass with ice.
1/2 oz Vodka
1/2 oz 151-Proof Rum
1/2 oz Yukon Jack
1/2 oz Cinnamon Schnapps
Stir.
Strain into chilled glass.

RED DEVIL
Fill glass with ice.
1/2 oz Vodka
1/2 oz Southern Comfort
1/2 oz Sloe Gin
1/2 oz Triple Sec
1/2 oz Peach Schnapps or Banana
Liqueur
Dash of Lime Juice or Grenadine
Fill with Orange Juice.
Shake.

RED DWARF
Fill glass with ice.
1 oz Rum or Citrus Rum
1 oz Peach Schnapps
1 oz Lemon Juice or Sour Mix
2 oz Orange Juice
Shake.
Strain into chilled glass.
Pour 1/2 oz Crème de Cassis down
spoon to bottom of drink.

RED EYE
1 1/2 oz Vodka
1 Egg
2 oz Bloody Mary Mix
Fill with cold Beer.
Shake.

RED EYE, KICK START, SHOT IN THE DARK, SPEEDBALL, HAMMERHEAD
In large coffee cup:
2 shots Espresso
Fill with Hot Black Coffee.

RED HEADED SLUT
Fill glass with ice.
3/4 oz Blended Whiskey
3/4 oz Black Raspberry Liqueur
3/4 oz Southern Comfort
Shake. Strain into chilled glass or
shot glass.

RED HEADED SLUT 2
Fill glass with ice.
1 oz Jägermeister
1 oz Peach Schnapps
1 oz Cranberry Juice
Shake. Strain into chilled glass or
shot glass.

RED LION
Fill glass with ice.
1 oz Gin
1 oz Orange Liqueur
1/2 oz Orange Juice
1/2 oz Lemon Juice
Shake.
Strain into chilled glass.

RED NEEDLE
2 oz Tequila
Fill to 1/2 inch from top with Ginger
Ale.
Top with Cranberry Juice.
Garnish with Lime.

RED PANTIES
Fill glass with ice.
1 1/2 oz Vodka or Peach,
   or Cranberry Vodka
1/2 oz Peach Schnapps
Dash of Grenadine
1 oz Orange Juice
1 oz Cranberry Juice
Shake.
Strain into chilled glass.

RED ROOSTER
Fill 1 shot glass with Gold Tequila.
Fill 1 shot glass with Orange Juice.
Fill 1 shot glass with Bloody Mary mix.
Drink in order given, one after the
other.

RED RUBY
Fill glass with ice.
2 oz Amaretto
2 tsp Grenadine
1 1/2 oz Orange Juice
1 1/2 oz Cranberry Juice
Fill with Ginger Ale.

RED RUM SONIC
Fill glass with ice.
2 oz Amber Rum
2 oz Cranberry Juice
Fill with equal parts Soda Water
and Tonic Water.
Garnish with a Lemon.
Orville Giddings

RED RUSSIAN aka SNOWBERRY
Fill glass with ice.
1 oz Vodka or Strawberry Vodka
1 oz Strawberry Liqueur
Fill with Milk or Cream.
Shake.

RED SILK PANTIES
Fill glass with ice.
1 1/2 oz Vodka or Cranberry,
   or Peach Vodka
1/2 oz Peach Schnapps
1 oz Cranberry Juice
Stir.
Strain into chilled glass.

RED SNAPPER
Fill glass with ice.
2 oz Gin
1 tsp of Horseradish
3 dashes of Tabasco Sauce
3 dashes of Worcestershire Sauce
Dash of Lime Juice
3 dashes of Celery Salt
3 dashes of Pepper
1 oz Clam Juice (optional)
Fill with Tomato Juice.
Shake.
Garnish with Lemon or Lime,
Celery or Cucumber and/or
Cocktail Shrimp.

RED TIDE
Fill glass with ice.
3/4 oz Light Rum
3/4 oz Dark Rum
3/4 oz Banana Liqueur
Dash of Pineapple Juice
Dash of Sour Mix
Fill with Cranberry Juice.

RED WINE COOLER
Fill glass 3/4 with ice.
Fill 3/4 with desired Red Wine.
Fill with Lemon-Lime Soda or
Ginger Ale.
Stir.
Garnish with Lime.

RED ZIPPER
Fill glass with ice.
1 oz Vodka or Cranberry Vodka
1 oz Galliano
Fill with Cranberry Juice.
Stir.
Garnish with Lime.

REFORM
Fill glass with ice.
1 1/2 oz Dry Sherry
3/4 oz Dry Vermouth
1-2 dashes of Orange Bitters
Stir and Strain into chilled glass.

RELEASE VALVE
Fill glass with ice.
1 oz Vodka or Pineapple Vodka
1 oz Rum or Pineapple Rum
Fill with Pineapple Juice.
Top with 1/2 oz Grenadine.

RENAISSANCE COCKTAIL
Fill glass with ice.
1 1/2 oz Gin
1/2 oz Dry Sherry
1 tbsp Cream
Shake.
Strain into chilled glass.
Sprinkle with Nutmeg.

RENDEZVOUS
Fill glass with ice.
1 1/2 oz Gin
1/2 oz Kirschwasser
1/2 oz Campari
Shake and Strain into chilled glass.
Garnish with Lemon Twist.

RESTORATION
Fill glass with ice.
1 oz Brandy
1 oz Black Raspberry Liqueur
Dash of Sour Mix
Fill with Red Wine.
Shake.
Strain into wine glass.
Garnish with Lemon Twist.

REVEREND
Fill glass with ice.
2 oz Bourbon
2 oz Sour Mix
Shake and strain.
Fill with Beer.

RHETT BUTTLER
Fill glass with ice
1 1/2 oz Southern Comfort
1 tsp Curacao
1/2 oz Lime Juice
1/2 oz Lemon Juice
1 tsp Sugar
Shake.
Strain into chilled glass.

RHODE ISLAND ICED TEA
Fill glass with ice.
3/4 oz Brandy
3/4 oz Vodka
3/4 oz Coffee Liqueur
Fill with Milk or Cream.
Shake.

RICKEY
Fill glass with ice.
2 oz Desired Liquor or Liqueur
Dash of Lime Juice
Fill with Soda Water.
Stir.

RIGOR MORTIS
Fill glass with ice.
1 1/2 oz Vodka or Citrus Vodka
1 oz Amaretto
Fill with equal parts Orange and
Pineapple Juice.
Shake.

RISING SUN
Fill glass with ice.
4 oz Sake
Fill with Orange Juice.
Pour 1/2 oz Grenadine down spoon
to bottom of drink.

RITZ FIZZ
Fill glass with ice.
1 oz Amaretto
1/2 oz Blue Curacao
1 oz Sour Mix
Shake.
Strain into chilled glass.
Fill with Champagne.
Garnish with Orange.

RITZ PICK-ME-UP
1 oz Cognac or Brandy
1 oz Orange Liqueur
2 oz Orange Juice
Fill with Champagne.

RIVER BERRY
Fill glass with ice.
1 oz Vodka
1 oz Wildberry Schnapps
4 oz Sour Mix
Shake.
Drop of Grenadine
Splash of Soda Water

RIVIERA
Fill glass with ice.
3/4 oz Rum or Citrus Rum
3/4 oz Orange Liqueur
3/4 oz Black Raspberry Liqueur
Stir.

R

ROASTED TOASTED ALMOND
aka BURNT ALMOND, ORGASM
Fill glass with ice.
1 oz Vodka
1 oz Coffee Liqueur
1 oz Amaretto
Fill with Milk or Cream.
Shake.

ROASTED TOASTED ALMOND
(frozen)
In Blender:
1/2 cup of Ice
1 oz Vodka
1 oz Coffee Liqueur
1 oz Amaretto
Scoop of Vanilla Ice Cream
Blend until smooth.
If too thick add Milk or Cream.
If too thin add ice or Ice Cream.

ROB ROY
(*CAUTION:* DRY can mean either
make drink with Dry Vermouth or
less Sweet Vermouth than usual.
PERFECT means use equal
amounts of Sweet and Dry
Vermouth. SWEET means use
more Sweet Vermouth than usual.)
Fill glass with ice.
2 oz Scotch Whiskey
1/2 oz Sweet Vermouth
Stir.
Strain into chilled glass or pour
contents (with ice) into short glass.
Garnish with Cherry or Lemon
Twist.

ROBSON
Fill glass with ice.
1 1/2 oz Jamaican Rum
1 tbsp Orange Juice
1 1/2 tsp Lemon Juice
1 tsp Grenadine
Shake.
Serve or strain into chilled glass.

ROCK LOBSTER (frozen)
In Blender:
1 cup of Ice.
1 oz Coconut Rum
1/2 oz Banana Liqueur
Dash of Grenadine
1/2 ripe peeled Banana
Dash of Pineapple and Orange
Juice
Blend until smooth.
Top with Dark Rum.

ROCKAWAY BEACH
Fill glass with ice.
1 1/2 oz Light Rum
1/2 oz Dark Rum
1/2 oz Tequila
1 oz Orange Juice
1/2 oz Pineapple Juice
1/2 oz Cranberry Juice
1 tsp Crème de Nouyax
Shake.
Garnish with Cherry.

ROCKET
Fill glass with ice.
2 oz Yukon Jack
Fill with Lemonade.
Float 1/2 oz 151-Proof Rum
on top.

ROCKY MOUNTAIN ROOTBEER
Fill glass with ice.
1 1/2 oz Vodka
1/2 oz Galliano
Fill with Cola.
Stir.

ROCKY ROAD
Fill glass with ice.
1 oz Hazelnut Liqueur
1 oz Crème de Cacao
Fill with Milk or Cream.
Shake.

ROLL ME OVER
Fill glass with ice.
1/2 oz Light Rum
1/2 oz Dark Rum
1/2 oz Coconut Rum
1/2 oz Banana Liqueur
1/2 oz Orange Liqueur
1/2 oz Melon Liqueur
Fill with Pineapple Juice.
Shake.

ROMAN CANDLE
Fill glass with ice.
1 oz Sambuca
1 oz Amaretto
Dash of Grenadine
Fill with Orange Juice.
Shake.
Top with Soda Water.

ROMAN CAPPUCCINO
1 1/2 oz Sambuca
Fill with Espresso.
Top with steamed Milk.
Garnish with 3 Coffee Beans.

ROMAN CAPPUCCINO (frozen)
In Blender:
1/2 cup of Ice
2 oz Sambuca
3 oz Espresso
Scoop of Vanilla or Coffee Ice Cream
Blend until smooth.

ROMAN COFFEE
2 oz Sambuca
Fill with hot Black Coffee.
Top with Whipped Cream.
Garnish with 3 Coffee Beans.

ROMAN HOLIDAY
Fill glass with ice.
3/4 oz Amaretto
3/4 oz Sambuca
3/4 oz Blackberry Brandy
Fill with Milk.
Shake.

ROMAN ICED TEA
Fill glass with ice.
1/2 oz Vodka
1/2 oz Gin
1/2 oz Rum
1/2 oz Triple Sec
1/2 oz Amaretto
Fill with equal parts Cranberry
Juice and Sour Mix.
Shake.
Top with Lemon-Lime Soda.

ROMAN RASTA COFFEE
1 oz Sambuca
1 oz Dark Rum
Fill with hot Black Coffee.
Top with Whipped Cream.

ROMAN RIOT
Fill glass with ice.
3/4 oz Amaretto
3/4 oz Sambuca
3/4 oz Galliano
Shake and Strain into chilled glass.

ROOT BEER
Fill glass with ice.
3/4 oz Vodka
3/4 oz Coffee Liqueur
3/4 oz Galliano
Fill with Cola.
Stir.

ROOT BEER FLOAT
Fill glass with ice.
1 oz Vodka
1 oz Root Beer Schnapps
1 oz Cream
Shake.
Top with 2 oz Cola.

ROOT BEER FLOAT 2
Place a scoop of Vanilla Ice Cream
in large glass.
2 oz Dark Rum
Fill with Root Beer.

ROOT OF ALL EVIL
Fill glass with ice.
2 oz Bourbon
Fill with Root Beer.

ROSÉ COOLER
Fill glass 3/4 with ice.
Fill 3/4 with Rosé Wine.
Fill with Ginger Ale
or Lemon-Lime Soda.
Garnish with Lime.

ROSE HALL
Fill glass with ice.
1 1/2 oz Dark Rum
1/2 oz Banana Liqueur
1 oz Orange Juice
1 tsp Lime Juice
Shake.
Serve or strain into chilled glass.
Garnish with a Lime.

ROSÉ SPRITZER
Fill glass 3/4 with ice.
Fill glass 3/4 with Rosé Wine.
Fill with Soda Water.
Garnish with Lime.

ROSY DAWN
Fill glass with ice.
1 oz Vodka or Rum
1 oz Gin
Dash of Grenadine
Dash of Lime Juice
Fill with Grapefruit Juice.
Shake.

ROXANNE
Fill glass with ice.
1 oz Vodka or Peach Vodka
1/2 oz Peach Schnapps
1/2 oz Amaretto
Fill with equal parts Orange Juice
and Cranberry Juice.
Shake.
Strain into chilled glass.

ROY ROGERS
Fill glass with ice.
Fill glass with Cola.
Dash of Grenadine
Garnish with Cherry.

ROYAL CANADIAN
Fill glass with ice.
1/2 oz Canadian Whiskey
1/2 oz Coffee Liqueur
1/2 oz Amaretto
Strain into chilled glass.

ROYAL GIN FIZZ
Fill glass with ice.
2 oz Gin
1/2 oz Orange Liqueur
1 Egg
1 oz Lemon Juice or Sour Mix
1 tsp Sugar Syrup
Shake.
Fill with Soda Water.

ROYAL SCREW
Fill glass 3/4 with ice.
2 oz Cognac
2 oz Orange Juice
Fill with Champagne.

ROYAL SHEET COFFEE
1 oz Amaretto
1 oz Coffee Liqueur
Fill with hot Black Coffee.
Top with Whipped Cream.
Sprinkle with Shaved Almonds.

ROYAL SMILE
Fill glass with ice.
1 oz Apple Brandy
1/2 oz Gin
1/2 oz Lemon Juice
1 tsp Grenadine
Shake.
Strain into chilled glass.

ROYAL SPRITZER
Fill glass 3/4 with ice.
1 oz Black Raspberry Liqueur
Fill 3/4 with Champagne.
Fill with Soda.
Garnish with Lime.

RUBY FIZZ
Fill glass with ice.
2 1/2 oz Sloe Gin
1/2 Egg White
1 tsp Grenadine
1 tsp Sugar Syrup
or Powdered Sugar
1 oz Lemon Juice
Shake.
Fill with Soda Water.

RUBY RED
Fill glass with ice.
1 1/2 oz Vodka or Grapefruit Vodka
1/2 oz Grenadine or Campari
Fill with Grapefruit Juice.
Shake.

RUDDY MIMOSA
1/2 oz Peach Schnapps
1 oz Orange Juice
1 oz Cranberry Juice
Fill with Champagne.
Garnish with Orange.

RUDE COSMOPOLITAN
Fill glass with ice.
3 1/2 oz Tequila
Dash Triple Sec
Dash Lime Juice
Dash Cranberry Juice or
Grapefruit Juice
Shake. Strain into chilled glass.
Garnish with Lime

R

Metric Measurement Conversion Chart on page 14

RUM AND COKE
Fill glass with ice.
2 oz Rum
Fill with Cola.
Garnish with Lime.

RUM DINGER
Fill glass with ice.
1 1/2 oz Dark Rum
1 1/2 oz Coffee Liqueur
Dash Ginger Ale
Stir

RUM-LACED CIDER
1 oz Dark Rum
1 oz Spiced Rum
Fill with hot Apple Cider.
Float Pat of Butter on top.
Sprinkle Cinnamon and whole
Cloves on top.

RUM MADRAS aka
BOG FOG
Fill glass with ice.
2 oz Rum or Citrus Rum
Fill with equal parts Orange and
Cranberry Juice.
Garnish with Lime.

RUM PUNCH
Fill glass with ice.
2 oz Amber Rum
Dash of Bitters
Tsp. Sugar
Dash of Lime Juice
Fill with Orange Juice
Pinch Nutmeg
Shake.

RUM PUNCH 2
Fill glass with ice.
2 oz Rum
Dash of Grenadine
Fill with equal parts Orange and
Pineapple Juice.
Shake
Splash with Lemon-Lime Soda.
Garnish with Lime.

RUM RUNNER
Fill glass with ice.
1/2 oz Light Rum
1/2 oz Dark Rum
1/2 oz Banana Liqueur
1/2 oz Blackberry Brandy
Dash of Grenadine
Dash of Sour Mix
Dash of Orange Juice
Shake.
Float 1/2 oz 151-Proof Rum
on top.

RUM RUNNER (frozen)
In Blender:
1 cup of Ice
1 oz Rum
1 oz Banana Liqueur
1/2 oz Blackberry Brandy
Dash of Grenadine
Dash of Lime Juice
Blend until smooth.
If too thick add liqueur or juice.
If too thin add ice.

RUMBALL
1 oz Dark Rum
1 oz Chocolate Liqueur
Stir.

RUMPELSTILTSKIN
1 oz 100-Proof Peppermint Schnapps
1 oz Bourbon

RUN, SKIP AND GO NAKED
Fill glass with ice.
1/2 oz Gin
1/2 oz Rum
1/2 oz Brandy
1/2 oz Triple Sec
Fill with Sour Mix (leaving 1/2 inch
from top).
Shake.
Top with Beer.

RUPTURED DUCK
Fill glass with ice.
1 oz Banana Liqueur
1 oz Crème de Nouyax
1 oz Cream
Shake.
Strain into chilled glass.

RUSSIAN
Fill glass with ice.
3/4 oz Vodka
3/4 oz Gin
3/4 oz White Crème de Cacao
Shake.
Strain into chilled glass.

RUSSIAN BANANA
Fill glass with ice.
3/4 oz Vodka or Banana Vodka
3/4 oz Banana Liqueur
3/4 oz Dark Crème de Cacao
1 oz Cream or Milk
Shake.
Strain into chilled glass.

RUSSIAN BEAR
Fill glass with ice.
1 oz Vodka or Chocolate Vodka
1 oz Dark Crème de Cacao
1 oz Heavy Cream
Shake.
Strain into chilled glass.

RUSSIAN COFFEE
2 oz Vodka
Fill with hot Black Coffee.
1/2 tsp of Sugar (optional)
Stir.
Top with Whipped Cream.
Garnish with Orange.

RUSSIAN NIGHTS aka
FLYING MADRAS
Fill glass with ice.
2 oz Vodka or Citrus Vodka
2 oz Cranberry Juice
2 oz Orange Juice
Fill with Champagne.
Garnish with Orange.

RUSSIAN PUSSY
Fill glass with ice.
2 1/2 oz Vodka or Vanilla Vodka
1/2 oz White Crème de Cacao
1 oz Milk or Cream
Shake. Strain into chilled glass.

RUSSIAN QUAALUDE
Fill glass with ice.
1 oz Vodka or Vanilla Vodka
1 oz Irish Cream
1 oz Hazelnut Liqueur
Fill with Milk.
Shake.

RUSSIAN QUAALUDE 2
Fill glass with ice.
1/2 oz Vodka or Vanilla Vodka
1/2 oz Coffee Liqueur
1/2 oz Amaretto
1/2 oz Hazelnut Liqueur
1/2 oz Irish Cream
1 oz Milk (optional)
Shake.

RUSSIAN QUAALUDE (floater)
1 oz Hazelnut Liqueur (bottom)
1 oz Irish Cream
1 oz Vodka or Vanilla Vodka(top)

RUSSIAN QUAALUDE (frozen)
In Blender:
1/2 cup of Ice
1/2 oz Vodka or Vanilla Vodka
1/2 oz Coffee Liqueur
1/2 oz Irish Cream
1/2 oz Hazelnut Liqueur
1/2 oz Tia Maria
1/2 oz Amaretto
Scoop of Vanilla Ice Cream
Blend until smooth.
If too thick add Milk or Cream.
If too thin add ice or Ice Cream.
Garnish with Shaved Chocolate or
Sprinkles.

RUSSIAN ROSE
Fill glass with ice.
2 oz Vodka or Citrus Vodka
1/2 oz Grenadine
Dash of Orange Bitters
Shake.
Strain into chilled glass.

RUSSIAN ROULETTE
Fill glass with ice.
1 oz Vodka
1/2 oz Drambuie
1/2 oz Galliano
Fill with equal parts Sour Mix and
Orange Juice.
Shake.
Garnish with Lemon.

RUSSIAN ROULETTE 2
Fill glass with ice.
1/2 oz Vodka or Orange Vodjka
1/2 oz Brandy or Cognac
1/2 oz Banana Liqueur
1 oz Sour Mix
1 oz Orange Juice
Shake.
Strain into chilled glass.

RUSSIAN SUNRISE
Fill glass with ice.
2 oz Vodka or Orange Vodka
Fill with Orange Juice.
Pour 1/2 oz Grenadine down spoon
to bottom of glass.
Garnish with Orange.

RUSTY NAIL
Fill glass with ice.
1 1/2 oz Scotch
1/2 oz Drambuie
Stir.

RUSTY NAIL COFFEE aka
HEATHER COFFEE
1 oz Scotch
1 oz Drambuie
Fill with hot Black Coffee.
Top with Whipped Cream.
Sprinkle with Cinnamon.

S. O. B.
1/3 oz Orange Liqueur or Triple Sec
1/3 oz Brandy
1/3 oz 151-Proof Rum

S. O. B. 2 (floater)
1 oz Orange Liqueur (bottom)
1 oz Southern Comfort (top)
Serve with Lemon or Lime wedge.
Bite fruit before drinking.

S. O. M. F. (floater)
1/2 oz Coffee Liqueur (bottom)
1/2 oz Irish Cream
1/2 oz Hazelnut Liqueur (top)

S. O. M. F. 2 (floater)
1/2 oz Blackberry Brandy
(bottom)
1/2 oz Amaretto
1/2 oz Triple Sec
1/2 oz Lime Juice (top)

S. O. S.
Fill glass with ice.
1 1/2 oz Vodka
1/2 oz Black Raspberry Liqueur
Fill with equal parts Cranberry
and Orange Juice.
Shake.

ST. PETERSBURG SUNDAE
(frozen)
In Blender: 1/2 cup of ice.
1 1/2 oz Vanilla Vodka
1/2 oz Amaretto
Scoop of Chocolate Ice Cream
Blend until smooth.
If too thick add Milk or Cream.
If too thin add ice or Ice Cream.
Garnish with Shaved Almonds.

SAINT MORITZ (floater)
1/2 oz Black Raspberry Liqueur
(bottom)
1/2 oz Milk or Cream (top)

SAKETINI
Fill glass with ice.
3 1/2 oz Gin or Vodka
1/2 oz Sake
Stir.
Strain into chilled glass
or pour contents (with ice)
into short glass.
Garnish with Lemon Twist
or Olives.

SAKI BOMB
Fill large glass 3/4 with beer.
Place shot glass filled with Saki.
on top of 2 chopsticks balanced on
top of the beer.
Slam hands on table
(not at my joint),
Until Saki enters beer....Drink.

SALTY BULL
Fill glass with ice.
2 oz Tequila
Fill with Grapefruit Juice.
Rub rim of second glass with Lime.
Dip rim in Kosher Salt.
Pour contents of first glass into
salted glass.
Garnish with Lime.

R
S

Metric Measurement Conversion Chart on page 14

SALTY DOG
Fill glass with ice.
2 oz Gin or Vodka
Fill with Grapefruit Juice.
Rub rim of second glass with Lime.
Dip rim in kosher salt.
Pour contents of first glass into
salted glass.
Garnish with Lime.

SALTY DOGITRON
Fill glass with ice.
2 oz Citrus Vodka
Dash of Grenadine
Fill with Grapefruit Juice.

SALTY JOHN
Fill glass with ice.
2 oz Whiskey
Fill with Grapefruit Juice.
Stir.
Pour into glass with salted rim.

SAMURAI
Fill glass with ice.
3 1/2 oz Citrus Vodka
1/2 oz Triple Sec
Stir.
Garnish with a Lemon.

SAN FRANCISCO
Fill glass with ice.
3/4 oz Sloe Gin
3/4 oz Dry Vermouth
3/4 oz Sweet Vermouth
Dash of Bitters
Dash of Orange Bitters
Shake.
Strain into chilled glass.

SAN JUAN (frozen)
In Blender:
1 cup of Ice
1 1/2 oz Amber Rum
1 oz Grapefruit Juice
1 oz Lime Juice
1/2 oz Cream of Coconut
Blend until smooth.
If too thick add juice.
If too thin add ice.
Float tsp 151-Proof Rum
on top.
Garnish with Lime.

SAN JUAN SUNSET
Fill glass with ice.
2 oz Rum or Citrus Rum
Fill with Orange Juice.
Float 1/2 oz Cherry Brandy
on top.

SAN SEBASTIAN
Fill glass with ice.
1 oz Gin
1 1/2 tsp Rum
1/2 tsp Triple Sec
1 tbsp Grapefruit Juice
1 tbsp Lemon Juice
Shake.
Strain into chilled glass.

SANCTUARY
Fill glass with ice.
1 1/2 oz Dubonnet Rouge
3/4 oz Amer Picon
3/4 oz Orange Liqueur
Shake.
Serve or strain into chilled glass.

SAND BLASTER
Fill glass with ice.
1 oz Rum or Citrus Rum
1 oz Jägermeister
Fill with Cola.
Stir.
Garnish with Lime.

SAND FLEA
Fill glass with ice.
1 oz Rumor Orange Rum
1/2 oz Apricot Brandy
1/2 oz Orange Liqueur
Dash of Grenadine.
Fill with equal parts Orange Juice
and Sour Mix.

SAND IN YOUR BUTT
Fill glass with ice.
1 oz Southern Comfort
1 oz Melon Liqueur
1 oz Pineapple Juice
Shake. Strain into shot glass.

SANGRIA 1
(Chill all ingredients prior to mixing.)
In a large punch bowl with a cake
of ice in it, mix:
2 750ml bottles of desired Red Wine
3 oz Curacao or Triple Sec
2 oz Brandy
1/2 cup Orange Juice
1/4 cup Lemon Juice
1/4 cup Sugar
2 oz Water
Stir until sugar dissolves.
Add an Orange and a Lemon sliced
thinly.
Add 1 qt Soda Water.

SANGRIA 2
Fill glass with ice.
1 oz Orange Liqueur
1/2 oz Brandy
Dash of Sour Mix
Dash of Orange Juice
Pinch Sugar
Fill with desired Red Wine.
Shake.
Splash with Soda Water.
Garnish with Orange and Lemon.

SANGRIA BLANCA
Fill glass with ice.
1 oz Peach or Orange Liqueur
Dash of Sour Mix
Dash of Orange Juice
Pinch Sugar
Fill with Desired White Wine.
Shake.
Splash with Soda.
Garnish with Peach slice.

SANGRITA
In Pitcher:
12 oz Tomato Juice
6 oz Orange Juice
2 oz Lime Juice
6-8 Dashes Worcestershire Sauce
5-20 Dashes Hot Sauce
Pinch of Salt
Pinch of Pepper
1-2 oz Grenadine (optional)
1/2 cup minced Onions (optional)
1/2 cup minced Hot Peppers (optional)
Stir. Chill. Strain into shot glass.
Drink Tequila. Chase with Sangrita.

Metric Measurement Conversion Chart on page 14

SANTA SHOT (floater)
3/4 oz Grenadine (bottom)
3/4 oz Green Crème de Menthe
3/4 oz Peppermint Schnapps (top)

SANTIAGO
Fill glass with ice.
1 oz Light Rum
1 oz Dark Rum
1 oz Triple Sec
1 oz Sour Mix
1/2 oz Lime Juice
2-3 dashes of Bitters
Shake.
Strain into chilled glass.
Garnish with Lime.

SANTIAGO 2
Fill glass with ice.
3/4 oz Light Rum
3/4 oz Dark Rum
3/4 oz Triple Sec
1 oz Sour Mix
1/2 oz Lime Juice
2-3 dashes of Bitters
Shake.
Strain into tall chilled glass.
Fill with Champagne.
Garnish with Lime.

SARATOGA
Fill glass with ice.
2 oz Brandy
1 oz crushed fresh or canned
Pineapple
1/2 tsp Maraschino Liqueur
2 or 3 dashes of Bitters
Shake.
Strain into chilled glass.

SATURN'S RING (floater)
1/2 oz Anisette (bottom)
1/2 oz Grenadine
1/2 oz Southern Comfort (top)

SAUCY SUE
Fill glass with ice.
2 oz Apple Brandy
1/2 tsp Apricot Brandy
1/2 tsp Pernod
Stir.
Strain into chilled glass.

SAVANNAH
Fill glass with ice.
2 oz Gin
1 Egg White
1 oz Orange Juice
Shake.
Strain into chilled glass.
Top with 1/2 oz White Crème de
Cacao.

SAVE THE PLANET
Fill glass with ice.
1 oz Vodka or Citrus Vodka
1 oz Melon Liqueur
1/2 oz Blue Curacao
Shake.
Strain into chilled glass.
Float 1/2 oz Green Chartreuse on
top.

SAVOY HOTEL (floater)
1/2 oz White Crème de Cacao (bottom)
1/2 oz Benedictine
1/2 oz Brandy (top)

SAVOY TANGO
Fill glass with ice.
1 1/2 oz Apple Brandy
1 oz Sloe Gin
Stir.
Strain into chilled glass.

SAZERAC
Fill glass with ice.
2 oz Bourbon
1 tsp Sugar
2 dashes of Bitters
Stir until sugar dissolves.
Coat inside of second glass
with Pernod.
Strain mixture into coated glass.
Garnish with Lemon Twist.

**SCARLET LETTER aka
CHAM CRAN CHAM,
BRUT AND BOGS**
Fill glass 3/4 with ice.
Fill glass 3/4 with Champagne.
Dash of Black Raspberry Liqueur
Fill with Cranberry Juice.

SCARLET O'HARA
Fill glass with ice.
2 oz Southern Comfort
Dash of Lime Juice (optional)
Fill with Cranberry Juice.
Garnish with Lime.

SCHOOL BUS
Fill glass with ice.
2 oz Amaretto
Fill with equal parts Beer
and Orange Juice.
Stir.
Garnish with unused number 2
pencil.

SCOOBY SNACK
Fill glass with ice.
1 oz Coconut Rum
1 oz Melon Liqueur
Dash of Pineapple Juice
Dash of Milk
Shake. Strain into shot glass.
Top with Whipped Cream.

SCORPION (frozen)
In Blender:
1/2 cup of Ice
1 oz Light Rum
1 oz Gin
1 oz Brandy
1 oz Orange Juice
1 oz White wine
1 oz Lemon Juice
1/2 oz Crème de Nouyax or
Orgeat Syrup
Blend until smooth.
Float 1/2 oz Dark Rum on top.
Garnish with gardenia.

SCORPION (floater)
1/2 oz Grenadine (bottom)
1 oz Blackberry Brandy
1/2 oz Vodka (top)

SCOTCH BIRD
1 1/2 oz Scotch
1/2 oz Triple Sec
Tsp powdered Sugar
Fill with Milk or Cream.
Shake.

S

SCOTCH COLLINS aka
JOE COLLINS, MIKE COLLINS
Fill glass with ice.
2 oz Scotch
Fill with Sour Mix.
Shake.
Splash with Soda Water.
Garnish with Orange and Cherry.

SCOTCH SOUR
Fill glass with ice.
2 oz Scotch
Fill with Sour Mix.
Shake.
Garnish with Orange and Cherry.

SCOTTI WAS BEAMED UP
Fill glass with ice.
1 1/2 oz Tequila
1/2 oz Galliano
Shake. Strain into shot glass.

SCOTTISH COFFEE
2 oz Drambuie or Scotch
or 1 oz of each
Fill with hot Black Coffee.
Top with Whipped Cream.
Sprinkle with Shaved Chocolate.

SCREAMER
Fill glass with ice.
1 1/2 oz Greek Brandy
1/2 oz Green Chartreuse
Stir.
Strain into chilled glass.

SCREAMING BANSHEE
Fill glass with ice.
1 oz Vodka or Banana Vodka
1 oz Banana Liqueur
1/2 oz White Crème de Cacao
Fill with Milk or Cream.
Shake.

SCREAMING BLUE MESSIAH
(floater)
1 1/2 oz 100-proof Goldschlager
(bottom)
1/2 oz Blue Curacao (top)

SCREAMING DEAD NAZI
DIGGING FOR GOLD
Fill glass with ice.
1/2 oz Grain Alcohol
1/2 oz 100-proof Peppermint
Schnapps
1/2 oz Jägermeister
1/2 oz Yellow Chartreuse
Shake. Strain into shot glass.

SCREAMING NAZI aka
DEAD NAZI
Fill glass with ice.
1 oz 100-Proof Peppermint
Schnapps
1 oz Jägermeister
Stir.
Strain into chilled glass.

SCREAMING ORGASM
Fill glass with ice.
1/2 oz Vodka or Vanilla Vodka
1/2 oz Coffee Liqueur
1/2 oz Amaretto or Orange Liqueur
1/2 oz Irish Cream
Fill with equal parts Milk
or Cream and Soda Water.

SCREAMING VIKING aka
SKYSCRAPER
Fill glass with ice.
2 oz Bourbon
2-3 dashes of Bitters
1/2 oz Lime Juice
Fill with Cranberry Juice.
Stir.
Garnish with Cucumber.

SCREAMING VIKING
Fill glass with ice.
2oz Vodka
1oz Dry Vermouth
1oz Lime Juice
Shake.
Strain into chilled glass.
Garnish with Celery and Cucumber
Ask customer if they would like the
Cucumber bruised

SCREAMING YELLOW MONKEY
Fill glass with ice.
1 oz Vodka or Banana,
or Vanilla Vodka
1 oz Banana Liqueur
1/2 oz White Crème de Cacao
Fill with Milk or Cream.
Shake.

SCREW-UP
Fill glass with ice.
2 oz Vodka or Citrus Vodka
Splash of Orange Juice
Fill with Lemon-Lime Soda.
Garnish with Orange.

SCREWDRIVER
Fill glass with ice.
2 oz Vodka
Fill with Orange Juice.
Garnish with Orange or Lime.

SCROPPINO (frpzen)
In Blender: 1/2 cup ice
2 oz Vodka
2 oz Champagne or Sparkling Wine
2-3 Tblsp Whipped Cream
Scoop desired Sorbet or Gelato
Blend until smooth.
Garnish with whipped cream,
And fresh fruit.

SCUMBUCKET
Fill glass with ice.
1 oz Beer
Dash of Bourbon
Dash of Sambuca
Dash of Red Wine
Dash Irish Cream
Shake. Strain into shot glass.

SEA BREEZE aka
CAPE GRAPE
Fill glass with ice.
2 oz Vodka
Fill with equal parts Cranberry and
Grapefruit Juice
Garnish with Lime.

SEA MONKEYS
In shot glass:
1 1/2 oz Goldschlager
1/2 oz Blue Curacao
Stir.

SEDUCTION (floater)
3/4 oz Hazelnut Liqueur (bottom)
3/4 oz Banana Liqueur
3/4 oz Irish Cream (top)

SELF-STARTER
Fill glass with ice.
2 1/2 oz Gin
1/2 oz Lillet Blanc
1 tsp Apricot Brandy
2-3 dashes of Pernod
Shake.
Strain into chilled glass.

SEPARATOR aka
DIRTY MOTHER
Fill glass with ice.
1 1/2 oz Brandy
3/4 oz Coffee Liqueur
1 oz Cream (optional)
Stir.

SEPTEMBER MORN
Fill glass with ice.
2 1/2 oz Rum
1/2 oz Lime Juice
1 tsp Grenadine
1 Egg White
Shake.
Strain into chilled glass.

SEVEN AND SEVEN
Fill glass with ice.
2 oz Seagram's 7 Whiskey
Fill with 7-up.
Garnish with Lemon.

727
Fill glass with ice.
1/2 oz Vodka
1/2 oz Coffee Liqueur
1/2 oz Irish Cream
1/2 oz Orange Liqueur
Shake.

747 (floater)
1/2 oz Coffee Liqueur (bottom)
1/2 oz Irish Cream
1/2 oz Hazelnut Liqueur (top)

SEVENTH AVENUE
Fill glass with ice.
1 oz Amaretto
1 oz Drambuie
1 oz Chocolate Liqueur
Fill with Milk or Cream.
Shake.

SEVENTH HEAVEN
Fill glass with ice.
1 1/2 oz Whiskey
1/2 oz Amaretto
Fill with Orange Juice.
Stir.

SEVILLA
Fill glass with ice.
1 oz Dark Rum
1 oz Sweet Vermouth
Shake.
Strain into chilled glass.
Garnish with Orange Twist.

SEVILLA 2
Fill glass with ice.
1 1/2 oz Rum
1 1/2 oz Port
1 egg
1/2 tsp Powdered Sugar
or Sugar Syrup
Shake.
Sprinkle Nutmeg on top.

SEWER RAT
Fill glass with ice.
1 oz Vodka
1/2 oz Peach Schnapps
1/2 oz Coffee Liqueur
Fill with Orange Juice.

SEX
Fill glass with ice.
1 oz Coffee Liqueur
1 oz Orange Liqueur
Stir.
Garnish with Orange.

SEX AT MY HOUSE
Fill glass with ice.
1 oz Amaretto
1 oz Black Raspberry Liqueur
Fill with Pineapple Juice.
Shake.
Garnish with Pineapple.

SEX AT THE BEACH
Fill glass with ice.
1/2 oz Vodka or Citrus Vodka
1/2 oz Southern Comfort
1/2 oz Peach Schnapps
1/2 oz Apple Brandy
1/2 oz Orange Liqueur
1/2 oz Orange Juice
1/2 oz Cranberry Juice
1/2 oz Milk or Cream
Shake.
Strain into chilled glass.

SEX IN A BUBBLEGUM
FACTORY
Fill glass with ice.
1 oz Light Rum
2/3 oz Apricot Brandy
1/2 oz Banana Liqueur
1/2 oz Blue Curacao
Fill with Lemon-Lime Soda.

SEX IN A DISABLED LOO
Fill glass with ice.
1 oz Gin
1 oz Vodka
1/2 oz Crème de Cassis
Fill with Lemonade.
Shake.
Garnish Lass or Bird with drink.

SEX IN A HOT TUB
Fill glass with ice.
1 oz Vodka or Raspberry Vodka
1/2 oz Peach Schnapps
1/2 oz Black Raspberry Liqueur
Dash of Cranberry Juice
Dash of Pineapple Juice
Shake.
Fill with Champagne.

SEX IN THE BASEMENT
Fill glass with ice.
1 1/2 oz Bourbon
1/2 oz Peach Schnapps
1/2 oz Grenadine
Fill with favorite sweet carbonated
beverage.

SEX IN THE BEDROOM
Fill glass with ice.
1 oz Coconut Rum
1 oz Black Raspberry Liqueur
Fill with Pineapple Juice.
Shake. Garnish with Cherry.

S

SEX IN THE GRAVEYARD
Fill glass with ice.
1/2 oz Vodka
1/2 oz Rum
1/2 oz Bourbon
1/2 oz Tequila
1/2 oz Blackberry Brandy
Dash of Sour Mix.
Fill with Cranberry Juice.
Shake.
Float 1/2oz of Green Chartreuse
(optional)

SEX IN THE PARKING LOT
Fill glass with ice.
1 oz Vodka or Apple Vodka
1/2 oz Black Raspberry Liqueur
1/2 oz Apple Brandy
Fill with equal parts Orange
and Cranberry Juice.
Shake.

SEX IN THE SNOW
Fill glass with ice.
1 1/2 oz Vodka or Peach Vodka
1/2 oz Peach Schnapps
Fill with equal parts Orange Juice
and
Milk or Cream.
Shake.

SEX IN THE WOODS
Fill glass with ice.
1 oz Vodka or Pineapple Vodka
1/2 oz Amaretto
1/2 oz Coffee Liqueur
Fill with Pineapple Juice.
Shake.

SEX MACHINE
Fill glass with ice.
3/4 oz Vodka or Vanilla Vodka
3/4 oz Coffee Liqueur
3/4 oz Orange Liqueur
Float 1/2 oz Milk or Cream on top.

SEX ON ACID
Fill glass with ice.
3/4 oz Jagermeister
3/4 oz Black Raspberry Liqueur
3/4 oz Melon Liqueur
Fill with equal parts Pineapple and
Cranberry Juice.
Shake.

SEX ON A BOAT
Fill glass with ice.
1 1/2 oz Spiced Rum
1/2 oz Banana Liqueur
Fill with Orange Juice
Shake.

SEX ON A FLORIDA BEACH
Fill glass with ice.
1oz Vodka or Citrus Vodka
1/2 oz Peach Schnapps
1/2 oz Melon Liqueur
Fill with equal parts Orange and
Pineapple Juice
Shake.

SEX ON THE BEACH
Fill glass with ice.
1 1/2 oz Vodka or Peach Vodka
1/2 oz Peach Schnapps
Fill with equal parts Cranberry and
Orange or Pineapple Juice.
Garnish with Orange or Pineapple.

SEX ON THE BEACH 2
Fill glass with ice.
1 oz Vodka or Pineapple Vodka
1/2 oz Melon Liqueur
1/2 oz Black Raspberry Liqueur
Fill with Pineapple Juice or equal
parts Pineapple and Cranberry
Juice.
Shake.
Garnish with Pineapple.

SEX ON THE BEACH 3
Fill glass with ice.
1 oz Vodka or Raspberry Vodka
1/2 oz Coffee Liqueur or Peach
Schnapps
1/2 oz Black Raspberry Liqueur
Fill with Pineapple Juice.
Shake.

SEX ON THE BEACH (Australian)
Fill glass with ice.
1 oz Blue Curacao
1 oz Pisang Ambon
Dash of Grenadine
Fill with Orange Juice.
Shake.

SEX ON THE BEACH IN WINTER
Fill glass with ice.
1 oz Vodka or Peach Vodka
1 oz Peach Schnapps
1/2 tsp Cream of Coconut
Fill with equal parts Pineapple and
Cranberry Juice.
Shake.

SEX ON THE LAKE
Fill glass with ice.
1 oz Rum or Banana Rum
1/2 oz Banana Liqueur
1/2 oz dark Crème de Cacao
Dash of Cream
Shake.
Strain into chilled glass.

SEX ON THE POOL TABLE
Fill glass with ice.
1 oz Vodka or Orange Vodka
1/2 oz Melon Liqueur
1/2 oz Blue Curacao
Fill with equal parts Orange
and Pineapple Juice.
Shake.

SEX ON THE SIDEWALK
Fill glass with ice.
1 oz Vodka or Cranberry Vodka
1/2 oz Melon Liqueur
1/2 oz Black Raspberry Liqueur
Fill with Cranberry Juice.
Shake.
Garnish with packaged condom.

SEX WITH AN ALLIGATOR
Fill glass with ice.
3/4 oz Jagermeister
3/4 oz Black Raspberry Liqueur
3/4 oz Melon Liqueur
Fill with equal parts Sour Mix and
Pineapple Juice.
Shake.

SEX WITH THE BARTENDER
Fill glass with ice.
1 oz Vodka
1/2 oz Coconut Rum
1/2 oz Orange Liqueur
Dash Secret Ingredient
Fill with equal parts Pineapple
Juice and Lemon-Lime Soda.
Garnish the Bartender with
Flowers, Jewelry, Cash, Sports Car.

SEXUAL GATOR (floater)
3/4 oz Black Raspberry Liqueur
(bottom)
Mix together:
1/2 oz Melon Liqueur and 1/2oz
Pineapple Juice
3/4 oz Jägermeister (top)

SEXY aka CARA SPOSA
Fill glass with ice.
1 oz Coffee Liqueur
1 oz Orange Liqueur
Fill with Milk or Cream.
Shake.
Garnish with Orange.

SEXY ALLIGATOR (floater)
1/4oz Black Raspberry Liqueur
(bottom)
Mix together:
1/2 oz Coconut Rum
1/2 oz Melon Liqueur
1/2 oz Pineapple Juice
1/4 oz Jägermeister (top)

SHADY LADY
Fill glass with ice.
1 oz Tequila
1 oz Melon Liqueur
Fill with Grapefruit Juice.

SHANGHAI
Fill glass with ice.
1 1/2 oz Dark Rum
1/2 oz Sambuca or Anisette
1/2 oz Lemon Juice
1 tsp Grenadine
Shake.
Strain into chilled glass.

SHANTE'GAF
Fill glass 3/4 with Ale or Beer.
Fill with Ginger Beer or
Lemon-Lime Soda.

SHARK ATTACK
Fill glass with ice.
2 oz Light Rum
Fill with Lemonade.
Float 1/2 oz Blue Curacao
on top.

SHARK BITE
Fill glass with ice.
2 oz Dark Rum
Dash of Grenadine
Fill with Orange Juice.
Shake.
Garnish with Orange and Cherry.

SHARK'S TOOTH
Fill glass with ice.
1 1/2 oz Dark Rum
1/2 oz Lime Juice
1/2 oz Lemon Juice
1/4 oz Grenadine
Shake.
Fill with Soda Water.

SHARK'S TOOTH 2
Fill glass with ice.
2 oz Dark Rum
Fill with Sour Mix.
Shake.
Top with 1/2 oz Grenadine.

SHARKY PUNCH
Fill glass with ice.
1 1/2 oz Apple Brandy
1/2 oz Whiskey
1 tsp Sugar Syrup
Shake.
Fill with Soda Water.

SHAVED BUSH
Fill glass with ice.
1/2 oz Light Rum or Vanilla Rum
1/2 oz Coffee Liqueur
1/2 oz Amaretto
1/2 oz White Crème de Cacao
1 oz Milk or Cream
Shake. Strain into shot glass.

SHERRY COCKTAIL
Fill glass with ice.
2 1/2 oz Cream Sherry
Dash of Bitters
Stir.
Strain into chilled glass.
Garnish with Orange Twist.

SHERRY TWIST
Fill glass with ice.
3 oz Sherry
1 oz Brandy
1 oz Dry Vermouth
1/2 tsp Curacao or Triple Sec
3 dashes of Lemon Juice
Shake.
Strain into chilled glass.
Sprinkle with Cinnamon.

SHILLELAGH aka BUSHWACKER
Fill glass with ice.
1 oz Irish Whiskey or Irish Mist
1 oz Irish Cream
Stir.

SHINEY NAVEL
Fill glass with ice.
2 oz Apple Brandy
Fill with Orange Juice.

SHIPWRECK
Fill glass with ice.
2 oz Coconut Rum
Fill with Pineapple Juice.
Top with 1/2 oz 151-Proof Rum.
Garnish with Pineapple.

SHIRLEY TEMPLE
Fill glass with ice.
Fill with Ginger Ale or
Lemon-Lime Soda.
Dash of Grenadine
Garnish with Cherry.

SHIVER SHOT
Find an attractive, desirable,
ample bust.
Ask permission to use it.
If yes, fill shot glass with Tequila.
Lick upper chest, and salt
moistened location.
Put Lime wedge in desired lips.
Place shot glass in cleavage.
Lick salt, drink shot, take Lime.
(No Hands)

S

Metric Measurement Conversion Chart on page 14

SHOGUN
1 1/2 oz Citrus Vodka
1/2 oz Orange Liqueur
1 oz Lime Juice or Sour Mix
Shake.

SHOT IN THE DARK
1/2 oz Yukon Jack
1/2 oz Orange Liqueur
1/2 oz hot Black Coffee

SHOT IN THE DARK, SPEED-BALL, HAMMERHEAD, KICK START, RED EYE,
In large coffee cup:
2 shots Espresso
Fill with Hot Black Coffee.

SIBERIAN
Fill glass with ice.
1 1/2 oz Vodka
1/2 oz Coffee Liqueur
1/2 oz Brandy
Stir.

SICILIAN COFFEE
1 oz Southern Comfort
1 oz Amaretto
Fill glass with hot Black Coffee.
Top with Whipped Cream.
Sprinkle with Shaved Almonds.

SICILIAN KISS
Fill glass with ice.
1 1/2 oz Southern Comfort
1/2 oz Amaretto
Stir.

SIDECAR
Fill glass with ice.
1 1/2 oz Brandy
1/2 oz Triple Sec
Fill with Sour Mix.
Shake.
Strain into chilled glass.
Garnish with Orange and Cherry.

SILK PANTIES
Fill glass with ice.
3/4 oz Peach Schnapps
3/4 oz Sambuca or Vodka
Stir.
Strain into chilled glass.

SILK PANTIES 2 aka WOO WOO
Fill glass with ice.
3/4 oz Vodka or Cranberry
   or Peach Vodka
3/4 oz Peach Schnapps
1 oz Cranberry Juice
Stir.
Strain into chilled glass.

SILK SHORTS
3/4 oz Vodka
3/4 oz Peach Schnapps
Stir.

SILKEN VEIL
Fill glass with ice.
1 oz Vodka
1 oz Dubonnet Rouge
Stir.
Garnish with twist.

SILVER BULLET
Fill glass with ice.
1 1/2 oz Tequila
1/2 oz White Crème de Menthe
Stir.
Serve or strain into chilled glass.

SILVER CLOUD
Fill glass with ice.
1/2 oz Vodka or Vanilla Vodka
1/2 oz Coffee Liqueur
1/2 oz White Crème de Cacao
1/ oz Amaretto
Fill with Milk.
Shake.
Top with Whipped Cream.

SILVER FIZZ
Fill glass with ice.
2 oz Gin
1 Egg White
2 oz Sour Mix
Shake.
Strain into chilled glass.
Fill with Soda Water.

SILVER FIZZ 2
Fill glass with ice.
2 oz Gin
1 Egg White
1/2 oz Sugar Syrup
or 1 tsp Sugar
1 oz Sour Mix
2 oz Cream or Milk
Shake.
Strain into chilled glass.
Splash with Soda Water.
Garnish with Orange and Cherry.

SILVER KING
Fill glass with ice.
1 1/2 oz Gin
1 Egg White
1 oz Lemon Juice
1/2 tsp Sugar Syrup
or Powdered Sugar
2 dashes of Orange Bitters
Shake.
Serve or strain into chilled glass.

SILVER SPIDER
Fill glass with ice.
1/2 oz Vodka
1/2 oz Light Rum
1/2 oz Triple Sec
1/2 oz White Crème de Menthe
Stir.
Serve or strain into chilled glass.

SILVERADO
Fill glass with ice.
1 1/2 oz Vodka or Citrus Vodka
1/2 oz Campari
Fill with Orange or Grapefruit Juice.
Shake.

SIMPLY BONKERS
Fill glass with ice.
1 oz Rum or Raspberry RUm
1 oz Black Raspberry Liqueur
1 oz Cream or Milk
Shake. Strain into shot glass.

SIMPLY EXQUISITE
Fill glass with ice.
3/4 oz Orange Liqueur
3/4 oz Banana Liqueur
3/4 oz Hazelnut Liqueur
Fill with Milk or Cream.
Shake.
Garnish with Orange and Banana.

SINGAPORE SLING
Fill glass with ice.
2 oz Gin
Splash Sloe Gin
3 oz Sour Mix
Shake.
Splash of Soda Water
Top with Cherry Brandy.
Garnish with Cherry and Lemon.

SINGAPORE SLING 2
Fill glass with ice.
1 1/2 oz Gin
1/2 oz Triple Sec
Dash of Lime Juice
Fill with equal parts Orange,
Pineapple Juice and Sour Mix.
Shake.
Top with Cherry Brandy
Garnish with Orange and Cherry.

SINK OR SWIM
Fill glass with ice.
1 1/2 oz Brandy
1/2 oz Sweet Vermouth
3 dashes of Bitters
Shake.
Strain into chilled glass.

SINNER
Fill glass with ice.
2 oz Vodka or Lemon Vodka
Dash of Sour Mix
Fill with Lemon-Lime Soda.

SIR WALTER
Fill glass with ice.
1 1/2 oz Brandy
3/4 oz Light Rum
1 tsp Curacao
1 tsp Grenadine
1 tsp Lemon or Lime Juice
Shake.
Serve or strain into chilled glass.

69ER
Fill glass with ice.
1 1/2 oz Rum or Citrus Rum
1/2 oz Peach Schnapps
Fill with Cola.

SIZZLER
Fill glass with ice.
1 oz Vodka
1 oz Bourbon
1 oz Beer
1 oz Lemonade
Stir. Strain into shot glass.

SKI LIFT
1 oz Peach Schnapps
1 oz Coconut Rum
Fill with Hot Chocolate.
Top with Whipped Cream.
Sprinkle with Shredded Coconut.

SKID MARK
Fill glass with ice.
3/4 oz Coffee Liqueur
3/4 oz Peppermint Schnapps
3/4 oz Jägermeister
Shake.
Strain into shot glass.

SKINNY DIPPING
Fill glass with ice.
1 1/2 oz Vodka or Peach Vodka
1/2 oz Peach Schnapps
1/2 oz Amaretto

Fill with equal parts Orange and
Cranberry Juice.
Stir.
Garnish with Orange.

SKIP AND GO NAKED
Fill glass with ice.
2 oz Gin
Fill with Orange Juice or Sour Mix
(leaving 1/2 inch from top).
Float Beer on top.
Garnish with Orange.

SKIP AND GO NAKED 2
Fill glass with ice.
2 oz Gin or Vodka
Dash of Grenadine
Fill with Sour Mix
(leaving 1/2 inch from top).
Float Beer on top.
Garnish with Lemon.

SKULL
Fill glass with ice.
1 1/2 oz Light Rum
1/2 oz Spiced Rum
Fill with equal parts Lemon Juice
And Lemon-Lime Soda.
Garnish with lime.

SKULL CRACKER
Fill glass with ice.
4 oz Rum or Citrus Rum
1 oz White Crème de Cacao
1 oz Pineapple Juice
1 oz Lemon Juice
Shake.
Garnish with Lime.

SKYLAB FALLOUT
Fill glass with ice.
1/2 oz Vodka
1/2 oz Gin
1/2 oz Rum
1/2 oz Tequila
1/2 oz Blue Curacao
1/2 oz Pineapple Juice
Shake. Strain into shot glass.

SKYSCRAPER aka
SCREAMING VIKING
Fill glass with ice.
2 oz Bourbon
2-3 dashes of Bitters
1/2 oz Lime Juice
Fill with Cranberry Juice.
Stir.
Garnish with Cucumber.

SLAMMERS
In shot glass:
1 oz Desired Liquor
1 oz Ginger Ale or Lemon-Lime
Soda
Cover glass with napkin and hand,
Then slam on bar top.
Drink while foaming.

SLEDGEHAMMER
Fill glass with ice.
1 oz Brandy
1 oz Apple Brandy
1 oz Dark Rum
2 dashes of Pernod
Shake.
Strain into chilled glass.

S

SLEDGEHAMMER 2
Fill glass with ice.
1 oz Gin
1 oz Coconut Rum
Dash of Grenadine
Fill with equal parts Pineapple and Orange Juice.
Shake.

SLEDGEHAMMER (floater)
1 oz Sambuca (bottom)
1 oz Cognac or Brandy (top)

SLEEPY HEAD
Fill glass with ice.
3 oz Brandy
Fill with Ginger Ale.
Garnish with Orange Twist.

SLIMEBALL
Make Lime Flavored Gelatin.
Replace 1 cup of water in the recipe with:
6 oz Vodka
2 oz Melon Liqueur
Chill until it coagulates.

SLIPPERY BLACK NIPPLE
(floater)
1 1/2 oz Black Sambuca (bottom)
1/2 oz Irish Cream (top)
Carefully drip a single drop of Grenadine in center (optional).

SLIPPERY DICK (floater)
1 1/2 oz Banana Liqueur (bottom)
1/2 oz Irish Cream (top)

SLIPPERY NIPPLE
Fill glass with ice.
1 1/2 oz Sambuca
1/2 oz Irish Cream
Shake.

SLIPPERY NIPPLE (floater)
1 1/2 oz Sambuca (bottom)
1/2 oz Irish Cream (top)
Carefully drop a single drop of Grenadine in center (optional).

SLOE BALL
Fill glass with ice.
1 oz Sloe Gin
1/2 oz Vodka
1/2 oz Gin
Dash of Sour Mix
1 oz Orange Juice
Shake.
Strain into chilled glass.

SLOE BOAT TO CHINA
Fill glass with ice.
1 1/2 oz Ginger Liqueur
1/2 oz Sloe Gin
Stir.
Fill with Lemon-Lime Soda.

SLOE BRANDY
Fill glass with ice.
2 oz Brandy
1/2 oz Sloe Gin
1 tsp Lemon Juice
Shake.
Strain into chilled glass.
Garnish with Lemon Twist.

SLOE COMFORTABLE SCREW BETWEEN THE SHEETS
Fill glass with ice.
Dash Vodka or Orange Vodka
Dash Southern Comfort
Dash Sloe Gin
Dash Rum
Dash Brandy
Dash Triple Sec
Dash Sour Mix
Fill with Orange Juice.
Shake.

SLOE COMFORTABLE FUZZY SCREW AGAINST THE WALL
Fill glass with ice.
1/2 oz Sloe Gin
1/2 oz Southern Comfort
1/2 oz Peach Schnapps
1/2 oz Vodka
Fill with Orange Juice.
Shake.
Top with 1/2 oz Galliano.

SLOE COMFORTABLE MEXICAN SCREW AGAINST THE WALL
Fill glass with ice.
1/2 oz Sloe Gin
1/2 oz Southern Comfort
1/2 oz Tequila
1/2 oz Vodka
Fill with Orange Juice.
Shake.
Top with 1/2 oz Galliano.

SLOE COMFORTABLE SCREW
Fill glass with ice.
1 oz Vodka
1 oz Southern Comfort
1/2 oz Sloe Gin
Fill with Orange Juice.
Garnish with Orange.

SLOE COMFORTABLE SCREW AGAINST THE WALL
Fill glass with ice.
1 oz Vodka
1 oz Southern Comfort
1/2 oz Sloe Gin
Fill with Orange Juice.
Shake.
Top with Galliano.
Garnish with Orange.

SLOE DOG
Fill glass with ice.
1 1/2 oz Vodka
1/2 oz Sloe Gin
Fill with Grapefruit Juice.
Shake.

SLOE GIN FIZZ
Fill glass with ice.
2 oz Sloe Gin
Fill with Sour Mix.
Shake.
Splash with Soda Water.
Garnish with Lemon.

SLOE POKE
Fill glass with ice.
2 oz Sloe Gin
Fill with Cola.

SLOE SCREW
Fill glass with ice.
1 1/2 oz Sloe Gin
or 3/4 oz Vodka
and 3/4 oz Sloe Gin
Fill with Orange Juice.
Stir.
Garnish with Orange.

Metric Measurement Conversion Chart on page 14

SLOE TEQUILA
Fill glass with ice.
1 1/2 oz Tequila
1/2 oz Sloe Gin
1 tsp Lime Juice
Shake.
Strain into chilled glass.
Garnish with Cucumber Peel.

SLOPPY JOE
Fill glass with ice.
3/4 oz Rum
3/4 oz Dry Vermouth
1/4 oz Triple Sec
1/4 oz Grenadine
1 oz Lime Juice
Shake.
Serve or strain into chilled glass.

SLOPPY JOE'S
Fill glass with ice.
1 oz Brandy
1 oz Port
1/2 tsp Triple Sec
1 oz Pineapple Juice
1/2 tsp Grenadine
Shake.
Strain into chilled glass.

SMELLY CAT
Fill glass with ice.
1 1/2 oz Citrus Vodka
1/2 oz Peach Schnapps
Dash of Cranberry Juice
Shake.
Strain into chilled glass.

SMITH AND KERNS
Fill glass with ice.
2 oz Coffee Liqueur
1 oz Cream
Shake.
Fill with Soda Water.

SMOOTH DRIVER
Fill glass with ice.
2 oz Vodka or Orange Vodka
Fill with Orange Juice.
Float 1/2 oz Orange Liqueur on top.

SMOOTH OPERATOR (frozen)
In Blender: cup of ice
3/4 oz Coffee Liqueur
3/4 oz Hazelnut Liqueur
3/4 oz Irish Cream
1/2 ripe peeled banana
Dash of Milk or Cream
Blend until smooth.

SMURF P.
Fill glass with ice.
1 oz Light Rum or Citrus Rum
1/2 oz Blueberry Schnapps
1/2 oz Blue Curacao
1 oz Sour Mix
Shake.
Strain into chilled glass.
Splash with Lemon-Lime Soda.

SNAKE BITE
Fill glass with ice.
2 oz Yukon Jack
Dash of Lime Juice
Shake.
Serve or strain into chilled glass.
Garnish with Lime.

SNAKE BITE 2
Fill glass with ice.
1 1/2 oz Bourbon
or Canadian Whiskey
1/2 oz Peppermint Schnapps
Stir.
Strain into chilled glass.

SNAKE BITE 3
Fill glass 3/4 with Hard Cider.
Fill glass with Ale.

SNEAKY PETE
Fill glass with ice.
2 oz Tequila
1/2 oz White Crème de Menthe
1 oz Pineapple Juice
Dash of Lime Juice
Shake.
Strain into chilled glass.
Garnish with Lime.

SNICKER
Fill glass with ice.
1 oz Hazelnut Liqueur
1 oz Irish Cream
1 oz Dark Crème de Cacao
Fill with Milk or Cream.
Shake.

SNICKER AT THE BAR (frozen)
In Blender:
1/2 cup of Ice
3/4 oz Coffee Liqueur
3/4 oz Irish Cream
3/4 oz Hazelnut Liqueur
1/4 cup peanuts
1 scoop of Vanilla Ice Cream
Blend until smooth.
If too thick add Milk.
If too thin add ice or Ice Cream.

SNO CAP (frozen)
In Blender: cup of ice.
1 oz Coffee Liqueur
3/4 oz Vodka
3/4 oz Irish Cream
Blend until smooth.
Garnish with non perils.
Bill Bona

SNOW CONE
Pack glass with crushed ice.
So that it is convex (arched)
Drizzle to make stripes
2 oz Spiced Rum
1/2 oz Banana Liqueur
1/2 oz Blue Curacao
Dash Sloe Gin or Grenadine
Serve with spoon.

SNOWBALL
Fill glass with ice.
1 oz Gin
1/2 oz White Crème de Menthe
1/2 oz Anisette
Fill with Milk or Cream.
Shake.

SNOWBALL 2
Fill glass with ice.
3/4 oz Brandy
3/4 oz Peppermint Schnapps
3/4 oz White Crème de Cacao
Shake.
Strain into shot glass.

S

SNOWBALL 3
Fill glass with ice.
1 oz Sambuca
1 oz White Crème de Cacao
1 oz Cream
Shake.
Strain into chilled glass.

SNOWBERRY aka RED RUSSIAN
Fill glass with ice.
1 oz Vodka or Strawberry Vodka
1 oz Strawberry Liqueur
Fill with Milk or Cream.
Shake.

SNOWBLOWER 2
Fill glass with ice.
1 oz Gin
3/4 oz Peppermint Schnapps
2 oz Cream of Coconut
Fill with Pineapple Juice.
Shake.

SNOWCAP (floater)
3/4 oz Tequila (bottom)
3/4 oz Irish Cream (top)

SNOWSHOE GROG
Fill glass with ice.
1 1/2 oz Bourbon or Brandy
1/2 oz Peppermint Schnapps
Stir.

SNUGGLER aka COCOANAPPS, ADULT HOT CHOCOLATE, PEPPERMINT KISS
2 oz Peppermint Schnapps
Fill with Hot Chocolate.
Top with Whipped Cream.
Sprinkle with Shaved Chocolate or Chocolate Sprinkles.

SOMBRERO
Fill glass with ice.
2 oz Coffee Liqueur
or Coffee Brandy
Fill with Milk or Cream.
Shake.

SONIC
Fill glass with ice.
1 oz desired Liquor or Liqueur
Fill with equal parts Soda Water
and Tonic Water.

SOUL KISS
Fill glass with ice.
1 oz Whiskey
1 oz Dry Vermouth
1/2 oz Dubonnet
3/4 oz Orange Juice
Shake.
Serve or strain into chilled glass.

SOUR (from scratch)
heaping tsp Sugar(superfine works best)
juice of a medium lemon
Fill glass with ice.
2oz desired liquor or Liqueur
Shake.
Garnish with Orange and Cherry.

SOUR
Fill glass with ice.
2 oz desired liquor or liqueur
Fill with Sour Mix.
Shake.
Garnish with Orange and Cherry.

SOUR APPLE MARTINI
Fill glass with ice.
3 1/2 oz Vodka or Apple Vodka
1/2 oz Sour Apple Liqueur
Shake
Strain into chilled glass.
Garnish with cherry.

SOUR BALL
Fill glass with ice.
1 oz Vodka or Citrus Vodka
1 oz Apricot Brandy
Fill with equal parts Sour Mix and
Orange Juice.
Shake.
Garnish with Orange and Cherry.

SOUR CHERRY MARTINI
Fill glass with ice.
2 1/2 oz Vodka or Cherry Vodka
1/2 oz Cherry Liqueur
1/2 oz Lemon Juice
Dash Cherry Juice
Shake. Strain into a chilled glass.
Garnish with Cherry.

SOUR GRAPES
Fill glass with ice.
3/4 oz Vodka
3/4 oz Black Raspberry Liqueur
3/4 oz Sour Mix
Shake.
Strain into chilled glass.

SOUR MIX
In Blender:
1 Egg White
1 cup of Water
1 cup of Lemon Juice
3 tbsp Sugar
Blend until sugar is liquefied.

SOUR PATCH MARTINI
Fill glass with ice.
1/2 oz Citrus Vodka
1/2 oz Orange Vodka
1/2 oz Raspberry Vodka
1/2 oz Strawberry Vodka
1oz Lemon Juice
1oz Sour Mix
Dash Cranberry Juice
Shake. Strain into chilled glass
rimmed with sugar.

SOUTH FORK COFFEE
1 oz Bourbon
1 oz Crème de Cacao
Fill with hot Black Coffee
Top with Whipped Cream.
Drizzle with Chocolate Syrup.

SOUTH OF FRANCE
Fill glass with ice.
1 oz Rum
1 oz B&B
1 tbsp Cream of Coconut
Fill with Pineapple Juice.
Shake.

SOUTH OF THE BORDER
Fill glass with ice.
1 1/2 oz Tequila
1/2 oz Coffee Liqueur
1oz Lime Juice
Shake.
Strain into chilled glass.

SOUTH PACIFIC

Fill glass with ice.
1 1/2 oz Dark Rum
1/2 oz Coconut Rum
Fill with equal parts Orange,
Cranberry, and Pineapple Juice.
Shake.
Garnish with Cherry and Orange.

SOUTHERN BEACH

Fill glass with ice.
1 oz Southern Comfort
1/2 oz Peach Schnapps
1/2 oz Amaretto
Dash of Pineapple Juice
Dash of Cranberry Juice
1 oz Orange Juice
Shake.
Strain into chilled glass.

SOUTHERN BELLE

Fill glass with ice.
1 oz Southern Comfort
1 oz Irish Cream

SOUTHERN BELLE 2

Fill glass with ice.
1 1/2 oz Bourbon or Southern
Comfort
1/2 oz Triple Sec
Dash of Grenadine
Fill with equal parts Pineapple
Juice
and Orange Juice or Sour Mix.
Shake.

SOUTHERN BRIDE

2 1/2 oz Gin
1 oz Grapefruit Juice
Dash of Grenadine
Shake.
Strain into chilled glass.

SOUTHERN BRIDE 2

Fill glass with ice.
2 oz Gin or Orange Gin
1/2 tsp Triple Sec or Curacao
2 dashes of Orange Bitters
Stir.
Strain into chilled glass.
Garnish with Lemon Twist.

SOUTHERN BULLDOG

Fill glass with ice.
1 oz Southern Comfort
1 oz Coffee Liqueur
Fill with Milk or Cream.
Shake.

SOUTHERN COMFORT
MANHATTAN

Fill glass with ice.
2 oz Southern Comfort
1/2 oz Dry Vermouth
Stir.
Strain into chilled glass or pour
contents (with ice) into short glass.
Garnish with Cherry or Lemon
Twist.

SOUTHERN COMFORT OLD
FASHIONED

Muddle together in glass:
Stemless Maraschino Cherry
Orange Slice
1/2 tsp Sugar
4 or 5 dashes of Bitters
Fill glass with ice.
2 oz Southern Comfort
Splash of Soda Water
Stir.

SOUTHERN MAIDEN

Fill glass with ice.
1 1/2 oz Bourbon
1/2 oz Triple Sec
2 oz Orange Juice
Fill with Pineapple Juice.
Shake.

SOUTHSIDE

Muddle together in glass:
6 Mint Leaves
1 tsp Sugar
Dash of Water
1 tbsp Lemon Juice.
Fill glass with crushed ice.
2 oz Bourbon
Fill with Spring Water.
Stir vigorously.

SOVEREIGN COFFEE

1 oz Black Raspberry Liqueur
1 oz Dark Crème de Cacao
Fill with hot Black Coffee.
Top with Whipped Cream.
Sprinkle with Shaved Chocolate or
Sprinkles.

SOVIET COCKTAIL

Fill glass with ice.
1 1/2 oz Vodka
1/2 oz Amontillado Sherry
1/2 oz Dry Vermouth
Shake.
Serve or strain into chilled glass.
Garnish with Lemon Twist.

SPANISH COFFEE aka
SUPER COFFEE

1 oz Coffee Liqueur
1 oz Cognac or Brandy
Fill with hot Black Coffee.
Top with Whipped Cream.
Garnish with Orange.

SPANISH COFFEE 2

3/4 oz Coffee Liqueur
3/4 oz Brandy
3/4 oz Orange Liqueur
Fill with hot Black Coffee.
Top with Whipped Cream.
Garnish with Orange.

SPANISH COFFEE 3

2 oz Tequila
Fill with hot Black Coffee.
Top with Whipped Cream.
Garnish with Lime.

SPANISH COFFEE 4

In a heat tempered glass or mug
Moisten rim of glass
with Orange slice
And sprinkle rim with Sugar.
1/2 oz 151 proof Rum
Ignite. Let burn for 10-15 seconds
and snuff, by covering
With plate or another glass.
1/2 oz Orange Liqueur
1/2 oz Dark Rum
Dash Coffee Liqueur
Fill with Hot Black Coffee
Top with Whipped Cream
Garnish with Orange.

SPANISH DYNAMITE

Fill glass with ice.
1 oz Tequila
1/2 oz Licor 43
1/2 oz Orange Liqueur or Triple Sec
Shake and Strain into chilled glass.
Garnish with Cinnamon Stick.

S

SPANISH FLY
Fill glass with ice.
1 oz Tequila
1 oz Amaretto
Stir.

SPANISH ICED COFFEE
Fill glass with ice.
1 oz Coffee Liqueur
1 oz Cognac or Brandy
Fill with Iced Coffee.
Add Cream or Milk and sugar or
sweetener to taste.

SPANISH MOSS
Fill glass with ice.
1 1/2 oz Tequila
1 oz Coffee Liqueur
or Coffee Brandy
Shake.
Strain into chilled glass.
Add 3 drops of Green Crème de
Menthe.

SPARKS
Fill glass 3/4 full with ice.
1 oz Peppered Vodka
Fill with Champagne.

SPATS
Fill glass with ice.
1 1/2 oz Rum or Citrus Rum
1/2 oz Melon Liqueur
Fill with equal parts Orange and
Pineapple Juice.
Shake.
Float 1/2 oz Sloe Gin on top.
Garnish with Orange or Pineapple
and Cherry.

SPECIAL ROUGH
Fill glass with ice.
1 1/2 oz Brandy
1 1/2 oz Apple Brandy
2 dashes of Pernod
Stir.
Strain into chilled glass.

SPEEDBALL, HAMMERHEAD, KICK START, RED EYE, SHOT IN THE DARK,
In large coffee cup:
2 shots Espresso
Fill with Hot Black Coffee.

SPEEDY aka JUMPER CABLE
Fill glass with ice.
2 oz 151-Proof Rum
Fill with Jolt Cola
Stir.
Garnish with Lime.

SPERM (floater)
1 1/2 oz Tequila (bottom)
1/2 oz Irish Cream (top)

SPERM BANK (floater)
1/2 oz Irish Cream (bottom)
1/2 oz White Crème de Cacao
1/2 oz Amaretto (top)
Place 1 drop of Grenadine in center
of glass.

SPHINX
Fill glass with ice.
2 oz Gin
2 tsp Dry Vermouth
2 tsp Sweet Vermouth
Stir.
Strain into chilled glass.

SPICY SWORD
In chilled glass: one whole
peeled baby banana.
In a mixing glass:
Fill glass with ice.
3 1/2 oz Pepper Vodka
1/2 oz Banana Liqueur
tsp Salsa
Dash hot sauce (optional)
Shake. Strain into chilled glass.

SPIKE
Fill glass with ice.
2 oz Tequila
Fill with Grapefruit Juice.
Stir.
Garnish with Lime.

SPILT MILK
1/2 oz Light Rum
1/2 oz Blended Whiskey
1/2 oz Irish Cream
1/2 oz Crème de Nouyax
or Amaretto
1 oz Milk or Cream
Shake.
Strain into chilled glass.

SPITTING HAMSTER
Fill glass with ice.
1 oz Tequila
1 oz Orange Liqueur
Dash Sambuca
Dash Green Crème de Menthe
Shake. Strain into chilled glass.

SPLEEF
Fill glass with ice.
2 oz Dark Rum
2 oz Orange Juice
Fill with Pineapple Juice.
Stir.
Garnish with Lime.

SPOOGE
Fill glass with ice.
1 oz Coconut Rum
1 oz Coffee Liqueur
1 oz Cream
Shake. Strain into shot glass.

SPRING ACTION
Fill glass with ice.
3/4 oz Southern Comfort
3/4 oz Apricot Brandy
3/4 oz Sloe Gin
Fill with Orange Juice.
Shake.

SPRING BREAK
Fill glass with ice.
2 oz Coconut Rum
Fill with equal parts Cranberry
Juice and Lemon-Lime Soda.

SPRING FLING
Fill glass with ice.
1/2 oz Vodka
1/2 oz Triple Sec
1/2 oz Apricot Brandy
Fill with equal parts Orange Juice
and Sour Mix.
Shake.

SPRING THAW (floater)
1 1/4 oz Yukon Jack (bottom)
1/2 oz Irish Cream
1/4 oz Vodka (top)
Nick G. Zeroulias

Metric Measurement Conversion Chart on page 14

SPRITZER
Fill glass 3/4 with ice.
Fill 3/4 with desired Wine.
Fill with Soda Water.
Garnish with Lime.

SPY'S DEMISE
Fill glass with ice.
1/2 oz Vodka
1/2 oz Gin
1/2 oz Rum
1/2 oz Sloe Gin
1 oz Sour Mix
Shake.
Strain into chilled glass.
Fill with Lemon-Lime Soda.

SQUID INK
Fill glass with ice.
1 oz Black Sambuca
1 oz Black Raspberry Liqueur
Stir.

STAR
Fill glass with ice.
1 1/2 oz Apple Brandy
1 1/2 oz Sweet Vermouth
2 dashes of Bitters
Stir.
Strain into chilled glass.

STAR WARS
Fill glass with ice.
3/4 oz Vodka or Peach
    or Orange Vodka
3/4 oz Southern Comfort
3/4 oz Orange Liqueur
Fill with Orange Juice.
Dash of Grenadine
Shake.
Garnish with Orange.

STARBOARD TACK
Fill glass with ice.
1 oz Spiced Rum
1 oz Coconut Rum
Fill with equal parts Cranberry
and Orange Juice.
Garnish with Orange.

STARBURSTS
Fill glass with ice.
3 1/2 oz Citrus Vodka or Citrus Rum
1/2 oz Amaretto
1 oz Cranberry Juice
Shake.
Strain into chilled glass.

STARLIGHT
Fill glass with ice.
1 1/2 oz Vodka
1/2 oz Black Sambuca
Stir.
Strain into chilled glass.
Garnish with Lemon Twist.

STARS AND STRIPES (floater)
1 oz Grenadine (bottom)
1 oz Heavy Cream
1 oz Blue Curacao (top)

STEALTH (floater)
1/2 oz Coffee Liqueur (bottom)
1/2 oz Banana Liqueur
1/2 oz Irish Cream
1/2 oz Orange Liqueur (top)

STEEL HELMET
Fill glass with ice.
1 oz Vodka
1 oz Coffee Liqueur
Fill with Milk or Cream.
Shake.
Top with Galliano.

STEEPLE JACK
Fill glass with ice.
2 oz Apple Brandy
2 oz Apple Cider
or Apple Juice
Dash of Lime Juice
Shake.
Strain into chilled glass.
Fill with Soda Water.
Garnish with Cinnamon Stick and
Lime.

STEVIE RAY VAUGHAN
Fill glass with ice.
1 oz Bourbon
1 oz Southern Comfort
1/2 oz Triple Sec
Dash of Sour Mix
Fill with Orange Juice.
Shake.

STILETTO
Fill glass with ice.
1 oz Rum or Banana Vodka
    or Citrus Vodka
1/2 oz Amaretto
1/2 oz Banana Liqueur
Fill with equal parts Orange Juice
and Pineapple Juice.
Shake.

STINGER
Fill glass with ice.
1 1/2 oz Brandy
1/2 oz White Crème de Menthe
Stir.
Serve or strain into chilled glass.

STOCK MARKET ZOO
Fill glass with ice.
1/2 oz Gin
1/2 oz Rum
1/2 oz Tequila
1/2 oz Bourbon
Dash of Grenadine
Dash of Orange Juice
Fill with Pineapple Juice.
Shake.
Strain into chilled glass.

STONE FENCE
Fill glass with ice.
2 oz Apple Brandy or Scotch
2 dashes of Bitters
Fill glass with cold cider.

STONEWALL
Fill glass with ice.
1 oz Dark Rum
2 oz Apple Cider
Stir.

STORM CLOUD
Fill glass with ice.
1 oz 151-Proof Rum
1 oz Coffee Liqueur
Stir.

S

STRAIGHT LAW
Fill glass with ice.
2 oz Dry Sherry
1 oz Gin
Stir.
Strain into chilled glass.
Garnish with Lemon Twist.

STRAWBERRY BLONDE (frozen)
In Blender:
1/2 cup of Ice
1 oz Strawberry Liqueur
1 oz White Crème de Cacao
1/2 cup fresh or frozen
Strawberries
Scoop of Vanilla Ice Cream
Blend until smooth.
If too thick add Milk or berries. If too thin add ice or Ice Cream.

STRAWBERRY CHEESECAKE
In Blender:
1/2 cup ice
1 1/2 oz Vanilla Vodka or Vodka
1/2 oz Strawberry Liqueur
2 tsp Strawberry Jam
2 Tblsp Cream Cheese
Blend until smooth.
Garnish with Graham Cracker.

STRAWBERRY COLADA
(frozen)
In Blender:
1/2 cup of Ice
2 oz Rum or Coconut Rum
2 tbsp Cream of Coconut
1/2 cup fresh or frozen
Strawberries
1 tbsp Vanilla Ice Cream
Blend until smooth.
If too thick add fruit or juice.
If too thin add ice or Ice Cream.
Garnish with strawberry.

STRAWBERRY DAIQUIRI
(frozen)
In Blender:
1 cup of Ice
1 1/2 oz Rum
1/2 oz Strawberry Liqueur
1/2 oz Lime Juice
1/2 cup fresh or frozen
Strawberries
Blend until smooth.
If too thick add berries or juice.
If too thin add ice.
Garnish with Lime and/or strawberry.

STRAWBERRY MARGARITA
(frozen)
In Blender:
1 cup of Ice
1 1/2 oz Tequila
1/2 oz Triple Sec
1/2 oz Lime Juice
1/2 cup fresh or frozen
Strawberries
Blend until smooth.
If too thick add juice or berries.
If too thin add ice.
Garnish with Lime and/or Strawberry.

STRAWBERRY MARTINI
Fill glass with ice.
3 1/2 oz Vodka or
Strawberry Vodka
Dash Strawberry Liqueur
tsp Strawberry Jam (optional)
Shake. Strain into a chilled glass.

STRAWBERRY SHORTCAKE
(frozen)
In Blender:
1/2 cup of Ice
1 oz Vodka or Strawberry Vodka
1 oz Strawberry Liqueur
1/2 cup fresh or frozen
Strawberries
Scoop of Vanilla Ice Cream
Blend until smooth.
If too thick add fruit or Milk.
If too thin add ice or Ice Cream.
Top with Whipped Cream.
Garnish with strawberry.

STREGA SOUR
Fill glass with ice.
1 1/2 oz Gin
1/2 oz Strega
2 oz Sour Mix
Shake.
Strain into chilled glass.

STUFFED TOILET (floater)
1/2 oz Coffee Liqueur (bottom)
1/2 oz Irish Cream
1/2 oz Tuaca (top)

STUMBLING F.
Fill glass with ice.
1 oz 151-Proof Rum
1 oz Jägermeister
1 oz 100-Proof Peppermint
Schnapps
Stir.
Strain into shot glass.

STUMBLING ISLANDER
Fill glass with ice.
1/2 oz Dark Rum
1/2 oz Spiced Rum
1/2 oz 151 Proof Rum
1/2 oz Coconut Rum
Dash of Lime Juice
Fill with equal parts Orange,
Pineapple, and Cranberry Juice.

STUMP BUSTER
Fill glass with ice.
1/2 oz Vodka
1/2 oz Gin
1/2 oz Rum
1/2 oz Tequila
Dash of Grenadine
Fill with Orange Juice.
Shake.
Garnish with Orange.

STUPID CUBE
Fill glass with ice.
1/2 oz Light Rum
1/2 oz Spiced Rum
1/2 oz Dark Rum
1/2 oz Amber Rum
Fill with equal parts Orange,
Grapefruit and Cranberry Juice.
Garnish with Lime, Lemon, Orange
and Cherry.

SUFFERING BASTARD
Fill glass with ice.
1 1/2 oz Dark Rum
1 oz 151-Proof Rum
1/2 oz Orange Curacao
or Triple Sec
1/2 oz Orgeat Syrup
Fill with equal parts Orange and
Lemon Juice.
Shake.
Garnish with Lime.

Metric Measurement Conversion Chart on page 14

SUFFRAGETTE CITY
Fill glass with ice.
2 oz Rum or Citrus Rum
1 oz Orange Liqueur
Dash of Grenadine
Dash of Lime Juice
Shake.
Strain into chilled glass.

SUGAR DADDY
Fill glass with ice.
1 oz Butterscotch Schnapps
1 oz Irish Cream
Dash of Coffee Liqueur
1 oz Milk
Shake.

SUGAR SYRUP
Mix 1 part Water
with 2 parts Sugar
(Works much better with hot water
and superfine sugar.)

SUICIDAL TENDENCIES
Fill glass with ice.
1 oz Grain Alcohol
1 oz Absinthe
Stir.

SUISSESSE
Fill glass with ice.
1 1/2 oz Pernod
2 oz Sour Mix
Shake.
Strain into chilled glass.
Fill with Soda Water.
Garnish with Lemon and Cherry.

SUMMER BREEZE
Fill glass with ice.
2 oz Rum
Fill with equal parts Cranberry and
Grapefruit Juice.
Garnish with Lime.

SUMMER SHARE
Fill glass with ice.
1 oz Vodka or Cherry Vodka
1 oz Rum or Pineapple Rum
1/2 oz Tequila
1 oz Orange Juice
1 oz Cranberry Juice
Dash of Apricot Brandy
Shake.
Fill with Lemon-Lime Soda.
Garnish with Orange.

SUMMER SOLSTICE SUNRISE
Fill glass with ice.
1 oz Vodka
1 oz Rum
Fill glass leaving 1/4 inch from top
with Orange, Pineapple and
Cranberry Juice.
Top with 1/2 oz Cherry Brandy.

SUN STROKE
Fill glass with ice.
1 1/2 oz Vodka or Citrus Vodka
1/4 oz Orange Liqueur
Fill with Grapefruit Juice.
Shake.

SUNBURST
Fill glass with ice.
1 1/2 oz Vodka or Grapefruit Vodka
1/2 oz Triple Sec
Fill with Grapefruit Juice.
Dash of Grenadine
Shake.

SUNDOWNER
Fill glass with ice.
2 oz Rum or Citrus Rum
Dash of Triple Sec
1 tsp Grenadine
3/4 oz Sour Mix
Shake and Strain into chilled glass.
Fill with Tonic Water.

SUNKEN TREASURE (floater)
1 oz Irish Cream (bottom)
1 oz Spiced Rum (top)

SUNNY DAY DREAM
Fill glass with ice.
2 oz Southern Comfort
Fill with Iced Tea.
Garnish with Lemon.
Mary Beth Dallas

SUNSPOT
Fill glass with ice.
1 1/2 oz Rum or Citrus Rum
1/2 oz Triple Sec
tsp Fresh Lemon Juice
Fill with Orange Juice.
Shake.

SUNTAN
Fill glass with ice.
2 oz Coconut Rum
Fill with Iced Tea.
Garnish with Lemon and Lime.

SUPER COFFEE aka SPANISH COFFEE
1 oz Coffee Liqueur
1 oz Cognac or Brandy
Fill with hot Black Coffee.
Top with Whipped Cream.
Garnish with Orange.

SURF RAT
Fill glass with ice.
3/4 oz Spiced Rum
3/4 oz Banana Liqueur
3/4 oz Coconut Rum
Fill with equal parts Orange,
Cranberry and Pineapple Juice.
Shake.

SURF'S UP
Fill glass with ice.
1 oz Coconut Rum
1/2 oz Banana Liqueur
1/2 oz White Crème de Cacao
Fill with equal parts Milk
and Pineapple Juice.
Shake.

SURFER ON ACID
Fill glass with ice.
1 oz Coconut Rum
1 oz Jägermeister
Fill with Pineapple Juice.
Shake.

SUSIE TAYLOR
Fill glass with ice.
2 oz Light Rum
1/2 oz Lime Juice
Fill with Ginger Ale.
Stir.
Garnish with Lemon.

SWAMP WATER
Fill glass with ice.
2 oz Rum or Orange Rum
1/4 oz Blue Curacao
1 oz Orange Juice
1/2 oz Lemon Juice
Shake.

S

SWAMP WATER 2
Fill glass with ice.
2 oz Green Chartreuse
Fill with Pineapple Juice or
Grapefruit Juice.
Shake.

SWEAT SOCK
Squeeze wet bar rag into shot
glass.

SWEATY MEXICAN LUMBERJACK
Fill glass with ice.
1 oz Tequila
1 oz Yukon Jack
3 dashes of Tabasco Sauce
Strain into shot glass.

SWEET CREAM (floater)
1 1/2 oz Coffee Liqueur (bottom)
1/2 oz Irish Cream (top)

SWEET PATOOTIE
Fill glass with ice.
1 oz Gin or Orange Gin
1/2 oz Triple Sec
1/2 oz Orange Juice
Shake.
Strain into chilled glass.

SWEET RELEASE
Fill glass with ice.
1 oz Vodka or Pineapple Vodka
1 oz Rum
Fill with Pineapple Juice.
Top with Sloe Gin.

SWEET TART
Fill glass with ice.
1 1/2 oz Vodka or Citrus Vodka
1/2 oz Black Raspberry Liqueur
2 oz Sour Mix
2 oz Cranberry Juice
Shake.
Fill with Lemon-Lime Soda.

SWEET TART 2
Fill glass with ice.
1 oz Vodka or Citrus Vodka
1/2 oz Orange Liqueur
1/2 oz Amaretto
Dash of Grenadine
Dash of Lime Juice
Fill with equal parts Sour Mix and
Lemon-Lime Soda.
Shake.

SWEET TEA
Sweetened Iced Tea

SWEDISH B J (floater)
1/2 oz Coffee Liqueur (bottom)
1/2 oz Banana Liqueur
1/2 oz Irish Cream
1/2 oz Swedish Vodka (top)
Top with Whipped Cream.
To drink, place hands behind back
and pick up using only mouth.

SWEDISH BEAR
Fill glass with ice.
1 1/2 oz Vodka or Vanilla Vodka
1/2 oz Dark Crème de Cacao
Fill with Milk or Cream.
Shake.

SWEDISH LULLABY
Fill glass with ice.
1 1/2 oz Swedish Punch
1 oz Cherry Liqueur
1/2 oz Lemon juice
Shake.
Strain into chilled glass.

SWIZZLE
Fill glass with ice.
2 oz Desired Liquor or Liqueur
2 Dashes Bitters
tsp Powdered Sugar
1 oz Lime Juice
Shake.
Fill with Soda Water.
Garnish with Lime.

T-BIRD
Fill glass with ice.
1/2 oz Vodka or Citrus Vodka
1/2 oz Orange Liqueur
1/2 oz Amaretto
2 oz Pineapple Juice
Dash of Cream (optional)
Shake.
Strain into chilled glass.

T L C
Fill glass with ice.
2 oz Tequila
Fill with Cola .
Garnish with Lime.

T. K. O.
Fill glass with ice.
2 oz Tequila
1 oz Coffee Liqueur
1 oz Ouzo
Stir.

T. N. T.
Fill glass with ice.
2 oz Tequila
Fill with Tonic Water.
Garnish with Lime.
*T.N.T. can also mean a Tangueray
Gin and Tonic*

TAHITI CLUB
Fill glass with ice.
2 oz Amber Rum
1/2 oz Lime Juice
1/2 oz Lemon Juice
1/2 oz Pineapple Juice
1/4 oz Maraschino Liqueur
Shake.
Garnish with Orange.

TAHITIAN APPLE
Fill glass with ice.
2 oz Light Rum
Fill with Apple Juice.

TAHITIAN ITCH
Fill glass with ice.
1 oz Bourbon
1 oz Rum
1/2 oz Orange Liqueur
2 oz Pineapple Juice
2 tbsp Lime Sherbet
Fill with Ginger Ale.

TAM-O-SHANTER
Fill glass with ice.
1 oz Irish Whiskey
1 oz Coffee Liqueur
Fill with Milk or Cream.
Shake.

TAMPA BAY SMOOTHIE
Fill glass with ice.
1 1/2 oz Vodka or Orange Vodka
1/2 oz Orange Liqueur
Dash of Grenadine
1 oz Orange Juice
Shake.
Strain into chilled glass.
Garnish with Orange and Cherry.

TANGERINE
Fill glass with ice.
2 oz Gin
1 tsp Grenadine
1 tsp Lime Juice
Fill with Sour Mix.

TANGERINE 2
Fill glass with ice.
1 oz Vodka or Orange Vodka
1/2 oz Orange Liqueur
1/2 oz Amaretto
Dash of Grenadine
Fill with Orange Juice.
Shake.

TANGO
Fill glass with ice.
1 1/2 oz Gin or Orange Gin
1/4 oz Dry Vermouth
1/4 oz Sweet Vermouth
1/2 tsp Curacao or Triple Sec
3/4 oz Orange Juice
Shake.
Serve or strain into chilled glass.
Garnish with Orange.

TANTALUS
Fill glass with ice.
1 oz Brandy
1 oz Forbidden Fruit
1 oz Lemon Juice
Shake.
Strain into chilled glass.

TARANTULA
Fill glass with ice.
3/4 oz Whiskey
3/4 oz Amaretto
3/4 oz Irish Cream
Stir.

TARNISHED BULLET
Fill glass with ice.
1/2 oz Tequila
1/2 oz Green Crème de Menthe
Stir.

TAWNY RUSSIAN aka GODMOTHER
Fill glass with ice.
1 1/2 oz Vodka
1/2 oz Amaretto
Stir.

TEACHER'S PET aka AGGRAVATION
Fill glass with ice.
1 oz Scotch
1 oz Coffee Liqueur
or Coffee Brandy
Fill with Milk or Cream.
Shake.

TEAR DROP
3 oz White Zinfandel
1 oz Peach Schnapps
Dash of Sour Mix
Fill with Soda Water.
Garnish with Lemon.

TEMPTATION
Fill glass with ice.
1 1/2 oz Whiskey
1/4 oz Triple Sec or Curacao
1/4 oz Dubonnet Rouge
1/4 oz Pernod
Shake.
Strain into chilled glass.
Garnish with Orange Twist and
Lemon Twist.

TEMPTER
Fill glass with ice.
1 1/2 oz Apricot Brandy
1 1/2 oz Port
Shake.
Serve or strain into chilled glass.

TENNESSEE
Fill glass with ice.
2 oz Whiskey
3/4 oz Maraschino Liqueur
1/2 oz Lemon Juice
Shake.

TENNESSEE LEMONADE
Fill glass with ice.
2 oz Bourbon
Fill with Lemonade.
Shake.

TENNESSEE MUD
1 oz Bourbon
1 oz Amaretto
Fill with hot Black Coffee.
Top with Whipped Cream.
Sprinkle with Brown Sugar.

TENNESSEE TEA
Fill glass with ice.
1/2 oz Bourbon
1/2 oz Dark Crème de Cacao
Fill with Cranberry Juice.
Stir.
Garnish with Lemon.

TEQUILA COLLINS
Fill glass with ice.
2 oz Tequila
Fill with Sour Mix.
Shake.
Splash of Soda Water
Garnish with Cherry and Orange.

TEQUILA GIMLET
Fill glass with ice.
2 oz Tequila
1 oz Lime Juice
Stir.
Serve or strain into chilled glass.
Garnish with Lime.

TEQUILA MANHATTAN
Fill glass with ice.
3 1/2 oz Tequila
1/2 oz Sweet Vermouth
Stir.
Strain into chilled glass or pour
contents (with ice) into short glass.
Garnish with Cherry.

S
T

Metric Measurement Conversion Chart on page 14

TEQUILA MARTINI aka TEQUINI
Fill glass with ice.
3 1/2 oz Tequila
1/2 oz Dry Vermouth
Stir.
Strain into chilled glass
or pour contents (with ice)
into short glass.
Garnish with Lemon Twist or
Orange Twist.

TEQUILA OLD FASHIONED
Muddle together in glass:
Stemless Maraschino Cherry
Orange Slice
1/2 tsp Sugar
4-5 dashes of Bitters
Fill glass with ice.
2 oz Tequila
Fill with Soda Water.
Stir.

TEQUILA PARALYZER
Fill glass with ice.
1 1/2 oz Tequila
1/2 oz Coffee Liqueur
2 oz Milk or Cream
Shake.
Top with 1-2 oz Cola.

TEQUILA POPPER aka TEQUILA BOOM BOOM aka TEQUILAZO aka GOLPEADO
In shot glass:
1 oz Tequila
1 oz Ginger Ale or Lemon-Lime
Soda
Cover glass with napkin and hand,
Then slam on bar top.
Drink while foaming.

TEQUILA QUENCHER
Fill glass with ice.
2 oz Tequila
Fill with equal parts Orange Juice
and Soda Water.
Garnish with Lime.

TEQUILA ROSE
Fill glass with ice.
2 oz Tequila
1/2 oz Lime Juice
Fill with Grapefruit Juice.
Shake.
Float 1/2 oz Grenadine on top.

TEQUILA SCREW-UP
Fill glass with ice.
2 oz Tequila
Splash Orange Juice
Fill with Lemon-Lime Soda
Garnish with Orange.

TEQUILA SHOOTER
Fill shot glass with Tequila.
Lick hand and pour small amount
of salt on moistened skin.
Have wedge of Lime or Lemon
ready.
1. Lick off salt
2. Drink shot
3. Bite and suck fruit wedge

TEQUILA SLAMMER aka TEQUILA BOOM BOOM aka TEQUILAZO aka POPPER
In shot glass:
1 oz Tequila
1 oz Ginger Ale or Lemon-Lime
Soda
Cover glass with napkin and hand,
Then slam on bar top.
Drink while foaming.

TEQUILA SOUR
Fill glass with ice.
2 oz Tequila
Fill with Sour Mix.
Shake.
Garnish with Cherry and Orange.

TEQUILA STINGER
Fill glass with ice.
1 1/2 oz Tequila
1/2 oz White Crème de Menthe
Stir.
Strain into chilled glass.

TEQUILA SUNRISE
Fill glass with ice.
2 oz Tequila
Fill with Orange Juice.
Pour 1/2 oz Grenadine down
spoon to bottom of glass.
Garnish with Orange.

TEQUILA SUNSET
Fill glass with ice.
2 oz Tequila
Fill with Orange or Grapefruit Juice.
Pour 1/2 oz Blackberry Brandy
down spoon to bottom of glass.

TEQUILA WITH TRAINING WHEELS
Pour shot of Tequila.
Slide the patron the salt shaker,
and a lemon or a lime on a napkin.

TEQUINI aka TEQUILA MARTINI
Fill glass with ice.
3 1/2 oz Tequila
1/2 oz Dry Vermouth
Stir.
Strain into chilled glass
or pour contents (with ice)
into short glass.
Garnish with Lemon Twist or
Orange Twist.

TERMINAL ICED TEA
Fill glass with ice.
1/2 oz Premium Vodka
1/2 oz Premium Gin
1/2 oz Premium Rum
1/2 oz Premium Tequila
1/2 oz Premium Orange Liqueur
2 oz Sour Mix
Top with Cola.
Garnish with Lemon.

TERMINATOR
Fill glass with ice.
1 oz Yukon Jack
1 oz Amaretto
1/2 oz Coconut Rum
1/2 oz Blue Curacao
Dash of Orange Juice
Shake.
Fill with Lemon-Lime Soda.

TERMINATOR 2
1/2oz Vodka or Citrus Vodka
1/2oz Gin
1/2oz Rum
1/2oz Orange Liqueur
1/2oz Coffee Liqueur
Dash Cranberry Juice
Fill almost to the top with Sour Mix
Shake
Top with 1/2oz Beer.

TEST-TUBE BABE
Fill glass with ice.
1 oz Tequila
or Southern Comfort
1 oz Amaretto
Strain into chilled glass.
Add 3-4 drops of Irish Cream or
Milk.

TEXAS MARY
Fill glass with ice.
2 oz Vodka or Peppered Vodka
1 oz Steak Sauce
tsp Horseradish
3 dashes of Tabasco Sauce
3 dashes of Worcestershire Sauce
Dash of Lime Juice
3 dashes of Celery Salt
3 dashes of Pepper
Fill with Tomato Juice.
Shake.

TEXAS TEA
Fill glass with ice.
1 oz Tequila
1/2 oz Vodka
1/2 oz Rum
1/2 oz Triple Sec
1 oz Sour Mix
Splash with Cola.
Garnish with Lemon.

THANKSGIVING
Fill glass with ice.
3/4 oz Gin
3/4 oz Dry Vermouth
3/4 oz Apricot Brandy
1/4 oz Lemon Juice
Shake.
Strain into chilled glass.
Garnish with Cherry.

THEY KILLED KENNY
Fill glass with ice.
1 1/2 oz Bourbon
1/2 oz Apple Brandy
1 oz Apple Juice
Fill with Lemon-Lime Soda.
Stir.

THIRD DEGREE
Fill glass with ice.
2 1/2 oz Gin
1/2 oz Dry Vermouth
1/2 tsp Pernod
Stir.
Strain into chilled glass.

THIRD RAIL
Fill glass with ice.
3/4 oz Brandy
3/4 oz Apple Brandy
3/4 oz Light Rum
1/4 tsp Pernod
Shake.
Strain into chilled glass.

38TH PARALLEL COFFEE
1/2 oz Brandy
1/2 oz Irish Cream
1/2 oz Dark Crème de Cacao
1/2 oz Black Raspberry Liqueur
Fill with hot Black Coffee.
Top with Whipped Cream.
Drizzle Chocolate Syrup on top.

THISTLE
Fill glass with ice.
1 1/2 oz Scotch
3/4 oz Sweet Vermouth
3 dashes of Bitters
Stir.
Strain into chilled glass.

THREE AMIGOS
Fill glass with ice.
3/4 oz Jose Cuervo
3/4 oz Ron Bacardi
3/4 oz Jack Daniels
Stir.
Strain into shot glass.

THREE KINGS (floater)
3/4 oz Coffee Liqueur (bottom)
3/4 oz Galliano
3/4 oz Cognac (top)

THREE MILES
Fill glass with ice.
1 oz Brandy
1 oz Rum
1 tsp Grenadine
1/4 tsp Lemon Juice
Shake.
Strain into chilled glass.

THREE MILE ISLAND aka
NUCLEAR MELTDOWN
Fill glass with ice.
1/2 oz Vodka
1/2 oz Gin
1/2 oz Rum
1/2 oz Tequila
1/2 oz Triple Sec
Fill with Sour Mix
or Pineapple Juice.
Shake.
Top with 1/2 oz Melon Liqueur.

THREE STORY HOUSE
ON FIRE (floater)
1/2 oz Crème de Nouyax
(bottom)
1/2 oz Banana Liqueur
1/2 oz Melon Liqueur
1/2 oz 151-Proof Rum (top)
Ignite.

THREE STRIPES
Fill glass with ice.
2 1/2 oz Gin
1/2 oz Dry Vermouth
1/2 oz Orange Juice
Shake.
Strain into chilled glass.

THREE WISE MEN
Fill glass with ice.
3/4 oz Johnnie Walker
3/4 oz Jim Beam
or Jack Daniels
3/4 oz Ron Bacardi
Stir.
Strain into chilled glass.

T

THREE WISE MEN 2
Fill glass with ice.
3/4 oz 100-proof Peppermint Schnapps
3/4 oz Jägermeister
3/4 oz 100-proof Cinnamon Schnapps
Stir. Strain into shot glass.

THREE WISE MEN AND THE MEXICAN PORTER
Fill glass with ice.
1/2 oz Johnnie Walker
1/2 oz Jim Beam
1/2 oz Jack Daniels
1/2 oz Jose Cuervo
Shake. Strain into shot glass.

THUG HEAVEN
Fill glass with ice.
1 oz Vodka or Citrus Vodka
1 oz Alize
Stir.

THUG PASSION
2 oz Cognac or Alize
Fill with Champagne.

THUMPER
Fill glass with ice.
1 1/2 oz Cognac or Brandy
1/2 oz Tuaca
Stir.
Garnish with Lemon Twist.

THUNDER
Fill glass with ice.
1 1/2 oz Brandy
1 tsp Sugar Syrup
or Powdered Sugar
1 Egg Yolk
1 pinch Cayenne Pepper
Shake.
Serve or strain into chilled glass.

THUNDER AND LIGHTNING
In shot glass:
1 oz 151-Proof Rum
1 oz 100-Proof Peppermint Schnapps

TIA TIA
Fill glass with ice.
1 oz Rum
1/2 oz Dark Rum
1/2 oz Dark Crème de Cacao
2 oz Pineapple Juice
1/2 oz Lime Juice
1/2 oz Sugar Syrup
Shake.

TIC TAC
Fill glass with ice.
1 oz Peppermint Schnapps
1 oz Anisette or Sambuca
Stir.
Strain into chilled glass.

TIDAL WAVE
Fill glass with ice.
1 oz Coconut Rum
1 oz Blackberry Brandy
Dash of Grenadine
Fill with Pineapple Juice.
Shake.

TIDAL WAVE 2
Fill glass with ice.
1 oz Vodka
1 oz Light Rum
1 oz Spiced Rum
1 oz Sour Mix
Fill with Cranberry Juice.
Shake.

TIDAL WAVE (frozen)
In Blender:
1/2 cup of Ice
3/4 oz Vodka
3/4 oz Gin
3/4 oz Southern Comfort
Dash of Grenadine
Scoop of Orange Sherbet
Blend until smooth.
If too thick add orange juice.
If too thin add ice or sherbet.

TIDBIT (frozen)
In Blender:
1/2 cup of Ice
1 oz Gin
1/4 oz Dry Sherry
Scoop of Vanilla Ice Cream
Blend until smooth.
If too thick add Milk.
If too thin add ice or Ice Cream.

TIE ME TO THE BEDPOST
Fill glass with ice.
1 oz Citrus Vodka
1 oz Coconut Rum
1 oz Melon Liqueur
1 oz Sour Mix
Shake.
Strain into chilled glass.

TIE ME TO THE BEDPOST BABY
Fill glass with ice.
1/2 oz Vodka
1/2 oz Southern Comfort
1/2 oz Melon Liqueur
1/2 oz Black Raspberry Liqueur
1/2 oz Sloe Gin
1/2 oz Cranberry Juice
1/2 oz Pineapple Juice
Shake.
Strain into chilled glass.

TIGER BALLS
Fill glass with ice.
1 oz Bourbon
1 oz Grain Alcohol
1 oz Beer
Shake. Strain into shot glass.

TIGER'S MILK
Fill glass with ice.
1 oz Amber or Dark Rum
1 oz Cognac or Brandy
4 oz Cream
1/4 oz Sugar Syrup
Shake.
Garnish with grated Nutmeg or Cinnamon.

TIGER'S MILK 2
Fill glass with ice.
2 oz Tuaca
Fill with Milk.
Shake.

TIGER'S TAIL
Fill glass with ice.
1 1/2 oz Pernod or Ricard
Dash of Curacao
or Triple Sec
Fill with Orange Juice.
Stir.
Garnish with Lime.

TIGHT SNATCH
Fill glass with ice.
1 1/2 oz Light Rum
1/2 oz Peach Schnapps
Fill with Pineapple Juice.
Shake.

TIJUANA BULLDOG
Fill glass with ice.
1 1/2 oz Tequila
1/2 oz Coffee Liqueur
Fill with equal parts Milk and Cola.
Shake.

TIJUANA GIMLET
Fill glass with ice.
2 oz Tequila
1/4 oz-1oz Lime Juice
Stir.
Strain into chilled glass or pour
contents (with ice) into short glass.
Garnish with Lime.

TIJUANA SUNRISE
Fill glass with ice.
2 oz Tequila
Fill with Orange Juice.
Stir.
Pour 1/4 oz Bitters down spoon to
bottom of glass.

TIJUANA TITTY TICKLER
Fill glass with ice.
3/4 oz Tequila
3/4 oz Triple Sec
3/4 oz Tuaca
Shake. Strain into shot glass.

TIKI BOWL
Fill glass with ice.
3/4 oz Light Rum
3/4 oz Dark Rum
1/2 oz Cherry Brandy
Fill with equal parts Orange and
Pineapple Juice.
Shake.

TINTORETTO
Puree 1/2 cup of fresh or canned
pears.
Pour into glass.
1/2 oz Pear Brandy
Fill with chilled Champagne.

TINY BOWL
1 1/2 oz Vodka
1 or 2 drops Blue Curacao
Garnish with 2 Raisins.

TIPPERARY
Fill glass with ice.
3/4 oz Irish Whiskey
3/4 oz Sweet Vermouth
3/4 oz Green Chartreuse
Stir well.
Strain into chilled glass.

TIVOLI
Fill glass with ice.
1 1/2 oz Bourbon
1/2 oz Aquavit
1/2 oz Sweet Vermouth
Dash of Campari
Shake.
Strain into chilled glass.

TO HELL YOU RIDE
Fill shot glass with Vodka
7-10 dashes of hot sauce

TOASTED ALMOND
Fill glass with ice.
1 oz Coffee Liqueur
1 oz Amaretto
Fill with Milk or Cream.
Shake.

TOASTED ALMOND (frozen)
In Blender:
1/2 cup of Ice
1 oz Coffee Liqueur
1 oz Amaretto
Scoop of Vanilla Ice Cream
Blend until smooth.
If too thick add Milk or Cream.
If too thin add ice or Ice Cream.

TOASTED MARSHMALLOW
Fill glass with ice.
3/4 oz Amaretto
3/4 oz Galliano
3/4 oz Banana Liqueur
Fill with Milk or Cream.
Shake.
Top with Soda Water.

TOBLERONE
Fill glass with ice.
3/4 oz Hazelnut Liqueur
3/4 oz Irish Cream
3/4 oz Coffee Liqueur
Tsp Honey
Fill with Milk or Cream.
Shake.

TOBLERONE (frozen)
In Blender:
1/2 cup of ice
3/4 oz Hazelnut Liqueur
3/4 oz Irish Cream
3/4 oz Coffee Liqueur
tsp Honey
Scoop Vanilla Ice Cream
Blend until smooth.

TOKYO EXPRESS (frozen)
In Blender:
1 cup of Ice
2 oz Dark Rum
1 oz Peach Schnapps
Dash of Grenadine
1 oz Sour Mix
2 oz Orange Juice
Blend 3-6 seconds on low speed.
Garnish with Orange, Lemon and
Cherry.

TOKYO ROSE
Fill glass with ice.
2 oz Dry Sake
1 oz Peach Schnapps
Fill with equal parts Orange
and Cranberry Juice.
Shake.

T

Metric Measurement Conversion Chart on page 14

TOKYO TEA
Fill glass with ice.
1/2 oz Vodka or Citrus Vodka
1/2 oz Gin
1/2 oz Rum or Citrus Rum
1/2 oz Tequila
1/2 oz Triple Sec
1/2 oz Melon Liqueur
Fill with Sour Mix.
Shake
Garnish with Lemon.

TOM AND JERRY
Beat an Egg White and an Egg
Yolk separately.
Fold together and place into mug.
1/2 oz Sugar Syrup
or 1 tsp Powdered Sugar
1 oz Dark Rum
1 oz Cognac or Brandy
Fill with hot Milk or hot Water.
Stir.
Garnish with Nutmeg.

TOM COLLINS
Fill glass with ice.
2 oz Gin
Fill with Sour Mix.
Shake.
Splash of Soda Water
Garnish with Orange and Cherry.

TOM MIX HIGH
Fill glass with ice.
2 oz Blended Whiskey
Dash of Grenadine
Dash of Bitters
Fill with Soda Water.
Garnish with Lemon.

TOOL
Fill glass with ice.
1 1/2 oz Tequila
Dash of Grenadine
Fill with Orange Juice.
Shake.
Float 1/2 oz Southern Comfort
on top.

TOOTSIE
Fill glass with ice.
2 oz Coffee Liqueur or Sabra
or Dark Crème de Cacao
Fill with Orange Juice.
Shake.
Garnish with Orange.

TOP BANANA
Fill glass with ice.
1 oz Vodka or Banana Vodka
1 oz Banana Liqueur
Fill with Orange Juice.
Shake.

TOP GUN
Fill glass with ice.
Dash of Vodka
Dash of Dark Rum
Dash of Coconut Rum
Dash of Southern Comfort
Dash of Peach Schnapps
Dash of Amaretto
Dash of Triple Sec
Fill with equal parts Orange and
Cranberry Juice.
Shake.

TOREADOR
Fill glass with ice.
1 1/2 oz Tequila
1/2 oz White Crème de Cacao
1/2 oz Cream
Shake.
Strain into chilled glass.
Top with Whipped Cream.
Sprinkle with Cocoa or Shaved
Chocolate.

TOREADOR 2
Fill glass with ice.
2 oz Brandy
1 oz Coffee Liqueur
1/2 Egg White
Shake.

TORONTO ORGY
Fill glass with ice.
1/2 oz Vodka or Vanilla Vodka
1/2 oz Coffee Liqueur
1/2 oz Orange Liqueur
1/2 oz Irish Cream
Shake.
Strain into shot glass.

TORPEDO
Fill glass with ice.
1 1/2 oz Apple Brandy
3/4 oz Brandy
Shake.
Strain into chilled glass.

TORQUE WRENCH
1 oz Melon Liqueur
1 oz Orange Juice
Fill with Champagne.
Garnish with Orange.

TONGUE STROKE
Fill glass with ice.
1 1/2 oz Brandy
Fill with equal parts Hard Cider
and Ginger Ale.
Stir.

TOVARICH
Fill glass with ice.
1 1/2 oz Vodka
3/4 oz Kummel
1/4 oz Lime Juice
Shake.
Strain into chilled glass.

TOXIC JELLYBEAN
Fill glass with ice.
3/4 oz Sambuca
3/4 oz Blackberry Brandy
3/4 oz Jägermeister
Shake. Strain into shot glass.

TOXIC SHOCK
Fill glass with ice.
1/2 oz Vodka
1/2 oz Citrus Vodka
1/2 oz Gin
1/2 oz Rum
1/2 oz Spiced Rum
1/2 oz Tequila
Fill with Sour Mix.
Shake.
Top with Lemon-Lime Soda

TOXIC WASTE
Fill glass with ice.
1/2 oz Coffee Liqueur
1/2 oz Galliano
1/2 oz Apricot Brandy
Fill with Orange Juice
(leaving 1/2 inch from top).
Shake.
Top with Cream.

TRADE WIND
Fill glass with ice.
1/2 oz Rum or Orange Rum
1/2 oz Galliano
1/2 oz Apricot Brandy
1/2 oz Orange Liqueur
Fill with Milk or Cream.
Shake.

TRADE WINDS (frozen)
In Blender:
1/2 cup of Ice
2 oz Amber Rum
1/2 oz Plum Brandy
1/2 oz Lime Juice
2 tsp Sugar Syrup
Blend until smooth.

TRAFFIC LIGHT
In three separate shot glasses.
1. 1 oz Vodka
   1/2 oz Melon Liqueur
2. 1 oz Vodka
   1/2 oz Orange Juice
3. 1 oz Vodka
   1/2 oz Cranberry Juice

TRAFFIC LIGHT 2 (floater)
1/2 oz Crème de Nouyax
(bottom)
1/2 oz Galliano
1/2 oz Melon Liqueur (top)

TRAFFIC LIGHT (floater)
1/2 oz Green Crème de Menthe
(bottom)
1/2 oz Banana Liqueur
1/2 oz Sloe Gin (top)

TRAIN WRECK
In Beer glass:
4 oz Mad Dog
Fill with Beer.

TRANCE
Fill glass with ice.
1 oz Jägermeister
1 oz Hypnotiq
Fill with Energy Drink.
Sprinkle pinch of Sugar over drink.

**TRANSFUSION aka
PURPLE PASSION**
Fill glass with ice.
2 oz Vodka or Citrus Vodka
Fill with equal parts
Grape Juice and Ginger Ale
or Soda Water.

TRAPPIST FRAPPE
Fill large stemmed glass (Red Wine
glass, Champagne saucer) with
crushed ice.
3/4 oz Coffee Liqueur
3/4 oz Hazelnut Liqueur
3/4 oz Irish Cream

TRAPPIST MONK
3/4 oz Coffee Liqueur
3/4 oz Hazelnut Liqueur
3/4 oz Irish Cream
Fill with hot Black Coffee.
Top with Whipped Cream.

TREE CLIMBER
Fill glass with ice.
1 oz Rum
1/2 oz Amaretto
1/2 oz White Crème de Cacao
Fill with Milk or Cream.
Shake.

TREE SMACKER
Fill glass with ice.
1 oz Rum or Citrus Rum
1/2 oz Peach Schnapps
1/2 oz Apple Brandy
Dash of Grenadine
Fill with equal parts Sour Mix,
Pineapple,
And Orange Juice.
Shake.
Top with 1/2 oz 151-Proof Rum.

TRILBY
Fill glass with ice.
1 1/2 oz Bourbon
1/2 oz Sweet Vermouth
2 dashes of Orange Bitters
Stir.
Strain into chilled glass.

TRIP TO THE BEACH
Fill glass with ice.
3/4 oz Vodka or Peach Vodka
3/4 oz Coconut Rum
3/4 oz Peach Schnapps
Fill with Orange Juice.
Shake.

TRIPLE PHAT LIMEADE
In a mixing glass:
tsp Sugar, 2 oz Fresh Lime Juice
Fill glass ice.
1 oz Citrus Vodka or Vodka
1 oz Cognac
1 oz Orange Liqueur
Shake. Strain into chilled glass.

TROIKA
Fill glass with ice.
1 oz Peach Vodka
1/2 oz Amaretto
1/2 oz Sloe Gin
Fill glass with Sour Mix.
Shake.

TROIS RIVIERES
Fill glass with ice.
1 1/2 oz Canadian Whiskey
3/4 oz Dubonnet Rouge
1/2 oz Triple Sec
Shake.
Serve or strain into chilled glass.
Garnish with Orange Twist.

TROLLEY
Fill glass with ice.
2 oz Bourbon
Fill with equal parts Cranberry and
Pineapple Juice.
Stir.

T

TROPHY ROOM COFFEE
1/2 oz Amaretto
1/2 oz Vandermint
1/2 oz Dark Rum
Fill with hot Black Coffee.
Top with Whipped Cream.
Dribble Coffee Liqueur on top.

TROPICAL BREEZE (frozen)
In Blender:
1/2 cup of Ice
1 1/2 oz Banana Liqueur
1 1/2 oz Crème de Nouyax
1/2 cup fresh or frozen Strawberries
Scoop of Vanilla Ice Cream
Blend until smooth.
If too thick add berries or juice.
If too thin add ice or Ice Cream.
Top with Whipped Cream.

TROPICAL COCKTAIL
Fill glass with ice.
3/4 oz White Crème de Cacao
3/4 oz Maraschino Liqueur
3/4 oz Dry Vermouth
Dash of Bitters
Stir.
Strain into chilled glass.

TROPICAL GOLD
Fill glass with ice.
1 1/2 oz Rum or Banana Rum
1/2 oz Banana Liqueur
Fill with Orange Juice.
Shake.

TROPICAL HOOTER
Fill glass with ice.
1 1/2 oz Coconut Rum
1/2 oz Melon Liqueur
Dash of Cranberry Juice
Dash of Pineapple Juice
Shake.
Strain into chilled glass.

TROPICAL LIFESAVER
Fill glass with ice.
3/4 oz Citrus Vodka
3/4 oz Coconut Rum
3/4 oz Melon Liqueur
Dash of Sour Mix
Fill with Pineapple Juice.
Shake.
Top with Lemon-Lime Soda

TROPICAL MARTINI
Fill glass with ice.
2 oz Pineapple Vodka
1 oz Coconut Rum
1/2 oz Banana Liqueur
Dash Orange Juice.
Shake. Strain into chilled glass.
Garnish with Pineapple and Cherry.

TROPICAL MOON (frozen)
In Blender:
1/2 cup of Ice
1 oz Dark Rum
1 oz coconut Rum
1/2 cup fresh or canned Pineapple
Scoop of Vanilla Ice Cream
Blend until smooth.
Float 1/2 oz Amaretto on top.
Garnish with Pineapple.

TROPICAL SCREW
Fill glass with ice.
2 oz Coconut Rum
Fill with Orange Juice.

TROPICAL STORM
Fill glass with ice.
1/2 oz Vodka
1/2 oz Gin
1/2 oz Rum
1/2 oz Tequila
1/2 oz Triple Sec
Dash of Cherry Brandy
Dash of Sour Mix
Shake.

TROPICAL STORM 2
Fill glass with ice.
1 1/2 oz Rum or Mango Rum
1/2 oz Blackberry Brandy
Fill with Grapefruit Juice.
Shake.
Garnish with Lime.

TROPICAL STORM 3
Fill glass with ice.
1 oz Dark Rum
1/4 oz Amber Rum
1/4 oz Coconut Rum
1/4 oz Galliano
1/4 oz Grenadine
Fill with equal parts Sour Mix,
Pineapple and Orange Juice.
Shake.
Garnish with Orange and Cherry.

TTT
Fill glass with ice.
1 1/2 oz Tequila
1/2 oz Triple Sec
Fill with Tonic Water.

TUACA COCKTAIL
Fill glass with ice.
1 oz Vodka
1 oz Tuaca
2 tbsp Lime Juice
Shake.
Strain into chilled glass.

TULIP
Fill glass with ice.
3/4 oz Apple Brandy
3/4 oz Sweet Vermouth
1 1/2 tsp Apricot Brandy
1 1/2 tsp Lemon Juice
Shake.
Strain into chilled glass.

TUMBLEWEED
Fill glass with ice.
1/2 oz Coffee Liqueur
1/2 oz Brandy
1/2 oz White Crème de Cacao
1/2 oz Hazelnut Liqueur
Fill with Milk.
Shake.

TUMBLEWEED (frozen)
In Blender:
1/2 cup of Ice
1/2 oz Coffee Liqueur
1/2 oz Brandy
1/2 oz White Crème de Cacao
1/2 oz Hazelnut Liqueur
Scoop of Vanilla Ice Cream
Blend until smooth.
If too thick add Cream or Milk.
If too thin add ice or Ice Cream.
Top with Whipped Cream.
Sprinkle with Shaved Chocolate
or Sprinkles.

Metric Measurement Conversion Chart on page 14

TURF
Fill glass with ice.
1 oz Gin
3/4 oz Dry Vermouth
1/4 oz Maraschino Liqueur
        (optional)
1/4 oz Anisette
1/4 oz Bitters
Stir.
Strain into chilled glass.

TURKEY SHOOT (floater)
1 1/2 oz 101-Proof Bourbon
(bottom)
1/2 oz White Crème de Menthe
(top)

TURTLE DOVE
Fill glass with ice.
1 1/2 oz Dark Rum
1/2 oz Amaretto
Fill with Orange Juice.
Shake.

TUXEDO
Fill glass with ice.
2 oz Fino Sherry
1/2 oz Anisette
1/4 oz Maraschino Liqueur
1/4 oz Bitters
Stir.
Strain into chilled glass.

24 KARAT NIGHTMARE aka 911
Fill glass with ice.
1 oz 100-Proof Cinnamon
Schnapps
1 oz 100-Proof Peppermint
Schnapps
Stir.

TWIN HILLS
Fill glass with ice.
1 1/2 oz Whiskey
2 tsp Benedictine
1 1/2 tsp Lemon Juice
1 1/2 tsp Lime Juice
1 tsp Sugar Syrup
or Powdered Sugar
Shake.
Strain into chilled glass.

TWIN SIX
Fill glass with ice.
2 oz Gin or Orange Gin
1/2 oz Sweet Vermouth
1 tsp Grenadine
1 tbsp Orange Juice
1 Egg White
Shake.
Strain into chilled glass.

TWISTED LEMONADE
CAUTION: people might want a
bottled concoction.
Fill glass with ice.
1 1/2 oz Citrus Vodka
1/2 oz Triple Sec
Fill with Sour Mix.
Shake.

TWISTER
Fill glass with ice.
2 oz Vodka or Lime Vodka
1/2 oz Lime Juice
Fill with Lemon-Lime Soda.
Stir.
Garnish with Lime.

252 (floater)
1 oz 101-proof Bourbon (bottom)
1 oz 151-Proof Rum (top)

TYPHOON
Fill glass with ice.
1/2 oz Gin or Lime Vodka
1/2 oz Sambuca
Dash of Lime Juice
Fill with Champagne.
Garnish with Lime.

UGLY DUCKLING
Fill glass with ice.
2 oz Amaretto
Fill with equal parts Milk or Cream
and Soda Water.
Stir.

ULANDA
Fill glass with ice.
2 oz Gin or Orange Gin
3/4 oz Orange Liqueur or Triple Sec
1/4 tsp Pernod
Shake.
Strain into chilled glass.

UNCLE SAM
1 oz Bourbon
1 oz Peach Schnapps
Dash of Lime Juice
Stir.

UNDER THE COVERS
Fill glass with ice.
1 oz Vodka or Sambuca
1 oz Irish Cream
1 oz Peach Schnapps
Shake.

UNDER CURRENT (floater)
1/2 oz Black Raspberry Liqueur
(bottom)
In separate glass mix:
1 oz Currant Vodka or Spiced Rum
1/2 oz Blue Curacao
Dash Pineapple Juice
Shake. Float on top.

UNDERTOW (floater)
1/2 oz Black Raspberry Liqueur
(bottom)
1 1/2 oz Blue Curacao (top)

UNION JACK
Fill glass with ice.
1 1/2 oz Gin
3/4 oz Sloe Gin
1/2 tsp Grenadine
Shake.
Strain into chilled glass.

UNION JACK 2
Fill glass with ice.
1 1/2 oz Gin
1/4 oz Crème de Yvette
Stir.
Strain into chilled glass.

UNION LEAGUE
Fill glass with ice.
1 1/2 oz Gin
1 oz Port
2-3 dashes of Orange Bitters
Stir.
Strain into chilled glass.
Garnish with Orange Twist.

T.
U

Metric Measurement Conversion Chart on page 14

UNIVERSAL
Fill glass with ice.
3/4 oz Vodka or Pineapple,
   or Grapefruit Vodka
3/4 oz Amaretto
3/4 oz Melon Liqueur
Fill with Grapefruit
or Pineapple Juice.
Shake.

UNPUBLISHED HEMINGWAY
2 oz Cognac
1/2 oz Orange Liqueur

UPSIDE DOWN MARGARITA aka HEAD REST
Rest head on bar.
Have friend pour ingredients into
mouth.
1 oz Tequila
1/2 oz Triple Sec
Dash of Lime Juice
Dash of Sour Mix
Dash of Orange Juice
Slosh around mouth.
Swallow!

URINALYSIS
Fill glass with ice.
1 1/2 oz Southern Comfort
1/2 oz Peppermint Schnapps
Stir.
Strain into chilled glass.

URINE SAMPLE
Fill glass with ice.
2 oz Amber Rum
1 oz Sour Mix
1 oz Pineapple Juice
Fill with Lemon-Lime Soda.

UZI (floater)
1/2 oz Coffee Liqueur (bottom)
1/2 oz Apricot Brandy
1/2 oz Ouzo (top)

VACATION
Fill glass with ice.
1 oz Spiced Rum
1 oz Coconut Rum
Fill with equal parts Cranberry,
And Pineapple Juice.
Shake.

VALENCIA
Fill glass with ice.
2 oz Apricot Brandy
1 oz Orange Juice
2-3 dashes of Orange Bitters
Shake.
Strain into chilled glass.
Add 3 oz chilled Champagne (optional).

VAMPIRE
Fill glass with ice.
1 1/2 oz Vodka or Raspberry,
   or Cranberry Vodka
1/2 oz Black Raspberry Liqueur
Fill with Cranberry Juice.
Shake.

VANCOUVER
Fill glass with ice.
2 oz Canadian Whiskey
1 oz Dubonnet Rouge
1/2 oz Lemon Juice
1/2 oz Egg White
1/2 tsp Maple or Sugar Syrup
3 dashes of Orange Bitters
Shake.

VANDERBILT
Fill glass with ice.
1 1/2 oz Brandy
3/4 oz Cherry Brandy
1 tsp Sugar Syrup
2 dashes of Bitters
Stir.
Strain into chilled glass.

VANILLA MARTINI
Fill glass with ice.
3 1/2 oz Vanilla Vodka
Dash White Crème de Cacao
Stir.
Strain into a chilled glass.
Float tsp Vanilla Ice Cream.

VANITY FAIR
Fill glass with ice.
1 1/2 oz Apple Brandy
1/2 oz Cherry Brandy
1/2 oz Cherry Liqueur
Shake.
Float 1 tsp Crème de Nouyax or
Amaretto on top.

VATICAN COFFEE
1 oz Cognac or Brandy
1 oz Hazelnut Liqueur
Fill with hot Black Coffee.
Top with Whipped Cream.

VEGAS B J
Fill glass with ice.
3/4 oz Rum or Citrus Rum
3/4 oz Jägermeister
3/4 oz Banana Liqueur
3/4 oz Orange Juice
3/4 oz Pineapple Juice
Shake. Strain into shot glass.

VELVET DRESS
Fill glass with ice.
1 oz Brandy
1/2 oz Coffee Liqueur
1/2 oz Triple Sec
Fill with Milk or Cream
Shake.

VELVET GAF
Fill glass 1/2 with Porter.
Fill glass 1/2 with Champagne.

VELVET GLOVE
Fill glass with ice.
1 oz Sloe Gin
1 oz White Crème de Menthe
1 oz Cream or Milk
Shake.
Strain into chilled glass.

VELVET HAMMER
Fill glass with ice.
1 oz Triple Sec or Curacao
1 oz White Crème de Cacao
1 oz Cream or Milk
Shake.
Strain into chilled glass.

VELVET HAMMER (frozen)
In Blender:
1/2 cup of Ice
1 oz Triple Sec or Curacao
1 oz White Crème de Cacao
Scoop of Vanilla Ice Cream
Blend until smooth.
If too thick add Milk or Cream.
If too thin add ice or Ice Cream.
Sprinkle with Shaved Chocolate.
Garnish with Orange.

Metric Measurement Conversion Chart on page 14

VELVET KISS
Fill glass with ice.
1 oz Gin
1/2 oz Banana Liqueur
1/2 oz Pineapple Juice
1 oz Cream
Dash of Grenadine (optional)
Shake.
Strain into chilled glass.

VENETIAN COFFEE
1 oz Brandy
1/2 oz Galliano
1/2 oz Triple Sec
Fill with hot Black Coffee.
Top with Whipped Cream.
Sprinkle with Cinnamon.

VENETIAN FRAPPE
Fill large stemmed glass (Red
Wine glass, Champagne saucer)
with crushed ice.
3/4 oz Brandy
3/4 oz Galliano
3/4 oz Triple Sec

VENETIAN SUNRISE
Fill glass with ice.
1 1/2 oz Grappa or Brandy
Fill with Orange Juice.
Pour 1/2 oz Campari down spoon
to bottom of glass.
Garnish with Orange.

VERMOUTH CASSIS
Fill glass with ice.
2 oz Sweet or Dry Vermouth
1 oz Crème de Cassis
Fill with Soda Water.
Stir.
Garnish with Lemon Twist.

VERONA
Fill glass with ice.
1 oz Gin
1 oz Amaretto
1/2 oz Sweet Vermouth
1 or 2 dashes of Lemon Juice
Shake.
Garnish with Orange.

VESPER AKA JAMES BOND MARTINI
Fill glass with ice.
3 oz Gin
1 oz Vodka
1/2 oz Blond Lillet
Shake.
Strain into chilled glass.
Garnish with Lemon Twist.

VIA VENETO
Fill glass with ice.
1 1/2 oz Brandy
1/2 oz Sambuca
1/2 oz Lemon Juice
1 tsp Sugar Syrup
1/2 Egg White
Shake.

VIBRATOR (floater)
1 1/2 oz Southern Comfort (bottom)
1/2 oz Irish Cream (top)

VICIOUS SID
Fill glass with ice.
1 1/2 oz Rum
1/2 oz Southern Comfort
1/2 oz Triple Sec
1 oz Lemon Juice
2 Dash Bitters.
Shake.

VICTOR
Fill glass with ice.
1 1/2 oz Gin
1/2 oz Brandy
1/2 oz Sweet Vermouth
Shake.
Strain into chilled glass.

VICTORY
Fill glass with ice.
1 1/2 oz Pernod
3/4 oz Grenadine
Shake.
Fill with Soda Water.

VIKING
Fill glass with ice.
1 1/2 oz Swedish Punch
1 oz Aquavit
1 oz Lime Juice
Shake.

VIRGIN
Fill glass with ice.
1 oz Gin
1/2 oz White Crème de Menthe
1 oz Forbidden Fruit
Shake.
Strain into chilled glass.
Garnish with Cherry.

VIRGIN BANANA ORANGE FROSTIE
In Blender:
1 cup of ice.
1/2 ripe peeled Banana
1/2 peeled Orange (minus seeds)
Dash of Grenadine
2 oz Milk or Cream
Blend until smooth.

VIRGIN MARY
Fill glass with ice.
1 tsp Horseradish
3 dashes of Tabasco Sauce
3 dashes of Worcestershire Sauce
Dash of Lime Juice
3 dashes of Celery Salt
3 dashes of Pepper
1 oz Clam Juice (optional)
Fill with Tomato Juice.
Pour from one glass to another
until mixed.
Garnish with Lemon and/or Lime,
Celery and /or Cucumber and /or
Cocktail Shrimp.

VIRGIN PIÑA COLADA (frozen)
In Blender:
1 cup of Ice
2 tbsp Cream of Coconut
1 cup fresh or canned Pineapple
1 tsp Vanilla Ice Cream (optional)
Blend until smooth.
If too thick add fruit or juice.
If too thin add ice.
Garnish with Pineapple and Cherry.

VIRGIN STRAWBERRY DAIQUIRI
(frozen)
In Blender:
1 cup of Ice
Dash of Lime Juice
1 cup of fresh or frozen
Strawberries
Blend until smooth.
If too thick add berries or juice.
If too thin add ice.
Garnish with Strawberry and/or
Lime.

U
V

Metric Measurement Conversion Chart on page 14

VISITOR
Fill glass with ice.
1 oz Vodka or Banana,
    or Orange Vodka
1/2 oz Orange Liqueur
1/2 oz Banana Liqueur
Fill with Orange Juice.
Shake.

VODKA COLLINS
Fill glass with ice.
2 oz Vodka
Fill with Sour Mix.
Shake.
Splash with Soda Water.
Garnish with Orange and Cherry.

VODKA COOLER
Fill glass with ice.
2 oz Vodka
1/2 oz Sweet Vermouth
Dash of Sour Mix
1/2 oz Sugar Syrup
or Powdered Sugar
Shake.
Fill with Soda Water.

VODKA GIBSON
(*CAUTION:* DRY usually means
less Vermouth than usual.
EXTRA DRY can mean even less
Vermouth than usual or
no Vermouth at all.)
Fill glass with ice.
2 oz Vodka
1/2 oz Dry Vermouth
Stir.
Strain into chilled glass
or pour contents (with ice)
into short glass.
Garnish with Cocktail Onion.

VODKA GIMLET
Fill glass with ice.
2 oz Vodka or Lime Vodka
1/2 oz Lime Juice
Stir.
Strain into chilled glass
or pour contents (with ice)
into short glass.
Garnish with Lime.

VODKA GRASSHOPPER aka FLYING GRASSHOPPER
Fill glass with ice.
1 oz Vodka
3/4 oz Green Crème de Menthe
3/4 oz White Crème de Cacao
Fill with Milk or Cream.
Shake.
Serve or strain into chilled glass.

VODKA MARTINI
(*CAUTION:* DRY usually means
less Vermouth than usual.
EXTRA DRY can mean even less
Vermouth than usual or
no Vermouth at all.)
Fill glass with ice.
3 1/2 oz Vodka
1/2 oz Dry Vermouth
Stir.
Strain into chilled glass
or pour contents (with ice)
into short glass.
Garnish with Lemon Twist or
Olives.

VODKA SAKETINI
Fill glass with ice.
2 oz Vodka
1/2 oz Sake
Stir.
Strain into chilled glass
or pour contents (with ice)
into short glass.
Garnish with Lemon Twist or Olives
or Cocktail Onions.

VODKA SLING
Fill glass 1/2 way with ice.
Place 2 fresh Sliced Pitted Cherries
around the inside of the glass.
2 oz Vodka or Cherry or Lime Vodka
1/2 oz Lime Juice
Fill glass with crushed ice.
Top with 1/2 oz Cherry Brandy.

VODKA SODA
Fill glass with ice.
2 oz Vodka or Currant Vodka
Fill with Soda Water.
Garnish with Lemon or Lime.

VODKA SONIC
Fill glass with ice.
2 oz Vodka or Lemon Vodka
Fill with equal parts Soda and Tonic
Water.
Garnish with Lemon or Lime.

VODKA SOUR
Fill glass with ice.
2 oz Vodka or Citrus Vodka
Fill with Sour Mix.
Shake.
Garnish with Cherry and Orange.

VODKA STINGER
Fill glass with ice.
1 1/2 oz Vodka or Mint Vodka
1/2 oz White Crème de Menthe
Stir.
Serve or strain into chilled glass.

VODKA TONIC
Fill glass with ice.
2 oz Vodka or Lime Vodka
Fill with Tonic Water.
Garnish with Lime.

VOLCANO
Fill glass with ice.
1 1/2 oz Brandy
1 oz Orange Juice
1 oz Pineapple Juice
1 oz Sour Mix
Dash of Grenadine
Dash of Lime Juice
Shake.
Top with 1/2 oz 151-Proof Rum.
Ignite.
Pour in 1/2 oz Champagne.

VOLGA BOATMAN
Fill glass with ice.
1 1/2 oz Vodka or Cherry Vodka
1 oz Cherry Liqueur
1 oz Orange Juice
Shake.
Strain into chilled glass.
Garnish with Cherry.

VOLGA COOLER
Fill glass with ice.
1 oz Vanilla Vodka
1/2 oz Banana Liqueur
1/2 oz Triple Sec
Fill with Lemon-Lime Soda.
Stir.

VOO DOO (floater)
1/2 oz Coffee Liqueur (bottom)
1/2 oz Irish Cream
1/2 oz Dark Rum (top)

VOO DOO 2 (floater)
1/2 oz Coffee Liqueur (bottom)
1/2 oz Dark Rum
1/2 oz 151-Proof Rum (top)

VOODOO DOLL
Fill glass with ice.
1 oz Vodka or Raspberry Liqueur
1 oz Black Raspberry Liqueur
Fill with equal parts Orange and
Cranberry Juice.
Shake.
Float 1/4 oz 151-Proof Rum.

VULCAN
Fill glass with ice.
1/2 oz Vodka
1/2 oz Gin
1/2 oz Coconut Rum
1/2 oz Southern Comfort
Fill with equal parts Grapefruit
Juice and Lemon-Lime Soda.
Stir.

VULCAN BLOOD
Fill glass with ice.
1 oz Vodka or Orange Vodka
1 oz Blue Curacao
Fill with Orange Juice.
Shake.

VULCAN MIND MELD
1 oz Sambuca
1 oz 151-Proof Rum
Ignite.

VULCAN MIND PROBE
Fill glass with ice.
1/2 oz Vodka
1/2 oz Gin
1/2 oz Coconut Rum
1/2 oz Melon Liqueur
Dash of Lime Juice
Shake.
Strain into chilled glass.

VULCAN MIND PROBE 2
Fill glass with ice.
1/2 oz Gin
1/2 oz Rum
1/2 oz Brandy
1/2 oz Triple Sec or Curacao
Fill with equal parts Sour Mix and Beer.

W. W. II
Fill glass with ice.
1 oz Vodka or Citrus Vodka
1 oz Triple Sec
1 oz Melon Liqueur
Dash of Lime Juice
Fill with Pineapple Juice.
Shake.

WADKINS GLEN
Fill glass with ice.
1 oz Vodka
1/2 oz Black Raspberry Liqueur
1/2 oz Banana Liqueur
Dash of Orange Juice
Dash of Cranberry Juice
Dash of Pineapple Juice
Shake.
Strain into chilled glass.
Garnish with Lime.

WAGON WHEEL
Fill glass with ice.
2 oz Southern Comfort
1 oz Cognac or Brandy
1 oz Sour Mix
1/2 oz Grenadine
Shake.
Strain into chilled glass.

WAIKIKI BEACHCOMBER
Fill glass with ice.
1 1/2 oz Gin or Orange Gin
1/2 oz Triple Sec
Fill with Pineapple Juice
Shake.

WALDORF
Fill glass with ice.
1 1/2 oz Bourbon
3/4 oz Pernod
1/2 oz Sweet Vermouth
Dash of Bitters
Stir.
Strain into chilled glass.

WALL STREET LIZARD
Fill glass with ice.
1/2 oz Vodka
1/2 oz Gin
1/2 oz Rum
1/2 oz Melon Liqueur
1/2 oz Blue Curacao
Stir.
Serve or strain into chilled glass.

WALLY WALLBANGER
Fill glass with ice.
1 oz Vodka or Citrus Vodka
1/2 oz Galliano
Fill with Orange Juice.
Shake.
Top with 1/2 oz 151-Proof Rum.

WANDERING MINSTREL
Fill glass with ice.
1/2 oz Vodka or Vanilla Vodka
1/2 oz Coffee Liqueur
1/2 oz Brandy
1/2 oz White Crème de Menthe
Stir.
Strain into chilled glass.

WANNA PROBE YA
Fill glass with ice.
1 oz Spiced Rum
1 oz Coconut Rum
Fill with equal parts Pineapple and
Cranberry Juice.
Stir.
Garnish with Lime.

WARD EIGHT
Fill glass with ice.
2 oz Whiskey
Dash of Grenadine
Fill with Sour Mix.
Shake.
Garnish with Cherry and Orange.

V

W

WARDAY'S COCKTAIL
Fill glass with ice.
1 oz Gin
1 oz Sweet Vermouth
1 oz Apple Brandy
1 tsp Yellow Chartreuse
Shake.
Strain into chilled glass.

WARM CREAMY BUSH
1 oz Irish Whiskey
1 oz Irish Cream
1 oz hot Coffee

WARSAW
Fill glass with ice.
1 1/2 oz Vodka or Lemon Vodka
1/2 oz Blackberry Liqueur
1/2 oz Dry Vermouth
1/4 oz Lemon Juice
Shake.
Strain into chilled glass.
Garnish with Lemon Twist.

WASHINGTON
Fill glass with ice.
1 1/2 oz Dry Vermouth
3/4 oz Brandy
1/2 tsp Sugar Syrup
2-3 dashes of Bitters
Stir.
Strain into chilled glass.

WATERBURY COCKTAIL
Fill glass with ice.
2 oz Cognac or Brandy
1/2 oz Lemon Juice
1 tsp Sugar Syrup
1/2 Egg White
2-3 dashes of Bitters
Shake.
Strain into chilled glass.

WATERFALL
Fill shot glass with desired Liquor
or Liqueur. (Tequila, Peppermint
Schnapps, Jägermeister, Whiskey)
Fill shot glass with desired chaser.
(beer, soda, juice, water, espresso)
Hold 1st glass between thumb and
forefinger. Hold 2nd glass between
forefinger and middle finger. Drink
from first glass and let second
glass flow into first glass.

WATERGATE COFFEE
1 oz Coffee Liqueur
1 oz Orange Liqueur
Fill with hot Black Coffee.
Top with Whipped Cream.

WATERMELON
Fill glass with ice.
1 oz Southern Comfort
1/2 oz Sloe Gin
Dash of Orange Juice
Fill with Pineapple Juice.
Shake.

WATERMELON 2
Fill glass with ice.
1 oz Vodka or Amaretto
1 oz Melon Liqueur
Fill with Cranberry Juice.
Stir.

WATERMELON 3
Fill glass with ice.
1 oz Vodka
1 oz Strawberry Liqueur
1 oz Sour Mix
1 oz Orange Juice
Shake.

WATERMELON SPIKED, LIQUOR SOAKED
Find whole ripe watermelon.
Lay on side
Make a circular cut into the oblong
top, make the diameter of the
whole just a little larger than the
circumference of the liquor bottle
neck.
Remove the cut plug (rind).
With a swift accurate move insert
desired spike (Vodka, Rum, Gin,
Tequila, Brandy, Bourbon).
Press bottle firmly into melon for a
tight as possible fit.
Bottle should drain slightly or
completely.
If it drains completely remove bottle
and replace the plug,
And tape securely with electrical or
duct tape.
If it drains slightly check back in a
couple hours or the next day.
When plugged and taped. Let sit
for 24 hours, rotating the melon
3 or 4 times.

WATERMELON MARTINI
Mash 1/4 cup of Fresh Watermelon
in glass.
Fill glass with ice.
2 1/2 oz Vodka
Dash Watermelon Schnapps (optional)
Dash Lime Juice (optional)

WEDDING BELLE
Fill glass with ice.
3/4 oz Gin or Orange Gin
3/4 oz Dubonnet Rouge
1/2 oz Cherry Brandy
1/2 oz Orange Juice
Shake.
Serve or strain into chilled glass.

WEDDING CAKE
Fill glass with ice.
1 1/2 oz Amaretto
1/2 oz White Crème de Cacao
Fill with equal parts Milk
and Pineapple Juice.
Shake.

WEEK ON THE BEACH
Fill glass with ice.
1 oz Rum or Citrus Rum
1/2 oz Peach Schnapps
1/2 oz Apple Brandy
Fill with equal parts Orange,
Cranberry and Pineapple Juice.
Shake.

WEEKEND AT THE BEACH
Fill glass with ice.
1 oz Rum or Citrus Rum
1 oz Peach Schnapps
Fill with equal parts Pineapple and
Orange Juice.
Shake.

Metric Measurement Conversion Chart on page 14

WEEP NO MORE
Fill glass with ice.
3/4 oz Brandy
3/4 oz Dubonnet
3/4 oz Lime Juice
1/4 tsp Cherry Liqueur (optional)
Shake.
Strain into chilled glass.

WELL RED RHINO (frozen)
In Blender:
1 cup of Ice
1 oz Vodka
1 oz Rum
1 oz Cream of Coconut
1 oz fresh or frozen
Strawberries
Dash of Cranberry, Lime and
Pineapple Juice
Blend until smooth.

WEMBLEY
Fill glass with ice.
1 1/2 oz Gin
3/4 oz Dry Vermouth
1/2 oz Apple Brandy
1/4 oz Apricot Brandy (optional)
Stir.
Strain into chilled glass.

WENCH
Fill glass with ice.
1 oz Spiced Rum
1 oz Amaretto
Shake. Strain into shot glass.

WEST INDIAN FRAPPE
Fill large stemmed glass (Red Wine
glass, Champagne saucer) with
crushed ice.
3/4 oz Light Rum
3/4 oz Banana Liqueur
3/4 oz Orange Liqueur

WEST INDIES YELLOWBIRD
Fill glass with ice.
1 oz Rum or Mango Rum
1 oz Banana Liqueur
Splash Galliano
1/2 tsp Sugar
Dash of Cream
Fill with equal parts Orange and
Pineapple Juice.
Shake.

WET CROTCH
Fill glass with ice.
3/4 oz Irish Cream
3/4 oz Triple Sec or Orange Vodka
3/4 oz Black Raspberry Liqueur
Shake. Strain into shot glass.

WET DREAM
1 oz Vodka
1/2 oz Black Raspberry LIqueur
1/2 oz Banana Liqueur
Fill with equal parts of Orange
Juice and Milk.
Shake.

WHALE'S TAIL
Fill glass with ice.
1 oz Vodka or Lime Vodka
1 oz Spiced Rum
1/2 oz Blue Curacao
1 oz Sour Mix
Fill with Pineapple Juice.
Shake.

WHARF RAT
Fill glass with ice.
1 oz Rum
1/2 oz Apricot Brandy
Dash of Grenadine
2 oz Sour Mix
Fill with Orange Juice.
Shake.
Garnish with Lime and Black
Licorice Whip.

WHEN HELL FREEZES OVER
(frozen)
In Blender:
1 cup of Ice
1 oz Cinnamon Schnapps
1 oz Banana Liqueur
1/2 ripe peeled Banana
Dash of Orange Juice
Dash of Cranberry Juice
Pinch ground Cinnamon
Blend until smooth.

WHIP COCKTAIL
Fill glass with ice.
1 1/2 oz Brandy
3/4 oz Sweet Vermouth
3/4 oz Dry Vermouth
1/2 tsp Curacao or Triple Sec
1/4 tsp Pernod
Stir.
Strain into chilled glass.

WHIPPET
Fill glass with ice.
1 1/2 oz Whiskey
1/2 oz Peppermint Schnapps
1/2 oz White Crème de Cacao
Shake.
Strain into chilled glass.

WHIRLAWAY
Fill glass with ice.
1 1/2 oz Bourbon
3/4 oz Curacao
2-3 dashes of Bitters
Shake.
Top with Soda Water.

WHISKEY AND BRANCH
Fill glass with ice.
2 oz Whiskey
Fill with water.
Stir.

WHISKEY AND WATER
Fill glass with ice.
2 oz Whiskey
Fill with Water.
Stir.

WHISKEY COLLINS
Fill glass with ice.
2 oz Whiskey
Fill with Sour Mix.
Shake.
Splash with Soda Water.
Garnish with Cherry and Orange.

WHISKEY DAISY
Fill glass with ice.
2 oz Whiskey
1 tsp Raspberry Syrup
or Grenadine or Red Currant Syrup
1/2 oz Lemon Juice
Shake.
Fill with Soda Water.
Float 1 tsp Yellow Chartreuse on top.
Garnish with Lemon wedge.

W

WHISKEY FIX
Fill glass with ice.
2 oz Blended Whiskey
or Blended Scotch Whiskey
1 oz Lemon Juice
1 tsp Powdered Sugar
Stir.
Garnish with Lemon.

WHISKEY HIGHBALL
Fill glass with ice.
2 oz Whiskey
Fill with Water or Soda Water
or Ginger Ale.

WHISKEY RICKEY
Fill glass with ice.
1 1/2 oz Whiskey
1/2 oz Lime Juice
1 tsp Sugar Syrup (optional)
Fill with Soda Water.
Stir.
Garnish with Lime.

WHISKEY SOUR
Fill glass with ice.
2 oz Whiskey
Fill with Sour Mix.
Shake.
Garnish with Cherry and Orange.

WHISKEY ZIPPER
Fill glass with ice.
1 1/2 oz Whiskey
Dash of Drambuie
Dash of Cherry Liqueur
Squeeze and drop Lemon Wedge
into drink.

WHISPER (frozen)
In Blender:
1/2 cup of Ice
1/2 oz Coffee Liqueur
1/2 oz Crème de Cacao
1/2 oz Brandy
Scoop of Vanilla Ice Cream
Blend until smooth.
If too thick add Cream or Milk.
If too thin add ice or Ice Cream.
Sprinkle with Shaved Chocolate.

WHITE BABY
Fill glass with ice.
1 oz Gin or Orange Gin
1 oz Triple Sec
1 oz Heavy Cream
Shake.
Strain into chilled glass.

WHITE BULL aka AMIGO
Fill glass with ice.
1 oz Tequila
1 oz Coffee Liqueur
Fill with Milk or Cream.
Shake.

WHITE CADILLAC
Fill glass with ice.
2 oz Scotch
Fill with Milk or Cream.
Stir.

WHITE CADILLAC 2
Fill glass with ice.
1 oz Triple Sec
1 oz White Crème de Cacao
1 oz Milk or Cream
Shake.
Strain into chilled glass.

WHITE CARGO (frozen)
In Blender:
1/2 cup of Ice
2 1/2 oz Gin
1/2 oz Maraschino Liqueur
1/2 oz Dry White Wine
Scoop of Vanilla Ice Cream
Blend until smooth.
If too thick add Milk or Cream.
If too thin add ice or Ice Cream.

WHITE CHOCOLATE MARTINI
Fill glass with ice.
3 1/2 oz Vodka or Chocolate Vodka
1/2 oz White Creme de Cacao
Stir.
Strain into chilled glass.
Garnish with Cherry.

WHITE CLOUD
Fill glass with ice.
2 oz Sambuca
Fill with Soda Water.
Stir.

WHITE DEATH
Fill glass with ice.
1 oz Vodka or Raspberry Vodka
1/2 oz White Crème de Cacao
1/2 oz Raspberry Schnapps
Stir.
Strain into chilled glass.

WHITE ELEPHANT
Fill glass with ice.
1 oz Vodka or Cinnamon Vodka
1 oz White Crème de Cacao
Fill with Milk.
Shake.

WHITE GHOST (frozen)
In Blender:
1 cup of Ice
1 1/2 oz Hazelnut Liqueur
3/4 oz White Crème de Cacao
1/4 oz Black Raspberry Liqueur
2 oz Cream
Blend.

WHITE HEART
Fill glass with ice.
1/2 oz Sambuca
1/2 oz White Crème de Cacao
2 oz Cream or Milk
Shake.
Strain into chilled glass.

WHITE HEAT
Fill glass with ice.
1 oz Gin or Orange Gin
1/2 oz Triple Sec
1/2 oz Dry Vermouth
1 oz Pineapple Juice
Shake.

WHITE JAMAICAN
Fill glass with ice.
1 oz Rum or Vanilla Rum
1 oz Coffee Liqueur
Fill with Milk or Cream.
Shake.

WHITE KNIGHT
Fill glass with ice.
3/4 oz Scotch
3/4 oz Drambuie
3/4 oz Coffee Liqueur
Fill with Milk or Cream.
Shake.

WHITE LADY
Fill glass with ice.
1 1/2 oz Gin
1/4 oz Cream
1 tsp Sugar Syrup
or Powdered Sugar
1/2 Egg White
Shake.
Strain into chilled glass.

WHITE LADY 2
Fill glass with ice.
1 oz Gin or Orange Gin
1 oz Triple Sec
1 oz Cream or Milk
Shake.
Strain into chilled glass.

WHITE LILY
Fill glass with ice.
1 oz Gin or Orange Gin
1 oz Rum
1 oz Triple Sec
1/4 tsp Pernod
Shake.
Serve or strain into chilled glass.

WHITE LION
Fill glass with ice.
1 1/2 oz Rum or Orange Rum
3/4 oz Lemon juice
1 tsp Powdered Sugar
1/2 tsp Grenadine
2-3 dashes of Bitters
Shake.
Strain into chilled glass.

WHITE MINK
Fill glass with ice.
1 oz Vodka
1/2 oz White Crème de Menthe
1/2 oz Galliano
Fill with Cream or Milk.
Shake.

WHITE MINK 2
Fill glass with ice.
1 oz Galliano
1 oz Triple Sec
1 oz Cream or Milk
Shake.
Strain into chilled glass.

WHITE MINNESOTA
Fill glass with ice.
2 oz White Crème de Menthe
Fill with Soda Water.
Stir.

WHITE OUT
Fill glass with ice.
1 1/2 oz Gin
1 oz White Crème de Cacao
Fill with Milk.
Shake.

WHITE ROMAN
Fill glass with ice.
1 oz Sambuca
1 oz Coffee Liqueur
Fill with Milk or Cream.
Shake.

WHITE ROSE
Fill glass with ice.
1 1/2 oz Gin or Lime Gin
3/4 oz Cherry Liqueur
2 oz Orange Juice
1/2 oz Lime Juice
1 tsp Sugar Syrup
1/2 Egg White
Shake.
Strain into chilled glass.

WHITE RUSSIAN
Fill glass with ice.
1 oz Vodka
1 oz Coffee Liqueur
Fill with Milk or Cream.
Shake.

WHITE RUSSIAN (frozen)
In Blender:
1/2 cup of Ice
1 oz Vodka
1 oz Coffee Liqueur
Scoop of Vanilla Ice Cream
Blend until smooth.
If too thick add Milk or Cream.
If too thin add ice or Ice Cream.
Sprinkle with Shaved Chocolate
or Sprinkles.

WHITE SPANIARD
Fill glass with ice.
1 oz Brandy
1 oz Coffee Liqueur
Fill with Milk or Cream.
Shake.

WHITE SPIDER
Fill glass with ice.
2 oz Vodka
1 oz White Crème de Menthe
Shake.
Strain into chilled glass.

WHITE SWAN
Fill glass with ice.
2 oz Amaretto
2 oz Milk or Cream
Shake.

WHITE TIGER
Fill glass with ice.
2 oz Tuaca
1 oz White Crème de Cacao
Dash Cream
Shake.
Strain into chilled glass.

WHITE TRASH
Fill glass with ice.
2 oz Southern Comfort
Fill with Milk.

WHITE WATER
Fill glass with ice.
1/2 oz Triple Sec
1 oz Pineapple Juice
Fill with White Wine.
Top with Lemon-Lime Soda.

WHITE WAY
Fill glass with ice.
3 oz Gin
1/2 oz White Crème de Menthe
Stir.
Strain into chilled glass.

W

Metric Measurement Conversion Chart on page 14

WHITE WITCH
Fill glass with ice.
1 oz Light Rum or Citurs Rum
1/2 oz White Crème de Cacao
1/2 oz Triple Sec
Squeeze 1/2 Lime into drink.
Fill with Soda Water.
Garnish with Mint Sprigs
dusted with Powdered Sugar.

WHY NOT
Fill glass with ice.
1 oz Gin
1 oz Apricot Brandy
or Dry Vermouth
1/2 oz Dry Vermouth
or Apricot Brandy
1 tsp Lemon Juice
Shake.
Strain into chilled glass.

WIBBLY WOBBLY WOO
Fill glass with ice.
1 oz Dark Rum
1 oz Brandy
Dash Green Chartreuse
Shake. Strain into a chilled glass.

WIDGET
Fill glass with ice.
1 1/2 oz Gin
1 1/2 oz Peach Schnapps
Stir.

WIDOW'S DREAM
Fill glass with ice.
2 oz Benedictine
1 Egg
Shake.
Strain into chilled glass.
Float 1 oz Cream on top.

WIDOW'S KISS
Fill glass with ice.
1 oz Brandy
1/2 oz Benedictine
1/2 oz Yellow Chartreuse
Dash of Bitters
Shake.
Strain into chilled glass.

WIKI WAKI WOO
Fill glass with ice.
1/2 oz Vodka or Citrus Vodka
1/2 oz 151-Proof Rum
1/2 oz Tequila
1/2 oz Triple Sec
1/2 oz Amaretto
Fill with equal parts Orange,
Cranberry,
and Pineapple Juice.
Shake.

WILD IRISH ROSE
Fill glass with ice.
1 1/2 oz Irish Whiskey
1 1/2 tsp Grenadine
1/2 oz Lime Juice
Stir.
Fill with Soda Water.

WILD THING
Fill glass with ice.
1 oz Vodka or Citrus Vodka
1/2 oz Rum or Citrus Rum
1/2 oz Triple Sec
Dash of Lime Juice
Dash of Sour Mix
Shake.
Fill with Cranberry Juice.

WILDEBEEST
Fill glass with ice.
Dash of Vodka
Dash of Amaretto
Dash of Southern Comfort
Dash of Jägermeister
Dash of Peach Schnapps
Fill with equal parts Orange,
Pineapple and Cranberry Juice.
Shake.

WILL ROGERS
Fill glass with ice.
1 1/2 oz Gin or Orange Gin
1/2 oz Dry Vermouth
Dash of Triple Sec
1 tbsp Orange Juice
Shake.
Strain into chilled glass.

WIND JAMMER
Fill glass with ice.
1 oz Dark Rum
1/2 oz White Crème de Cacao
2 oz Pineapple Juice
1 oz Cream
Shake.
Garnish with Pineapple.

WIND SURF
4 oz White Wine
Dash of Triple Sec
Fill with equal parts Pineapple
Juice and Soda Water.
Stir.

WINDEX
Fill glass with ice.
1 1/2 oz Vodka or Citrus Vodka
1/4 oz Blue Curacao
Strain into shot glass.
Splash with Soda Water.

WINDEX 2
Fill glass with ice.
1 oz Vodka or Citrus Vodka
1 oz Rum or Citrus Rum
1/2 oz Blue Curacao
Dash of Lime Juice
Fill with Lemon-Lime Soda
Use paper towel as coaster.

WINDY CITY
Fill glass with ice.
1 1/4 oz Whiskey
Dash of Triple Sec
2 oz water
Garnish with Lemon Twist.

WINE COOLER
Fill glass 3/4 with ice.
Fill 3/4 with desired Wine.
Fill with Ginger Ale
or Lemon-Lime Soda.
Garnish with Lime.

WINE SPRITZER
Fill glass 3/4 with ice.
Fill 3/4 with desired Wine.
Fill with Soda Water.
Garnish with Lime.

WINTER FROST (frozen)
In Blender:
1/2 cup of Ice
3/4 oz Brandy
3/4 oz White Crème de Cacao
3/4 oz White Crème de Menthe
Scoop of Vanilla Ice Cream
Blend until smooth.

Metric Measurement Conversion Chart on page 14

WOLFHOUND
Fill glass with ice.
1 oz Irish Whiskey
3/4 oz Dark Crème de Cacao
1 oz Milk or Cream
Shake.
Top with 1 oz Soda Water.

WOMBAT
Pulverize 6 oz of Fresh Watermelon
(minus seeds) in glass.
2 oz Dark Rum
1/2 oz Strawberry Liqueur
3 oz Orange Juice
3 oz Pineapple Juice
Shake well.

WOO WOO aka
SILK PANTIES 2
Fill glass with ice.
1 1/2 oz Vodka or Citrus Vodka
      or Peach Vodka
1/2 oz Peach Schnapps
2 oz Cranberry Juice
Stir.
Serve or strain into chilled glass.

WOODEN SHOE
2 oz Vandermint
Fill with Hot Chocolate.
Top with Whipped Cream.
Drizzle Chocolate Syrup on top.

WYOMING SWING
COCKTAIL
Fill glass with ice.
1 1/2 oz Sweet Vermouth
1 1/2 oz Dry Vermouth
3 oz Orange Juice
1/2 oz Sugar Syrup
Shake.

WYOOTER HOOTER
Fill glass with ice.
2 oz Bourbon
Dash of Grenadine
Fill with Lemon-Lime Soda.

XALAPA PUNCH
In Sauce Pan over low heat:
2 cups of Hot Black Tea
Add rind of 2 Oranges (use carrot
peeler or cheese grater)
Heat for 5 minutes.
Let cool.
Add 1 cup of Honey or Sugar (stir
until dissolved)
Pour into punch bowl with ice.
Add:
1 Quart Amber Rum
1 Quart Apple Brandy
1 Quart Dry Red Wine
Diced Orange and Lemon
Serves 40

XANADU (floater)
1/2 oz Galliano (bottom)
1/2 oz Orange Liqueur
1/2 oz Amaretto (top)

XANGO
Fill glass with ice.
1 1/2 oz Rum or Citrus Rum
1/2 oz Triple Sec
1 oz Grapefruit Juice
Shake.
Strain into chilled glass.

XANTHIA
Fill glass with ice.
3/4 oz Gin
3/4 oz Cherry Brandy
3/4 oz Yellow Chartreuse
Shake.
Serve or strain into chilled glass.

XAVIER
Fill glass with ice.
3/4 oz Coffee Liqueur
3/4 oz Crème de Nouyax
3/4 oz Orange Liqueur
Fill with Milk or Cream.
Shake.

XERES
Fill glass with ice.
2 oz Dry Sherry
Dash of Orange Bitters
Stir.
Strain into chilled glass.

XYLOPHONE (frozen)
In Blender:
1/2 cup of Ice
1 1/2 oz Tequila
1 oz White Crème de Cacao
1 oz Sugar Syrup
Scoop of Vanilla Ice Cream
Blend until smooth.
If too thick add Milk or Cream.
If too thin add ice or Ice Cream.

XYZ
Fill glass with ice.
1 1/2 oz Rum or Citrus Rum
1/2 oz Triple Sec
1/2 oz Lemon Juice
Shake and Strain into chilled glass.

Y 2 K
Fill glass with ice.
1 1/2 oz Yukon Jack
1/2 oz Coffee Liqueur
Shake. Strain into shot glass.

Y. I.
Fill glass with ice.
1/2 oz Vodka
1/2 oz Coconut Rum
1/2 oz Melon Liqueur
1/2 oz Black Raspberry Liqueur
Dash of Pineapple and Cranberry
Juice
Shake.
Strain into shot glass.

YALE COCKTAIL
Fill glass with ice.
1 1/2 oz Gin
1/2 oz Dry Vermouth
1 tsp Blue Curacao
or Cherry Brandy
Dash of Bitters
Stir.

YARD OF FLANNEL
In sauce pan over low heat:
2 pints of Ale (do not boil)
Blend in a separate bowl:
4 oz Amber Rum
3 oz Super Fine Sugar
1/2 tsp ground Nutmeg
4 Eggs
1/2 tsp Ginger or Cinnamon
Beat well.
Pour mixture in heated pitcher.
Slowly add hot ale.
Stir constantly.
Serves 4.

W
X
Y

Metric Measurement Conversion Chart on page 14

YASHMAK
Fill glass with ice.
1 1/2 oz Rye Whiskey
3/4 oz Dry Vermouth
1/2 oz Pernod
3 dashes of Bitters
1/2 tsp Sugar Syrup
Shake.

YELLOW BIRD
Fill glass with ice.
3/4 oz Vodka or Citrus
    or Orange Vodka
3/4 oz White Crème de Cacao
3/4 oz Orange Juice
3/4 oz Cream
1/2 oz Galliano
Shake.
Strain into chilled glass.

YELLOW BIRD (frozen)
In Blender:
1 cup of Ice
1 oz Rum or Pineapple Vodka
1/2 oz Coffee Liqueur
1/2 oz Banana Liqueur
2 tbsp Cream of Coconut
1/2 cup fresh or canned Pineapple
Blend until smooth.

YELLOW FEVER
Fill glass with ice.
2 oz Vodka or Citrus Vodka
Fill with Lemonade.
Stir.
Garnish with Lemon.

YELLOW JACKET aka KENTUCKY SCREWDRIVER, BLACK-EYED SUSAN
Fill glass with ice.
2 oz Bourbon
Fill with Orange Juice.

YELLOW JACKET 2
Fill glass with ice.
1/2 oz Jägermeister
1/2 oz Bärenjäger
1/2 oz Coffee Liqueur
Stir.
Strain into chilled glass.

YELLOW PARROT
Fill glass with ice.
1 oz Apricot Brandy
1 oz Pernod
1 oz Yellow Chartreuse
Shake.
Strain into chilled glass.

YELLOW RATTLER
Fill glass with ice.
1 oz Gin or Orange Gin
1 oz Dry Vermouth
1 oz Sweet Vermouth
3 oz Orange Juice
Shake.
Strain into chilled glass.

YELLOW RUSSIAN aka JUNGLE JIM
Fill glass with ice.
1 oz Vodka or Banana Vodka
1 oz Banana Liqueur
Fill with Milk or Cream.
Shake.

YELLOW SNOW
Fill glass with ice.
2 oz Vodka or Pineapple Vodka
Fill with equal parts Pineapple
Juice and Milk.
Shake.

YELLOW SUBMARINE
Fill glass with ice.
1 oz Peach Schnapps
1 oz Banana Liqueur
Fill with equal parts Orange and
Pineapple Juice.
Shake.

YO MAMA
Fill glass with ice.
2 oz Orange Vodka
Fill with Soda Water.
Float 1/2 oz Orange Juice on top.

YODEL
Fill glass with ice.
2 oz Fernet Branca
2 oz Orange Juice
Stir.
Fill with Soda Water.
Garnish with Orange.

YOG
Fill glass with ice.
2 oz Yukon Jack
Fill with equal parts Orange and
Grapefruit Juice.
Shake.

YOKOHAMA MAMA
Fill glass with ice.
1 1/2 oz Brandy
1/2 oz Melon Liqueur
Dash of Amaretto
Dash of Grenadine
Fill with equal parts Orange
and Pineapple Juice.
Shake.

YORSH
2 oz Vodka
Fill with Beer.

ZAMBOANGA HUMMER
Fill glass with ice.
1/2 oz Amber Rum
1/2 oz Gin
1/2 oz Brandy
1/2 oz Curacao or Triple Sec
2 oz Orange Juice
2 oz Pineapple Juice
1/2 oz Lemon Juice
1 tsp Brown Sugar
Shake.

ZANZIBAR
Fill glass with ice.
2 1/2 oz Dry Vermouth
1 oz Gin
1/2 oz Lemon Juice
1 tsp Sugar Syrup
3 dashes of Bitters
Shake.
Strain into chilled glass.
Garnish with a Lemon Twist.

ZAZA
Fill glass with ice.
1 1/2 oz Gin or Orange Gin
1 1/2 oz Dubonnet
1/2 oz Triple Sec
2 oz Orange Juice
Shake.
Strain into chilled glass.

ZAZARAC
Fill glass with ice.
1 oz Whiskey
1/4 oz Rum
1/4 oz Anisette
1/4 oz Sugar Syrup
3 dashes of Bitters
1 oz Water
Stir.
Garnish with Lemon.

ZHIVAGO STANDARD
Fill glass with ice.
1 1/2 oz Vodka or Lime Vodka
1/2 oz Kummel
1/2 oz Lime Juice
Stir.
Strain into chilled glass.
Garnish with Olive.

ZIPPER
1 oz Tequila
1 oz Orange Liqueur or Triple Sec
1/2 oz Milk or Cream
Shake.
Strain into shot glass.

ZIPPER HEAD
Fill glass with ice.
1 1/2 oz Vodka
1/2 oz Black Raspberry Liqueur
Fill with Soda Water.
Supposed to be drunk in one shot
through a straw.

ZOMBIE
Fill glass with ice.
1 oz Light Rum
1 oz Dark Rum
1/2 oz Triple Sec or Curacao or
Apricot Brandy
Dash of Crème de Nouyax
or Grenadine
2 oz Orange Juice
2 oz Sour Mix
or Pineapple Juice
Shake.
Top with 1/2 oz 151-Proof Rum.
Garnish with Lemon, Orange and
Cherry.

ZONKER
Fill glass with ice.
1 oz Vodka or Citrus Vodka
1 oz Triple Sec
1 oz Amaretto
1 oz Cranberry Juice
Shake.
Strain into chilled glass.

ZOO
Fill glass with ice.
1/2 oz Gin
1/2 oz Rum
1/2 oz Tequila
1/2 oz Bourbon
Dash of Grenadine
Fill with equal parts Orange and
Pineapple Juice.
Shake.

ZOOM
Fill glass with ice.
1 1/2 oz Brandy
1/4 oz Honey
1/2 oz Cream
Shake.
Strain into chilled glass.

ZUMA BUMA
Fill glass with ice.
1 1/2 oz Citrus Vodka
1/2 oz Black Raspberry Liqueur
Fill with Orange Juice.
Splash of Cranberry Juice

Y

Z

Metric Measurement Conversion Chart on page 14

 NON-ALCOHOLIC DRINKS

Below is an index of non-alcoholic drink recipes that can be found in alphabetical order in this book.

ARNOLD PALMER

BEACH BLANKET BINGO

CAFE AU LAIT

CAFE MOCHA

CAFFE AMERICANO

CAFFE LATTE

CAPPUCCINO

DOUBLE CAPPUCCINO

DOUBLE ESPRESSO

ESPRESSO CON PANNO

FRAPPE

FROZEN CAPPUCCINO

HAMMERHEAD

ICE CREAM COFFEE

ICE CREAM FLOAT

ICE CREAM SODA

ICED COFFEE MOCHA

JULIUS

KICKSTART

LATTE

LEMONADE

LIMEADE

LIME RICKEY

MILKSHAKE

MOCHACCINO

MULLED CIDER

RASPBERRY LIME RICKEY

RED EYE

ROY ROGERS

SHIRLEY TEMPLE

SHOT IN THE DARK

SPEEDBALL

SWEET TEA

VIRGIN BANANA

VIRGIN MARY

VIRGIN PINA COLADA

VIRGIN STRAWBERRY DAIQUIRI

Martinis and Martini Style Libations

At first "Martini" only referred to a straight up gin drink. Then came the Vodka Martini which is now the most popular. The ingredients never varied that much, the spirit (gin, vodka), ice and a little Vermouth, maybe a dash of juice. Sure, there were some interesting garnishes (olives, onions, lemon, chili pepper, orange, lime), but plain and classic, the Martini has remained for decades.

The Martini (straight up drink) Explosion of the 90's changed the drink forever. All the rules changed. People are calling rum and liqueur based drinks served straight up Martinis. You can find veteran bartenders saying things like "A Cosmopolitan is not a Martini," and on one level, they are right, but they will be left behind because the Martini (straight up drink) movement is too big.

Here are the rules as they exist today:

1. If you serve it in a Martini glass and there is no whiskey in it you can call it a Martini.

2. They can be any color of the rainbow.

3. They can be very potent, or have their strength dramatically cut with low octane liqueurs and mixers.

SECRET #1 — Perfect Pour Every time

Waste will take down an establishment from within. Every mixed up order, miss-made drink, every drop not drained from a bottle, and every over pour add up to money going down the sink.
Are you ready? This is so simple.

1. Take your Martini glass and fill it with water to the level to which you will be pouring.
2. Now take out 2 tsp(10ml) of water (this is what you will be gaining from the chilling process).
3. Take the mixing glass you would be using to mix your Martinis in the future in, and fill it with ice (I prefer a 16oz Pint/Boston Shaker glass).
4. Pour the water filled Martini glass into the ice filled mixing glass.
5. Now mark the side of the mixing glass with a marker or paint. This is where you want your liquid with ice to come to every time you make a Martini. Leave this marked glass next to your mixing area for reference.

SECRET #2 — Chilled Glasses

Nothing enhances a perfectly made Martini more than a nice chilly glass. If you can, refrigerate your glasses 20-30 minutes before needed. If you do not have room behind the bar, ask your chef or manager if you can keep glasses in the walk-in refrigerator, but keep the glasses in the dishwasher racks (the last thing you need is broken glass in the fridge).

If you have no place cool to keep your glasses, line up as many as you can safely on the bar where they are not likely to get knocked over and fill them with ice and water. They will be ready in 30 seconds.

SECRET #3 — The Shake

You need to shake all the new Martini (straight up) drinks. You have your ingredients in the glass. You have secured the mixing cup to the glass. Now pick them up — one hand on the glass, one hand on the cup — and let's get a little shaking going on.

The trick is getting a little rhythm going. Try up and down like a piston in an engine. Try horizontally in front of yourself, in and out. Practice and choose whichever you feel better with (your fingers are going to go numb if you practice with ice)....and always keep in mind, the longer you shake a drink the more diluted from the melting ice it will become.

SECRET #4 — The Chop Stir

The Classic Martini are not shaken unless the guest has specifically requested their Martini shaken. Got that Mr. Bond?

You will not find this bartending secret in print in any other publication available.

You really need the restaurant grade two piece strainer and the foot long or better bar spoon.

Let's say someone has ordered a Dry Sapphire Martini up. First, start chilling a Martini glass, unless you already have one awaiting the cocktail. You then fill a mixing glass with ice, gin and vermouth.

1. Place the spoon (bowl down) in the drink.

2. Place the strainer over the mixing glass so the spoon either sticks out the larger hole or sticks out between the lip of the glass and the strainer.

3. Place your hand over the strainer and the glass, in a manner so that the strainer and glass are fixed and not moving, as if you were picking up a baseball or a apple

4. With your other hand grab the spoon handle and vigorously drive it up and down to agitate the contents of the glass. I would say depending on your speed, 8 to15 movements should correctly mix your drink.

5. Remove spoon and strain your Martini into the chilled glass.

A SALUTE TO THE BIG APPLE!

BIG APPLE MARTINIS

APPLE MARTINI
Fill glass with ice.
4 oz Apple Vodka
Dash Dry Vermouth or Apple Liqueur (optional)
Stir
Strain into chilled glass
Or pour contents (with ice)
Into short glass.
Garnish with apple slice.

CARAMEL APPLE MARTINI
Fill glass with ice.
3 1/2 oz Vodka
Dash Apple Cider or Apple Juice
Shake
Dip rim of chilled glass in caramel or
Drizzle onto inside of glass.
Strain into chilled glass.

DIRTY SOUR APPLE MARTINI
Place 1/4 diced skinless Granny Smith Apple
in mixing glass and mash.
Fill glass with ice.
3 1/2 oz Vodka
1/2 oz Sour Apple Liqueur
Shake vigorously.
Strain into chilled glass.

SOUR APPLE MARTINI
Fill glass with ice.
3 1/2 oz Vodka
1/2 oz Sour Apple Liqueur
Shake
Strain into chilled glass.
Garnish with cherry.

Martini Section

Martini and Martini-Style Favorites

Below is an index of Martini and Martini-style recipes that can be found in alphabetical order in this book.

Martini Section

NAPOLEON
NEGRONI
NEWBURY
NINETEEN
NINOTCHKA
NUCLEAR KAMIKAZE
THE "O" MARTINI
OLIVER TWIST
OPERA
ORANGE MARTINI
PAISLEY MARTINI
PARADISE
PARISIAN
PARK AVENUE
PASSION MARTINI
PEACH MARTINI
PEACHES & CREAM MARTINI
PEAR MARTINI
PEARL DIVER
PEPPER MARTINI
PINEAPPLE COSMOPOLITAN
PINEAPPLE MARTINI
PINK GIN
PINK LEMONADE MARTINI
PINK PANTHER
PLAZA
POLLYANNA
POLO
POMEGRANATE MARTINI
PRINCE'S SMILE
PRINCETON
PURPLE ELASTIC THUNDER
PURPLE KAMIKAZE
PURPLE MARTINI
PURPLE RUSSIAN
PUSSY SUPREME
QUEEN
RACQUET CLUB
RASPBERRY COSMOPOLITAN
RASPBERRY MARTINI
RED HEADED SLUT
RENDEZVOUS
RUDE COSMOPOLITAN
RUSSIAN PUSSY
SAKETINI

SAMURAI
SCREAMING VIKING
SELF-STARTER
SOUR APPLE MARTINI
SOUR CHERRY MARTINI
SOUR PATCH MARTINI
SOUTHERN BRIDE
SPICY SWORD
SPHINX
STRAWBERRY MARTINI
TANGO
TEQUILA MARTINI
THANKSGIVING
THIRD DEGREE
THREE STRIPES
TRIPLE PHAT LIMEADE
TROPICAL MARTINI
TURF
TWIN SIX
ULANDA
UNDERCURRENT
UNION JACK
VANILLA MARTINI
VELVET KISS
VERONA
VESPER
    aka JAMES BOND MARTINI
VICTOR
VIRGIN
VODKA MARTINI
VOLGA BOATMAN
WARSAW
WATERMELON MARTINI
WEMBLEY
WHITE CHOCOLATE MARTINI
WHITE HEAT
WHITE TIGER
WHITE WAY
WHY NOT
WIBBLY WOBBLY WOO
WILL ROGERS
WOO WOO
YALE COCKTAIL
YELLOW RATTLER
ZANZIBAR

HOT DRINKS

Below is an index of hot drink recipes
that can be found in alphabetical order in this book.

FROZEN DRINKS

Below is an index of frozen drink recipes that can be found in alphabetical order in this book.

175

🥃 SHOTS, SHOOTERS, 🥃 QUICKIES ᴀɴᴅ FLOATERS

SECRET #1 — You can make any kind of shot

Just so you know, every drink is a potential shooter or shot. Any Martini, coffee drink, iced tea variation, etc., can be made into a shot.

Here is the secret: All you have to do is resize your cocktail.

Let's use a typical 2 oz(6 cl) shot glass, and let's take a random drink we can all picture -- a VODKA SOUR. The drink typically is served on ice in a tall glass with 2 oz(6cl) of spirit (vodka) and the rest Sour Mix. So to fit it into a 2 oz glass we will use 1 1/2 oz (4.5 cl) Vodka and a dash of the mixer (Sour Mix).

So:
VODKA SOUR SHOOTER
Fill glass with ice.
1 1/2 oz(4.5cl) Vodka
Dash Sour Mix
Shake.
Strain into shot glass.

SECRET #2 — Multi-shot Multi-tasking

One more quick lesson if you need to make 2-4 drinks, double-quadruple the recipe to save mixing time.

SECRET #3 — Wow your customers and friends

If you have four people who want shots, you can make a rather stiff drink like a TOKYO ICED TEA or a LONG SLOE COMFORTABLE FUZZY SCREW AGAINST THE WALL WITH SATIN PILLOWS THE HARD WAY by the directions in the book, and then just strain it into 4 shot glasses. Memorize a couple crazy drinks like these and whip them together, set them in front of your customers or guests, and you are money.

SECRET #4 — Layering & Floating

All liquids have a specific gravity making it more or less dense than other liquids (See chart on next page).

That is how, when making a B-52 (floater), the Irish Cream sits on top of the coffee liqueur and the orange liqueur sits on top of the Irish Cream.

Let me talk you through a B-52. You are going to need a small volume glass like a shot, pony, sherry, small stemmed cocktail, small martini, or small champagne flute.

- Pour 1/2 oz coffee liqueur in the glass.
- Take the bowl of a spoon and hold it horizontally just above the coffee liqueur.
- Pour the 1/2 oz of Irish Cream on the hovering spoon.
- Take a step back and look at what you did....pretty cool?
- Either rinse off the spoon or wipe it off with a clean bar rag.
- All right, hold the spoon just as before over the Irish Cream and gently pour the 1/2 oz orange liqueur. The last two often mix a little. That is how it is done. I have used a butter knife before as well as a maraschino cherry with stem instead of a spoon.

Also if your preparing for a party and you have some time before hand you can put the ingredients of a layered drink in the glass and refrigerate it and they will separate, some drinks it works better than others make a tester first and try it out.

GRAVITY INDEX FOR POUSSE-CAFE'

POUSSE CAFE' *is French term for*
a glass of liqueurs arranged in layers.

Below is a partial list of liqueurs, their color and their density (weights) which could aid you if you are attempting to create your own layered drinks.

The higher the gravity number, the more dense the liqueur.

Liqueur	Color	Gravity
Amaretto Bols	Brown	1.0710
Apricot Brandy Liqueur Bols	Amber	1.0605
Bailey's Irish Cream	Milky Brown	1.0540
Banana Liqueur Bols	Yellow	1.0942
Blue Curacao Bols	Blue	1.0677
Cacao Brown Bols	Dark Brown	1.0981
Cacao White Bols	Clear	1.0812
Cherry Brandy Liqueur Bols	Red	1.0456
Frangelico Hazelnut Liqueur	Amber	1.06505
Gosling's Black Seal Rum	Black	0.95362
Grand Marnier Cordon Rouge, Centenaire, Cinquantenaire	Orange/Amber	1.03300
Lychee Liqueur Bols	Clear	1.0661
Melon Liqueur Bols	Bright Green	1.0513
Triple Sec Bols	Clear	1.0797
Vanilla Liqueur Bols	Clear	1.0817

Dear Liquor Companies: if you do not see your product listed here it is because you never got back to me -- S.K.C.

SHOTS, SHOOTERS AND QUICKIES

Now you have the knowledge to make thousands of shooters. Listed below are drinks that are typically served as shots and can be found in alphabetical order in this book:

- A BAT AND A BALL
- A-BOMB
- ABC
- AFTER EIGHT
- AFTER FIVE
- AFTERBURNER
- AGENT 99
- ALICE IN WONDERLAND
- ANGEL KISS
- ANGEL WING
- ANGEL TIT
- ANTI-FREEZE
- APPLE PIE
- ASSASSIN
- AUNT JEMIMA
- AVALANCHE
- B-12
- B-50
- B-51
- B-52
- B-52 ON A MISSION
- B-52 WITH A MEXICAN TAILGUNNER
- B-52 WITH BOMBAY DOORS
- B-53
- B-54
- B-55
- B-57
- BANANA SANDWICH
- BATTERED BRUISED AND BLEEDING
- BAZOOKA
- BAZOOKA JOE
- BEACH HUT MADNESS
- BEAM ME UP SCOTTI
- BEARHUG
- BELFAST BOMBER
- BELLY BUTTON SHOT
- BEVERLY HILLBILLY
- BIG BAMBOO
- BIKINI LINE
- BISCUIT NECK
- BLACK FOREST
- BLACK SABBATH
- BLACK TIE
- BLOOD CLOT
- BLOW JOB
- BLUE KAMIKAZE
- BLUE MEANIE
- BODY SHOT
- BOILERMAKER
- BOOTLEGGER
- BRAIN
- BRAIN ERASER
- BRAIN TUMOR
- BRAIN WAVE
- BRAVE BULL
- BROKEN DOWN GOLF CART
- BUCKING BRONCO
- BUFFALO SWEAT
- BULL SHOT
- BULLFROG
- BURNING BUSH
- BUSH DIVER
- BUSTED CHERRY
- BUSTED RUBBER
- BUTTER BALL
- BUTTER SHOT
- CAMSHAFT
- CANDY CANE

- CAPITAL PUNISHMENT
- CARROT CAKE
- CARTEL BUSTER
- CELTIC COMRADE
- CEMENT MIXER
- CEREBRAL HEMORRHAGE
- CHAMBERED ROUND
- CHAOS
- CHARRO
- CHASTITY BELT
- CHERRY BOMB
- CHERRY COLA FROM HELL
- CHICKEN SHOT
- CHINESE TORTURE
- CHOCOLATE CAKE
- CHOCOLATE RATTLESNAKE
- CHUPACABRA
- CLAM SHOT
- CLOUDS OVER SCOTLAND
- CONCORD
- COOKIE MONSTER
- COPENHAGEN
- CRAMP RELIEVER
- CRANBERRY KAMIKAZE
- CREATURE FROM THE BLACK LAGOON
- CRIPPLER
- CUM DROP
- D.O.A.
- DAISY CUTTER
- DALLAS ALICE
- DC-3
- DC-9
- DC-10
- DEAD NAZI
- DEAD RAT
- DEATHWISH
- DEEP SEA
- DEEP THROAT
- DEPTH CHAMBER
- DEPTH CHARGE
- DICKIE TOECHEESE
- DIRTY HARRY
- DIRTY SILK PANTIES
- DOLI
- DOUBLEMINT BJ
- DR.J
- DR P. FROM HELL
- DUCK FART
- DUSTY ROSE
- DYING NAZI FROM HELL
- E.T.
- EAT HOT DEATH
- EAT THE CHERRY
- EMBRYO
- ENERGIZER
- F-16
- F-52
- FACE ERASER
- FAHRENHEIT
- FAIRCHILD
- FESTERING SLOBOVIAN HUMMER
- FIFTH AVENUE
- FIRE AND ICE
- FIRE IN HE HOLE
- FIREBALL

- FIERY KISS
- FIRESTORM
- FLAMING BLUE J.
- FLAMING HOOKER
- FLAMING LAMBORGHINI
- FLAMING NORIEGA
- FOUR HORSEMAN
- FOURTH OF JULY
- FREDDY KRUGER
- FREEDOM FIGHTER
- FUEL-INJECTION
- FUZZY MOTHER
- G-SPOT
- G-STRING
- GASOLINE
- GERMAN LEG SPREADER
- GHETTO BLASTER
- GHOSTBUSTER
- GINGERBREAD MAN
- G.S.COOKIE
- GOLPEADO
- GORILLA FART
- GUILLOTINE
- GUMDROP
- H.D.RIDER
- HAITIAN ASSISTANT
- HAMMER
- HAND JOB
- HAND RELEASE
- HAPPY JACK
- HARBOR LIGHTS
- HARD CANDY
- HARD NIPPLE
- HARD ON
- HARI KARI
- HEAD BANGER
- HEAD ROOM
- HEADREST
- HIGH JAMAICAN WIND
- HOG SNORT
- HOGBACK GROWLER
- HOLE IN ONE
- HOMECOMING
- HONEY BEE
- HOT TAMALE
- HOT YOUNG LADY
- HUSSIE
- ICE BOAT
- INDIAN SUMMER
- INTERNATIONAL INCIDENT
- INVERTED NAIL
- IRISH CAR BOMB
- IRISH FLAG
- IRISH MARIA
- IRON CROSS
- J.OFF
- J.FROST
- JAMAICAN TEN SPEED
- JAWBREAKER
- JELLO SHOTS
- JELLY BEAN
- JELLY FISH
- JET FUEL
- JEZEBEL
- JIZZ
- KAMIKAZI
- KEY LIME SHOOTER
- KILLER BEE
- KILLER COOL AID
- L.A.P.D.

- L.S.D.
- LADY LUCK
- LAYER CAKE
- LEFT HOOK
- LEG SPREADER
- LEMON BOMB
- LEMON DROP
- LEWINSKY
- LICORICE STICK
- LIFE-SAVER
- LIQUID ASPHALT
- LIQUID COCA
- LIQUID CRACK
- LITTLE GREEN MEN
- LITTLE PURPLE MEN
- LOCH NESS MONSTER
- LUGER
- M-16
- MAD COW
- MAGGOT
- MEXICAN BOILERMAKER
- MEXICAN FLAG
- MEXICAN MISSILE
- MIDNIGHT COWBOY
- MIDNIGHT SUN
- MIND ERASER
- MIND OBLITERATOR
- MOCHA MINT
- MONK SLIDE
- MONKEY WRENCH
- MOTHER LOVE
- MUDSLIDE
- MUFF DIVER
- MULE SKINNER
- NAKED G.S
- NASTY GIRL
- NESI
- NETHERLAND
- NEUTRON BOMB
- 911
- NINJA
- NO TELL MOTEL
- NUCLEAR KAMIKAZE
- NUTS AND BERRIES
- NUTS AND CREAM
- NUTTY CHINAMAN
- NUTTY JAMAICAN
- OATMEAL COOKIE
- 110 IN THE SHADE
- OPENING
- ORANGE DROP
- ORGASM
- OYSTER SHOT
- P.M.S.
- PAGO PAGO
- PAINT BALL
- PAIR OF JACKS
- PANTY BURNER
- PEANUT BUTTER AND JELLY
- PEARL NECKLACE
- PECKERHEAD
- PEZ
- PHANTOM
- PICKLED BRAIN
- PINK SNAPPER
- PITBULL ON CRACK
- PLEASURE DOME
- POINT
- POLISH BUTTERFLY
- POOP DECK
- POPPER
- PORT AND STARBOARD
- POUSSE CAFE
- PRAIRIE CHICKEN
- PRAIRIE FIRE
- PRAIRIE OYSTER

- PUMPKIN PIE
- PURPLE ALASKAN
- PURPLE BUNNY
- PURPLE HELMETED WARRIOR
- PURPLE HOOTER
- PURPLE NIPPLE
- PUSSY GALORE
- QUICK F.
- QUICKIE RAINBOW
- RASPBERRY BERET
- RASPBERRY GIMLET
- RASTA MAN
- RAZORBACK HOGCALLER
- REBEL YELL
- RED BEER SHOOTER
- RED DEATH
- RED HEADED SLUT
- ROMAN RIOT
- ROYAL SMILE
- RUMBALL
- RUMPELSTILTSKIN
- RUPTURED DUCK
- RUSSIAN PUSSY
- RUSSIAN QUAALUDE
- S.O.B.
- S.O.M.F.
- SAINT MORITZ
- SAKI BOMB
- SAMURAI
- SAND IN YOUR BUTT
- SANTA SHOT
- SATURN'S RING
- SAVOY HOTEL
- SCOOBY SNACK
- SCORPION
- SCOTTI WAS BEAMED UP
- SCREAMER
- SCREAMING BLUE MESSIAH
- SCREAMING DEAD NAZI
- SCREAMING NAZI
- SCUMBUCKET
- SEA MONKEYS
- SEDUCTION
- 727
- 747
- SEX
- SEXUAL GATOR
- SHAVED BUSH
- SHIVER SHOT
- SHOGUN
- SHOT IN THE DARK
- SILK PANTIES
- SILK SHORTS
- SILVER BULLET
- SILVER SPIDER
- SIMPLY BONKERS
- SIZZLER
- SKID MARK
- SKYLAB FALLOUT
- SLAMMERS
- SLEDGEHAMMER
- SLIMEBALL
- SLIPPERY BLACK NIPPLE
- SLIPPERY DICK
- SLIPPERY NIPPLE
- SLOPPY JOE
- SMURF P.
- SNOWBALL
- SNOWCAP
- SOUR GRAPES
- SOUTH OF THE BORDER
- SPANISH DYNAMITE

- SPANISH FLY
- SPANISH MOSS
- SPERM
- SPERM BANK
- SPILT MILK
- SPOOGE
- SPRING THAW
- SQUID INK
- STARS AND STRIPES
- STEALTH
- STUFFED TOILET
- STUMBLING F.
- SUICIDAL TENDENCIES
- SUNKEN TREASURE
- SWEAT SOCK
- SWEATY MEXICAN LUMBERJACK
- SWEET CREAM
- SWEDISH BJ
- TEMPER
- TEQUILA POPPER
- TEQUILA SHOOTER
- TEQUILA SLAMMER
- TEQUILA WITH TRAINING WHEELS
- TEST-TUBE BABE
- THREE AMIGOS
- THREE KINGS
- THREE STORY HOUSE FIRE
- THREE WISEMEN
- THREE WISEMEN AND THE MEXICAN PORTER
- THUNDER AND LIGHTNING
- TIC TAC
- TIE ME TO THE BEDPOST
- TIGER BALLS
- TIJUANA TITTY TICKLER
- TINY BOWL
- TO HELL YOU RIDE
- TORONTO ORGY
- TOXIC JELLYBEAN
- TRAFFIC LIGHT
- TROPICAL HOOTER
- TURKEY SHOOT
- 24 KARAT NIGHTMARE
- 252
- UNCLE SAM
- UNDERTOW
- UPSIDE DOWN MARGARITA
- URINALYSIS
- UZI
- VEGAS BJ
- VIBRATOR
- VOO DOO
- VULCAN MIND MELD
- VULCAN MIND PROBE
- WWII
- WALL STREET LIZARD
- WANDERING MISTRAL
- WARM CREAMY BUSH
- WATERFALL
- WENCH
- WET CROTCH
- WHIPPET
- WHITE DEATH
- WOO WOO
- XANADU
- XANTHIA
- XYZ
- Y2K
- Y.I.
- ZIPPER
- ZIPPERHEAD
- ZOOM

DESSERT DRINKS

A new fad has emerged in the ever-changing restaurant scene. Sweet dessert drinks are being offered to cap off the dining experience. They can be martini style, frozen or even hot drinks, just as long as they are sweet. The following is a list of my favorite sweet recipes that you can feel confident serving as dessert. The recipes that can be found in alphabetical order in this book.

- ABBY ROAD
- ADULT HOT CHOCOLATE
- ALEXANDER
- ALMOND ENJOY
- AMARIST
- AMBER MARTINI
- ANGEL KISS
- ANGEL WING
- ANGEL'S LIPS
- APPLE PIE
- ASIAN MARTINI
- AUGUST MOON
- B-52(floater)
- B-52 (frozen)
- B-52(coffee)
- BANANA CREAM PIE
- BANANA CREAM PIE MARTINI
- BELLINI
- BLACK ROSE
- BRANDY ALMOND MOCHA
- BROWN SQUIRREL
- CAFE AMORE
- CAFE FOSTER
- CARAMEL APPLE MARTINI
- CARROT CAKE
- CHERRY PIE
- CHERRY TART
- CHOCOLATE BANANA FREEZE
- CHOCOLATE COVERED CHERRY
- CHOCOLATE CHAOS
- CHOCOLATE MARTINI
- CLIMAX
- COOKIES AND CREAM
- CREAMSICLE
- DEEP DARK SECRET
- ECSTASY
- FIREBALL
- FRENCH KISS
- FRENCH MARTINI
- FROSTED ROMANCE
- FROZEN CAPPUCCINO
- FUDGESICLE
- GINGERBREAD MAN
- G. S. COOKIE
- GRASSHOPPER
- GUMMY MARTINI
- GUN RUNNER COFFEE
- HEAVENLY SEX
- HELLO NURSE
- HOT APPLE PIE
- HOT PEPPERMINT PATTY
- HOT SEX
- HOT SHOT
- INDIAN SUMMER
- JELLY DOUGHNUT
- KEOKE COFFEE
- KEY LIME MARTINI
- KEY LIME PIE
- KISS
- LA MOSCA
- LADY LUCK
- LEMON DROP
- MENAGE a TROIS
- MINT CHOCOLATE CHIP ICE CREAM
- MONTE CRISTO COFFEE
- MOON CHASER
- MOUND BAR
- NAUGHTY HULA PIE
- NUT AND HONEY
- NUTCRACKER
- NUTS AND BERRIES
- OATMEAL COOKIE
- PEACH COLADA
- PEACH MARTINI
- PEAR MARTINI
- PEARL DIVER
- PINEAPPLE DAIQUIRI
- POP-SICLE
- PUMPKIN PIE
- QUEEN
- RASPBERRY BELLINI
- RASPBERRY CHEESECAKE
- RASPBERRY KISS
- RED DWARF
- ROMAN RIOT
- RUSSIAN BANANA
- SCOOBY SNACK
- SCROPPINO
- SEX
- SICILIAN COFFEE
- SMOOTH OPERATOR
- SNOW CONE
- SOUR APPLE MARTINI
- SOVEREIGN COFFEE
- STRAWBERRY CHEESECAKE
- STRAWBERRY SHORTCAKE
- SUGAR DADDY
- TIE ME TO THE BEDPOST
- TOASTED ALMOND
- TOASTED MARSHMALLOW
- TOBLERONE
- TRAPPIST MONK
- TRIPLE PHAT LIMEADE
- TROPHY ROOM COFFEE
- TROPICAL MOON
- UNDER CURRENT
- VELVET HAMMER
- WINTER FROST
- YELLOW BIRD
- ZOOM

 **BEER**

ALES:

Ale: A top fermented beer. Ale is similar to lager, but usually richer, heavier and more complex. Ale can vary from blond to black in color. It is brewed in the 60*-75* range

Alt: Means "old" in German and refers to a traditional brewing process which dates back to pre 1840's which is when Lagers were starting to brew. It is fermented warm, but aged cold.

Barley Wine: A strong ale, copper to amber colored. Should be sipped like a brandy. A great winter warmer with complex sweetness and bitterness. A wide spectrum of tastes from maple to prune. It can improve with age.

Biere de Garde: From Northwest France, it is medium to strong in alcohol content and straw to copper colored. Biere de Garde is generally in the Ale family, but some are made with the lager process. Both types are bottle conditioned, laid on its side to age.

Bitter: Straw to red amber in color. Ordinary bitter is low to medium in alcohol content, while Extra Special Bitter is medium to high. Low to medium bitterness with low carbonation.

Black & Tan: A mixture of stout or porter with a light or pale ale. A layered drink when made from scratch, a mixture when bottled. SEE: RECIPES: Black & Tan, and Half & Half SEE: MIXING: Floating.

Brown Ale: There are two distinctly different Brown Ale families. Northern England is known for their reddish, medium bodied, nutty or fruity beer. While Southern England is known for their darker, sweeter, lighter bodied product.

Hefe: Means "yeast" in German. An unfiltered wheat beer, cloudy and bottle-conditioned with yeast. Tastes of clove or citrus are prevalent. Pour to evacuate the sediment out of the bottom; squeeze a lemon wedge into the creamy head.

Imperial: SEE Stout

India Pale Ale: Created to endure voyages from England to India during British rule. Pale or golden to deep copper in color. Quite hoppy, with nuances of fruit and/or flowers. Alcohol strength is evident.

Lambic or Lambiek: Straight Lambic: Referred to taste wise as horsey, sweaty or tart. Can range from well-carbonated to almost flat, but always pale and sour.

Gueuze or Geuze: A blend of lambics, it carries all the properties of the straight lambics in a smoother more complex package.

Fruit: A blend of lambics (usually young and old) with fruit added. Tart and pale. Varieties include Kriek (cherry), Framboise (raspberry), Peche (peach), Faro (candy sugar), Vigneronne or Muscat (grape), Cassis (black currant), Mirabelle (plum), Fraises (strawberry), Exotic (pineapple) Apricot, Banana.

Old Ale: A broad term for the rich traditional strong ale from England. Originally brewed in the 17th-century for consumption during the winter months.

Pale Ale: Color ranges from golden to copper. European versions tend to be heavily malted, and the American versions tend to lean toward a more prevalent abundance of hops. Both may have a fruitiness about them. SEE: India Pale Ale

Porter: A blend of three ales (old, new and week). Medium brown to black. Usually very hoppy and very malty. Often sharp with a hint of burnt charcoal flavor. Strong in flavor and alcohol content. Porter is the predecessor of modern day stout.

Scotch Ale: Amber to red to dark brown in color. A broad term. Usually these beers are sweet and rich with a creamy head. More malty than hoppy.

Stout: Very dark to black. Origins in 18th-century London. Tastes range from charcoal to molasses with a malty sweetness to a bitter sweetness. Serve warm. Stout was born from Porter.

Dry Stout or Irish Stout: Deep dark red to black opaque, with a rich creamy head, Roasty with a medium to high hop flavor balanced by hints of coffee and/or caramel. Lower in calories and alcohol content than commonly thought.

Imperial or Russian: Very dark or black. Originally created for export to frozen Russian climates. It is heavy and rich with undertones of coffee, cocoa and or burnt black currant. Strong in flavor and alcohol content.

Milk Stout or Sweet Stout: Very dark amber to black with a creamy head. Malty sweet, and not dry, often with caramel or semi-sweet chocolate overtones.

Oatmeal Stout: A stout with any amount of oatmeal added. Originally a heavy, sweet beer marketed for lactating mothers. Heavy bitter ones as well as lighter easier drinking ones are being crafted by micro-breweries today.

Trappist: This fruity heavily sedimented ale is dark, rich, and strong. True Trappist is brewed at Trappist monasteries in Belgium under centuries-old guidelines. Serve mild to warm 55-60 F.

Wheat Beer: A general term for any beer made with wheat malts. Pale straw to deep copper or brown. Usually cloudy, but some are clear, Usually highly carbonated, but some are rather low. Often yeasty and tart, but taste can vary greatly.

White Beer or Witbier: Originates from Belgium and is a kind of wheat beer. Color can vary from pale to golden, with a creamy head. Taste is usually a contrast of citrus and spices like coriander, nutmeg, and/or clove.

LAGERS:

Lager: Bottom fermented beer, named for the German word (lagern) "to store". It is aged at cool temperatures that give it a smooth refined taste.

Bock: Traditionally brewed in Germany in the spring at the peak of barley and hop development. A full-bodied, stronger richer lager.

Doppelbock: Doublebock, very full-bodied and extra strong. Can be amber, red amber, dark brown. Often sweet and creamy, sometimes fruity or tangy.

Dry Beer: A Japanese variation on the German Diat Pils. Now produced extensively in the U.S. Enzymes are added during the production converting more of the malt into alcohol, making a drier beer with less after taste.

Dunkel: Refers to any dark lager from deep red to black. Full-bodied with heavy malt character. Clean and crisp with caramel undertones. Sometimes they are well hopped, but almost always bitter. Note: Some dark wheat beers(ale) are referred to as Dunkel.

Ice Beer: At first a German product, with their Eisbock, a strong dark note worthy brew. Now made extensively in the U.S. Slightly higher in alcohol content due to the process of partial freezing during production. The ice is removed, yielding a stronger beer.

Light Beer: A pale watery, low-calorie, low-strength, pilsner style beer. An American original. Some light beers are actually the companies normal product, with water added.

Malt Liqueur: A term made up in America to call beer that's alcohol content exceeds the governmental guidelines. Usually pale, strong, and cheap.

Marzen/Vienna/Octoberfest : Amber to pale copper. Very malty, and medium to strong in potency. Brewed in March to be ceremoniously imbibed in late September and early October.

Pizen (Pilsen, Pilsner): Originates from Pilsner, Czechoslovakia. Pale to golden, elegantly dry, and crisp with a flowery finish. The most copied and widely brewed beer style in the world.

CIDERS:

Hard Cider: Actually apple wine, produced from fermented apples. Platinum to deep yellow to deep copper in color, 2.5% to 14% alcohol by volume. Flavors vary, featuring melon, citrus, herbs, caramel, spices and flowers.

Perry: A sparkling alcoholic pear flavored drink. Pear Cider. English.

MALTERNATIVES:
ALTERNATIVE FLAVORED
MALT BEVERAGES and DESIGNER BEERS

Just so you know, these are all basically beer that has been filtered until tasteless and designer flavored. They may say that they are hard lemonade, or they may have logos on them from huge rum, vodka or whiskey distillers, but there is none of their famous product in them. They are produced in large by the big American beer manufacturers for the individual companies who can now get their hard liquor logos everywhere a beer logo can go getting around the strict liquor ad laws.

The sad by-product of these sweet designer beers is that they are taking up all the space in bars and stores where the small batch or micro brews were once available.

It's like what corporate music has done for radio.

DRINK RECIPES WITH BEER

All these recipes are in
alphabetical order throughout the book.

110 IN THE SHADE
AMERICAN SNAKEBITE
APHRODISIAC
BMW
BEER BUSTER
BLOODY BASTARD
BLOODY BREW
BOILERMAKER
CHANNEL
CINCINNATI
COLORADO BULLDOG
DEPTH CHAMBER
DEPTH CHARGE
DIESEL
DOG'S NOSE
DOUBLE TROUBLE
DR. P.
DR. P. FROM HELL
GLAM TRASH
GRAVEYARD
HALF & HALF
HOP, SKIP AND GO NAKED
HOT DOG
HUSSIE
ICE CREAM FLOAT
IRISH CAR BOMB
IRISH RUSSIAN
MEXICAN BOILERMAKER
MOJO
NASCAR DAD
PINK HOTEL
PURPLE NASTY
RED BEER
RED BEER SHOOTER
RED EYE
REVEREND
RUN, SKIP AND GO NAKED
SCHOOL BUS
SCUMBUCKET
SHANTE'GAF
SIZZLER
SKIP AND GO NAKED
SNAKEBITE
STRIP AND GO NAKED
TIGER BALLS
TRAIN WRECK
VELVET GAF
YORSH
VULCAN MIND PROBE
YARD OF FLANNEL

☻ COGNAC ☻

Cognac (kon yak) is a brandy produced in the vicinity of Cognac in western France. Cognacs are aged in wooden barrels and will improve in quality until they are 50 or 60 years old. Cognacs do not age in the bottle. Therefore a bottle of cognac bottled in 1990 at age 20, is still age 20 in the year 2000. The alcohol content of bottled cognacs range from 80-94 proof.

Below are listed some of the various grades of cognac.

V.S. 3 Star: (Very Special) 4-8 years old.

V.S.O.P.: (Very Superior Old Pale) or V.O. (Very Old) No brandy in the blend. May be less than 4 years 6 months old.

Napoleon: 6-25 years old.

X.O.: (Extra Old) May be 10-70 years old.

Reserve: 20-25 year old.

Extra: 20-50 years old.

Rare: 35-40 years old.

Remember these are guidelines and not rules.

Listed below are some of the major cognac houses and their finest products:

Beaulon . . . . .Cognac Rare
Camus . . . . .Extraordinaire
CCG . . . . .Meukow X.O.
Chabasse . . . . .Bowen Extra
Courvoisier . . . . . . .Collection Erte
Dor . . . . .Reserve No.11
Duboigalant . . . . . . .Tres Rare Grande Champagne
Dupuy . . . . .Rochas X.O. Fine Champagne
Pierre Frapin . . . . . .Cuvee Rabelais
Gautier . . . . .Tradition Rare
Paul Giraud . . . . . . .Tres Rare
Hennessy . . . . .Richard Hennessy
Hine . . . . .Family Reserve Grande Champagne
Guy Lheraud . . . . . .Tres Vieille Reserve Du Paradis
Martell . . . . .Creation
Moyet . . . . .Grande Champagne Tres Vieille
Normandin-Mercier . .Grande Champagne Vieille 43 degrees
Paulet . . . . .Lalique
Remy Martin . . . . . . .Louie XIII

The Wine Advocate's Vintage Guide

1970-2002® (Current as of 12/31/04)

By Robert M. Parker, Jr.

"Robert Parker is easily the single most influential person in the world of wine."

— *Paul Levy, The Observer*

"By Dint of Talent and a Formidable Capacity for Thoroughness, Robert M. Parker, Jr. has become one of the most respected American wine authorities."

— *The New York Times*

"The world's most experienced and trustworthy palate."

— *London Times*

"When Robert Parker spits, people listen....Parker has revolutionized American wine criticism to the genteel and snobbish world, Parker brought the forthright tastes of a middle class American ... the stringent standards of a fanatic, the high moral purpose of a reformer."

— *Newsweek*

"The most powerful and influential critic in any field."

— *60 Minutes II*

The Wine Avocate Rating System

Robert Parker's rating system employs a 50-100 point quality scale. It is my belief that the various twenty (20) point rating systems do not provide enough flexibility and often result in compressed and inflated wine ratings. The Wine Advocate takes a hard, very critical look at wine, since I would prefer to underestimate the wine's quality than to overestimate it. The numerical ratings are utilized only to enhance and complement the thorough tasting notes, which are my primary means of communicating my judgments to you.

96 - 100 — An extraordinary wine of profound and complex character displaying all the attributes expected of a classic wine of its variety. Wines of this caliber are worth a special effort to find, purchase, and consume.

90 - 95 — An outstanding wine of exceptional complexity and character. In short, these are terrific wines.

80 - 89 — A barely above average to very good wine displaying various degrees of finesse and flavor as well as character with no noticeable flaws.

70 - 79 — An average wine with little distinction except that it is a soundly made. In essence, a straightforward, innocuous wine.

60 - 69 — A below average wine containing noticeable deficiencies, such as excessive acidity and/or tannin, an absence of flavor, or possibly dirty aromas or flavors.

50 - 59 — A wine deemed to be unacceptable.

Scores in parentheses indicate that the wine was tasted from barrel.

Tasting Notes and Ratings

When possible all of my tastings are done in peer-group, single-blind conditions, (meaning that the same types of wines are tasted against each other and the producers' names are not known). The ratings reflect an independent, critical look at the wines. Neither price nor the reputation of the producer/grower affect the rating in any manner. I spend three months of every year tasting in vineyards. During the other nine months of the year, six and sometimes seven-day workweeks are devoted solely to tasting and writing. I do not participate in wine judgings or trade tastings for many reasons, but principal among these are the following: (1) I prefer to taste from an entire bottle of wine, (2) I find it essential to have properly sized and cleaned professional tasting glasses, (3) the temperature of the wine must be correct, and (4) I prefer to determine the time allocated to the number of wines to be critiqued.

The numeral rating given is a guide to what I think of the wine vis-à-vis its peer group. Certainly, wines rated above 85 are very good to excellent, and any wine rated 90 or above will be outstanding for its particular type. While some have suggested that scoring is not well suited to a beverage that has been romantically extolled for centuries, wine is no different from any consumer product. There are specific standards of quality that full-time wine professionals recognize, and there are benchmark wines against which others can be judged. I know of no one with three or four different glasses of wine in front of him or her, regardless of how good or bad the wines might be, who cannot say, "I prefer this one to that one." Scoring wines is simply taking a professional's opinion and applying some sort of numerical system to it on a consistent basis. Scoring permits rapid communication of information to expert and novice alike.

The score given for a specific wine reflects the quality of the wine at its best. I often tell people that evaluating a wine and assigning a score to a beverage that will change and evolve in many cases for up to 10 or more years is analogous to taking a photograph of a marathon runner. Much can be ascertained but, like a picture of a moving object, the wine will also evolve and change. Wines from obviously badly corked or defective bottles are retasted, since a wine from a single bad bottle does not indicate an entirely spoiled batch. Many of the wines reviewed have been tasted many times, and the score represents a cumulative average of the wine's performance in tastings to date. **Scores, however, do not reveal the important facts about a wine. The written commentary that accompanies the ratings is a better source of information regarding the wine's style and personality, its relative quality vis-à-vis its peers, and its value and aging potential than any score could ever indicate.**

Here then is a general guide to interpreting the numerical ratings:

90-100 is equivalent to an A and is given only for an outstanding or special effort. Wines in this category are the very best produced of their type. There is a big difference between a 90 and 99, but both are top marks. As you will note through the text, there are few wines that actually make it into this top category because there are not many great wines.

80-89 is equivalent to a B in school and such a wine, particularly in the 85-89 range, is very, very good; many of the wines that fall into this range often are great values as well. I have many of these wines in my personal collection.

70-79 represents a C, or average mark, but obviously 79 is a much more desirable score than 70. Wines that receive scores between 75 and 79 are generally pleasant, straightforward wines that lack complexity, character, or depth. If inexpensive, they may be ideal for uncritical quaffing.

Below 70 is a D or F, depending on where you went to school. For wine, it is a sign of an imbalanced, flawed, or terribly dull or diluted product that will be of little interest to the discriminating consumer.

In terms of awarding points, my scoring system gives every wine a base of 50 points. The wine's general color and appearance merit up to 5 points. Since most wines today are well made, thanks to modern technology and the increased use of professional oenologists, they tend to receive at least 4, often 5 points. The aroma and bouquet merit up to 15 points, depending on the intensity level and dimension of the aroma and bouquet as well as the cleanliness of the wine. The flavor and finish merit up to 20 points, and again, intensity of flavor, balance, cleanliness, and depth and length on the palate are all important considerations when giving out points. Finally, the overall quality level or potential for further evolution and improvement—aging—merits up to 10 points.

Scores are important for the reader to gauge a professional critic's overall qualitative placement of a wine vis-à-vis its peer group. However, it is also vital to consider the description of the wine's style, personality, and potential. No scoring system is perfect, but a system that provides for flexibility in scores, if applied by the same taster without prejudice, can quantify different levels of wine quality and provide the reader with one professional's judgment. **However, there can never be any substitute for your own palate nor any better education than tasting the wine yourself.**

THE WINE ADVOCATE'S VINTAGE GUIDE©
(as of August 2005)
2003-1970

	REGION	2003	2002	2001	2000	1999
Bordeaux	St. Julien/Pauillac St. Estephe	95T	88T	88R	98T	88R
	Margaux	91T	88T	89E	95T	89R
	Graves	90T	87T	88R	97T	88R
	Pomerol	84E	85E	90E	96T	88R
	St. Emilion	90I	87E	90E	98T	88R
	Barsac/Sauternes	95E	95E	98T	88E	88E
Burgundy	Côte de Nuits (Red)	NT	93T	84E	85E	91E
	Côte de Beaune (Red)	NT	90T	77C	80C	93E
	White	NT	92I	86E	88R	89E
Rhône	North-Côte Rôtie, Hermitage	96T	78C	89E	87E	95T
	South-Châteauneuf du Pape	94E	58C	96T	98E	90E
	Beaujolais	95I	86C	75C	91R	89R
	Alsace	NT	89T	91R	90R	87R
	Loire Valley (Sweet White)	NT	90R	82C	84R	84R
	Champagne	NT	90T	83E	87E	87E
Italy	Piedmont	NT	75C	91T	94E	90T
	Tuscany	NT	75C	88T	88E	94E
	Germany	88R	92T	98T	87R	88R
	Vintage Port	NT	NT	N.V.	92T	N.V.
Spain	Rioja	NT	76C	94E	86E	86E
	Ribera del Duero	NT	78C	95E	87C	88C
Aust	South Austraila	90E	95T	95T	88C	88E
California-N. Coast	Cabernet Sauvignon	92I	95E	96T	78C	88T
	Chardonnay	90R	90E	90E	87C	89R
	Zinfandel	90R	90R	90E	83C	90E
	Pinot Noir	91R	92E	92E	88R	90E
Ore	Pinot Noir	88T	92I	85E	86E	92E
Wash	Cabernet Sauvignon	NT	89T	92T	89R	90T

Robert M. Parker, Jr's. The Wine Advocate, P.O. Box 311, Monkton, Md. 21111 © Copyright 2003

ABOUT VINTAGE CHARTS

This vintage chart should be regarded as a very general overall rating slanted in favor of what the finest producers were capable of producing in a particular viticultural region. Such charts are filled with exceptions to the rule ... astonishingly good wines from skillful or lucky vintners in years rated mediocre, and thin, diluted, characterless wines from incompetent or greedy producers in great years.

THE WINE ADVOCATE'S VINTAGE GUIDE©

(as of August 2005)
2003-1970

1998	1997	1996	1995	1994	1993
87T	84R	96T	92T	85C	78C
86T	82R	88T	88E	85C	77C
94T	86R	86E	89E	88E	86C
96T	87R	85E	92T	89T	87C
96T	86R	87T	88E	86T	84C
87E	89E	87E	85E	78E	70C
83C	90R	92T	90T	72C	85C
82C	89R	92T	88T	73C	80C
84R	89R	92T	93R	77C	72C
90T	90E	86R	90T	88C	58C
98E	82C	82C	92T	86C	85C
84C	87R	82C	87C	85C	80C
90R	87R	87R	89R	90R	87R
84R	88R	91R	88R	87R	86R
86C	86R	91T	90E	N.V.	88E
92E	94E	95T	87C	77C	86E
86C	95E	78R	88T	85C	86C
85R	88R	93R	87R	90R	87R
N.V.	89T	N.V.	N.V.	92T	N.V.
82C	86R	85R	90R	90R	87R
88T	86R	92R	90R	90R	87R
95E	88R	90E	87R	90R	87R
85R	94C	90T	94T	95E	93T
89R	92C	87C	92C	88C	90C
86C	85E	89E	87R	92R	90R
89R	90E	88R	88R	92R	88R
89T	87C	83C	76C	92R	89R
90T	88T	88T	86R	90R	87R

KEY (General Vintage Chart)

100-96 = Extraordinary
90-95= Outstanding
80-89= Above Average to Excellent
70-79= Average
60-69= Below Average
59 or below = Appalling

Explanations of

C = Caution, too old
E = Early maturing and accessible
I = Irregular, even among best wines
T = Tannic or youthful, slow to mature
R = Ready to drink
NV = Non-vintage
? = No impression yet formed

THE WINE ADVOCATE'S VINTAGE GUIDE©
(as of August 2005)
2003-1970

	REGION	1992	1991	1990	1989	1988
Bordeaux	St. Julien/Pauillac St. Estephe	79C	75R	98T	90E	87R
	Margaux	75C	74R	90E	86E	85R
	Graves	75C	74R	90R	89R	89R
	Pomerol	82R	58C	96R	96R	89R
	St. Emilion	75C	59C	98R	88R	88R
	Barsac/Sauternes	68C	70C	96T	90R	98T
Burgundy	Côte de Nuits (Red)	69C	86T	93R	87R	79C
	Côte de Beaune (Red)	82R	72E	92R	88R	86C
	White	90R	70C	87R	92T	82R
Rhône	North-Côte Rôtie, Hermitage	78R	92R	92T	92T	92R
	South-Châteauneuf du Pape	78C	65C	95R	94T	88R
	Beaujolais	77C	88C	86C	92C	86C
	Alsace	85R	75R	93R	93R	86R
	Loire Valley (Sweet White)	80R	75R	90R	92R	88R
	Champagne	N.V.	N.V.	96R	90R	88R
Italy	Piedmont	74C	76C	96R	96T	90R
	Tuscany	72C	85C	90R	72C	89R
	Germany	90R	85E	92E	90E	89R
	Vintage Port	95E	90E	N.V.	N.V.	N.V.
Spain	Rioja	85R	76R	87R	90R	87R
	Ribera del Duero	82R	74R	89R	88C	87C
Aust	South Australia	87R	89R	88R	88C	85C
California-N. Coast	Cabernet Sauvignon	93E	94T	94E	84E	75E
	Chardonnay	92C	85C	90C	76C	89C
	Zinfandel	90R	91R	91R	83C	82C
	Pinot Noir	88R	86R	86R	85C	87C
Wash Ore	Pinot Noir	88R	87C	90C	86C	88C
	Cabernet Sauvignon	89R	85C	87R	92R	88R

Robert M. Parker, Jr's. The Wine Advocate, P.O. Box 311, Monkton, Md. 21111 © Copyright 2003

THE WINE ADVOCATE'S VINTAGE GUIDE©
(as of December 31, 2004)
2003-1970

1987	1986	1985	1983	1982	1981
82R	94T	90R	86R	98R	85R
76R	90T	86R	95R	86R	82R
84R	89E	90R	89R	88R	84R
85C	87T	88R	90R	96R	86R
74C	88E	87R	89R	94R	82R
70R	94T	85R	88T	75R	85R
75C	65C	87R	75C	75C	50C
79C	72C	87R	78C	80C	74C
79R	90R	89R	85C	88C	86C
86R	84C	90R	89C	85C	75C
60C	78C	88R	87C	70C	88C
85C	84C	87C	86C	75C	83C
83C	82C	88R	93R	82C	86C
82R	87R	88R	84C	84C	82C
N.V.	89R	95R	84C	90R	84C
85C	78R	90R	75C	92R	80R
73C	84C	93R	80C	86C	82C
82R	80R	85R	90R	80R	82R
N.V.	N.V.	95R	92R	86R	N.V.
82C	82R	82C	74C	92C	92C
88C	77C	85C	85C	87C	84C
87C	90R	86C	76R	83C	85C
90E	90R	90T	76C	86R	85R
75C	90C	84C	85C	85C	86C
90C	87C	88C	78C	80C	82C
86C	84C	86C	85C	84C	83C
72C	85C	87C	90C	84C	86C
90R	78R	86R	92R	78C	-

KEY (General Vintage Chart)	**Explanations of**
100-96 = Extraordinary	C = Caution, too old
90-95= Outstanding	E = Early maturing and accessible
80-89= Above Average to Excellent	I = Irregular, even among best wines
70-79= Average	T = Tannic or youthful, slow to mature
60-69= Below Average	R = Ready to drink
59 or below = Appalling	NV = Non-vintage
	? = No impression yet formed

THE WINE ADVOCATE'S VINTAGE GUIDE©
(as of August 2005)
2003-1970

	REGION	1980	1979	1978	1975	1970
Bordeaux	St. Julien/Pauillac St. Estephe	78R	85R	87R	89T	87R
	Margaux	79C	87R	87R	78E	85R
	Graves	78C	88R	88R	89T	87R
	Pomerol	79C	86R	84R	94R	90R
	St. Emilion	72R	84R	84R	85R	85R
	Barsac/Sauternes	85R	75R	75R	90T	84R
Burgundy	Côte de Nuits (Red)	84C	77C	88C	50C	82C
	Côte de Beaune (Red)	78C	77C	86R	50C	82C
	White	75C	88C	88C	65C	83C
Rhône	North-Côte Rôtie, Hermitage	83C	87C	98R	73C	90C
	South-Châteauneuf du Pape	77C	88C	97R	60C	88C
	Beaujolais	60C	80C	84C	-	-
	Alsace	80C	84C	80C	82C	80C
	Loire Valley (Sweet White)	72C	83C	85C	-	-
	Champagne	N.V.	88C	N.V.	90C	85C
Italy	Piedmont	70C	86R	95T	65C	84R
	Tuscany	70C	75C	85C	84C	84C
	Germany	65R	84R	72C	85R	80C
	Vintage Port	84R	N.V.	83C	82R	90R
Spain	Rioja	75C	79C	84C	84C	90C
	Ribera del Duero	85C	-	-	-	-
Aust	South Australia	88C	-	-	-	-
California-N. Coast	Cabernet Sauvignon	87C	80R	92R	85R	92R
	Chardonnay	88C	83C	86C	86C	83C
	Zinfandel	82C	83C	86C	60C	89C
	Pinot Noir	85C	80C	84C	-	-
Ore	Pinot Noir	86C	-	-	-	-
Wash	Cabernet Sauvignon	-	-	-	-	-

Robert M. Parker, Jr's. The Wine Advocate, P.O. Box 311, Monkton, Md. 21111 © Copyright 2003

KEY (General Vintage Chart)

100-96 = Extraordinary
90-95= Outstanding
80-89= Above Average to Excellent
70-79= Average
60-69= Below Average
59 or below = Appalling

Explanations of

C = Caution, too old
E = Early maturing and accessible
I = Irregular, even among best wines
T = Tannic or youthful, slow to mature
R = Ready to drink
NV = Non-vintage
? = No impression yet formed

Parker Speaks on Wine
HOW TO STORE WINE

Wine has to be stored properly if it is to be served in a healthy condition. All wine enthusiasts know that subterranean wine cellars that are vibration free, dark, damp and kept at a constant 55 degrees F are considered perfect for wine. However, few of us have our own castles and such perfect accommodations for our beloved wines. While such conditions are ideal, most wines will thrive and develop well under other circumstances. I have tasted many old Bordeaux wines from closets and basements that have reached 65-70 degrees F in summer, and the wines have been perfect. In cellaring wine, keep the following rules in mind and you will not be disappointed with a wine that has gone over the hill prematurely.

First of all, in order to safely cellar wines for ten years or more keep them at 65 degrees F, perhaps 68, but no higher. If the temperature rises to 70 degrees F, be prepared to drink your red wines within ten years. Under no circumstances should you store and cellar white wines more that 1 to 2 years at temperatures above 70 degrees F. Wines kept at temperatures above 65 degrees F will age faster, but unless the temperature exceeds 70 degrees F, will not age badly. If you can somehow get the temperatures down to 65 degrees F or below, you will never have to worry about the condition of your wines. At 55 degrees F, the ideal temperature according to the textbooks, the wines actually evolve so slowly that your grandchildren are likely to benefit from the wines more than you. Constancy in temperature is most essential, and any changes in temperature should occur slowly. White wines are much more fragile and much more sensitive to temperature changes and higher temperatures than red wines. Therefore, if you do not have ideal storage conditions, buy only enough white wine to drink over a 1 to 2 year period.

Second, be sure that your storage area is odor free, vibration free, and dark. A humidity level above 50% is essential; 70-75% is ideal. The problem with a humidity level over 75% is that the labels become moldy and deteriorate. A humidity level below 40% will keep the labels in great shape, but will cause the corks to become very dry, possibly shortening the potential lifeline of your wine. Low humidity is believed to be nearly as great a threat to a wine's health as high temperature. There has been no research to prove this, and limited studies I have done are far from conclusive.

Third, always bear in mind that wines from vintages which have produced powerful, rich concentrated, full bodied wines travel and age significantly better than wines from vintages that produced lighter weight wines. It is often traumatic for a fragile, lighter styled wine from either Europe or California to be transported transatlantic or cross country, whereas the richer, more intense, bigger wines from the better vintages seem much less travel worn after their journey.

The important thing for you as a consumer to remember, after inspecting the bottle to make sure it appears to be healthy, is to stock up on wines as quickly as they come on the market and to approach older vintages with a great deal of caution and hesitation unless you have absolute faith in their condition and provenance.

THE QUESTION OF HOW MUCH AGING

The majority of wines made in the world taste best when they are just released or consumed within one to two years of the vintage. Many wines are drinkable at five, 10 or even 15 years of age, but based on my experience only a small percentage are more interesting and more enjoyable after extended cellaring, than they were when originally released.

It is important to have a working definition of what the aging of wine actually means. I define the process as nothing more than the ability of a wine, over time, to (1) develop more pleasurable nuances, (2) expand and soften in texture, and in the case of red wines, exhibit an additional melting away of tannins, and (3) reveal a more compelling aromatic and flavor profile. in short, the wine must deliver additional complexity, increased pleasure, and more interest as an older wine than it did when released. Only such a performance can justify the purchase of a wine in its youth for the purpose of cellaring it for future drinking. Unfortunately, just a tiny percentage of the world's wines fall within this definition of aging.

It is fundamentally false to believe that a wine cannot be serious or profound if it is drunk young. In France, the finest Bordeaux, northern Rhône Valley wines (particularly Hermitage and Côte Rhône), a few red burgundies, come Chateauneuf du Papes, and surprisingly, many of the sweet white Alsace wines and sweet Loire Valley wines do indeed age well and are frequently much more enjoyable and complex when drunk five, 10 or even 15 years after the vintage. But virtually all other French wines, from Champagne to Côtes du Rhône, from Beaujolais to the "petits châteaux" of Bordeaux, to even the vast majority of red and white burgundies, are better in their youth.

The French have long adhered to the wine drinking strategy that younger is better. Centuries of wine consumption, not to mention gastronomic indulgences, have taught the French something that Americans and Englishmen have failed to grasp; most wines are more pleasurable and friendly when young than old.

The French know that the aging and cellaring of wines, even those of high pedigree, are often fraught with more disappointments than successes. Nowhere is this more in evidence than in French restaurants.

This phenomenon is not limited to France. Similar drinking habits prevail in the restaurants of Florence, Rome, Madrid and Barcelona. Italians and Spaniards also enjoy their wines young. This is not to suggest that Italy does not make some wines that improve in the bottle. In Tuscany, for example, a handful of Chiantis and some of the finest new breed Tuscan red wines (i.e., the famed Cabernet Sauvignon called Sassicaia) will handsomely repay extended cellaring, but most never get the opportunity. In the Piedmont section of northern Italy, no one will deny that an fine Barbaresco or Barolo improves after a decade in the bottle. But by and large, all of Italy's other wines are meant to be drunk young, a fact that Italians have long known and that you should observe as well.

All this impacts on the following notion. Unlike any other wine consumers in the world, most American wine enthusiasts, as well as many English consumers, fret over the perfect moment to drink a wine. **There is none.** Most modern day vintages, even age-worthy Bordeaux or Rhône Valley wines, can be drunk when released. Some of them will improve, but many will not. If you enjoy drinking a 1995 Pomerol now, then who could be so foolish as to suggest that you are making an error because the wine will be appreciably better in five to 10 years?

In America and Australia, winemaking is much more dominated by technology. White a handful of producers still adhere to the artisanal, traditional way of making wine as done in Europe, most treat the vineyard as a factory and the winemaking as a manufacturing process. As a result, such techniques as excessive acidification, brutally traumatic centrifugation, and eviscerating sterile filtration are routinely utilized to produce squeaky clean, simplistic, sediment-free, spit-polished, totally stable yet innocuous wines with statistical profiles that fit neatly within strict technical parameters. Yet it is these same techniques that denude wines of their flavors, aromas and pleasure-giving qualities. Moreover, they reveal a profound lack of respect for the vineyard, the varietal, the vintage, and the wine consumer, who after all, is seeking pleasure, not blandness.

In both Australia and California, the alarming tendency of most Sauvignon Blancs and Chardonnays to collapse in the bottle and drop their fruit within two to three years of the vintage has been well documented. Yet some of California and Australia's most vocal advocates continue to advise wine consumers to cellar and invest (a deplorable word when it comes to wine) in Chardonnays and Sauvignon Blancs. It is a stupid policy. If the aging of wine is indeed the ability of a wine to become more interesting and pleasurable with time, then the rule of thumb to be applied to American and Australian Sauvignon Blancs and Chardonnays is that they must be drunk within 12 months of their release unless the consumer has an eccentric fetish for fruitless wines with blistering acidity and scorchingly noticeable alcohol levels.

Even in Burgundy there are probably no more that two dozen producers who make their wines in such a manner that they improve and last for more than a decade. Many of these wines can withstand the test of time in the sense of being survivors, but they are far less interesting and pleasurable at age 10 than they were at two or three. Of course, the producers and retailers who specialize in these wines will argue otherwise, but they are in the business of selling. Do not be bamboozled by the public relations arm of the wine industry or the fallacious notion that red wines all improve with age. If you enjoy them young, and most likely you will, then buy only quantities needed for near-term consumption.

America's most famous dry red wine, however, is not Pinot Noir but Cabernet Sauvignon, particularly that grown in California and to a lesser extent in Washington State. The idea that most California Cabernet Sauvignons improve in the bottle is a myth. Nonetheless, the belief that all California Cabernet Sauvignons are incapable of lasting in the bottle is equally unfounded. Today no one would be foolish enough to argue that the best California Cabernets cannot tolerate 15 or 20, even 25 or 30 years of cellaring, especially in the case of the 1991's and 1994's.

I frequently have the opportunity to taste 20 to 30 year old California Cabernet Sauvignons, and they are delicious. But have they significantly improved because of the aging process? A few of them have, though most still tend to be relatively grapy, somewhat monolithic, earthy, and tannic at age 20. Has the consumer's patience in cellaring these wines for all those years justified both the expense and the wait? Lamentably, the answer will usually be no. Most of these wines are no more complex or mellow than they were when young.

I am afraid the consumer who patiently waits for the proverbial "miracle in the bottle" will find that wine cellaring can all too frequently be an expensive exercise in futility.

If you think it over, the most important issue is why so many of today's wines exhibit scant improvement in the aging process. While most have always been meant to be drunk when young, I am convinced that much of the current winemaking philosophy has led to numerous compromises in the winemaking process. The advent of micropore sterile filters, so much in evidence at every modern winery, may admirably stabilize a wine, but regrettably, these filters also destroy the potential of a wine to develop a complex aromatic profile. When they are utilized by wine producers who routinely fertilize their vineyards excessively, thus overcropping, the results are wines that reveal an appalling lack of bouquet and flavor.

The prevailing winemaking obsession is to stabilize wine so it can be shipped to the far corners of the world 12 months a year, stand upright in over-heated stores indefinitely, and never change or spoil if exposed to extremes of heat and cold, or unfriendly storage conditions. For all intents and purposes, the wine is no longer alive. This is fine, even essential, for inexpensive jug wines, but for the fine-wine market, where consumers are asked to pay $30 or more for a bottle of wine, it is a winemaking tragedy. These stabilization and production techniques thus impact on the aging of wine because they preclude the development of the wine's ability to evolve and become more complex, tasty, profound and enjoyable beverage.

HOW TO SERVE WINE

There are really no secrets for proper wine service - all one needs is a good corkscrew, clean, odor free glasses, an idea of the order of service - light to full, and whether a wine needs to be aired or allowed to breathe. The major mistakes that most Americans, as well as most restaurants, make are 1) fine white wines are served entirely too cold, 2) fine red wines are served entirely too warm, and 3) too little attention is given to the glass into which the wine is poured. (It might contain a soapy residue or stale aromas picked up in a closed china closet or cardboard box.) All of these things can do much more to damage the impact of a fine wine and its subtle aromas that you might imagine.

The Parker Exhale Test — An effective method of testing a glass for off-odors is simply to exhale in the glass. The mouth's moist warm air will usually temporarily fog up the glass and vaporize any invisible cardboard cupboard or soapy aromas (which will be easy to discern by keeping your nose in the glass) in what appears to be an otherwise sparkling clean glass. As remarkably efficient as this exam can be, it should be done with considerable discretion when drinking at another's expense. Most people tend to think that the wine must be opened and allowed to "breathe" well in advance of serving. Some even think a wine must be decanted, a rather elaborate procedure but only essential if sediment is present in the bottle. With respect to breathing or airing wine, I am not sure anyone has all the answers. Certainly, no white wine requires any advance opening and pouring. With red wines, 15-30 minutes after being opened and poured into a clean, odor- and soap-free wine decanter is really all that is necessary. There are of course examples which can always be cited where the wine improves for 7 to 8 hours, but these are quite rare.

Although these topics seem to dominate much of the discussion in wine circles, a much more critical aspect for me is the appropriate temperature of the wine and of the glass in which it is to be served. The temperature of red wines is very important, and in America's generously heated dining rooms, temperatures are often 75-80 degrees F. higher than is good for a fine red wine. A red wine served at such a temperature will taste flat and flabby, with its bouquet diffuse and unfocused. The alcohol content will also seem higher than it should. The ideal temperature for most red wines is from

62 to 67 degrees F; light red wine such as Beaujolais should be
chilled to 55 degrees F. For white wines, 55-60 degrees F is perfect,
since most will show all their complexity and intensity at this tem-
perature, whereas if they are chilled to below 45 degrees F, it will
be difficult to tell, for instance, whether the wine is a Riesling or
Chardonnay.

In addition, there is the all-important issue of the glasses in which the wine is to be served. An all-purpose, tulip-shaped glass of 8 to 12 ounces is a good start for just about any type of wine, but think the subject over carefully. If you go to the trouble and expense of finding and storing wine properly, shouldn't you treat the wine to a good glass? The finest glasses for both technical and hedonistic purposes are those made by the Riedel company of Austria. I have to admit I was at first skeptical about these glasses. George Riedel, the head of his family's crystal business, claims to have created these glasses specifically to guide (by specially designed rims) the wine to a designated section of the palate. These rims, combined with the general shape of the glass, emphasize and promote the different flavors and aromas of a given varietal.

All of this may sound absurdly high-brow or esoteric, but the effect of these glasses on fine wine is profound. I cannot emphasize enough what a difference they make.

For more complete information about prices and models, readers can get in touch with **Riedel Crystal of America**, P. O. Box 446, 24 Aero Road, Bohemia, NY 11716; telephone number - **(631) 567-7575**. For residents or visitors to New York City, Riedel has a showroom at 41 Madison Avenue (at 26th Street).

Two other good sources for fine wine glasses include **St. George Crystal** in Jeannette, PA (telephone **(724) 523-6501**) and the superb all-purpose **Cristal d'Arques Oenologist glass.** For more information on the latter glass, readers should contact Grand Cru Imports, Souderton, PA (telephone **(215) 723-2033**). Another fine glassware source is Spiegelau from Germany. For information on where their glasses are sold, readers should visit their website, **www.Spiegelau.com**.

And last but not least, remember: No matter how clean the glass appears to be, be sure to rinse the glass or decanter with unchlorinated well or mineral water just before it is used. A decanter or wine glass left sitting for any time is a wonderful trap for room and kitchen odors that are undetectable until the wine is poured and they yield their off-putting smells. That, and soapy residues left in the glasses, have ruined more wines than any defective cork or, I suspect, poor storage from an importer, wholesaler or retailer. I myself put considerable stress on one friendship simply because I continued to complain at every dinner party about the soapy glasses that interfered with the enjoyment of the wonderful Bordeaux being served.

THE FINE WINE RETAILER

A serious wine merchant is the consumer's most under-rated ally and resource. With the excessive influence of wine writers, many fine merchants who (1) do their homework, (2) taste seriously, and (3) are passionate about finding superior wine and educating their clients, have not been utilized to the extent they should be. Obviously, I'm not referring to retailers that are in the business only to "sell," regardless of the wine's quality. Our country has never had as many well-informed, experienced and wine-loving retailers as it does today. Their advice should be taken seriously, as the best merchants will stand behind the products they sell.

Glossary of Wine Terms

acetic: Wines, no matter how well made, contain quantities of acetic acidity that have a vinegary smell. If there is an excessive amount of acetic acidity, the wine will have a vinegary smell and be a flawed, acetic wine.

acidic: Wines need natural acidity to taste fresh and lively, but an excess of acidity results in an acidic wine that is tart and sour.

acidity: The acidity level in a wine is critical to its enjoyment and livelihood. The natural acids that appear in wine are citric, tartaric, malic, and lactic. Wines from hot years tend to be lower in acidity, whereas wines from cool, rainy years tend to be high in acidity. Acidity in a wine can preserve the wine's freshness and keep the wine lively, but too much acidity, which masks the wines flavors and compresses its texture, is a flaw.

aftertaste: As the term suggests, the taste left in the mouth when one swallows is the aftertaste. This word is a synonym for length or finish. The longer the aftertaste lingers in the mouth (assuming it is a pleasant taste), the finer the quality of the wine.

aggressive: Aggressive is usually applied to wines that are either high in acidity or have harsh tannins, or both.

angular: Angular wines are wines that lack roundness, generosity, and depth. Wine from poor vintages or wines that are too acidic are often described as being angular.

aroma: Aroma is the smell of a young wine before it has had sufficient time to develop nuances of smell that are then called its bouquet. The word aroma is commonly used to mean the smell of a relatively young, unevolved wine.

astringent: Wines that are astringent are not necessarily bad or good wines. Astringent wines are harsh and coarse to taste, either because they are too young and tannic and just need time to develop, or because they are not well made. The level of tannins (if it is harsh) in a wine contributes to its degree of astringence.

austere: Wines that are austere are generally not terribly pleasant wines to drink. An austere wine is a hard, rather dry wine that lacks richness and generosity. However, young Rhônes are not as austere as young Bordeaux.

balance: One of the most desired traits in a wine is good balance, where the concentration of fruit, level of tannins, and acidity are in total harmony. Balanced wines are symmetrical and tend to age gracefully.

barnyard: An unclean, farmyard, fecal aroma that is imparted to a wine because of unclean barrels or unsanitary winemaking facilities.

berrylike: As this descriptive term implies, most red wines have an intense berry fruit character that can suggest blackberries, raspberries, black cherries, mulberries, or strawberries and cranberries.

big: A big wine is a large-framed, full-bodied wine with intense and concentrated feel on the palate. Most red Rhône wines are big.

blackcurrant: A pronounced smell of blackcurrant fruit is commonly associated with certain Rhône wines. It can vary in intensity from faint to very deep and rich.

body: Body is the weight and fullness of a wine that can be sensed as it crosses the palate. full-bodied wines tend to have a lot of alcohol, concentration, and glycerin.

Botrytis cinerea: The fungus that attacks the grape skins under specific climatic conditions (usually alternating periods of moisture and sunny weather). It causes the grape to become superconcentrated because it causes a natural dehydration. Botrytis cinerea is essential for the great sweet white wines of Barsac and Sauternes. It rarely occurs in the Rhône Valley because of the dry, constant sunshine and gusty winds.

bouquet: As a wine's aroma becomes more developed from bottle aging, the aroma is transformed into a bouquet that is hopefully more than just the smell of the grape.

GLOSSARY OF WINE TERMS

brawny: A hefty, muscular, full-bodied wine with plenty of weight and flavor, although not always the most elegant or refined sort of wine.

briery: I think of California Zinfandel when the term briery comes into play, denoting that the wine is aggressive and rather spicy.

brilliant: Brilliant relates to the color of the wine. A brilliant wine is one that s clear, with no haze or cloudiness to the color.

browning: As red wines age, their color changes from ruby/purple to dark ruby, to medium ruby, to ruby with an amber edge, to ruby with a brown edge. When a wine is browning it is usually fully mature and not likely to get better.

carbonic maceration: This vinification method is used to make soft, fruity, very accessible wines. Whole clusters of grapes are put into a vat that is then filled with carbonic gas. This system is used when fruit is to be emphasized in the final wine in contrast to structure and tannin.

cedar: Rhône reds can have a bouquet that suggests either faintly or overtly the smell of cedarwood. It is a complex aspect of the bouquet.

chewy: If a wine has a rather dense, viscous texture from a high glycerin content, it is often referred to as being chewy. High-extract wines from great vintages can often be chewy, largely because they have higher alcohol hence high levels of glycerin, which imparts a fleshy mouthfeel.

closed: The term closed is used to denote that the wine is not showing its potential, which remains locked in because it is too young. Young wines often close up about 12-18 months after bottling, and depending on the vintage and storage conditions, remain in such a state for several years to more than a decade.

complex: One of the most subjective descriptive terms used, a complex wine is a wine that the taster never gets bored with and finds interesting to drink. Complex wines tend to have a variety of subtle scents and flavors that hold one's interest in the wine.

concentrated: Fine wines, whether they are light-, medium-, or full-bodied, should have concentrated flavors. Concentrated denotes that the wine has a depth and richness of fruit that gives it appeal and interest. Deep is a synonym for concentrated.

corked: A corked wine is a flawed wine that has taken on the smell of cork as a result of an unclean or faulty cork. It is perceptible in a bouquet that shows no fruit, only the smell of musty cork, which reminds me of wet cardboard.

cuvée: Many producers in the Rhône Valley produce special, deluxe lots of wine or a lot of wine from a specific grape variety that they bottle separately. These lots are often referred to as cuvées.

decadent: If you are an ice cream and chocolate lover, you know the feeling of eating a huge sundae of rich vanilla ice cream lavished with hot fudge and real whipped cream. If you are a wine enthusiast, a wine loaded with opulent, even unctuous layers of fruit, with a huge bouquet, and a plump, luxurious texture can be said to be decadent.

deep: Essentially the same as concentrated, expressing the fact that the wine is rich, full of extract, and mouth filling.

delicate: As this word implies, delicate wines are light, subtle, understated wines that are prized for their shyness rather than for an extroverted, robust character. White wines are usually more delicate than red wines. Few Rhône red wines can correctly be called delicate.

diffuse: Wines that smell and taste unstructured and unfocused are said to be diffuse. When red wines are served at too warm a temperature they often become diffuse.

dumb: A dumb wine is also a closed wine, but the term dumb is used more pejoratively. Closed wines may need only time to reveal their richness and intensity. Dumb wines may never get any better.

earthy: May be used in both a negative and a positive sense; however, I prefer to use earthy to denote a positive aroma of fresh, rich, clean soil. Earthy is a more intense smell than woody or truffle scents.

GLOSSARY OF WINE TERMS

elegant: Although more white wines than red are described as being elegant, lighter-styled, graceful, balance red wines can be elegant.

extract: Everything in a wine besides water, sugar, alcohol and acidity.

exuberant: Like extroverted, somewhat hyper people, wines too can be gushing with fruit and seem nervous and intensely vigorous.

fat: When the Rhône has an exceptionally hot year for its crop and the wines attain a super sort of maturity, they are often quite rich and concentrated, with low to average acidity. Often such wines are said to be fat, which is a prized commodity. If they become too fat, that is a flaw and they are then called flabby.

flabby: A wine that is too fat or obese is a flabby wine. Flabby wines lack structure and are heavy to taste.

fleshy: Fleshy is a synonym for chewy, meaty, or beefy. Tthe wine has a lot of body, alcohol and extract and usually a high glycerin content. Châteauneuf-du-Pape and Hermitage are particularly fleshy wines.

floral: Wines made from the Muscat or Viognier grape have a flowery component, and occasionally a red wine will have a floral scent.

focused: Both a fine wine's bouquet and flavor should be focused. Focused simply means that the scents, aromas, and flavors are precise and clearly delineated. If they are not, the wine is like an out-of-focus picture-diffuse, hazy, and possibly problematic.

forward: A wine is said to be forward when its charm and character are fully revealed. While it may not be fully mature yet, a forward wine is generally quite enjoyable and drinkable. Forward is the opposite of backward. Accessible is a synonym for forward.

foudre: Large oak barrels that vary enormously in size but are significantly larger than the normal oak barrel used in Bordeaux or the piece used in Burgundy. They are widely used in the Rhône Valley.

fresh: Freshness in both young and old wines is a welcome and pleasing component. A wine is said to be fresh when it is lively and cleanly made. The opposite of fresh is stale. fruity: A very good wine should have enough concentration of fruit so that it can be said to be fruity. Fortunately, the best wines will have more than just a fruity personality.

full-bodied: Wines rich in extract, alcohol, and glycerin are full-bodied wines. Most Rhône wines are full-bodied.

garrigue: In the southern Rhône Valley and Provence, this is the landscape of small slopes and plateaus. This Provençal word applies to these windswept hilltops/slopes inhabited by scrub-brush and Provençal herb outcroppings. The smell of garrigue is often attributed to southern Rhône Valley wines. Suggesting more than the smell of herbes de Provence, it encompasses an earthy/herbal concoction of varying degrees of intensity.

green: Green wines are wines made from underripe grapes; they lack richness and generosity as well as having a vegetal character. Green wines are infrequently made in the Rhone, although vintages such as 1977 were characterized by a lack of ripening.

hard: Wines with abrasive, astringent tannins or high acidity are said to be hard. Young vintages of Rhône wines can be hard, but they should never be harsh.

harsh: If a wine is too hard it is said to be harsh. Harshness in a wine, young or old, is a flaw.

hedonistic: Certain styles of wine are meant to be inspected; they are introspective and intellectual wines. Others are designed to provide sheer delight, joy, and euphoria. Hedonistic wines can be criticized because in one sense they provide so much ecstasy that they can be called obvious, but in essence, they are totally gratifying wines meant to fascinate and enthrall-pleasure at its best.

herbaceous: Many wines have a distinctive herbal smell that is generally said to be herbaceous. Specific herbal smells can be of thyme, lavender, rosemary, oregano, fennel, or basil and are common in Rhône wines.

GLOSSARY OF WINE TERMS

herbes de Provence: Provence is known for the wild herbs that grow prolifically through- out the region. These include lavender, thyme, sage, rosemary, and oregano. It is not just an olfactory fancy to smell many of these herbs in Rhône Valley wines, particularly those made in the south.

hollow: Also known as shallow, hollow wines are diluted and lack depth and concentration. honeyed: A common personality trait of specific white Rhône wines, a honeyed wine is one that has the smell and taste of bee's honey.

hot: Rather than meaning that the temperature of the wine is too warm to drink, hot denotes that the wine is too high in alcohol and therefore leaves a burning sensation in the back of the throat when swallowed. Wines with alcohol levels in excess of 14.5% often taste hot if the requisite depth of fruit is not present.

inox vats: This is the French term for stainless steel vats that are used for both fermentation and storage of wine.

intensity: Intensity is one of the most desirable traits of a high-quality wine. Wines of great intensity must also have balance. They should never be heavy or cloying. Intensely concentrated great wines are alive, vibrant, aromatic, layered, and texturally compelling. Their intensity adds to their character, rather than detracting from it.

jammy: When wines have a great intensity of fruit from excellent ripeness they can be jammy, which is a very concentrated, flavorful wine with superb extract. In great vintages such as 1961, 1978, 1985, 1989, 1990, and 1995, some of the wines are so concentrated that they are said to be jammy.

Kisselguhr filtration system: This is a filtration system using diatomaceous earth as the filtering material, rather than cellulose, or in the past, before it was banned, asbestos.

leafy: A leafy character in a wine is similar to a herbaceous character only in that it refers to the smell of leaves rather than herbs. A wine that is too leafy is a vegetal or green wine.

lean: Lean wines are slim, rather streamlined wines that lack generosity and fatness but can still be enjoyable and pleasant.

lively: A synonym for fresh or exuberant, a lively wine is usually young wine with good acidity and a thirst-quenching personality.

long: A very desirable trait in any fine wine is that it be long in the mouth. Long (or length) relates to a wine's finish, meaning that after you swallow the wine, you sense its presence for a long time. (Thirty seconds to several minutes is great length.) In a young wine, the difference between something good and something great is the length of the wine.

lush: Lush wines are velvety, soft, richly fruity wines that are both concentrated and fat. A lush wine can never be an astringent or hard wine.

massive: In great vintages where there is a high degree of ripeness and superb concentration, some wines can turn out to be so big, full-bodied, and rich that they are called massive. A great wine such as the 1961 or 1990 Hermitage La Chapelle is a textbook example of a massive wine.

meaty: A chewy, fleshy wine is also said to be meaty.

monoepage: This term describes a wine made totally of one specific varietal.

monopole: Used to denote a vineyard owned exclusively by one proprietor, the word monopole appears on the label of a wine made from such a vineyard.

morsellated: Many vineyards are fragmented, with multiple growers owning a portion of the same vineyard. Such a vineyard is often referred to as a morsellated vineyard.

mouth-filling: Big, rich, concentrated wines that are filled with fruit extract and are high in alcohol and glycerin are wines that tend to texturally fill the mouth. A mouth-filling wine is also a chewy, fleshy, fat wine.

musty: Wines aged in dirty barrels or unkept cellars or exposed to a bad cork take on a damp, musty character that is a flaw.

GLOSSARY OF WINE TERMS

nose: The general smell and aroma of a wine as sensed through one's nose and olfactory senses is often called the wine's nose.

oaky: Many red Rhône wines are aged from 6 months to 30 months in various sizes of oak barrels. At some properties, a percentage of the oak barrels may be new, and these barrels impart a toasty, vanillin flavor and smell to the wine. If the wine is not rich and concentrated, the barrels can overwhelm the wine, making it taste overly oaky. Where the wine is rich and concentrated and the winemaker has made a judicious use of barrels, however, the results are a wonderful marriage of fruit and oak.

off: If a wine is not showing its true character, or is flawed or spoiled in some way, it is said to be "off."

overripe: An undesirable characteristic; grapes left too long on the vine become too ripe, lose their acidity, and produce wines that are heavy and balance. This can happen frequently in the hot viticultural areas of the Rhône Valley if the growers harvest too late.

oxidized: If a wine has been excessively exposed to air during either its making or aging, the wine loses freshness and takes on a stale, old smell and taste. Such a wine is said to be oxidized.

peppery: A peppery quality to a wine is usually noticeable in many Rhône wines that have an aroma of black or white pepper and a pungent flavor.

perfumed: This term usually is more applicable to fragrant, aromatic white wines than to red wines. However, some of the dry white wines (particularly Condrieu) and sweet white wines can have a strong perfumed smell.

pigéage: A winemaking technique of punching down the cap of grape skins that forms during the beginning of the wine's fermentation. This is done several times a day, occasionally more frequently, to extract color, flavor, and tannin from the fermenting juice.

plummy: Rich, concentrated wines can often have the smell and taste of ripe plums. When they do, the term plummy is applicable.

ponderous: Ponderous is often used as a synonym for massive, but in my usage a massive wine is simply a big, rich, very concentrated wine with balance, whereas a ponderous wine is a wine that has become heavy and tiring to drink.

precocious: Wines that mature quickly are precocious. However the term also applies to wines that may last and evolve gracefully over a long period of time, but taste as if they are aging quickly because of their tastiness and soft, early charms.

pruney: Wines produced from grapes that are overripe take on the character of prunes. Pruney wines are flawed wines.

raisiny: Late-harvest wines that are meant to be drunk at the end of a meal can often be slightly raisiny, which in some ports and sherries is desirable. However, a raisiny quality is a major flaw in a dinner wine.

rich: Wines that are high in extract, flavor, and intensity of fruit.

ripe: A wine is ripe when its grapes have reached the optimum level of maturity. Less than fully mature grapes produce wines that are underripe, and overly mature grapes produce wines that are overripe.

round: A very desirable character of wines, roundness occurs in fully mature wines that have lost their youthful, astringent tannins, and also in young wines that have soft tannins and low acidity.

savory: A general descriptive term that denotes that the wine is round, flavorful, and interesting to drink. shallow: A weak, feeble, watery or diluted wine lacking concentration is said to be shallow.

sharp: An undesirable trait, sharp wines are bitter and unpleasant with hard, pointed edges.

silky: A synonym for velvety or lush, silky wines are soft, sometimes fat, but never hard or angular.

smoky: Some wines, either because of the soil or because of the barrels used to age the wine, have a distinctive smoky character. Côte Rôtie and Hermitage often have a roasted or smoky quality.

GLOSSARY OF WINE TERMS

soft: A soft wine is one that is round and fruity, low in acidity, and has an absence of aggressive, hard tannins.

spicy: Wines often smell quite spicy with aromas of pepper, cinnamon, and other well-known spices. These pungent aromas are usually lumped together and called spicy.

stale: Dull, heavy wines that are oxidized or lack balancing acidity for freshness are called stale.

stalky: A synonym for vegetal, but used more frequently to denote that the wine has probably had too much contact with the stems, resulting in a green, vegetal, or stalky character to the wine.

supple: A supple wine is one that is soft, lush, velvety, and very attractively round and tasty. It is a highly desirable characteristic because it suggests that the wine is harmonious.

tannic: The tannins of a wine, which are extracted from the grape skins and stems, are, along with a wine's acidity and alcohol, its lifeline. Tannins give a wine firmness and some roughness when young, but gradually fall away and dissipate. A tannic wine is one that is young and unready to drink.

tart: Sharp, acidic, lean, unripe wines are called tart. In general, a wine that is tart is not pleasurable.

thick: Rich, ripe, concentrated wines that are low in acidity are often said to be thick.

thin: A synonym for shallow; it is an undesirable characteristic for a wine to be thin, meaning that it is watery, lacking in body, and just diluted.

tightly knit: Young wines that have good acidity levels, good tannin levels, and are well made are called tightly knit, meaning they have yet to open up and develop.

toasty: A smell of grilled toast can often be found in wines because the barrels the wines are aged in are charred or toasted on the inside.

tobacco: Some red wines have the scent of fresh tobacco. It is a distinctive and wonderful smell in wine.

troncais oak: This type of oak comes from the forest of Troncais in central France.

unctuous: Rich, lush, intense wines with layers of concentrated, soft, velvety fruit are said to be unctuous.

vegetal: An undesirable characteristic, wines that smell and taste vegetal are usually made from unripe grapes. In some wines, a subtle vegetable garden smell is pleasant and adds complexity, but if it is the predominant character, it is a major flaw.

velvety: A textural description and synonym for lush or silky, a velvety wine is a rich, soft, smooth wine to taste. It is a very desirable characteristic.

viscous: Viscous wines tend to be relatively concentrated, fat, almost thick wines with a great density of fruit extract, plenty of glycerin, and high alcohol content. If they have balancing acidity, they can be tremendously flavorful and exciting wines. If they lack acidity, they are often flabby and heavy.

volatile: A volatile wine is one that smells of vinegar as a result of an excessive amount of acetic bacteria present. It is a seriously flawed wine.

woody: When a wine is overly oaky it is often said to be woody. Oakiness in a wine's bouquet and taste is good up to a point. Once past that point, the wine is woody and its fruity qualities are masked by excessive oak aging.

—**Robert Parker**

**Please note your future wine selections, or
your comments on wines already tasted:**

_____

_____

_____

_____

_____

_____

_____

_____

_____

_____

_____

_____

_____

_____

_____

_____

_____

_____

_____

The World's Greatest Wine Values
by Robert M. Parker, Jr.
(This list is organized by wine producing region)

BORDEAUX

St.-Estèphe: Meyney, Les-Ormes-de-Pez, Phélan-Ségur, Tronquoy-Lalande Pibran

St.-Julien: Clos du Marquis, Gloria, Hortevie

Margaux and the Southern Medoc: d'Angluder, La Gurgue, Labégorcé-Zédé

Graves: Bahans Haut-Brion, La Louvière, Picque-Caillou

Moulis and Listrac: Fourcas-Loubaney, Gressier Grand Poujeaux, Maucaillou, Poujeaux

Médoc and Haut-Médoc: Beaumont, Le Boscq, Lanessan, Latour St.-Bonnet, Moulin Rouge, Potensac, Sociando-Mallet, La Tour de By, Tour Haut-Caussan, Tour du Haut-Moulin, Vieux-Robin

Pomerol: Bonalgue, L'Enclos

St.-Emilion: Pipean

Fronsac and Canon-Fronsac: Canon de Brem, Dalem, La Dauphine, Fontenil, La Grave, Haut-Carles, Mazeris, Moulin-Haut-Laroque, Moulin-Pey-Labrie, du Pavillon, Pez-Labrie, Rouet Les Trois-Croix, La Vieille-Cure

Lalande-de-Pomerol: Bel-Air, Bertineau-St.-Vincent, de Chambrum, du Chapelain, La Fleur-Bouard, Grand-Ormeau, Jean de Gué Cuvée Prestige, Haut-Chaigneau, Les Hauts-Conseillants, La Sergue

Côtes de Bourg: Fougas-Maldoror, Guerry, Haut-Maco, Mercier, Roc des Cambes, Tayac-Cuvée Prestige

Côtes de Blaye: Bel-Air La Royère, Bertinerie, Clos Lascombes, Garreau, Gigault Cuvée Viva, Grands Marechaux, Pérenne, Peyraud, Roland La Garde, La Rose-Bellevue, La Tonnelle

Bordeaux Premières Côtes and Supérieurs: Carsin, Carsin Black Label, Clos Chaumont, Domaine de Courteillac, Le Doyenné, De La Garde, Jonqueyrès Marjosse Parenchère Cuvée Raphaël, Le Pin Beausoleil, Plaisance, Prieuré-Ste.-Anne, Recougne, Reignac Cuvée, Speciale Reynon

Côtes de Castillon: d'Aigulhe, Brisson, Cap de Faugè res, Dubois-Grimon, Le Pin de Belcier, Pitray, Sainte-Colombre, Veyry, Vieux-Champ-de-Mars

Barsac/Sauternes: Bastor-Lamontagne, Doisy-Dubroca, Haut-Claverie, de Malle

Entre-Deux-Mers (dry white wines): Bonnet, Bonnet-Cuvée Réserve, Tertre-Launay, Turcaud

Generic Bordeaux: Bonnet, La Cour d'Argent, Thébot, Thieuley

Miscellaneaous: Branda (Puisseguin-St.-Emilion), La Griffe de Cap d'Or (St.-George St.-Emilion,), Marsau (Côtes de Francs), La Mauriane (Puisseguin-St.-Emilion), La Prade (Côtes de Francs)

RED BURGUNDY

Saint-Romain Appellation (Côte de Beaune): Bernard Fevre St.-Romaine), Alain Gras (St.-Romaine), Taupenot Père et Fils (St.-Romain, René Thévenin (Monthélie St.-Romain)

Saint-Aubin Appellation (Côte de Beaune): Jean-Claude Bachelet (St.-Aubin Derrière la Tour), Raoul Clerget (St.-Aubin Les Frionnes), Marc Colin (St.-Aubin), Larry-Pillot (St.-Aubin), Langoureau-Gilles Bouton (St.-Aubin en Remilly), Henri Prudhon (St.-Aubin Les Frionnes, St.-Aubin Sentiers de Clou), Domaine Roux Père et Fils (St.-Aubin), Gérard Thomas (St.-Subin Les Frionnes)

Rully (Côte Chalonnaise): Michel Briday (Rully), Domaine de la Folie (Rully Clos de Bellecroix), Jacqueson (Rully Les Chaponnieres, Rully Les Cloix), Domaine de la Rénard (Rully Premier Cru), Antonin Rodet (Rully), Château de Rully (Rully). Domaine de Rully St.-Micheal (Rully Les Champs Cloux, Rully Clos de Pelleret)

The World's Greatest Wine Values

by Robert M. Parker, Jr.

(This list is organized by wine producing region)

RED BURGUNDY *continued*

Mercurey (Côte Chalonnaise): Château de Chamirey (Mercurey), Chartron et Trébuchet (Mercurey Clos des Hayes), Faiveley (Mercurey Clos des Myglands, Mercurey Clos du Roi, Mercurey La Croix Jacquelet, Mercurey LA Framboisière, Mercurey Les Mauvarennes), Michel Julliot (Mercurey Clos des Barraults, Mercurey Clos Tonnerre), Domaine de Meix Foulot (Mercurey Clos du Château de Montaigu, Mercurey Les Veleys), Domaine de a Monette (Mercurey), Domaine de Suremain (Mercurey Clos L'Eveque, Mercurey Clos Voyen)

Givry Appellation (Côte Chalonnaise): Jean Chofflet (Givry), Domiane Joblot (Givry Clos du Bois Chevaux, Givry Clos du Cellier aux Moines, Givry Clos de la Servoisine), Louis Latour (Givry), Thiery Lespinasse (Givry en Choué), Gerard Mouton (Givry), Domaine Veuve Steinmaier (Givry Clos de la Baraude), Domaine Thenard (Givry Cellier aux Moines, Givry Clos St.-Pierrem, Givry Les Bois Chevaux)

Beaujolais: Domaine Bacheard - Georges Duboeuf (Fleurie), René Berrod (Moulin à Vent), Rene Berrod-Les Roches du Vivier (Fleurie), Guy Braillion (Chenas), Domaine des Brureaux (Chenas), Manoir du Carra-Sambardier (Beaujolais-Villages), Domaine des Champs Grilles-J. G. Revillon (St.-Amour), Domaine Chauver-Georges Duboeuf (Moulin à Vent), Michel Chiguard Les Moriers (Fleurie), Clos de la Roilette-F. Coudert (Fleurie), Domaine de la Combe-Remont - Georges Duboeuf (Chenas), Château des Deduits - Georges Duboeuf (Fleurie), Jean Descombes - Georges Duboeuf (Morgon), Domaine Diochon (Moulin à Vent), Domaine des Grandes Vignes - J. C. Nesme (Brouilly), Domaine du Granit - A. Bertolla (Moulin à Vent), Domaine des Héritiers-Tagent - Georges Duboeuf (Moulin à Vent), Jacky Janoder (Moulin à Vent), Domaine de la Madone - J. Bererd (Beaujolais), Château Moulin à Vent - Jean-Pierre Bloud (Moulin à Vent), Domiane des Terres Dorées - J. P. Brun (Beaujolais-Villages), Domaine de la Tour du Bief - Georges Duboeuf (Moulin a Vent), Jacques Trichard (Morgon)

WHITE BURGUNDY

Jean-Claude Bachelet (St-Aubin Les Champlots), Michel Briday (Rully-Grésigny), Château de Chamirey (Mercurey), Chatron et Trébuchet (Rully Chaume, St.-Aubin, St.-Aubin La Chatenière), Raoul Clerget (St.-Aubin Le Charmois), Marc Colin (St.-Aubin La Chatenière), Joseph Drouhin (Mâcon La Forêt, Rully), Faiveley Bourgogne, Mercurey Clos Rochette), Domaine de la Folie (Rully Clos de Bellecroix, Fully Clos St.-Jacques), Jean Germain (St.-Romaine Clos Sous Le Château), Alain Gras (St.-Romaine), Jacqueson (Rully-Grésigny), Louis Jadot (Bourgogne Blanc), Robert Jayer-Gilles (Bourgogne Hautes Côtes de Beaune, Bourgogne Hautes Cotes de Nuits), Michel Julliot (Mercurey), Louis Latour (Mâcon Lugny, Montagny, St.-Veran), Lequin-Roussot (Santenay Premier Cru), Moillard (Montagny Premier Cru), Bernard Morey (St.-Aubin), Jean-Marc Morey (St.-Aubin Le Charmois), Michel Niellon (Chassagne-Montrachet), Prieur-Brunet (Sanrenay-Clos Rousseau), Henri Prudhon (St.-Aubin), Francois et Jean-Marie Raveneau (Chablis), Antonin Rodet (Bourgogne Blanc, Montagny), Château de Rully (Rully), Domaine de Rully St.-Michel (Rully Les Cloux, Rully Rabourcé), Château de la Saule (Montagny), Erienne Sauzer (Puligny-Montrachet), Gerard Thomas (St.-Aubin Murgers des Dents de Chien), Jean Vachet (Montagny les Coeres), Aubert de Villaine (Bourgogne Aligoté, Bourgogne Le Clous)

LOIRE VALLEY
- terrific dry, crisp, virgin whites (no oak) -

Muscadet: Michel Bahuand, Domaine de la Borne, Andre-Michel Brégeon, Château de Chasseloir, Chèreau-Carré, Joseph Drouard, Domaine de l'Ecu, Domaine du Fief Guérin, Marquis de Goulaine, Domaine Les Hautel Noëlles, Château de la Mercredière, Louis Métaireau, Domaine Les Mortaine, Domaine des Mortiers-Gobin, Château La Noë, Domaine La Quilla, Sauvion Cardinal Richard, Domaine le Rossignol, Sauvion Château de Cléray, Domaine des Sensonnieres, Domain de la Vrillonnière

Sancerre: Paul Cotat, Château du Nozet-Ladoucette, Edmond Vatan

Savennieres: Domaine des Baumard (Clos du Papillon, Trie Spéciale), Clos de la Coulée de Sérrant (N. Joly), Domaine du Closel (Clos du Papillon)

Vouvray: Domain Bourillon-Dorléans, Philippe Foreau Clos Naudin, Gaston Huet

The World's Greatest Wine Values

by Robert M. Parker, Jr.

(This list is organized by wine producing region)

LANGUEDOC-ROUSSILLON

- gutsy red wines, improving whites -

Domaine l'Aiguelière-Montpoyroux (Coteaux du Languedoc), Gilbert Alquier-Cuvée Les Bastides (Faugères), Domaine d'Aupillac (Vin de Pays), Château La Baroone (Corbières), Château Bastide-Durand (Corbières), Domaine Bois Monsieur (Coteaux du Languedoc), Château de Calage (Coteaux du Languedoc), Château de Campuget Cuvée Prestige (Costières de Nimes), Domaine Capion (Vin de Pays), Domaine Capion Merlot (Vin de Pays), Château de Casenove (Côtes du Roussillon), Les Chemins de Bassac Pierre Elie (Vin de Pays), Domaine La Colombetre (Vin de Pays), Daniel Domergue (Minervois), Château Donjon Cuvée Prestige (Minervois), Château des Estanilles (Faugeres), Château des Estanilles Cuvée Syrah (Faugères), La Grange des Péres (Vin de Pays-Herault), Château Hèléne Cuvée Héléne de Troie (Vin de Pays), Domaine de l'Hortus (Coteaux du Languedoc), Château des Lanes (Corbières), Domaine Maris (Minervois), Mas Amiel (Maury), Mas des Bressades Cabernet Sauvignon, Mas des Bressades Syrah, Mas de Daumas Gassac (L'Hérault), Mas Jullien Les Cailloutis (Coteaux du Languedoc), Mas Jullien Les Dedierre (Corteaux du Languedoc), Château d'Oupia Cuvée des Barons (Minervois), Château Les Palais (Corbieres), Château Les Palais Cuvée Randolin (Corbières), Château de Paraza Cuvée Speciale (Minervois), Dr. Parté Mas Blanc (Banyuls), Domaine Peyre Rose Clos des Sistes (Coteaux du Languedoc), Domaine Peyre Rose Clos Syrah (Coteaux du Languedoc), Château Routas Agrippa (Coteaux Varois), Château Routa Infernet (Coteaux Varois), Château Routas Truffière (Coteaux Varois), Prieuré de St.-Jean de Babian (Vin de Pays), Catherine de Saint-Juery (Coteaux du Languedoc), Château La Sauvagéonne (Coteaux du Languedoc), Château Le Thou (Vin de Pays d'Oc), Domaine La Tour Boisée Cuvée Marie-Claude (Minervois)

CALIFORNIA

Alderbrook (Sauvignon Blanc, Chardonnay), Amador Foothill Winery (White Zinfandel), Arrowood Domaine du Grant Archer (Chardonnay, Cabernet Sauvignon), Bel Arbors - Fetzer (Zinfandel, Sauvignon Blanc, Merlot), Belvedere (Chardonnay Cuvées), Beringer (Knights Valley Chardonnay, Sauvignon Blanc, Meritage white, Gamay Beaujolais), Bonny Doon (Clos de Gilroy, Ca'Del Solo cuvées, Pacific Rim Riesling), Carmenet (Colombard), Cartlidge & Browne (Chardonnay, Merlot, Zinfandel), Cline (Côtes d'Oakley), Duxoup (Gamay, Charbono), Edmunds St.-John (New World and Port o'Call reds, Pinot Grigio and El Nino whites), Estancia (Chardonnay cuvées, Meritage red), Fetzer (Sundial Chardonnay), Guenoc (Petite Sirah, Zinfandel), Hess Collection (Hess Select Chardonnay, Cabernet Sauvignon), Husch Vineyard (Chenin Blanc, Gewüztraminer, La Ribera Red), Kendall-Jackson (Vintner's Reserve Chardonnay, Fumé Blanc, Vistner's Reserve Zinfandel), Kenwood (Sauvignon Blanc), Konocti (Fumé Blanc), Laurel Glen (Counterpoint and Terra Rosa proprietary red wines), Liberty School--Caymus (Cabernet Sauvignon, Sauvignon Blanc, Chardonnay), J. Lohr (Gamay, Cypress Chardonnay), Marietta Cellar (Old Vine Red, Zinfandel, Cabernet Sauvignon), Mirassou (white burgundy--Pinot Blanc), Monterey Vineyard (Classic cuvées of Merlot, Cabernet Sauvignon, Chardonnay, Sauvignon Blanc, and Zinfandel, generic Classic White and Classic Red), Moro Bay Vineyards (Chardonnay), Mountain View Winery (Sauvignon Blanc, Chardonnay Pinot Noir, Zinfandel), Murphy-Goode (Fume Blanc), Napa Ridge (Chardonnay, Cabernet Sauvignon, Sauvignon Blanc), Parducci (Sauvignon Blanc), Robert Pecota (gamay), J. Pedroncelli (Sauvignon Blanc, Zinfandel, Cabernet Sauvignon), Joseph Phelps (Vins du Mistral cuvées), R. H. Phillips (Night Harvest cuvée of Chardonnay and Sauvignon Blanc), Château Souverain (Chardonnay, Merlot, Cabernet Sauvignon, Sauvignon Blanc), Ivan Tamas (Trebbiano, Fumé Blanc, and Chardonnay), Thentadue (Old Patch Red, Zinfandel, Cariguane, Sangiovese, Petite Sirah, Merlot, Salute Proprietary Red Win, N. V. Alexander Valley red), Westwood (Barbera)

WASHINGTON STATE

Arbor Crest (Merlot), Columbia Creat (Chardonnay, Sauvignon Blanc/Semillon, Merlot), L'Ecole No. 41 (Semillon), Hogue (Chardonnay, Merlot, Chenin Blanc, Dry Riesling, Fumé Blanc)

SPAIN

Abadia Retuerta (Prumicia, Rivola), Argicola de Borja (Vina Borgia, Vina Borsao), Agricola Falset Marca (Etim), Albet I. Noya (Cava Brut Reserve),

The World's Greatest Wine Values

by Robert M. Parker, Jr.

(This list is organized by wine producing region)

SPAIN *continued*

Joan d'Anguera (La Planella), Bodegas Aragoneas (Monte Corba), Capafons (Masia Esplanes), Capcanes (Mas Donis Barrica), Casa Castillo (Monastrell), Casa de la Ermita (Tinto), Castano (Hecula, Solana), Bodegas Martin Codax (Burgans Albarino), Dehesa Gago, Dominico de Eguren (Codice, Protocolo Tinto), El Cep (Marques de Gelida), Erate (Crianza, Gewurztraminer), Farina (Colegista Tinto), Bodegas Godeval (Vina Godeval), Garmona (Gessami), Granja Filliboa (Albarino), Finca Luzon (Merlot), Castillo de Maluenda (Vina Alarba), Bodegas Nekeas (Vega Sindoa cuvées), Palacio de Menade (Rueda), Pazo de Senorans (Albarino), Pergolas (Crianza Old Vines), Real Sitio de Ventosilla (Prado Rey), Castell de Remes (Gotim Bru), Herencia Remondo (Rioja, Tempranillo), Telmo Rodrigueez (Basa Rueda, Dehesa Gago), Sierra Cantabria (Rioja, Rioja Crianza), Bodegas Solar de Urbezo (Vina Urbezo), Tresantos, Valminor (Albarino), Bodegas Vina Alarba (Old Vines Grenache, Vina Alarba), Vina Mein (Vina Mein), Bodegas Y Vinedos Solabal (Rioja Crianza), Vinicola del Priorat (Onix)

ITALY

Giovanni Abrigo (Dolcetto Diano d'Alba Sori Crava), Alario (Dolcetto d'Alba Costa Fiore), Allegrini (Vaipolicello), Almondo (Arneis cuvées), Altesino (Rosso di Altesino), Ambra (Barco Reale, Carmignano San Cristina), Anselmi (San Vincenzo), Apollonio (Copertino), Badabing (Bianco, Russo), Badia a Coilbuono (Chianti Cetamura), Boschis (Dolcetto cuvees), Ca del Vispo (Chainti Colli Senesi Rovai), Castello di Cacchiano (Rosso Toscano), Le Calcinaio (Vernaccia Vigna Al Sassi), De Calvane (Chianti Classico Riserva Il Trecione), La Carraia (Sangiovese), I Casciani (Chanti di Montespertoli), Catalci Madonna (Montepulciano d'Abruzzo), Cavalchina (Bianco di Custoza), Censio (Chanti Erte), Clerico Dolcetto Laughe Visari), Coffele (Chardonnay, Soave), Colli Amerini (Carbio), Colognole (Chianti Rufina), Coppo (Barbera d'Asti l'Avvocata), Corrina (Bianco Vergine di Baldichiana, Sangioves), Elisabetta (Aulo Rosso, Le Marze Bianco), Falesco (Poggio dei Gelsi Est! Est! Est!, Vitiano), Fontaleoni (Chianti, Rosso di San Gimignano), Nino Franco (Prosecco di Valdobbiadene Rustico), Gini (Soave Classico), Laila (Rosso Piceno), Lamborghini (Truscone), Lanari (Fibbio), Lucignano (Chianti Classico Colli Fiorentini), Maculan (Pinot et Toi), Di Majo Norante (Biblos, Ramitello, Sangiovese San Giorgio), A'Mano (Primitivo), Manzone Dolcetto d'Alba), Marcarini (Dolcetto d'Alba Fontanazza), Monte Antico (Monte Antico), La Montecchia (Cadetto), Cantina Monrubio (Rosso), Tenute Montepulischio (Verdicchio di Matelica), Giacomo Mori (Chianti), I. Mori (Chianti, Chianti Colli Fiorentini), Nalles and Magre-Miclara (Chardonnay Lucia, Pinot Bianco Lucia, Pinot Grigo Lucia), Parusso (Dolcetto d'Alba), Elio Perrone (Biagaro, Moscato Clarte), Petrolo (Terre di Galatrona), Piazzano (Chianti Classico Reserva Rio Camarata, Chianti Rio Camarata), Pieropan (Soave Classico), Pira (Dolcetto d'Alba Vigna Fornaci), Poderi Alasia (Arneis Roero, Sauvignon, Camillona), Poggio Turana (IGT), Pojer and Sandri (Chardonnay, Muller Thurgan, Nosiola, Traminer), Maso Poli (Chardonnay, Pinot Grigio), Promessa (Negroamaro, Rosso Salente), Pruntto (Barbera d'Asti Hulot, Dolcetto d'Alba), Tenuta Le Querce (Aglianico), Rebuil (Prosecco Valbobbiadene), Revello (Barbera d'Alba, Dolcetto d'Alba), Rocca di Fabbri (Sangiovese Satiro), Ronchi di Menzano (Chardonnay, Pinot Grigio, Tocai Friuliaco), Castel di Salve (Rosso del Salentino Priante, Rosso del Salentino Santi Mediei), San Biagio (Chianti Colli Senesi), San Fabiano (Chianti Putto), Feudi di San Gregorio (Falanghina), Fattoria San Lorenzo (Montepuliano), Sandrone (Dolcetto d'Alba), Santa Cristina (Rosso), Saracco (Moscato d'Asti), Scavino (Rosso, Rosso Corale), Fattoria Le Sorgenti (Chianti Colli Fiorentini), Sportoletti Assisi Rosso), Tamellini (Scave Superiore), Taurino (Notarpanaro, Salice Salentino), Tavignano (Rosso Piceno, Verdicchio dei Castelli di Jesi Misco), Tiefenbrunner (Pinot Bianco, Pinor Grigio), Cantina Tollo (Montepulciano d'Abruzzo Collect Secco, Sangiovese Villa Diana), Gianolio Tomaso (Arneis, Barbera d'Alba, Dolcetto d'Alba, Nebbiolo d'Alba), Tormaresca (Bianco, Rosso), Giuseppe Traverse (Moscaro d'Asti Vigna Canova), Villa del Borgo (Chardonnay, Merlot, Pinot, Grigio, Refosco), Villa Giada (Barbera d'Asti cuvées), Villa Matilde (Falerno del Massico), Villamaga (Rosso Paceno), Zardetto (Prosecco Brut), Zemmer (Chardonnay, Pinot, Grigo, Sauvignon), Zenato (Valpolicella Classico)

SICILY and SARDINIA

Argiolas (Costere, Perdera Selegas Vermentino), Colosi (Rosso), Morgante (Nero d'Avola), Planeta (Rosso la Segreta), Santa Anastasia (Passomaggio),

The World's Greatest Wine Values
by Robert M. Parker, Jr.
(This list is organized by wine producing region)

SICILY AND SARDINIA *continued*

Cantina Santadi (Vermentino Cala Silente), Tasca d'Almeria (Regaleali Bianco, Regaleali Rosso, Regaleali Rose)

AUSTRALIA

Berry Estates (Semillon), Brown Brothers (Cabernet Sauvignon, Chardonnay King Valley, Muscat Lexia), Jacobs Creek (various cuvées), Peter Lehmann (Cabernet Sauvignon, Shiraz), Lindermans (Chardonnay Bin 65), Michelton (Semmillon/Chardonnay), Montrose (Cabernet Sauvignon, Chardonnay, Shiraz), Orlando (Cabernet Sauvignon Jacob's Creek, Chardonnay Jacob's Creek), Oxford Landing (Cabernet Sauvignon, Chardonnay), Rosemount (various cuvées), Rothbury Estate (Chardonnay Broken Back Vineyard, Shiraz), Seppelt (various cuvées), Tyrells (Long Flat Red), Wolf Blass (Cabernet Sauvignon, Yellow Label, Shiraz President's Selection), Wyndham Estates (Cabernet Sauvignon Bin 444, Chardonnay Bin 222), Yalamba Clocktower Port

SOUTH AMERICA

Argentina: Bodega Weiner (Cabernet Sauvignon), Erchart (Cabernet Sauvignon)

Chile: Casa Lapostelle (Sauvignon Blanc), Cousino Macul (Cabernet/Merlot Finis Terrae, Cabernet Sauvignon Antiguas Reserva)

GLOSSARY of Drink Terms

Absinthe or Absenta: A green (from plant chlorophyll), highly proofed (120-170) beverage which turns milky white when water is added. Banned almost globally, it can be found legally in Spain, Denmark, Portugal, the Czech Republic and Andorra. It contains wormwood which is made up mostly of thujone (closely related to THC). Created in Switzerland by a French doctor in 1792.

Advokaat: a mixture of brandy, milk, eggs, vanilla and sugar. Can be bought pre-mixed in a bottle

Agwa: A South American liqueur which contain guarana, ginseng and coca. Highly caffeinated.

Akvavit or Aquavit ("Water of Life"): A clear to pale yellow Scandinavian liquor. Made much like vodka then flavor infused (caraway, dill, coriander). Served in shots, ice cold.

Ale: A rather broad term. A group in the beer family. Typically stronger than lager (the other half of the beer family). A beverage containing malt and hops that has been top-fermented.

Alize: A bottled mixture of fruit juices and Cognac 32-proof. French. Means "gentle trade wind".

Alcohol by Volume: used to measure the alcohol content of a beverage. A 100 proof Vodka would be 50% alcohol by volume. And a wine at 12% ABV would be 24 proof.

Amaretto: Originally from Italy, made from apricot pits and herbs with an almond and vanilla taste.

Amer Picon: A French cordial with a bitter orange flavor.

Anisette: A very sweet liqueur made from anise seed. Tastes like black licorice.

Aperitif: Originally referring to wine, but may mean any alcoholic beverage taken to stimulate the appetite before a meal.

Armagnac: Brandy from Gascony, France. A smaller growing area than the well known Cognac region. Due to difference in the distillation process, Armagnac usually has a fruitier or fuller taste than cognac which distills out many of the underlying nuances.

Aurum: A brandy-based, orange and saffron flavored Italian liqueur.

Babycham: A sparkling alcoholic pear flavored drink. Pear cider.

Barenjager: German "Bear Hunter", a vodka-based, honey-flavored liqueur.

Barley Wine: A dark, rather strong ale.

Beer: A generic term for an alcoholic beverage brewed from malt and flavored by hops. Encompasses ales (I.P.A., lambic, porter, stout, etc.) and lagers (bock, light beer, malt liquor, pilsner, etc).

Benedictine: A liqueur produced by monks. Made with a secret formula of 27 plants and spices.

Bhang: Indian cannabis wine.

Bitters: A general term for a bitter-tasting, alcoholic liquid made of herbs, bark, roots, plant extracts, flowers and fruits. There are many types available and they are usually used as a cocktail ingredient.

Black Raspberry Liqueur: A deep purple, brandy-based liqueur made with berries, spices and honey. Chambord is the most popular.

Blanc: French for white wine.

Blue Curacao: An orange flavored blue colored liqueur. From the Dutch West Indies.

Blended Whiskey: A whiskey or whisky made by blending 2 or more straight whiskeys, or a whiskey mixed with a neutral spirit (ethyl alcohol). American, Canadian and Scotch whiskey can be blends. Irish whiskeys are not blended; they are married.

Body: The weight or consistency of a wine.

Bourbon: Corn-based whiskey, solely American made. Aged a minimum of two years, but usually aged four years or more. Named after Bourbon County, Kentucky. Most are made to 120-160 proof and then diluted with water to a lower proof.

Brandy: An alcoholic liquor, either distilled from wine or from fermented fruit. A very broad term. Prized bottles of rare cognac and the myriad of sweet, colored, fruit brandies are all under this term. Some are liquors, and some are liqueurs.

Brut: Very dry champagne.

Byrrh: A French wine made from bark, quinine and herbs.

Cachaca or Pinga: Means "burning water", a Brazilian sugar cane brandy.

Cactus Whiskey: Tequila

Calvados: A French apple brandy

Campari: A brilliant, red, bitter, Italian, 41 proof aperitif. Developed by Gaspare Campari in Milan in 1860.

Canadian Whiskey: Lighter in taste and color than American whiskeys. Can be made from corn, wheat, rye or barley. Aged a minimum of three years, but usually aged four to six years. Always blended, either before or after aging.

Cava: Sparkling champagne-like wine from Spain.

Chambord: A French black raspberry liqueur.

Chartreuse: An herb liqueur. Developed by Cathusian monks in 1605. Comes in yellow or green. Said to contain 130 herbs and spices. "The Elixir of Long Life."

Claret or Clairet: A light, red wine from Bordeaux, France.

Coffee Liqueur: A dark brown sweet spirit, some have undertones of vanilla, orange or almond. Kahlua and Tia Maria are the two most popular ones.

Cognac: Brandy from the Cognac region of France. See Cognac section.

Cointreau: An upscale, French orange liqueur. In the Curacao family.

Cordial: A sweetened, flavored, liquor-based spirit. A liqueur. A straight liqueur drink taken to stimulate or enhance a warm of friendly situation.

Corkage: A fee charged by an establishment to a guest who brings his own wine.

Corked: Refers to wine ruined by a faulty cork. Air has entered the bottle.

Cream of Coconut: A coconut base or syrup used for many exotic drinks; most popular is the Pina Colada. Usually comes in cans.

Crème de nananas: A rum-based, pineapple-flavored liqueur.

Crème de Cacao: A liqueur which comes in either dark or white (clear). Made from cacao and vanilla.

Crème de Cassis: A liqueur made with European Black Currants.

Crème de Menthe: A liqueur which comes in either green or white (clear). Made from peppermint.

Crème de Mure: A sweet, blackberry-flavored liqueur.

Crème de Nouyax: A brilliant, red liqueur made with almonds.

Curacao or Triple Sec: A liqueur made from orange peels. Originally from the Dutch West Indies. Comes in blue, orange, green and clear. Cointreau is the finest one.

Cynar: An Italian liqueur made with artichokes and herbs.

Dash: Approximately 1/4 teaspoon.

Decant: To pour out a bottle of wine into another container to aerate it, or to remove sediment.

Drambule: A liqueur made from Scotch whisky and heather honey and herbs. It is sweet and spicy with an anise taste.

Dry: Pertaining to wine. Without sweetness. Low in residual sugar.

Dry Vermouth or French Vermouth: A brandy-laced, white wine flavored with 50 or more herbs and spices (wormwood, ginger, cloves, rose petals, camomile, forget-me-not, angelica, sage, etc.)

Dubonnet: An aromatic wine from France. It comes in red (rouge) and white (blanc). Refrigerate after opening.

Dumb: A wine opened before maturation.

Dutch Courage: British slang from Anglo-Dutch wars. Now used as a term for a drink before a challenge.

Espresso: A strong coffee made by forcing steam through grounds.

Falernum: 1. A spicy sweetener from Barbados with almonds and ginger undertones. 2. A historic wine from ancient Rome.

Fermentation: A chemical reaction when alcohol comes from a sitting substance (grapes).

Finish: The last taste left by a drink in the mouth.

Fino: Pale sherry. Most often from Portugal or Spain.

Flabby: A watery-tasting wine.

Forbidden Fruit: A liqueur made with brandy, honey and shaddock (grapefruit).

Framboise: Means "raspberry". This can be either a raspberry liqueur or a raspberry beer (lambic).

Frangelico: A golden liqueur made with hazelnuts, vanilla, orange and coffee. Originally made by a hermit monk from Italy.

Galliano: A sweet and spicy, bright yellow, Italian liqueur. It is brandy-based and made with a secret recipe of over 30 herbs, flowers, spices, roots and berries.

Garnish: A garnish is no more than a decoration, sometimes functional, either eaten or squeezed into a drink.

Ginger Beer: A non/low alcoholic drink made of ginger and sugar.

Gin: Originally from the Netherlands. It is distilled from grain (mostly corn, but some are rye or barley). Can be flavored with juniper, orange, angelica, caraway, coriander, anise, cassia, almonds, cinnamon, ginger, fennel and/or oris. No two gins are made exactly the same.

Goldschlager: High proof, clear, cinnamon schnapps with floating flecks of gold leaf, created in Switzerland.

Goldwasser: "Gold water." An herb-flavored liqueur with gold leaf floating about. Anise and caraway, or citrus and spice are the most pronounced flavors. Originally from Poland.

Gomme: Same as Simple Syrup.

Grain Alcohol: Made from sugar or other starches. Usually distilled to 200 proof and then diluted with water to bottled proof.

Grand Marnier: A highly-prized, cognac-based triple orange liqueur.

Grappa: Italian brandy made from the by-products of wine-making. There are hundreds of kinds and thousands of brands. Some are terribly harsh and unaged. Others are mellowed with age. Taste is different because of all the different grapes each producer will use.

Grenadine: A sweet, red syrup originally made with pomegranates from Grenada. Most are alcohol-free.

Hazelnut Liqueur: A sweet, syrupy, amber-colored spirit. Some have hints of vanilla, honey or chocolate. Frangelico would be the premier hazelnut liqueur.

Hpnotiq: A blue bottled mixture of Cognac, Vodka, and Fruit juices. 34-Proof.

Irish Cream: A silky liqueur made from Irish whiskey and cream. Some are made with toffee, honey or chocolate. Bailey's would be the most popular brand.

Irish Mist: A brown liqueur made with Irish whiskey, heather honey, citrus and sweet herbs.

Irish Whiskey: A triple distilled liquor aged no less than 3 years. Some are aged into their teens. If you are very lucky, there are some 36 year olds to be had. Irish whiskey can be a single malt or a blend.

Jägermeister: "Hunt Master." A German liqueur made of 56 herbs, roots, resins, seeds, spices and fruits from the four corners of the earth. It is a klosterlik or a form of bitters. It is usually taken chilled in shots, or as a cocktail ingredient.

Kahlua: A coffee liqueur with hints of vanilla and chocolate - one of Mexico's most popular exports.

Kirsch or Kirschwasser: A clear or reddish-brown liqueur distilled from black cherries.

Kummel: Originally from Holland (the Netherlands). A clear, sweet liqueur made from caraway, anise, cumin and fennel.

Kwai Feh: A lychee-flavored liqueur.

Lager: A rather broad term. A group in the beer family. Typically lighter than ale (the other half of the beer family). A beverage containing malt and hops that has been bottom fermented.

Legs: (tears) The trails left running down the inside of a wine glass after swirling the wine.

Length: The time the flavor of a wine stays on the palate.

Licor 43: A Spanish brandy-based liqueur with 43 ingredients, with a prominent vanilla-citrus flavor.

Lillet: A French aperitif made of wine, brandy, fruit and herbs. Comes in red (rouge) and white (blanc).

Limoncello: An Italian alcoholic beverage made with lemons and sugar. Taken ice cold after a meal or over fruit. Often homemade.

Liqueur or cordial: A syrupy, sweet alcoholic beverage usually liquor-based, or more specifically, brandy-based. Something as special as rare Grand Marnier as well as generic peppermint schnapps would fall into this category. They can be created by maceration, infusion or percolation. With flavoring agents such as fruit, oils, leaves, nuts, herbs, spices, barks, flowers and roots.

Liquor: Any alcoholic beverage that has been distilled (grain alcohol, vodka, gin, rum, tequila, mezcal, whiskey and some brandy). Usually 80 - 190 proof.

Madeira: A blended and fortified Portuguese wine.

Magnum: A wine bottle size: 1.5 liters. Equals two standard bottles.

Maraschino: A clear, bitter liqueur made from cherries and their pits.

Marc: French brandy made from the by-products of the wine-making process. See Grappa.

Married: Refers to blending of ingredients as in whiskey. They marry whiskeys together to make a blend.

Marsala: A full-bodied, fortified red wine from Sicily.

Mead: Arguably the first alcoholic beverage. Made from honey, herbs and water.

Metaxa: A sweetened Greek brandy.

Mezcal: A liquor distilled in Mexico. Developed by Spaniards. Made with Agave plants. Tequila is mezcal, but mezcal is not always tequila. Tequila has stricter guidelines about location of production and contents of liquor. Sometimes bottles contain a worm (gusano) which lives in the agave plants. The worm is supposed to bring luck to the person who swallows it....yummmmmm....

Midori: A melon-flavored liqueur from the Japanese house of Suntory.

Mist: A term meaning "on the rocks" (preferably with shaved or crushed ice). Coming from the fact that certain clear liqueurs cloud or mist when poured over ice.

Muddle: Meaning to mix together or mash together.

Neat: Another ways to say straight, no ice, not mixed, not chilled.

Night Cap: Usually a friendly suggestion or offering for a drink to end of the evening. Any drink could be a night cap.

Orange Liqueur: The most common are Triple Sec and Curacao. The best are Grand Marnier and Cointreau.

Orgeat: An almond-citrus flavored sweetener.

Ouzo: A clear, anise-flavored, Greek liqueur. Some recipes are made with mixtures of the following: grapes, fennel seeds, nutmeg, cardamon, coriander, cinnamon, nuts, mint, berries and anise.

Passion Fruit Liqueur: A citrus-based liqueur made in the United States, Australia, the Azores and France.

Peppermint Schnapps: A light, sweet, mint-flavored liqueur.

Pernod: A French, anise-flavored liqueur.

Pilsner: Originally a light, crisp, delicious beer from Czechoslovakia. The method of production has been imitated worldwide. Now the name has been bastardized and is being used by thousands of beer producers to describe their product.

Pimm's: A bottled, fortified liqueur drink. There were six different ones made. Now only #1 which is gin-based and # 6 which is vodka-based remain in production.

Pisang Ambon: An Indonesian green-colored, banana and herb-flavored liqueur.

Pony: Means one ounce. Also refers to a certain glass.

Port: A rich, sweet, fortified wine originally from Portugal. There are four main kinds of port: tawny, ruby, vintage and white.

Potcheen Poteen Poitin: Irish moonshine. The real thing is 160 proof or more. There are some available to purchase legally.

Pousse-Cafe: Refers to either a layered drink or an alcoholic drink taken with coffee.

Proof: A term used to denote alcohol content. 80-proof liquor would be 40% alcohol, meaning 40% of the contents of the bottle would be pure alcohol. Bottled wine at 12% alcohol by volume would be 24-proof.

Punt: The indent at the bottom of a wine bottle.

Raki or Arak Araka, Arrak, Araki, Ariki, Tsipouro, Tsikoudia: A distilled beverage made from the by-products of the wine-making process. All basically the same, but given different names. Has a range from the Orient to Greece. Some contain anise. Some illegally made in Crete are said to have hallucinogenic properties.

Robe: The color or look of a given wine.

Rosso: Italian for red wine.

Rouge: French for red wine.

Rum: Liquor made from molasses or sugar cane. Originally from the West Indies. Aged six months to 20 years. 70 to 150 proof.
> *Light, white or silver:* Clear, aged six months to one year.
> *Amber or gold:* Aged at least three years. Color comes from barrel aging or added caramel or both.
> *Anejo:* Usually a blend. Aged four to 10 years
> *Spiced:* There are many kinds: pepper, rosemary, vanilla, cinnamon and clove.
> *Dark Rum:* Aged five to seven years. Usually made from a blend of different batches.
> *Jamaican:* Dark rum from Jamaica.
> *Demerara:* High proof rum from Guyana.

Rum Cream Liqueur: a sweet Rum-based liqueur which can have hints of chocolate, coconut, coffee, vanilla, peanuts, bananas and cinnamon.

Rye: In the United States, a whiskey made from at least 51% rye that has been aged at least two years in oak barrels and can be diluted with water to no less than 80-proof. These rules do not apply anywhere else.

Sabra: An orange-chocolate liqueur from Israel.

Safari: A yellow, Dutch, fruit liqueur flavored with mangoes, limes and papaya.

Sake: Wine made from fermented rice. It is actually a type of beer. Traditionally served warm.

Sambuca: A clear or black Italian liqueur. Made from grape distillates, elderberries and anise. Traditionally served straight in a snifter with three coffee beans.

Sappy: A young wine that shows great promise for aging.

Schnapps: (U.S., Australia) A common name for a wide range of liqueurs, usually light-bodied, often colored and sweetly flavored. (Europe): "Mouthful" (German) Schnaps is a distilled clear liquor. Much different than American schnapps.

Scotch: Can be bottled from a singular batch (single malt) or from many different batches (blend). 20 to 30 single malts can be used to make a blend. They are blended to mellow for the consumer. If a blend has a year on it, it refers to the youngest single malt in the blend.

Single malts can be classified into 10 or 20 categories or areas, from taste clusters to river sides. The major ones are as follows. Lowland (generally the lightest and softest), Highland (most numerous with a very wide variation in flavor), Islay (generally the heaviest, full-bodied), Speyside (noted for their complexity), Cambeltown (two distillers left making a medium to heavy, full-bodied scotch).

Each different single malt has a unique taste. Scotch also ages better than any other liquor.

Shot: A type of drink, typically thrown down the throat. A pour of one to two ounces.

Sloe Gin: A sweet, bright red, gin-based liqueur, flavored with sloe plums.

Soda Water or Club Soda: Carbonated water. Water with bubbles. Effervescent. Sometimes coming in flavors.

Sour mix: They come in powder and liquid form. Essential at bars.

Southern Comfort: A liqueur made from bourbon, peach and citrus. Created by M. W. Heron, a bartender in New Orleans.

Spirit: Any alcohol that is distilled. An alcoholic beverage that is not wine or beer.

Splash: Approximately a 1/2 teaspoon.

Stout: A rather dark ale.

Strega ("Witch"): A spicy, sweet Italian liqueur made from over 70 herbs and spices. It gets its intense yellow color from actual saffron.

Sugar Syrup or Simple Syrup: Basically liquefied sugar. Simply mix sugar to water 2 to 1.

Sulfites: A naturally occurring additive to wine. Protects against harmful organisms and oxygen damage and helps wine last longer.

Swedish Punch: A Scandinavian liqueur made with either rum or Arak and wine, tea, lemon and spices. Some recipes have 30 or more ingredients. Usually stored for months before drunk.

Sweet Vermouth or Italian Vermouth: A brandy-laced white wine (yes! white wine) flavored with 50 or more herbs and spices (wormwood, ginger, cloves, rose petals, camomile, forget-me-not, angelica, sage, etc). It gets its color from oxidation or added dye.

Tannin: A natural acid that escapes the grape skins and stems into the juice and add color as well as tartness to the wine.

Tea: a drink made by soaking the dried leaves of a tea plant in hot water. Tea can be made with other kinds of plants as well.

Tears: (legs) The trails left running down the inside of a glass after swirling the wine.

Tequila: Invented by Spaniards in Mexico. It is derived from the Blue Agave plant (not a cacti). The best are 100% agave which would be stamped on the label. Some are merely 51% agave (mixto). Tequila is mezcal from a particular region and made to certain specifications. If produced two feet outside the region, it is mezcal, not tequila.
> *Anejo:* aged at least one year in wood.
> *Blanco:* (white or silver) usually unaged or under 60 days old.
> *Joven abocado:* young (like blanco) but colored with additives.
>> Usually labeled gold.
> *Muy Anejo:* aged two to four years in wood.
> *Reposado:* (rested) barrel aged two months to 3 years to
>> achieve mellowness and color.

Tia Maria: A rum-based, coffee liqueur from Jamaica.

Tinto: Portugese for red wine.

Tonic Water: A carbonated quinine-citrus flavored nonalcoholic beverage.

Top: Means to add ingredient to top of a drink, approximately a teaspoon to an ounce if alcoholic. Approximately two tablespoons or more if referring to whipped cream. Other nonalcoholic ingredients equal to 1 ounce.

Triple Sec or Curacao: A liqueur made from orange peels. Originally from the Dutch West Indies. Grand Marnier would be a top shelf orange liqueur.

Tuaca: An Italian brandy-based liqueur, flavored with citrus, nuts, vanilla and milk.

Ullage: 1. The space between the cork of a wine bottle and the wine.
              The space between the bottle cap and the beer.
         2. The first and/or last beer out of a keg, that you throw away.

Van der Hum: A South African brandy-based orange liqueur. Flavored with herbs and spices.

Vandermint: A Dutch chocolate-mint liqueur.

Vermouth: A wine which has had brandy added as well as 50 or more herbs and spices.

Vin: French for wine.

Vino: Italian and/or Spanish for wine.

Vintage: The year of the grape harvest in a given wine. Non-vintage means grapes from two or more years were used.

Vodka: "Water of Life" or "Dear Little Water". An unaged, neutral, colorless liquor. Can be distilled from wheat, rye, barley, potatoes, sugar cane or corn. Vodka is distilled to 190 proof, then it has demineralized water added. Therefore, 80 proof vodka is more water than pure distilled spirit. This makes the notion of purity as questionable as the distillery's water source. Vodka's origin cannot be pinpointed, but can be narrowed down to Persia, Poland or Russia.

Wein: German for wine.

Whisky or Whiskey: A liquor distilled from cereal grains (wheat, rye, corn, oats, barley). A general term covering whisky or whiskeys from all over the globe. American, Canadian, Irish or Scotch.

Wine: A fermented juice of any various kinds of grapes or other fruit.

Wort: Beer before it is fermented. The mixture of water, barley, hops and sugar.

Yukon Jack: A liqueur with a Canadian whisky base. Flavored with citrus and herbs.

Zubrowka, Zubrovka: A yellow Polish, Hungarian or Russian vodka made with bison grass.

Zymurgy(n): the science or study of fermentation

GLOSSARY of Bar, Club & Restaurant Lingo

86, Eight Six, 86'ed(adj): all out of a product, there is no more, can refer to a customer who was thrown out or ejected from an establishment. e.g., "Maria,... 86 veal saltimbocca, tell the twisted sisters and Francis,... 86 veal saltimbocca."

A.A., Alcoholics Anonymous: Get help if you need it (212) 870 3400
www.alcoholics-anonymous.org

AL-ANON: friends and family of alcoholics (800) 245-4656
or www.al-anon.alteen.org

abbeverate(v): to get a person a drink, to offer a drink, or provide a drink. e.g., "I'm going to abbeverate our guests before they die of thirst."

Action(n): slang, for gambling or adult fun e.g., "I'm on a business trip from Philly. I've never been to Bangor before; any action around here?"

After Party: refers to a little get together after a shift. Restaurant staff parties are notorious for their craziness. Nothing is more fun than a house full of drunken waitresses.....nothing

A List(n): slang, an imaginary list of the best, be it people, places, or things.   SEE: B List

A Few Cans Short of a Six Pack, A Few Sandwiches Short of a Picnic (adj): slang for a person without all their faculties.

Alcohol Abuse: Said in jest when a beer tips over, or a drink is spilled by mistake. A pun.

Amand, Saint, aka Amandus, Amand of France: Patron Saint of Bartenders, Bar Staff, Bar Keepers, Inn Keepers, Wine Makers, Wine Merchants, Feast Day 6 February.

Amateur Night(n): refers to a night that bartenders have to deal with idiots that cannot hold their drink. New Years eve is traditionally referred to as an Amateur night, because many of the people out, don't go out that often.

Annihilated: very, very drunk

Aquanaut(n): beads of condensation on a cold drink that fall, usually hitting the person who is raising the drink to their mouth

ASAP(acronym): As Soon As Possible

ASSCAN(acronym): Act Surprised, Show Concern, Admit Nothing

ATF(acronym): Alcohol Tobacco and Fire arms, Law enforcement

After Hours: refers to period of time after closing time, or to an illegal bar or house that serves and charges for alcohol after all the establishments have closed.

All Day: restaurant slang, means total of like dishes being prepared. e.g. "I need two more cheeseburgers." "That's six All Day?"

All Star: user of many substances, they drink beer, wine, liquor, liqueurs, cider, etc., etc.

Alligator Arms(n): slang, for cheap person. arms can't reach pocket.

B List(n): slang, an imaginary list of the second best, be it people, places, or things. SEE: A List

Bacchus: Roman God of Wine and Barley. Celebrate 3 January. SEE: Dionysus

BAC, BAL: Blood Alcohol Content, Blood Alcohol Level. A measurement of how much alcohol is in the bloodstream.   Milligrams of alcohol per 100 milliliters of blood.

Back of the House(n): This refers to the parts of the restaurant the customers do not usually have access to: the kitchen, prep area, dishroom, offices, store rooms. Can also refer to the personnel who work in those areas

Bail: (n)The money a defendant or a good friend of the defendent pays as surety that they will show up in court at a later date. (v)Or to leave a place or abort a mission. To Bail

Balance, Bank Balance: when you add and subtract all the transaction for a register or terminal, credit slips, payouts, tips, original bank, it should all balance. If it doesn't balance something is wrong.

Band Rat: slang, derogatory term for someone who follows a musical group around. A groupie.

Bandwidth(n): slang, a persons work limits.. e.g., "Sarah you have another four top at table 53." "Neil you are pushing my bandwidth."

Banging(adj): slang, very attractive, hot, nice, blazing. e.g., "Look at that banging chick at the hostess station, she is fine."

Bank: the money given to bartender to put in the register at the start of a shift or slang for a pocketful of money.

Banned: means never to return, do not return...ever. Not common. If you have been banned from a club you have been very bad.

Bar back: a bartender helper, restocks and runs errands for bartender, can receive anywhere between 10%-25% of bar tips or is compensated in pre arranged amount, duties can vary from bouncing, running food, getting ice, calling police, running to the bank or the market. They can make or break a busy night.

Barista: a coffee bartender, maker of espresso, cappuccinos and latte, etc.

Bar Fly: one who frequents or hangs at a bar, usually a dingy, seedy bar.

Bar Hopping: the act of drinking and jumping or moving from bar to bar.

Bar Spoon: a rather long, usually spiral handled, small bowled spoon, an essential tool

Bar Time: Bar time is usually 5-10 minutes faster than the rest of the clocks in the time zone. It doesn't matter what your watch says. It's a bar, its bar time, don't argue.

Beat(adj): slang, uninteresting, lame, boring, tired. e.g., "This joint is beat, lets go to Dooley's."

Beer Run(v): the act of leaving the party to gather more refreshments for the party. Money is often collected from party people prior.

Belt(n): a shot of a straight liquor CAUTION: (v) also means sharp blow with a fist.

Bender(n): staying drunk an extended amount of time.

Benjamin(n): slang, $100. One hundred dollars American

Bent(adj): referring to someone not being right somehow, mad, drunk, deviant, corrupt.

Bevvy(n): beverage.

B.O.Y.C.(n. acronym): Beverage of Your Choice

Beveraging: slang, to drink. e.g., "Are you beveraging this evening?" "Why yes I am, I'll have a V.S.O.P."

Binge Drinking(v): the act of drinking large amounts of alcohol at one time. Could be an hour or a weekend. I managed to do it for 15 years.

Bistro(n): a small laid back informal European style restaurant. Believed to be taken from Russian: Bistro means fast

Bitch Fuel(n): slang, sweet high alcohol drinks especially the pre-bottled kind. SEE: Tart Fuel

Bitchin'(adj): slang, cool, awesome. e.g., "That is one bitchin' Camaro you got there cornbread."

Blast(n): slang, a good time, fun. e.g., "Its a blast watching Matt trying to pick up girls.î

Bling, Bling Bling(n): slang, jewelry, flashy jewelry.

Blitzed: drunk as in a intense campaign of drunkeness.

Blotto: drunk as in blotted or soaked up with drink.

Blow Out(n): a big party.

Blue Laws(n): Old laws that govern moral behavior, including alcohol serving, and drunkenness.

Bogarting(v): the act of using something and not sharing with others

Bomb, to(v): slang to screw up, mess up. e.g., "I bombed on stage last night, my jokes had no flow. I was waiting for the rotten produce to fly."

Bomb, the, Bomb Diggy, Bombdiggity(a): slang, the best, the best ever. e.g. "That party was the bomb, Cognac, Caviar, and Honeys."

Bombed: drunk as in scattered mentally by drink.

Booted(a): thrown out, ejected, asked to leave SEE Knock Boots

Bootleggers(n): Someone who makes an illegal version of something. Someone who produces, homemade liquor or copies of movies, music discs, watches, clothes.

Boozeheimers(n): slang, when you forget what you are talking about, because of your inebriation

Bounce: 1.(v) slang, the action of being a bouncer/doorman. 2.(v) to leave.

Bounced: thrown out, ejected, asked to leave

Bouncer(n): Establishment employee, doorman, one who keeps order by verbal, physical means.

Brasserie(n): french brewery

Break Camp(v): slang, to leave, to go. e.g., "Ladies, I was thinking the bar is fully stocked at my loft, and this joints getting tired, what do you say, lets break camp."

Breastrant(n): slang, a restaurant with scantily clad waitstaff.

Brew(n): beer

Brown Bottle Flu(n): hangover sick from that brown bottle.

Bumped: loosing your place in line for reservations, usually because someone had a connection, and you didn't.

Bus, Bus Boy, Bus Girl (v,n): slang, to clean tables, person who cleans tables, among other duties.

Bust Ass(v): slang, to work really hard. "We are overbooked for reservations tonight, plus there is a seafood convention in town, we are going to have to bust ass."

Buzzed: slang, mildly drunk

B.Y.O.B(n,acronym): Bring Your Own (Booze, beer, bottle, broad, boy, bitch, beverage)

By The Neck(adj): bottled beer no glasses, drink out of the bottle.

C. Note(n): a hundred dollar bill American $100. Or a hundred pounds English.

Cafe(n): an establishment that serves coffee food, and possibly drink.

Cage Dancer(n): a female who dances in a sectioned off area, strictly for atmosphere.

Cake(n): money, dough, loot. e.g., "I got the drinks today boys, I'm rolling in cake this week."

Call(adj): Refers to named spirit used in a drink. Above well liquor. Beefeater or Tanqurey would be Call Gin, where as the low budget Gin in the speed rack would be Well. SEE Well:

Campers: People who linger at a table usually immersed in conversation, or staring into each other's eyes. Not a problem unless they are keeping people at work who could go home, or when there is a wait for tables.

Can(n): slang, rest room. (v) slang, to fire from employment. Past tense: canned. (n) Caution: also means buttocks or rear.

Carafe(n): a glass bottle with a flared opening used to serve wine.

Cappuccino(n): fresh, strong, black coffee with steamed milk and froth on top.

Carbonated(adj): effervesent, with bubbles. A drink with carbon dioxide added or occurring naturally. Soda, beer and champagne are all carbonated.

Cashed Out(a): a term used to state that the money register has done its last transaction, and closing procedures have commenced.

Cervesa(n): "Sir Vay Sah" spanish, beer

Chaser, Back: something to drink on the side to follow your libation. e.g. "Can I have your best bourbon neat with a soda water back?"

Check: slang, restaurant bill or tab SEE: Damages

Chew and Screw(n): Dine and Dash , Walk Out. This is when someone orders eats and/or drinks and leaves without paying their bill. An arrestable offense, some places your more liable to be beaten then prosecuted.

Chill, Chill Out(v): slang, to hang out, be at ease, relax. e.g. "Let's get another bottle of Shiraz and chill before we head back to the suite."

Chimneyfish(n): one who smokes like a chimney and drinks like a fish.

Chocolate(n): a substance made with cocoa berry seeds, sugar, milk, and water. Originally from Mexico, Central and South America.

Choir Practice(n): slang, used to tell someone you have something to do which might be looked upon as less than forthright, or used to tell someone your busy without disclosing your intentions.

Chrissy(n): Cristal Champagne.

Chug(v): the act of drinking in a fast or hurried manner.

Church Key(n): a thin, solid metal combination bottle and can opener.

Class 6(n): the classification that alcoholic beverages would fall under in the military.

Clinking, Clinky: the act of tapping two glasses together, which makes the holders of both glasses drink. It is poor manners not to put glass to mouth after clinking. SEE: Tapping:

Clip Joint: a nightclub, or bar that is way overpriced, a price gouging joint. Sometimes employed by over-friendly people who encourage the clients to buy them drinks. Can also mean a gambling spot with fixed tables.

Clusterfest(n): slang, an unorganized screwed up situation, usually occurs when too much input comes from too many people who think they are helping, but are not.

Clutch(a): slang, very important and good. e.g., "That was clutch when you jumped into the service bar, it made all the difference tonight."

Comp., Complimentary (adj): Usually refers to a gift of food, and/or drink and/or entrance at a certain establishment. Usually given to VIPs, or used as a marketing device to create business. Sometimes things are also comped to try to make up for shortcomings.

Completely Wrecked(adj): drunk to the point of no return. messy.

Cougar(n): slang, an older woman who hits on much younger men.

Counter Monkey(n): slang, derogatory, order takers at fast food joints

Covers(n): dinners, speaking in numbers. e.g. "We did 50 covers at the bar tonight."

Cover Charge(n): an entrance fee.

Coyote Ugly(adj): slang, waking up to someone so ugly, you want to gnaw off your own arm to get away rather than wake them.

Crocked: slang, drunk. As in disabled by drink

Curls, 12oz curls, 16oz curls(v): slang drinking beer.

Cut Off(v): the bartender shut you down, no more drinks for you, you have been cut off

Cut the Rug(v): to dance

Cutting Shapes(adj): slang, dancing well, looking good on the dance floor.

Damages(n): the cost, the bill, how much money you owe.

Dance(v): CAUTION: can mean to move rhythmically to music, or to fight.

Dead Soldier: an empty beer bottle. SEE: Soldier and Wounded Soldier

Designated Driver(n): Someone who stays sober to drive, leaving others to indulge in drink.

Deuce(n): slang, table of two

Diddly, Diddly Squat, Diddly Shit(n): slang, nothing, zero, zilch, none. e.g."That prick that drank all the expensive Scotch left us diddly for a tip."

Digits(n): slang, numbers, usually phone number or your bill or tab at a bar.

Dine and Dash(n): Chew and Screw, Walk Out, this is when someone orders eats and/or drinks and leaves without paying their bill. An arrest able offense, some places your more liable to be beaten then prosecuted.

Dionysus: Greek God of Wine and Barley. 3 January SEE: Bacchus

Distillation(n): a process to purify or separate a substance by heating.

Dive(n): A lower class drinking establishment. Could be warm and friendly or full of trouble.

Dog Breath(n): slang, after a full night of drinking and smoking, you wake up with dog breath.

Doggie Bag(n): packed up leftovers from a restaurant.

Dough(n): money

Down Low(adj): slang, for hush hush, covert, mums the word.

Down Time(n): military, time off, a break from work.

Down with(adj): slang to comprehend or be in agreement, sympathetic, liking to participate. e.g. "There is a major party in Southie tonight, I'm heading there know, are you down with that?"

Draw(n): the used bank, cash register draw.

Dressed for Drinks, D. for D.(adj): when a female is dressed hotly or suggestively.

Drizunk(adj): slang, drunk as in urban drunk

Droddle, Drottle(n): slang, the contents of a glass after it has been abandoned.

D.U.I., D.W.I. (n,acronym): Driving Under the Influence, Driving While Intoxicated. These are criminal charges you can face if you drink and drive.

Eighty Six, 86, 86'ed(adj): all out of a product, there is no more, can refer to a customer who was thrown out or ejected from establishment.

Effervescent(adj): carbonated, with bubbles. A drink with carbon dioxide added or occurring naturally. Soda, beer, and champagne are all carbonated.

Enophile or Oenophile(n): One with a great love for wine. A connoisseur of wine

Eye Opener(n): A heavy drinkers first drink of the day

Faced, Shit Faced(adj): drunk

Faded(adj): slang, drunk as in gradual lose of brilliance, vitality, or consciousness.

Fag(n): CAUTION:American: derogatory slang for homosexual. 2. English: Slang means cigarette.

Fermentation(n): a chemical reaction were fungi(yeast) produces alcohol from a sitting starch(sugar)

Fin(n): Five dollar $5 American note, can also mean $500.

Fire It(v): means start cooking it, kitchen term used amongst cooks, and wait staff.

Fizzage(adj): slang, carbonation. e.g."This cola is flat, no fizzage at all."

Flea(n): slang, a bad tipper.

Floaties(n): slang, foreign matter that shouldn't be, but is floating in a drink. SEE: Goobies

Flow(n): slang, money, cash, funds. e.g., "I'd love to stay and do 12oz curls with you all night, but I gots no flow."

Fly(adj): pretty, handsome, hot, fashionable, cool, hip. "This joint is awesome -- fly drinks, fly music, fly girls -- you're going to have to drag me out of here."

Four Top (n): slang, table of four

Freddy: a pint of beer, more specifically a Heineken. Freddy Heineken d.5 Jan 2002

Free Pour(v): to pour a drink without a measuring device, measuring by eye and memory.

Free Zone(n): slang, the time starting from when a girl starts getting drinks bought for her by strangers until it stops usually measured in years. Zone of time her looks will get drinks bought for her.

Freshie, Fresh One(n): slang, a new drink, another drink.

Front(v): 1. Slang to put on an act, faking, pretending. 2. Slang, to give out without compensation usually with a promise to payback in the future.

Front of the House(n): refers to the part of a restaurant that a customer sees. The bar area, dining rooms, host/hostess station. SEE: Back of the House.

Fubar: Fouled Up Beyond All Recognition or Repair(adj): e.g. Waitress: "What happen to that sirlion for my six top?" Cook: "I burned it. It was fubar."

G(n): a grand. American $1000. Also slang for girl or guy. e.g. "Yo, G. Is walking around with two Gs in his pocket."

Gassed(adj): drunk as in filled up, or poisoned with.

Gig(n): slang, job, prearranged get together, particularly musical. e.g., "The boys got a gig tonight. They are opening for Morphine at the Middle East."

Giggle Juice, Giggle Water: Liquor any alcoholic beverage.

Gin Mill(n): slang, a bar usually working class or blue collar.

Glass Someone(v): To hit with a bottle, or drink glass. e.g. "I shut that bitch off and she tried to glass me."

Gone(adj): very drunk, as in beyond hope, or ruined.

Goobies(n): slang, foreign matter that shouldn't be but is floating in a drink. SEE: Floaties.

Greenbacks(n): paper money, American

Grill Monkey(n): slang, a low paid griller of food, usually in a fast food restaurant. SEE: Counter Monkey.

Grinder aka Hoagie, Sub, Submarine, Hero, Torpedo, Poor Boy, Italian Sandwich, Sarney(n): (Slang) an elongated sandwich made by slicing a thin loaf of bread lengthwise.

Groove(v): slang, to dance(n) a pleasant niche

Ground Control(n): someone who remains sober or at least coherent and baby sits an indulger.

Hair of the Dog(n): refers to a drink taken to fight a hangover. SEE: Eye opener

Hammered(adj): slang, drunk. As in worked over by drink.

Happy Hour(n): A allotted time a bar runs drink and/or food specials.

Harmless(adj): slang, means make it decaf on that coffee, unleaded

Hat Stand(n): slang, someone who stands and doesn't move much. A wallflower.

Head: CAUTION 1.(n) boating term for rest room. 2. (v) Slang term for sexual activity. 3. (n) foam on top of a drink.

Hen Party(n): Women only party, usually a Bachelorette party. See Stag Party

Hob Nob(v): slang, to rub elbows, mingle, make the rounds. e.g., "I can tell by the stack of business cards in your hand and the lipstick marks on your cheek that you have been out hob nobbing."

Honey(n): slang, a person who you are sexually attracted to or just sweet on in general.

Honked(adj): drunk

Honky Tonk(adj,n): a dive, a less than reputable establishment.

Hooch(n): alcoholic drink, specifically illegally made alcoholic drink.

Hook Me Up(v): to give, to help out. e.g., "That bartender rocks, she made me the best Manhattan I've had in months, and slid me some inside info on the horse race. She hooked me up."

Hook Up(v): to get together with another person for a common purpose. Often used sexually.

Hopping(adj): slang, jumping, happening, rocking. e.g., "Where were you last night?. The cafe was hopping, you should have been there."

Hoopla(n): excitement, noisy celebration, jovial commotion.

Hophead(n): a beer afficianado

Hullabaloo(v,n): excitement, a loud party, a group commotion

Ice Cream Habit(adj): someone who indulges only occasionally.

In Check(adj): slang keep things right, the way they should be. e.g. "If I was not here to keep the staff in check this restaurant would have folded years ago."

In the Alley(adj): refers to a side dish, kitchen talk. e.g. "I need a chicken sandwich with guacamole and salsa in the alley."

In the Bag(adj): drunk, comes from either the paper bag your alcohol comes in or from captured or killed game goes in a bag.

In the House(adj): slang, present. To emphasize presence.

In The Weeds(adj,n): weeded, beyond busy, playing catch up. Hectic and unpleasant working climate.

Intoxicoligist(n): Bartender

Inventory(n), Taking Inventory(v): Liquor inventory is usually done weekly, monthly, or quarterly. Depending on the practices of each individual restaurant.

Jailbait(n): A person younger than the age of consent, a minor.

Jam(v): 1. slang(v),an impromptu music session. 2.(n) a singular song. 3. Slang(n), a problem or predicament.

Jammed(adj): slang, very busy. e.g. "My bar was jammed from the time I opened the door until we ran out of beer at 3 am."

Jamming(adj): pertaining to a bar. Very busy, non-stop work.

Java(n): slang coffee

Jive(v): slang, trivial conflict. e.g., "That freak friend of yours gives me jive after his forth bevvy every time" SEE: Static

Joe, Cup of Joe(n): slang for coffee

John(n): Men's room, toilet, lavatory, lav, can, bathroom, privy, head.

St. John of God: Patron Saint of Alcoholics, Alcoholism, booksellers, publishers, firefighters and nurses. Feast day is 8 March.

Joint(n): slang, can either mean an eating and/or drinking establishment, or a marijuana cigarette

Jug Bug(n): slang, for fruit flies, they tend to get into sweet liqueur bottles.

Juice(n): 1. Respect, power, influence. 2. Steroids 3. Fruit Juice

Juiced(adj): drunk, as in juiced up.

Jump On the Grenade(v): This is when you distract an undesirable friend of someone your buddy is interested in by ANY means possible, so that they might have a chance to get better acquainted. Also SEE "Take One For the Team" "Nightclub Kamikaze"

K(n): $1000. American

Kegger, Keg Party(n): a party with a keg of beer to drink.

Killer(adj): awesome, pretty cool. e.g., "You need to taste this drink George made up. It's killer."

Knackered(adj): beat, exhausted

Knock Boots(v): slang, to get close and face to face with.

Knock Off(adj): a fake, a copy, a cheaper item. e.g., "Some bars pour knock off Amaretto."

Lace(v): term used to add something extra to a drink. e.g., "Would you please lace my coffee with Sambuca?"

La La Land((n): a state of drunkenness. A different plane.

Lambasted(adj): slang, drunk, to be beat thrashed or whipped by drink.

Large(n): slang $1000. One thousand, American. e.g. "I have 6 large in my pocket that says you can't make it to the border in under a half hour."

Last Call(n): Your last chance for the bartender to get you anything. The night is coming to an end. When the bartender says it is over, It is over.

Lavatory: Bathroom. rest room,

St. Lawrence: Patron Saint of Cooks, Chefs, Restaurateurs, Students, Wine Makers, and Brewers. Feast Day is 10 August.

Lettuce(n): paper money, American SEE: Cabbage

Liquored Up(adj): drunk

Lip(v): slang verbal abuse.

Lit(adj): drunk

Loaded(adj): drunk

Loly Water(n): (Australian) soda, pop, tonic, soft drink

Loo(n): Bathroom, rest room, privy, head.

Looped(adj): slang, drunk.as in knocked stupid by drink, loopy

Lounge Lizard(n): one who frequents chic or trendy establishments. Can also be a womanizer

Lush(n): someone who drinks a lot, someone who indulges in drink.

Mad (adj): slang, means extremely, very, many, large. e.g. "That honey in red on the upper dance floor has mad moves. Look at her go."

Marry, Marrying the bottles(v): slang, to condense two or more bottles into less containers. It is an illegal, but common practice.

St. Martha: Patron Saint of Waitress, Waiters, travelers, maids and Innkeepers. Feast Day is 29 July.

MC, Master of Ceremonies(n): the man with the microphone 1. Rapper 2. A host of an event

Meat Market(n): A bar where people hook up or pick up each other on some regular basis.

M.I.A.: Missing in Action, or Missing in Alcohol

Mickey Finn(n): old slang, for a drink that has been drugged to incapacitate someone.

Mob Scene(adj): slang for an extremely busy bar, nightclub or establishment.

Mojo: a groove, or flow, to be synchronous with your environment. e.g., "That cook pumped out 170 covers all by himself, he really had his mojo on."

Money(a): slang, great, wanted, the best. e.g., "You are so money, you need to keep a baseball bat handy to keep the chicks off you."

St. Monica: Patron Saint of Alcoholics, Alcoholism, homemakers, disappointing children. Feast day is 27 August.

Mull(v): To crush, grind and mash.

Name your poison (phrase): What do you want to drink?

Nightclub Kamikazi (n): slang This is when you distract an undesirable friend of someone your girlfriend is interested in by ANY means possible, so that they might have a chance to get better acquainted. Also SEE: Take One For the Team and Jump on the Grenade

Nineteenth Hole, 19th Hole: slang, a bar, or clubhouse on or near the golf course.

Nip(n): a small bottled portion of a given beverage.

Niterie: slang, nightclub.

NFL(adj): No Frigging Lime. Used when ordering a drink. e.g., "I'll have a painfully dry tippy topshelf Vodka Martini with a twist and a Cuba Libre N.F.L. please."

No Dice: a refusal, no way

Nooner(n): a midday drink. CAUTION: can mean midday sex

Nursing a drink: drinking in a rather slow fashion. Keeping the drink alive.

Oenology or Enology(n): the science of wine and its production.

Off the Hook, Off the Hinges(adj): great, crazy or amazing, e.g., "When Donny and Jeff were working, that place was off the hook -- the body shots, the stripping waitress, the blazing, smoking room."

Oktoberfest(n): A yearly, two week German beer festival. It is the largest public festival in the world. Six million attend annually.

On A Leash(adj): kitchen slang, to go, food packed to go.

On The Fly(adj): kitchen slang. I need it right now, I need it yesterday, hurry hurry hurry.

On The House(adj): Slang for a complimentary offering. Usually for good customers, friends or V.I.P.s

On the Q.T.: quiet, don't broadcast, be discreet. e.g., "My girl will be showing up soon, could you cash out this tab, and start a new one, I'd like to keep it on the Q.T."

On The Rocks(adj): slang, on ice.

One For the Road(a): slang, one more drink before I leave. "Hey bartender, I'll have one for the road, and then cash me out please."

O.U.I.: Operating Under the Influence

Out of It (adj): slang, drunk as in out of the game, can't play, sidelined by drink.

Out of Order (adj): someone who is incapacitated by drink.

Out to Lunch (a): slang, crazy, gone mentally

OSHA: Occupational Safety and Health Administration

Packy, Package Store: a retail alcohol store.

Pasteurization: a preservative heat treatment.

Peet: to drink. From "A Clockwork Orange"

Perfect: a prefix to describe a drink made with equal amounts sweet and dry vermouth.

Phat (adj): slang, awesome, wicked nice, very excellent, attractive.

Pickled: drunk as in thoroughly marinated.

Pie Eyed: drunk to the point of eyes looking like slits or slices of pie.

Pissed: Caution: drunk (English), mad, angry (American)

Plastered: drunk, affected greatly

Ploughed, or plowed : drunk, as in plowed under

Polluted: drunk as in ruined by the consumption of alcohol.

Pop, Soda Pop: sweetened carbonated non-alcoholic drinks

Popped: slang, to get arrested. e.g., "I got popped for my third DWI, I'm looking at least at a six month bid, maybe thirty months."

Premium, Super Premium, Top Call: These are just designations of cost levels for booze used by corporate run establishments.

Prohibition: Prohibition of alcohol in the U.S. 1920-1933. The 18th Amendment stopped the consumption of alcohol, and the 21st Amendment repealed it.

Pub Crawl: Usually refers to a group of individuals drinking from establishment to establishment.They can be impromptu or organized events with guidelines.

Puma(n): slang, a young girl at a bar or gathering that is actively seeking affection. SEE: Cougar

Pushing Tin: slang, 1. drinking a lot of canned beer.

Raincheck: slang, to postpone until a later date. Perhaps in the future. A written entitlement for an out of stock item or reentry to a postponed sporting event.

R&R(n): military slang. Rest and Recreation or Relaxation

Rave(n): a nighttime, early morning dance happening, usually fueled by loud dance music, flashing lights and drugs.

Regulars(n): customers that frequent your establishment, they can be your regulars if they come in on only your shifts or house regulars if they come in at anytime.

RSVP: Respondez S'il Vous Plait (Lit. Please respond)

Roadie, Road Soda(n): a drink to go.

Roll(v): CAUTION: 1. means to leave, get going. 2. to be taken advantage of and robbed.

Rot Gut: refers to a cheap or below average straight drink, usually liquor or wine.

Rummy: slang, a habitual heavy drinker thought to be stupid.

SNAFU(acronym): military slang, Situation Normal, All Fucked Up

Sarnie(n): sandwich

Sauce(n): slang, alcoholic beverage

Sauced, On the Sauce(adj): drinking, drunk on the sauce

Sausage Party aka Sword Fight(n): hetro male slang, a party or establishment with way too many males and not nearly enough females.

Sawbuck: slang $10 American note.

Scalper(n): one who resells tickets privately, an illegal practice some places, price gouging for popular events. Sometimes selling counterfeit tickets

Schmooze, Shmooze: to chat, or converse, in a manner to make connections or gain.

Scoff(v): to eat with a fast manner. e.g., "I'm lucky to be able Scoff a meatball on a three minute break at this bartending gig."

Sea Monster(n): slang, a really really drunk girl that is incoherent and will not leave you alone.

Sediment(n): a natural and common collection of particles at the bottom of a wine bottle.

See A Man About a Horse(v): slang, you'll have to excuse me.

Seedy(adj): tired, worn-out, poor, shabby, low brow, morally degraded.

Service Bar: This is where the wait staff gets there drinks for their tables. Can be separate from main bar or one in the same.

Shark, Pool Shark(n): a very capable player, One who can kick most every ones ass at pool.

Shellacked(adj): drunk, having a good coat of alcohol applied

Shenanigans(n): slang, light-hearted foolish behavior, Hijinx, Tom Foolery, mischievousness.

Shimmy, Shimmie(v): slang, dance. e.g., "Enough with the martinis let's shimmy"

Shindig(n): slang, a large noisy festive party with dancing

Shit-Faced(adj): drunk to the point of not being able to represent oneself.

Shoot the Breeze, Shit, Bull(v): slang, to pass time talking

Short-Changed: This is when the person who is making the monetary transaction gives the payer less money than is due by mistake or on purpose.

Shotgun, Shotgunning a Beer(v): to drink in an extremely swift manner.

Sideways(adj): drunk, to the point of losing balance, or even incapacitation.

Skanking (n): slang, dancing to Reggae or Ska music

Sketchy(adj): slang, suspiciuos, perhaps dangerous. e.g.,"That sketchy dude that comes in Friday afternoons and guzzles drafts and tips like a Canadian, asked Gina out yesterday, she laughed in his face."

Skip Out, Chew and Screw, Dine and Dash, Walk Out: this is when someone orders eats and/or drinks and leaves without paying their bill. An arrest able offense, some places your more liable to be beaten then prosecuted.

Skulled(adj): drunk, to the point of empty headedness

Slammed(adj): very busy, "My bar gets slammed every night the B's are at the Fleet Center"

Slammin'(adj): slang, very attractive, hot, nice, blazing, smoking, on fire.

Smashed(adj): drunk, as in drunk and unrepairable

Snarf, Splurt(v): slang, if you snork your drink and it comes out your nose.

Snork(v): to accidentally inhale your drink up into your nasal cavities.

Soak(v): to overcharge, fleece, rob, rip-off.

Soiree(n): a evening gathering/party

Soldier(n): a full beer bottle, SEE: Dead Soldier and Wounded Soldier.

Soup to Nuts: slang, for everything. A multiple course meal used to start with Soup and end with Nuts, with a lot of stuff in between. Better than just the Treatment, but equal to the Works. SEE: the Treatment, the Works

Soused(adj): drunk, as in being wet from being plunged into beverage.

Spanked(adj): This is a term used to describe what happened to you, after a very busy night bartending. e.g., "I got spanked hard this evening."

Speakeasy(n): slang, illegal drinking establishment during prohibition.

Speed Rack(n): Metal troths usually made of stainless steel that hold bottles, usually strategically placed and filled with the most used cocktail ingredients.

Spent(adj): drunk, tired, or done

Spotters(n): hired people sent in to establishment under the guise of customers to spy on the help, Usually reporting back to the owners, management at a later date.

Spuckie AKA Grinder, Hoagie, Sub, Submarine, Hero, Torpedo, Poor Boy, Italian Sandwich,Sarney: Slang, an elongated sandwich made by slicing a thin loaf of bread lengthwise

Spun(adj): drunk, as in dizzy drunk

Stag Party(n): Men only party, usually a bachelor party, with or without female entertainment. SEE Hen Party.

Static(n): slang, unwanted or undesirable feedback from someone.

Stewed(adj): drunk, as if marinated and cooking in beverage.

Stiff(n): hated drunk that doesn't tip.

Stoked(a): excited, psyched. e.g., "I was so stoked that you showed. I didn't know what to do with half an open keg of stout."

Stoned(adj): drunk, or under thje influence of marijuana

Stoinkered(adj): slang, hung over, feeling haggard

Super Size(adv): tall drink, big drink

Swilly(adj): drunk and unattractive due to inebriation

Syrup(n): a street or house party drink served in a baby bottle. Containing liquor, over the counter drugs, and candy.

Tab(n): slang, the check, bill, damages, what is owed.

Tag and Release(v): slang, the practice of meeting, flirting with prospective love/sex interests and and stopping short of physical contact.

Tailgate Party(n): a party centered around a social, musical, or sporting event where the partying is done by or with vehicles.

Take One For the Team(v): this is when you distract the friend of a person your buddy is interested in so they might have a chance of getting better acquainted. Also SEE Jump On the Grenade, and Nightclub Kamikaze

Talent(n): slang, goodlooking girls, or guys e.g., "Hold on guys It looks like some fresh talent is entering our watering hole."

Tanked(adj): drunk as in the person is holding their drink like a water tank.

Tap: (adj) draft as in beer. CAUTION:(v) slang, sexual intercourse

Tapped(adj): out of money, no more flow.

Tapping(v): the act of tapping two glasses together, which makes the holders of both glasses drink. It is poor manners not to put glass to mouth after tapping. SEE: Clinking:

Taste(n): 1/4 oz of a bottled liquor or liqueur poured into a short glass. Usually given to a good customer at no charge. Otherwise not given out. Draft beer tastes are usually given out, 2oz at a time to help a customer choose a beer.

Tart Fuel:(n) slang, young ladies drink. Usually rather sweet. SEE: Bitch Fuel

Tear(as in ripping)(v): slang, a binge, a prolonged drunken binge

Teetotaler(n): nondrinker, one who practices abstinence from alcohol.

Ten(adj): slang, for a perfect score in a specimen rating. Could be a drink, a dish, a person.

Tenderloin(n): a tender cut of meat which runs down the back of the animal's spinal column. This is where your Filet Mignon and your Chateaubriand comes from.

Tie One On(v): slang, get drunk, taken from early times where people tied drinking cups around their neck.

Tight(adj): 1. describes a person who doesn't tip well 2. someone you are pretty close to.

Tip, Tipping (Income): See page 12

Tipple(n): a single serving of drink. e.g., "Would either of you young ladies like a tipple?"

Tired(adj): describes a played scene, nothing happening, lame.

Toast: 1. (v)a verbally expressed wish or observation shared amongst peers, agreed upon or excepted by all present by drinking at the same time 2.(adj): inoperable, dead, no good

Toasted: (adj) 1. past tense of toast 2. drunk

Top Off: (v) to fill the glass or freshen the drink.

Top Shelf: (adj) Refers to the best or finest liquor or liqueur. Which are kept on the top shelf of many establishments.

Toss Cookies: (v) to upchuck

Train Wreck:(n) a drunk who has been badly beaten up, multiple injuries.

Trashed(adj): drunk as in made useless or worthless by drink.

Treatment, the(n): slang, the manner a guest is usually treated. Every establishment has a basic procedure. Greet the guest/customer, offer seating to dine, a beverage if there is a wait. Perhaps an offer to sit and play cards/dominos, then a massage. The Treatment can vary greatly. SEE: the Works.

Trip The Light Fantastic (v): to dance

Trolling(v): slang, to be out there, to lure a man or women who would be looking for a person to dance with, flirt with, have a drink with.

Turn Over, Help(n): one of the best ways to judge management/owners of Restaurant/Pubs/Night Clubs/Bars is there employee turn over rate. If a majority of the help don't leave. You can assume people are making money, and the work conditions are tolerable.

Turn Over, Tables(n): Wait staff are usually given sections to work, 2-8 tables. Every time a party leaves and a new party comes, is a turn over. Turning over tables is crucial to wait staffs income.

Tweak:(v)1. to manipulate for the betterment. e.g., Good chefs are always tweaking recipes. (adj) 2. To be charged with energy, good or bad. e.g., I'm tweaking of this third espresso.

Twisted(adj): drunk as in not right, not straight

Two-Fisted(adj): slang, someone who drinks two drinks at a time.

Under the Table(adj): drunk as in on the floor drunk.

Underground(n): counterculture, alternative resistance, socially deviant. "I know this underground club that serves absinthe and laced brownies. By 4 am, everybody is naked."

Verbal Diarrhea (n): slang, to talk on and on incessantly

Vibrations, Vibes(n): unspoken instinctive feelings. e.g. "Those girls were throwing some crazy vibes, I can't put my finger on it, something is up."

Vinyl(n): a gramophone record. SEE: Wax

Walk Out(n): Dine and Dash, Chew and Screw, this is when someone orders eats and/or drinks and leaves without paying their bill. An arrestable offense, some places your more liable to be beaten then prosecuted.

Walking Papers(n): slang, Pink slip, notice of dismissal. termination of employment

Wasabi(n): green Japanese horseradish

Wasted(adj): drunk as in ruined

Watering Hole(n): a place to get a drink, usually a bar or pub.

Wax(n): slang, a gramophone record. SEE: Vinyl

Weeded(n): in the weeds, beyond busy, playing catch up. Often happens to wait staff when two or more parties are seated at the same time (people who seat parties are supposed to stagger or spread the parties around so as not to weed the wait staff, and to spread the wealth.) Weeding also happens because a place is short staffed and they keep seating people even though they are over their heads in customers. A single person can weed a server by making requests one after another and monopolizing the servers time instead of asking for everything at once. This is a very hated customer.

Weeper(n): slang, a wine bottle with a leaky cork. Usually caused by a cork that has shrunk. This doesn't mean the contents have spoiled, but they very well might have.

Weisenheimer(n): slang, an obnoxious know it all SEE: Wise Ass

Well(adj): This refers to generic spirit that is used in a basic drink. If someone orders a gin and tonic, and doesn't care what kind of gin is used. They get this kind of gin. It could a good gin, but most likely it will be a inexpensive brand. It varies from establishment to establishment. SEE: Call

Wet Goods(n): slang, packaged intoxicating beverages.

White Lightning(n): bootleg corn whiskey.

Windbag(n): a person who does not exhaust from talking incessantly. SEE: Verbal Diarrhea

Wingding(n): a jubulent party, gathering or festival.

Wing Dings(n): usually chicken wings frozen and processed.

Wiped Out(adj): drunk and/or exhausted.

Wise Ass(n): slang, someone who thinks their banter is clever or humorous, even though others may not. SEE: Weisenheimer:

Word(adj): used to give validity, viewed as truthful, or used to show agreement with. e.g. , "Word, this is the best party I've ever been to,...have you seen my pants?"

Working Girl(n): prostitute.

Works, the(n): slang, like the Treatment except better, an elevated experience. the Whole Nine Yards. With a hot dog it would mean mustard, onions, relish, catsup, chili maybe cheese.

Wounded Soldier(n): a beer that has been opened, partially consumed and left to die. SEE: Soldier, and Dead Soldier.

Wrecked(adj): drunk, ruined by drink.

X: 1. symbol for kiss. 2. slang for ecstasy (MDMA). 3. Roman numeral 10. 4. A generic symbol for alcohol or poison.

Zigzagged(adj): under the influence, stoned

Zonked (adj): drunk, drugged, high

INDEX OF DRINKS LISTED BY INGREDIENT

Use this index to find all of the drinks listed in this book by the ingredients they contain. The ingredients and the drinks are listed in alphabetical order.

DRINKS LISTED IN ALPHABETICAL ORDER

● AMARETTO

Abby Road
Abby Road Coffee
ABC
Alabama Slammer
Alien Orgasm
Almond Enjoy
Almond Kiss
Almond Mocha Coffee
Amaretto Sour
Amarist
Amber Martini
Ambush Coffee
Amore-Ade
August Moon
B-54
B-57
Bahama Mama
Bali Hai
Banana Frost
Beach Hut Madness
Bend Me Over
Biscuit Neck
Black Magic
Black Tie
Bocci Ball
Boss
Boston Iced Tea
Boston Massacre
Boston Tea Party
Brain Eraser
Brandy Almond Mocha
Broken Down Golf Cart
Brown Squirrel
Bubble Gum
Bungee Jumper
Burnt Almond
Butternut Coffee
Café Amore
Café Magic
Café Venitzio
Café Zurich
Capital Punishment
Casino Coffee
Cherry Life-Savor
Chocolate Covered Cherry
Chocolate Squirrel
Christian's Coffee
Climax
Coca Lady
Cocoetto
Cool Aid
Crazy Broad
Cuddler
Cupid's Potion
Day at the Beach
DC-10
Death Row
Depth Chamber
Dingo
Dizzy Buddha
Dr. P.
Dr. P. From Hell
Dreamsicle
Earthquake
East Side
Electric Cool Aid
F Me Hard
F.E.D.X.
Fern Gully
Ferrari
57 Chevy
57 T-Bird
Filby
Firery Kiss
Flaming Lamborghini
Foxy Lady
French Connection
French Connection Coffee
Full Moon
Gandy Dancer
Gilligan's Isle
Godchild
Godfather
Godmother
Golden Bull
Golden Torpedo
Grand Alliance
Grand Am
Gumdrop
Gummy Bear
Hammerhead
Hard On
Hardcore
Hasta La Vista Baby
Hawaiian
Hawaiian Punched

Heart Throb
Hello Nurse
Homecoming
Hooter
Hurricane
Hussie
Irish Headlock
Italian Coffee
Italian Delight
Italian Iced Coffee
Italian Sunrise
International Incident
Jackalope
Jaeger Monster
Jamaican Mule
Killer Cool Aid
King's Cup
Komaniwanalaya
Lake Street Lemonade
Latin Lover
Laser Beam
Lethal Injection
Liquid Pants Remover
Lobotomy
Long Sloe Comfortable
    Fuzzy Screw Against
    The Wall With A Kiss
Long Sloe Comfortable
    Fuzzy Screw Against
    The Wall with Satin
    Pillows The Hard Way
Lounge Lizard
Moon Chaser
Marlon Brando
Midway Rat
Milano Coffee
Mongolian Mother
Monkey Wrench
Moonbeam
Mooseberry
Moresque Cafe
Mountain Red Punch
Muff Diver
Multiple Orgasm
Mutual Orgasm
Nasty Girl
Naughty Hula Pie
Nutcracker
Nuts and Cream
Nutty Colada
Old Groaner
Old Groaner's Wife
Orgasm
Otter Rocker
Outrigger
Palm Beacher
Panda Bear
Panty Burner
Paranoia
Peckerhead
Persuader
Pimlico Special
Pineapple Bomb
Pineapple Bomber
Pink Almond
Pink Paradise
Pontiac
Pop-sicle
Prison Bitch
Pterodactyl
Purple Alaskan
Purple Matador
Rasbaretta
Red Death
Red Ruby
Rigor Mortis
Ritz Fizz
Roasted Toasted Almond
Roman Candle
Roman Holiday
Roman Iced Tea
Roman Riot
Roxanne
Royal Canadian
Royal Sheet Coffee
Russian Quaalude
S. O. M. F.
St. Petersburg Sundae
School Bus
Screaming O.
Seventh Avenue
Seventh Heaven
Sex At My House
Sex In The Woods
Shaved Bush
Sicilian Coffee
Sicilian Kiss
Silver Cloud

Skinny Dipping
Sour Apple
Southern Beach
Spanish Fly
Sperm Whale At The Barn
Spilt Milk
Starbursts
Stiletto
Sweet Tart
T-Bird
Tangerine
Tarantula
Tawney Russian
Tennessee Mud
Terminator
Test-Tube Babe
Toasted Almond
Toasted Marshmallow
Top Gun
Tree Climber
Trophy Room Coffee
Tropical Moon
Turtle Dove
Ugly Ducking
Universal
Vanity Fair
Verona
Watermelon
Wedding Cake
Wench
White Swan
Wiki Waki Woo
Wildebeest
Xanadu
Yokohama Mama
Zonker

● ANISETTE

Angel Face
Apple Margarita
Apple Pie
Apres Ski
Bartman
Candy Apple
Café Zurich
Corpse Reviver
Cranapple Cooler
Deauville
Depth Bomb
Diki Diki
Dream Cocktail
Earthquake
Good And Plent-e
Grand Apple
Green Apple
Gumdrop
Happy Jack
Hole In One
Honeymoon
Hot Apple Pie
Hot Apple Toddy
Ichbien
Indian Summer
Jack Rose
Jack-In-The-Box
Jelly Bean
Johnnie
Joll-e Rancher
Ladies
Liberty Cocktail
Licorice Stick
Luger
Marconi Wireless
Mexican Jumping Bean
Mike Tyson
Moonlight
Mule's Hind Leg
Narragansett
Oom Paul
Pernod Frappe
Princess Mary's Pride
Prince's Smile
Royal Smile
Saturn's Ring
Saucy Sue
Savoy Tango
Sex At The Beach
Shanghai
Sharky Punch
Sledgehammer
Snowball
Special Rough
Star
Steeple Jack
Stone Fence

Third Rail
Tic Tac
Torpedo
Tulip
Turf
Tuxedo
Vanity Fair
Very Joll-e Rancher
Warday's Cocktail
Week On The Beach
Wembly
Xalapa Punch
Zazarac

● **APRICOT BRANDY**

Angel Face
Antiquan Kiss
Apricot Frappe
Apricot Sour
Babbie's Special
Black Witch
Boomer
Bossa Nova
Boston Cocktail
Charlie Chaplin
Cruise Control
Darb
Devil's Tail
Elmer Fudpucker
Father Sherman
Favorite
Festival
Fifth Avenue
Flamingo
Frankenjack
Golden Dawn
Golden Daze
Gradeal Special
Hop Toad
Hotel California
Indian Summer Hummer
Iron Cross
Jamaican Delight
Jump Up And Kiss Me
Katinka
KGB
Kyoto
Layer Cake
Leave It To Me
Lebanese Coffee
Life Line
Mai Tai
Mother Sherman
Mule's Hind Leg
Naked Lady
Nevins
Pancho Villa
Paradise
Pendennis Club
Pink Whiskers
Porch Climber
Prince's Smile
Professor and Maryann
Red Cloud
Sand Flea
Saucy Sue
Self-Starter
Sex in a Bubblegum Factory
Sour Ball
Spring Action
Spring Fling
Summer Share
Tempter
Thanksgiving
Toxic Waste
Trade Wind
Tulip
Uzi
Valencia
Wembly
Wharf Rat
Why Not
Yellow Parrot
Zombie

● **BANANA LIQUEUR**

Alien Urine Sample
Antiquan Smile
Assassin
Atomic Waste
Baja Margarita
Banana Boat
Banana Cow
Banana Cream Pie
Banana Daiquiri
Banana Frost
Banana Popsicle
Banana Sandwich
Banana Sombrero
Banana Strawberry Daiquiri
Banshee
Bazooka
Bazooka Joe
Beam Me Up Scotti
Black Barracuda
Blow Job
Boardwalk Breezer
Bubble Gum
C-Drop
Café Foster
Capri
Caribbean Champagne
Caribbean Dream Coffee
Caribbean Screw
Chiquita
Chocolate Banana Freeze
Climax
Coco Loco
Copenhagen Pousse Café
Creamsicle
Dirty Banana
Dirty Monkey
Dizzy Buddha
Empire State Slammer
Fidel's Martini
Fru Fru
Funky Monkey
Fuzzy Monkey
Gandy Dancer
Gilligan
Goombay Smash
Gorilla
Hairy Ape
Hawaiian Eye
Head Room
Jamaican Ten Speed
Jolly Roger
June Bug
Jungle Jim
Key West
Kiwi
L. A. Sunrise
La Jolla
Lady Luck
Leisure Suit
Life-Saver
Limbo
Love Potion
Maxim's
Meister-Bation
Metal Helmet
Miami Vice
Mick
Monkey Juice
Moonpie
Nasty Girl
New York Slammer
Nightingale
The "O" Martini
Pacific Pacifier
Pain In The Ass
Paint Ball
Pilot Boat
Piñata
Port Pelican
Pussy Galore
Red Devil
Red Tide
Rock Lobster
Rose Hall
Rum Runner
Ruptured Duck
Russian Banana
Russian Roulette
Screaming Banshee
Screaming Yellow Monkey
Seduction
Sex In A Bubblegum Factory
Sex On A Boat
Sex On The Lake
Simply Exquisite
Slippery Dick
Stealth
Stiletto
Surf Rat
Surf's Up
Swedish B J
Three Story House On Fire
Toasted Marshmallow
Top Banana
Traffic Light
Tropical Breeze
Tropical Gold

Vegas B J
Velvet Kiss
Visitor
Volga Cooler
Wadkins Glen
West Indian Frappe
West Indies Yellowbird
Wet Dream
When Hell Freezes Over
Yellow Bird
Yellow Russian
Yellow Submarine

● **BEER**

110 in the Shade
American Snakebite
Aphrodisiac
BMW
Beer Buster
Bloody Bastard
Bloody Brew
Boilermaker
Channel
Cincinnati
Colorado Bulldog
Depth Chamber
Depth Charge
Diesel
Dog's Nose
Double Trouble
Dr. P.
Dr. P. From Hell
Glam Trash
Graveyard
Hop Skip And Go Naked
Hot Dog
Hussie)
Ice Cream Float
Irish Car Bomb
Irish Russian
Mexican Boilermaker
Mojo
NASCAR Dad
Pink Hotel
Purple Nasty
Red Beer
Red Beer Shooter
Red Eye
Reverend
Run Skip And Go Naked
School Bus
Scumbucket
Shante' Gaf
Sizzler
Skip And Go Naked
Snakebite
Strip and Go Naked
Tiger Balls
Train Wreck
Velvet Gaf
Yorsh
Vulcan Mind Probe
Yard Of Flannel

● **BENEDICTINE**

Aunt Jemima
B & B
C & B
Energizer
Frisco Sour
Froupe
Golden Caddie With
   Double Bumpers
Golden Dream
   (With Double Bumpers)
Gypsy
Highland Coffee
Honeymoon
Honolulu
Hoot Man
Kentucky Colonel
Marmalade
Monk's Coffee
Monte Carlo
Mule's Hind Leg
Oh, Henry
Pleasure Dome
Preakness
Queen Elizabeth Wine
Quiet Nun
Rainbow
Savoy Hotel
Twin Hills
Widow's Dream
Widow's Kiss

DRINKS LISTED IN ALPHABETICAL ORDER

● BLACKBERRY BRANDY

Atomic Bodyslam
Black Barracuda
Black Dog
Black Eye
Black Martini
Black Prince
Black Sheep
Blackjack
Bongo
Cadiz
Canadian Blackberry Fizz
Channel
Chi-Chi
Cough Drop
Cramp Reliever
Cure-All
Dark Eyes
Elvira
Good And Plent-e
Houndstooth
Jelly Bean
Life-Saver
Miami Vice
Mule Skinner
Naked Lady
Pain In The Ass
Pixie Stick
Poop Deck
Purple Jesus
Rattlesnake
Roman Holiday
Rum Runner
S. O. M. F.
Scorpion
Tequila Sunset
Tidal Wave
Toxic Jellybean
Tropical Storm
Warsaw

● BLACK RASPBERRY LIQUEUR

Abby Road
Abby Road Coffee
Belmont
Black Forest
Black Martini
Black Rose
Black Sheep
Blackberry Swizzle
Bon Bon
Broken Heart
Brut And Bogs
Busted Rubber
Café Marseilles
Candy Ass
Cham Cran Cham
Chocolate Mess
Coca
Cosmopolitan (South Beach)
Cranium Meltdown
Doctor's Elixir
Dry Arroyo
Dusty Road
Dusty Rose
Ecstacy
Elysee Palace
F.E.D.X.
Firecracker
Frankenberry
French Dream
French Martini
French Summer
Frosted Romance
Frutti Nueb
Gloomlifter
Go Girl
Grape Crush
Grape Nehi
Greatful D.
Happy Feller
Hollywood
Hollywood Martini
Hot Raspberry Dream
Hot Tub
Indian Summer Hummer
Jelly Doughnut
Key West
Killer Cool Aid
Killer Whale
Kir Royale
Lady Boy Martini
Lady Luck

Left Bank
Little Purple Men
Lobotomy
Macaroon
Mad Max
Madtown Milkshake
Menage a Trois
Midnight Dream
Mocha Berry Frappe
Nervous Breakdown
Nuts And Berries
Oral Sex on the Beach
Panabraitor
Paris Match
Parrot Head
Passionate Screw
Peanut Butter and Jelly
Pez
Phantom
Pink Missile
Purple Alaskan
Purple Dream
Purple Haze
Purple Hooter
Purple Matador
Purple Nipple
Purple Rain
Purple Russian
Raspberry Beret
Raspberry Cheesecake
Raspberry Colada
Raspberry Gimlet
Raspberry Kiss
Raspberry Lime Rickey
Raspberry Margarita
Raspberry Sherbet
Raspberry Smash
Raspberry Soda
Raspberry Sombrero
Raspberry Torte
Restoration
Riviera
Royal Spritzer
S. O. S.
Saint Moritz
Scarlet Letter
Sex at My House
Sex In A Hot Tub
Sex In The Parking Lot
Sex On The Beach
Sex On The Sidewalk
Simply Bonkers
Sour Grapes
Sovereign Coffee
Squid Ink
Sweet Tart
38th Parallel Coffee
Tie Me To The Bedpost Baby
Vampire
Wadkins Glen
Wet Crotch
Wet Dream
White Ghost
Y. I.
Zipper Head
Zuma Buma

● BLACK SAMBUCA

Creature From The Black Lagoon
Dark Secret
Dragoon
Eclipse
Phantom
Slippery Black Nipple
Squid Ink
Starlight

● BLUE CURACAO

Adios Mother
Agent 99
Air Gunner
Alaskan Iced Tea
Alien Urine Sample
Anti-Freeze
Assassin
Battered Bruised And Bleeding
Bazooka Joe
Big Kahuna
Bimini Ice-T
Blue Bayou
Blue Bijou
Blue Canary
Blue Daiquiri

Blue Hawaiian
Blue Kamikaze
Blue Lady
Blue Lemonade
Blue Margarita
Blue Meanie
Blue Shark
Blue Tail Fly
Blue Valium
Catalina Martini
Champagne Super Nova
Chi-Chi
Code Blue
Daisy Cutter
Deep Sea
Desert Sunrise
Dickie Toecheese
Dirty Ashtray
Flaming Blue J.
Flaming Lamborghini
Fourth of July
Frostbite
Gangrene
Go-Go Juice
Grape Sour Ball
Green Eyes
Green Goblin
Head Wind
Hog Snort
Kentucky Swampwater
L.A.P.D.
Leprechaun
Malibu Wave
Moody Blue
Moon Racker
Neon
Ninja Turtle
Nuclear Kamikaze
Oil Slick
Out Of The Blue
Paint Ball
Pan Galactic Gargle Blaster
Polish Butterfly
Pousse Café
Purple Armadillo
Purple Flirt
Purple Helmeted Warrior
Purple Margarita
Purple Rain
Purple Thunder
Ritz Fizz
Save The Planet
Screaming Blue Messiah
Sea Monkeys
Sex In A Bubblegum Factory
Sex On The Beach
Sex On The Pool Table
Shark Attack
Skylab Fallout
Smurf P.
Stars And Stripes
Swamp Water
Terminator
Tiny Bowl
Vulcan Blood
Wall Street Lizard
Whale's Tail
Windex
Yale Cocktail

● BOURBON

American Sour
Armored Car
Bambini Aruba
Beehive
Bible Belt
Biscuit Neck
Black Dog
Black-Eyed Susan
Black Sabbath
Bomb
Bootlegger
Boss
Bourbon Manhattan
Bourbon Old Fashion
Bourbon Satin
Brass Knuckles
Brighton Punch
Buffalo Sweat
Capital Punishment
Caribou Screw
Cherry Tart
Cowboy
Deathwish
Fedora
Fiji Fizz
Forester

● **BRANDY**

DRINKS LISTED IN ALPHABETICAL ORDER

● BRANDY (continued)
Widow's Kiss
Winter Frost
Yokohama Mama
Zamboanga Hummer
Zoom

● BUTTERSCOTCH SCHNAPPS
Buttafinger
Butter Ball
Butter Shot
Butternut Coffee
Carrot Cake
Gingerbread Man
Jamaican Bobsled
Neutron Bomb
Oatmeal Cookie
Sugar Daddy

● CHAMPAGNE
Ambrosia
April In Paris
Bali Hai
Barracuda
Bellini
Bird Of Paradise
Black Prince
Black Velvet
Bronco Cocktail
Brut And Bogs
Caribbean Champagne
Cham Cran Cham
Champagne Cocktail
Champagne Super Nova
Chicago
Concorde
Death In The Afternoon
Diamond Fizz
Dry Arroyo
Elysee Palace
F.E.D.X.
Flirtini
Flying Madras
French Lift
French 95
French 75
Frozen Bikini
Glenda
Golf Ball
Golden Showers
Grand Alliance
Grand Mimosa
Hawaiian Mimosa
Honeydew
Hot Tub
King's Peg
Kir Royale
Lobotomy
London Special
Mad Max
Maxim's
Maxim's A Londres
Me So Horney
Melon Royale
Metropolis Martini
Mimosa
Mind Obliterator
Moscow Mimosa
Nantucket Red
Nelson's Blood
One Seventy
Pan Galactic Gargle Blaster
Peach Mimosa
Pink Slip
Poinsettia
Prince Of Wales
Ritz Fizz
Ritz Pick-Me-Up
Royal Screw
Royal Spritzer
Ruddy Mimosa
Russian Nights
Santiago
Scarlet Letter
Sex In A Hot Tub
Sparks
Thug Passion
Tintoretto
Torque Wrench
Typhoon
Valencia
Velvet Gaf
Volcano

● CHARTREUSE (YELLOW and GREEN)
Dead Rat
Death Mint
Flaming Lamborghini
French Dragon
Golden Dragon
Green Dragon
Green Lizard
Jewel
Jewel of the Nile
Lollipop
Mexican Missile
Pago Pago
Pousse Café
Rainbow
Razorback Hogcaller
Save The Planet
Screamer
Screaming Dead Nazi
    Digging for Gold
Swampwater
Tipperary
Warday's Cocktail
Whiskey Daisy
Widow's Kiss
Xanthia
Yellow Parrot

● CHERRY BRANDY
Ankle Breaker
Black Cat
Blood And Sand
Busted Cherry
Candy Cane
Casablanca
Cherry Blossom
Cherry Cola
Cherry Cola From Hell
Cherry Hooker
Cherry Pie
Cherry Screw
Cherry Swizzle
Cherry Tart
Chinese Cocktail
Chocolate Covered Cherry
Copenhagen Pousse Café
Double-D
Dr. Funk
Electric Cool Aid
Fantasio
Fiji Fizz
Fireball
Forester
Harlem Cocktail
Hawaiian Nights
Hit-It
Honolulu
Hudson Bay
Hunter's Cocktail
Huntress Cocktail
Ideal
Kiss
Kiss In The Dark
Ladyfinger
Lawhill
Major Tom
Merry Widow
Mojo
Mon Cherie
Mountain Red Punch
Night Train
Nightmare
No Problem
Orange Oasis
Pancho Villa
Polynesian
Porch Climber
Purple Bunny
San Juan Sunset
Singapore Sling
Summer Solstice Sunrise
Swedish Lullaby
Tiki Bowl
Top Hat
Tropical Storm
Vanderbilt
Vanity Fair
Vodka Sling
Volga Boatman
Wedding Belle
Weep No More
White Rose
Xanthia
Yale Cocktail

● CINNAMON SCHNAPPS
Afterburner
Apple Pie
Beverly Hill
Canadian Cider
Candy Apple
Carrot Cake
Fahrenheit 5
Fireball
Firestorm
Firery Kiss
French Tickler
Gingerbread Man
Glam Trash
Gold Rush
Hot Tamale
Hot Young Lady
Jawbreaker
Left Hook
Liquid Crack
911
Oatmeal Cookie
Peach Cobbler
Pumpkin Pie
Red Death
Sugar Daddy
Three Wise Men
24 Karat Nightmare
When Hell Freezes Over

● COFFEE
Abby Road Coffee
After Five Coffee
Almond Mocha Coffee
Ambush Coffee
Aspen Coffee
Aspen Hummer
B-52 Coffee
Bailey's And Coffee
Bavarian Coffee
BBC
Black Rose
Brandy Almond Mocha
Brazilian Coffee
Butt Munch
Butternut Coffee
Café Amore
Café Barbados
Café Diablo
Café Foster
Café Gates
Café Grande
Café Italia
Café Magic
Café Marseilles
Café Orleans
Café Reggae
Café Royale
Café Theatre
Café Venitzio
Café Zurich
Cajun Coffee
Calypso Coffee
Canadian Coffee
Caribbean Dream Coffee
Casino Coffee
Charro
Christian's Coffee
Coffee Alexander
Curley's Delight Coffee
Dublin Coffee
Dutch Coffee
Espresso Martini
French Coffee
French Connection Coffee
French Iced Coffee
Gaelic Coffee
Greek Coffee
Gun Runner Coffee
Heather Coffee
Highland Coffee
Irish Coffee
Irish Coffee Royale
Irish Gentleman
Irish Iced Coffee
Irish Maiden Coffee
Irish Mocha Cooler
Irish Money Coffee
Irish Monk Coffee
Irish Skipper Coffee
Israeli Coffee
Italian Coffee
Italian Iced Coffee
Jamaican Coffee
Kahlua Coffee

236

COFFEE LIQUEUR
(continued)Swedish BJ
Sweet Cream
T. K. O.
Tam-O-Shanter
Teacher's Pet
Three Kings
Tijuana Bulldog
Toasted Almond
Toblerone
Tootsie
Toreador
Toronto Orgy
Toxic Waste
Trappist Frappe
Trappist Monk
Tumbleweed
Uzi
Velvet Dress
Voo Doo
Wandering Minstrel
Watergate Coffee
Whisper
White Bull
White Jamaican
White Knight
White Roman
White Russian
White Spaniard
Xavier
Y 2 K
Yellow Bird
Yellow Jacket

COGNAC
ABC
Amber Cloud
B-57
Between The Sheets
C & B
Café Amore
Café Diablo
Café Royale
Café Zurich
Capoeira
Concorde
Copenhagen Pousse Café
Corpse Reviver
Eggnog
Elysee Palace
Fat Cat
Fish House Punch
French Coffee
French Connection
French Connection Coffee
French Dragon
French Iced Coffee
French 75
G & C
Godchild
Grand Apple
Jizz
Keoke Cappuccino
Keoke Coffee
King Kong Coffee
King's Peg
Lallah Rookh
Paris Match
Petrifier
Phoebe Snow
Picon Fizz
Pierre Collins
Port In A Storm
Rainbow
Ritz Pick-Me-Up
Royal Screw
Russian Roulette
Sledgehammer
Spanish Coffee
Spanish Iced Coffee
Three Kinds
Thug Passion
Thumper
Tiger's Milk
Tom And Jerry
Unpublished Hemingway
Vatican Coffee
Wagon Wheel
Waterbury Cocktail

CRÉME de CASSIS
Diesel
El Diablo
Gin Cassis

Italian Sunrise
Kir
Mississippi Mule
Ostend Fizz
Parisian
Pink Panther
Purple Heather
Purple Nasty
Red Dwarf
Vermouth Cassis

CRÉME de CACAO
Alexander
Alexander The Great
Almond Enjoy
Almond Mocha Coffee
Angel Kiss
Angel Wing
Angel's Tit
Apres Ski
Aunt Jemima
Avalanche
Banshee
Barbary Coast
Beetle Juice
Black Cow
Blow Job
Blue Tail Fly
Boston Massacre
Bourbon Satin
Brandy Alexander
Brown Cow
Brown Squirrel
Bushwacker
Café Gates
Café Grande
Café Reggae
Café Theatre
Calypso Coffee
Candy Ass
Capoeira
Capri
Caribbean Dream Coffee
Casino Coffee
Chocolate Banana Freeze
Chocolate Corvette
Chocolate Covered Banana
Chocolate Covered Cherry
Chocolate Martini
Chocolate Mess
Chocolate Rattlesnake
Chocolate Squirrel
Climax
Coffee Alexander
Coney Island
Cookies And Cream
Cream Dream
Cricket
Dirty Banana
Everglades Special
Eye-Opener
Fantasio
Fat Cat
Festival
Fifth Avenue
57 Chevy
Flying Grasshopper
Fox River
Foxy Lady
Frost Bite
Frosted Romance
Fruitbar
Fudgesicle
Funky Monkey
G-String
Gaelic Coffee
Golden Caddie
Golden Caddie
  With Double Bumpers
Golden Gate
Gorilla
Grand Occasion
Grasshopper
Gumdrop
H. Bar
Hot Peppermint Patty
Hot Raspberry Dream
Houndstooth
Irish Angel
Irish Mocha Cooler
Irish Monkey Coffee
Irish Skipper Coffee
Jackalope
Jaguar Milk
Jelly Fish
Jockey Club

Keoke Cappuccino
Keoke Coffee
Kremlin Cocktail
Kretchma
Layer Cake
Liebfraumilch
Love Potion #9
Maxim
Mint Chocolate Chip
  Ice Cream
Mocha Berry Frappe
Mocha Mint
Mon Cherie
Moonbeam
Mound Bar
Mudslide
Muff Diver
Mutual Orgasm
Naughty Hula Pie
Night Train
Ninja
Ninotchka
Nocturnal
Oil Slick
OR-E-OH Cookie
Orgasm
Pago Pago
Panama
Panda Bear
Peach Alexander
Peach Velvet
Pearl Necklace
Peppermint Pattie
Peppermint Patty
Pimlico Special
Pink Squirrel
Pleasure Dome
Pousse Café
Purple Bunny
Purple Dream
Pussy Galore
Quaalude
Rainbow
Raspberry Kiss
Rocky Road
Russian
Russian Banana
Russian Bear
Russian Pussy
Savannah
Savoy Hotel
Screaming Banshee
Screaming Yellow Monkey
Sex On The Lake
Shaved Bush
Silver Cloud
Skull Cracker
Snicker
Snowball
South Fork Coffee
Sovereign Coffee
Sperm Whale At the Bank
Strawberry Blonde
Surf's Up
Swedish Bear
Tennessee Tea
38th Parallel Coffee
Tia Tia
Tootsie
Toreador
Tree Climber
Tropical Cocktail
Tumbleweed
Velvet hammer
Vodka Grasshopper
Wedding Cake
Whippet
Whisper
White Cadillac
White Chocolate Martini
White Death
White Elephant
White Ghost
White Heart
White Out
White Witch
Wind Jammer
Winter Frost
Wolfhound
Xylophone
Yellow Bird

CRÉME de MENTHE
(WHITE AND GREEN)
After Eight

DRINKS LISTED IN ALPHABETICAL ORDER

● **GIN** *(continued)*

Cable Car
California Iced Tea
California Lemonade
Chain Lightning
Champagne Super Nova
Chaos
Chelsea Sidecar
Cherry Swizzle
Clam Digger
Code Blue
Damn-The-Weather
Darb
Darth Vader
Deep Sea
Diamond Fizz
Diamond Head
Diki Diki
Dirty Ashtray
Dirty Dog
Dirty Martini
Dirty Water Martini
Dog's Nose
Dry Martini
Dubonnet Cocktail
Dundee
Eclipse
Edith Day
Electric Lemonade
Emerald Forest
English Screwdriver
F Me Hard
Fallen Angel
Fare-Thee-Well
Favorite
Fifty Fifty
Filby
Fine and Dandy
Flamingo
Florida
Florida Iced Tea
Fog Cutter
Fog Horn
Frankenjack
French 95
French 75
Fubar
Gale Force
Gentle Ben
Gibson
Gimlet
Gin And Tonic
Gin Buck
Gin Cassis
Gin Daisy
Gin Fizz
Gin Rickey
Go-Go Juice
Golden Dawn
Golden Daze
Golden Fizz
Golden Gate
Golf
Gradeal Special
Grand Passion
Grass Skirt
Graveyard
Great Secret
Greatful D.
Greyhound
Harlem Cocktail
Hawaiian
Hoffman House
Honolulu
Hop-Skip-And-Go-Naked
Hudson Bay
Hurricane
Iceball
Ideal
Income Tax
Irish Tea
James Bond Martini
Jewel
Jewel Of The Nile
Jiggy Cockfighter
Jockey Club
Judge, Jr.
Jupiter Cocktail
KGB
Killer Cool Aid
Kiss In The Dark
Knickerbocker
Kyoto
Lady Boy Martini
Ladyfinger
Lasky
Leap Frog

Leap Year
Leave It To Me
'Lectric Lemonade
Left-Handed Screwdriver
Lillet Nouyax
Lime Rickey
Little Devil
London Stinger
Lone Tree
Long Beach Iced Tea
Long Comfortable Screw
  Against The Wall
Long Sloe Comfortable
  Fuzzy Screw Against
  Wall With A Kiss
Long Sloe Comfortable
  Fuzzy Screw Against
  The Wall With Satin
  Pillows The Hard Way
Long Island Iced Tea
Long Island Lemonade
Los Angeles Iced Tea
Loudspeaker
Mac Daddy
Maiden's Blush
Maiden's Prayer
Mainbrace
Martinez
Martini
Maurice
Maxim
Melon Cocktail
Miami Ice
Mich
Mississippi Mule
Moll
Mongolian Mother
Montmarte
Montreal Club Bouncer
Mount Fuji
Mule's Hind Leg
Naked Lady
Napoleon
Negroni
Newbury
Nightmare
Nineteen
Nineteen-Pick-Me-Up
Ninja Turtle
Nuclear Meltdown
Oliver Twist
Opera
Orange Blossom
Orange Buck
Orange Oasis
Orsini
Ozark Mountain Punch
Paisley Martini
Pall Mall
Pancho Villa
Paradise
Parisian
Park Avenue
Peach Blow Fizz
Pegu Club
Pendennis Club
Petrifier
Pineapple Martini
Pink Gin
Pink Lady
Pink Panther
Pink Pussycat
Pink Rose
Pixie Stick
Plaid
Plaza
Pollyanna
Polo
Prince's Smile
Princeton
Punt E Mes Negroni
Purple Helmeted Warrior
Purple Rain
Queen
Queen Elizabeth
R. Royce
Racquet Club
Radioactive Iced Tea
Ramos Fizz
Raspberry Lime Rickey
Red Baron
Red Cloud
Red Lion
Red Snapper
Renaissance Cocktail
Rendezvous
Roman Iced Tea

Rosy Dawn
Royal Gin Fizz
Royal Smile
Run, Skip and Go Naked
Russian
Saketini
Salty Dog
San Sebastian
Savannah
Scorpion
Self-Starter
Silver Fizz
Silver King
Singapore Sling
Skip and Go Naked
Skylab Fallout
Sledgehammer
Sloe Ball
Snowball
Snowblower
Southern Bride
Sphinx
Spy's Demise
Stock Market Zoo
Straight Law
Strega Sour
Stump Buster
Sweet Patootie
Tangerine
Tango
Terminal Iced Tea
Thanksgiving
Third Degree
Three Mile Island
Three Stripes
Tidal Wave
Tidbit
Tom Collins
Toxic Shock
Tropical Storm
Turf
Twin Six
Typhoon
Ulanda
Union Jack
Union League
Velvet Kiss
Verona
Vesper
Victor
Virgin
Vulcan
Vulcan Mind Probe
Waikiki Beachcomber
Wall Street Lizard
Warday's Cocktail
Wedding Belle
Wembly
White Baby
White Cargo
White Heat
White Lady
White Lily
White Out
White Rose
White Way
Why Not
Will Rogers
Xanthia
Yale Cocktail
Yellow Rattler
Zamboagna Hummer
Zanzibar
Zaza
Zoo

● **GIN** (Citrus)
Electric Lemonade

● **GIN** (LIME)
Albatross
Bimini Iced Tea
Bottom Line
Hop-Skip-and-Go-Naked
Lime Rickey (alcoholic)

● **GIN** (ORANGE)
Kyoto
Leap Year
Left-Handed Screwdriver
Naked Lady 2
Nightmare
Ninja Turtle

DRINKS LISTED IN ALPHABETICAL ORDER

• IRISH CREAM
(continued)

Colorado Bulldog
Concord
Cookie Monster
Cuddler
Curley's Delight Coffee
DC-10
Depth Chamber
Designer Jeans
Dragoon
Duck Fart
Dusty Road
Dusty Rose
Dying Nazi From Hell
E. T.
Energizer
Erie Canal
F-16
Face Eraser
Flaming Lamborghini
Freedom Fighter
French Dream
Fuzzy Navel with Lint
G. S. Cookie
Gaelic Coffee
Ghostbuster
Ginger Bread Man
Gingerbread Man
Good Fortune
Gun Runner Coffee
Gun Runner Iced Coffee
Hard Nipple
Head Room
Homecoming
Hot Young Lady
International Incident
IRA Cocktail
Irish Car Bomb
Irish Cow
Irish Cream Soda
Irish Flag
Irish Gentleman
Irish Headlock
Irish Maiden Coffee
Irish Maiden Ice Coffee
Irish Maria
Irish Monk
Irish Monk Coffee
Irish Rover
Irish Skipper Coffee
J. Off
Jamaican Ten Speed
Jelly Doughnut
Jelly Fish
Jezebel
Jizz
Kingston Coffee
Left Bank
Lewinsky
Licorice Whip
Loch Ness Monster
Lube Job
M-16
Madtown Milkshake
Maggot
Menage a Trois
Millionaire's Coffee
Mint Chocolate Chip Ice
    Cream
Monk Slide
Monkey Juice
Mound Bar
Mudslide
Mudsling
Multiple Orgasm
Nesi
Neutron Bomb
Nutcracker
Nuts and Berries
Nutty Bitch
Nutty Chinaman
Nutty Irish Cooler
Nutty Irishman
Nutty Irishman Coffee
Oatmeal Cookie
Orgasm
Paint Ball
Peaches and Cream
Peanut Butter and Jelly
Pickled Brain
Point
Pond Scum
Pumpkin Pie
Purple Nipple
Pussy Galore
Quick F

Rattlesnake
Russian Quaalude
S. O. M. F.
Screaming O.
Scumbucket
Seduction
727
747
Shillelagh
Slippery Black Nipple
Slippery Dick
Slippery Nipple
Smooth Operator
Snicker
Snicker At The Bar
Sno Cap
Snowcap
Southern Belle
Sperm Whale
Sperm Whale At The Bank
Spilt Milk
Spring Thaw
Stealth
Stuffed Toilet
Sugar Daddy
Sunken Treasure
Swedish B J
Sweet Cream
Tarantula
Test-Tube Babe
38th Parallel Coffee
Toblerone
Toronto Orgy
Trappist Frappe
Trappist Monk
Under The Covers
Vibrator
Voo Doo
Warm Creamy Bush
Wet Crotch

• IRISH MIST
Bungee Jumper
Bushwacker
Dublin Coffee
Erie Canal
I For An I
Irish Brogue
Irish Fix
Irish Skipper Coffee
Niagara Falls
Shillelagh

• IRISH WHISKEY
Ambush Coffee
Belfast Bomber
Bloody Molly
Boston Massacre
Bushwacker
Commando Fix
Curley's Delight Coffee
Dublin Coffee
Erie Canal
Fairchild
Freedom Fighter
Gaelic Coffee
Gun Runner Coffee
Gun Runner Iced Coffee
I For An I
IRA Cocktail
Irish Angel
Irish Brogue
Irish Buck
Irish Car Bomb
Irish Coffee
Irish Coffee Royale
Irish Fix
Irish Gentleman
Irish Headlock
Irish Iced Coffee
Irish Maiden Coffee
Irish Maiden Iced Coffee
Irish Manhattan
Irish Mocha Cooler
Irish Money Coffee
Irish Monk
Irish Monk Coffee
Irish Rover
Irish Spring
Kerry Cooler
Leprechaun
Nutty Irishman
Nutty Irishman Coffee
Paddy Cocktail

Shillelagh
Tam-O-Shanter
Tipperary
Warm Creamy Bush
Wild Irish Rose
Wolfhound

• JÄGERMEISTER
Afterburner
Assisted Suicide
Beverly Hill
Bee Sting
Black Sabbath
Buckhead Root Beer
Camshaft
Chupacabra
Crazy Red Head
Creature From The Black
    Lagoon
D. O. A.
Darth Vader
Dead Nazi
Dr. J.
Dying Nazi From Hell
Four Horsemen
Freddy Kruger
German Leg Spreader
Haitian Assistant
Hand Release
Jaeger Monster
Jaeger Salsa
Jaegerita
Killer Bee
Kung Fu
Left Hook
Lewinsky
Liquid Asphalt
Liquid Coca
Liquid Crack
Loch Ness Monster
Meister-Bation
Mike Tyson
Nesi
Oatmeal Cookie
Oil Slick
Pitbull On Crack
Sand Blaster
Screaming Dead Nazi
    Digging For Gold
Screaming Nazi
Skid Mark
Stumbling F.
Surfer Taking A Trip
Three Wise Men
Toxic Jellybean
Vegas B J
Wildebeest
Yellow Jacket

• MELON LIQUEUR
Albatross
Alien Orgasm
Alien Secretion
Alien Urine Sample
Anti-Freeze
Artificial Intelligence
Atomic Waste
Bart Simpson
Battered Bruised And
    Bleeding
Bleacher Creature
Broken Down Golf Cart
Bubble Gum
Cheap Shades
Clouds Over Scotland
Cool Aid
Crocodile Cooler
Dizzy Buddha
E. T.
Electric Cool Aid
Electric Watermelon
F Me Hard
Fairchild
Frutti Nueb
Gangrene
Ghostbuster
Green Apple
Green Demon
Green Goddess
Green Kamikaze
Green Mary
Green Mountain Melon
Green Russian
Green Sneakers

DRINKS LISTED IN ALPHABETICAL ORDER

• MILK OR CREAM
(continued)

Russian Quaalude
Saint Moritz
St. Petersburg Sundae
Scooby Snack
Scotch Bird
Screaming Banshee
Screaming O.
Screaming Yellow Monkey
Separator
Seventh Avenue
Sex At The Beach
Sex Machine
Sexy
Shaved Bush
Silver Cloud
Silver Fizz
Simply Bonkers
Simply Exquisite
Smith and Kerns
Smooth Operator
Snicker
Snowball
Snowberry
Sombrero
Southern Bulldog
Spilt Milk
Spooge
Stars And Stripes
Steel Helmet
Sugar Daddy
Surf's Up
Swedish Bear
Tam-O-Shanter
Teacher's Pet
Tiger's Milk
Tijuana Bulldog
Toasted Almond
Toasted Marshmallow
Toblerone
Tom and Jerry
Toreador
Toxic Waste
Trade Wind
Tree Climber
Tumbleweed
Ugly Duckling
Velvet Dress
Velvet Glove
Velvet Hammer
Velvet Kiss
Virgin Banana Orange
    Frostie
Vodka Grasshopper
Wedding Cake
West Indies Yellow Bird
Wet Dream
White Baby
White Bull
White Cadillac
White Elephant
White Ghost
White Heart
White Jamaican
White Knight
White Lady
White Mink
White Out
White Roman
White Russian
White Spaniard
White Swan
White Trash
Widow's Dream
Wind Jammer
Wolfhound
Xavier
Yellow Bird
Yellow Russian
Yellow Snow
Zipper
Zoom

• ORANGE LIQUEUR
A-Bomb
ABC
Agent 99
Agent O.
Alice In Wonderland
Amarist
Appendectomy
April In Paris
Aspen Coffee
Assassin
B-12

B-52
B-52 Coffee
B-52 On A Mission
B-52 With A Mexican
    Tailgunner
B-52 With Bombay Doors
B-53
Barbarella
Bearhug
Bikini Line
Bitch Fight
Black Lady
Blood Orange Martini
Blow Job
Boston Iced Tea
Boston Massacre
Boston Sidecar
Boston Tea Party
Brazilian Coffee
Bronco Cocktail
Busted Rubber
Butterball
Café Diablo
Café Gates
Café Grande
Captain Mariner
Cara Sposa
Cartel Buster
Chaos
Chiquita
Chocolate Martini
Cruise Control
Curley's Delight Coffee
Dallas Alice
Dangerous Liaisons
Death Row
Deep Throat
Devil's Punch
Dirty Harry
Dream Cocktail
Energizer
Express
Fascination
57 Chevy
57 T-Bird
Fine And Dandy
French Coffee
French Connection
French Tickler
Full Moon
Glenda
Golden Margarita
Goldrush
Grand Am
Grand Apple
Grand Mimosa
Grand Occasion
G-Spot
Haitian Assistant
Happy Feller
High Roller
Hoopla
Hot Sex
Irish Flag
Jaegerita
Johnnie
King Kong Coffee
Kowloon
La Bamba
Laser Beam
Leap Year
Lemon Drop Martini
Lollipop
Loudspeaker
Malibu Monsoon
Maxim's
Maxim's A Londres
Meadowlark Lemon
Millionaire's Coffee
Mimosa
Monk's Coffee
Monte Cristo Coffee
Mooseberry
Multiple Orgasm
Napoleon
Northern Lights
Orange Margarita
Pacific Pacifier
Parisian Frappe
Passionate Point
Pernod Flip
Platinum Blonde
Prince Igor
Queen Elizabeth
Quaalude
Red Lion
Ritz Pick-Me-Up
Riviera

Royale Gin Fizz
S. O. B.
Sanctuary
Sand Flea
Sangria Blanca
Screaming Orgasm
727
Sex
Sex At The Beach
Sex Machine
Sex With The Bartender
Sexy
Shogun
Shot In The Dark
Simply Exquisite
Smooth Driver
Spanish Coffee
Spanish Dynamite
Star Wars
Stealth
Suffragette City
Sun Stroke
Sweet Tart
T-Bird
Tahitian Itch
Tampa Bay Smoothie
Tangerine
Terminal Iced Tea
Top Hat
Toronto Orgy
Trade Wind
Ulanda
Unpublished Hemingway
Visitor
Vodka Grand Marnier
Watergate Coffee
West Indian Frappe
Xanadu
Xavier
Zipper

• PEACH SCHNAPPS
Alien Orgasm
Alien Urine Sample
Antiquan Kiss
Atomic Waste
Bermuda Triangle
Bitch Fight
Brain
Bumble Bee
Catalina Margarita
Cerebral Hemorrhage
Cheap Shades
Comfortable Fuzzy Screw
    Against The Wall
Cool Aid
Corkscrew
Crazy Red Head
Cuban Peach
Dirty Silk Panties
F Me Hard
Fish House Punch
Forbidden Jungle
French Martini
Frozen Bikini
Fru Fru
Fruitbar
Fuzzy Astronaut
Fuzzy Bastard
Fuzzy Fruit
Fuzzy Guppie
Fuzzy Kamikaze
Fuzzy Monkey
Fuzzy Navel
Fuzzy Navel with Lint
Georgia Peach
Ghostbuster
Glass Tower
Glenda
Golden Daze
Hairy Navel
Halley's Comfort
Hand Job
Harmony
Hasta La Vista, Baby
Heatwave
Hollywood
Irish Spring
Joll-e Rancher
Juicy Fruit
June Bug
Killer Cool Aid
Leprechaun
Long Sloe Comfortable
    Fuzzy Screw Against the
    Wall with a Kiss

244

RUM (COCONUT)
(continued)

Luau
Malibu Driver
Malibu Sunset
Miami Vice
Moon Chaser
Mound Bar
Mount Vesuvius
Nasty Girl
Ninja Turtle
No Problem
"O" Martini
P. M. S.
Paranoia
Passionate Screw
Peach Colada
Pink Paradise
Pink Slip
Radioactive Iced Tea
Rock Lobster
Sex With The Bartender
Scooby Snack
Shipwreck
Ski Lift
Sledgehammer
South Pacific
Spooge
Spring Break
Starboard Tack
Strawberry Colada
Stumbling Islander
Suntan
Surf Rat
Surf's Up
Surfer Taking A Trip
Terminator
Tidal Wave
Tie Me to The Bedpost
Trip To The Beach
Tropical Screw
Top Gun
Tropical Hooter
Tropical Moon
Tropical Storm
Vacation
Vulcan
Vulcan Mind Probe
Wanna Probe Ya
Y. I.

RUM (DARK)

American Graffiti
Antiquan Kiss
Antiquan Smile
Apple Cooler
Artificial Intelligence
Atomic Bodyslam
Bahama Mama
Banana Cow
Beacon Hill Blizzard
Big Bamboo
Black Barracuda
Black Iced Tea
Black Sabbath
Black Stripe
Black Witch
Blizzard
Boardwalk Breezer
Bob Marley
Bomb
Bos'n Mate
Bull's Milk
Bushwacker
Café Barbados
Café Foster
Café Reggae
Caribbean Dream Coffee
Caribbean Madras
Caribbean Screw With
    A Sunburn
Chocolate Corvette
Chinese Cocktail
Coco Loco
Colorado MF
Dark and Stormy
Deep Dark Secret
Designer Jeans
Dizzy Buddha
Don Juan
Dr. Funk
Dutch Pirate
East Indian
Eggnog

Fascination
Fedora
Fern Gully
Fiji Fizz
Fireside
Fish House Punch
Florida Punch
.44 Magnum
Fu Manchu
Fuzzy Bastard
Goombay Smash
Guana Grabber
Head Wind
Heatwave
Henry Morgan's Grog
High Jamaican Wind
Hot Buttered Rum
Hot Toddy
Hummer
Hurricane
Indian Summer Hummer
Jackalope
Jade
Jamaica Cooler
Jamaica Me Crazy
Jamaican
Jamaican Bobsled
Jamaican Dust
Jamaican Milk Shake
Jamaican Mule
Jamaican Pine
Jamaican Wind
Jolly Roger
Jump Me
Jump Starter
Jump Up And Kiss Me
Kentucky Cooler
Key Largo
Key West
Kingston Coffee
Komaniwanalaya
L. A. Sunrise
Lethal Injection
Liquid Pants Remover
Lounge Lizard
Mai Tai
Menage a Trois
Midnight Cowboy
Modern
Monga Monga
Monkey Juice
Monkey Special
Montego Bay Coffee
Moon Chaser
Moose Milk
Nasty Girl
Navy Grog
Nutty Jamaican
Oil Slick
Open Grave
Otter Rocker
Outrigger
Palm Beacher
Panama
Paradise Punch
Parisian Blonde
Parisian Frappe
Pilot Boat
Pink Veranda
Planter's Punch
Port Antonio
Rainforest
Ranch Valencia Rum Punch
Red Tide
Robson
Rock Lobster
Rockaway Beach
Roman Rasta Coffee
Root Beer Float
Rose Hall
Rum-Laced Cider
Rum Runner
Rumball
Santiago
Scorpion
Sevilla
Shanghai
Shark Bite
Shark's Tooth
Sledgehammer
South Pacific
Spleef
Stonewall
Stumbling Islander
Stupid Cube
Suffering Bastard
Tai Tia

Tiger's Milk
Tiki Bowl
Tokyo Express
Tom and Jerry
Top Gun
Trophy Room Coffee
Tropical Moon
Tropical Storm
Turtle Dove
Voo Doo
Wind Jammer
Wombat
Zombie

RUM (LIGHT)

Adios Mother
Alaskan Iced Tea
American Graffiti
Antiquan Kiss
Apple Cooler
Artificial Intelligence
B. M. P.
Bacardi Cocktail
Bahama Mama
Bambini Aruba
Banana Colada
Banana Daiquiri
Banana Split
Banana Strawberry Daiquiri
Barbary Coast
Bartman
Bat Bite
Bee's Knees
Between The Sheets
Bimini Ice-T
Black Jamaican
Black Martini
Black Rose
Blast
Bleacher Creature
Bloody Marisela
Blue Bijou
Blue Hawaiian
Bog Fog
Bongo
Bos'n Mate
Boston Cooler
Boston Iced Tea
Boston Sidecar
Box Car
Brass Monkey
Buckaroo
Bulldog
California Cool Aid
California Iced Tea
Calypso Coffee
Caribbean Champagne
Caribbean Screw With
    A Sunburn
Casablanca
Catfish
Cherry Blossom
Chi-Chi
Chocolate Colada
Coca Lady
Coco Loco
Coconut Cream Frappe
Code Blue
Coffee Colada
Coral Sea
Corkscrew
Creamsicle
Cricket
Cruise Control
Cuba Libra
Cuban Peach
Daiquiri
Deep Dark Secret
Devil's Tail
Dirty Ashtray
Dr. Funk
Dr. P.
East Side
El Salvador
Electric Watermelon
Everglade's Special
Eye-Opener
Fair and Warmer
Fern Gully
57 Chevy
57 T-Bird
Flamingo
Flim Flam
Florida

DRINKS LISTED IN ALPHABETICAL ORDER

● **RUM** (ORANGE)
(continued)
Trade Wind
White Lion

● **RUM** (PINEAPPLE)
Outrigger
Pineapple Bomb
Pineapple Daiquiri
Pineapple Passion
Release Valve
Summer Solstice Sunrise

● **RUM** (RASPBERRY)
Raspberry Colada
Raspberry Daiquiri
Simply Bonkers

● **RUM** (SPICED)
Apple Cooler
Bad Attitude
Banging The Captain 3
 Ways On The Comforter
Barbados Punch
Barbary Coast
Bermuda Triangle
Bimini Iced Tea
Captain Mariner
Cream Soda
Dr. P.
Firecracker
Gangrene
Hammerhead
Latin Lover
Lethal Injection
Parrot Head
Pez
Pineapple Bomber
Rum-Laced Cider
Sex On A Boat
Starboard Tack
Stumbling Islander
Stupid Cube
Sunken Treasure
Surf Rat
Tidal Wave
Toxic Shock
Vacation
Wanna Probe Ya
Wench
Whale's Tail

● **RUM** (VANILLA)
Banana Split (frozen)
Creamsicle
Lallah Rookh
Night Train
Peach Cobbler
Shaved Bush
White Jamaican

● **SAMBUCA**
Agent 99
B-53
Barbarella
Beach Hut Madness
Bearhug
Café Diablo
Cancun
Fire-In-The-Hole
Flaming Lamborghini
Four Horsemen
Freddy Kruger
Glass Tower
Hammer
Head Banger
Ice Ball
Jelly Bean
La Mosca
Liquid Asphalt
Little Green Men
Little Purple Men
Mike Tyson
Moresque Cafe
Roman Candle
Roman Cappuccino
Roman Coffee
Roman Holiday
Roman Rasta Coffee

Roman Riot
Scumbucket
Shanghai
Silk Panties
Sledgehammer
Slippery Nipple
Snowball
Squid Ink
Tic Tac
Toxic Jellybean
Typhoon
Under The Covers
Via Veneto
Vulcan Mind Meld
White Cloud
White Heart
White Roman

● **SCOTCH**
Aggravation
Barbary Coast
Bit Of Honey
Black Tie
Black Watch
Blood and Sand
Bloody Josephine
Bomb
Dry Rob Roy
Dude
Dundee
Flying Scott
Gail Warning
Godfather
Heather Coffee
Highland Coffee
Highland Fling
Hoot Man
Hot Nail
Hot Scotch
Inverted Nail
Italian Stallion
Joe Collins
Jolly Roger
L. S. D.
London Sour
Mamie Taylor
Marlon Brando
Miami Beach
Mike Collins
Modern
Morning Glory
Paisley Martini
Polly's Special
Prince Edward
Purple Heather
Rob Roy
Rusty Nail
Rusty Nail Coffee
Scotch Collins
Scotch Sour
Scottish Coffee
Stone Fence
Teacher's Pet
Thistle
Three Wise Men
Whiskey Fix
White Cadillac
White Knight

● **SLOE GIN**
Alabama Slammer
American Graffiti
Black Hawk
Chaos
Charlie Chaplin
Death Row
Eclipse
Empire State Slammer
F Me Hard
Firecracker
Hawaiian Garden's Sling
Hawaiian Punched
Johnnie
Kiss The Boys Goodbye
Lady Boy Martini
Lemonade (Modern)
Long Sloe Comfortable
 Fuzzy Screw Against
 The Wall With A Kiss

Long Sloe Comfortable
 Fuzzy Screw Against
 The Wall with Satin
 Pillows The Hard Way
Love
McClelland
Mexican Flag
Mich
Modern
Moll
Monogolian Mother
Moulin Rouge
New York Slammer
Panty Dropper
Pink Floyd
Purple Margarita
Red Death
Red Devil
Ruby Fizz
San Francisco
Savoy Tango
Singapore Sling
Sloe Ball
Sloe Boat To China
Sloe Brandy
Sloe Comfortable Fuzzy
 Screw Against The Wall
Sloe Comfortable Mexican
 Screw Against The Wall
Sloe Comfortable Screw
Sloe Comfortable Screw
 Against The Wall
Sloe Dog
Sloe Gin Fizz
Sloe Poke
Sloe Screw
Sloe Tequila
Spats
Spring Action
Spy's Demise
Sweet Release
Tie Me To The Bedpost
 Baby
Traffic Light
Troika
Union Jack
Velvet Glove
Watermelon

● **SOUTHERN
 COMFORT**
Alabama Slammer
American Graffiti
Apple Polisher
Avalanche
Banging The Captain 3
 Ways On The Comforter
Bazooka
Bible Belt
Blood Clot
Bootlegger
Bubble Gum
Bucking Bronco
Coca
Comfortable Fuzzy Screw
 Against The Wall
Comfortable Screw
Cool Aid
Crankin' Wanker
Crazy Broad
Dingo
Dizzy Buddha
Double-D
Earthquake
Electric Cool Aid
57 Chevy
57 T-Bird
Flaming Blue J.
Gasoline
Golden Bull
Gorilla Fart
Green Meany
Gummy Bear
Halley's Comfort
Hammerhead
Harbor Lights
Hawaiian
Hawaiian Punched
Jelly Bean
Jezebel
Laser Beam
Lion Tamer
Liquid Pants Remover

248

DRINKS LISTED IN ALPHABETICAL ORDER

● TEQUILA (continued)
White Bull
Wiki Waki Woo
Xylophone
Zipper
Zoo

● TRIPLE SEC
Alabama
Alabama Slammer
Ambrosia
American Sour
Amore-Ade
August Moon
Balalaika
Barbados Punch
Bay City Bomber
Beachcomber
Betsy Ross
Between The Sheets
Bible Belt
Big Bamboo
Big Kahuna
Black Iced Tea
Bleacher Creature
Bos'n Mate
Boston Sidecar
Box Car
Brass Knuckles
Burnout Bitch
Cadiz
California Iced Tea
Cable Car
Canada Cocktail
Casablanca
Catfish
Chain Lightning
Chelsea Sidecar
Chicago
Chinese Cocktail
Chiquita
Climax
Commando Fix
Coral Sea
Cosmopolitan
Creamsicle
Crippler
Cruise Control
Cupid's Potion
Damn-The-Weather
Darth Vader
Deauville
Diablo
Diamond Head
Dr. Funk
Dream Cocktail
Drooling Passionate Lady
East India
East Indian
Electric Cool Aid
Electric Lemonade
Electric Watermelon
Eye-Opener
Fair And Warmer
Fare-Thee-Well
Fedora
Fine And Dandy
Flim Flam
Florida
Florida Iced Tea
Fog Cutter
.44 Magnum
Fox Trot
Frankenjack
Fu Manchu
Fuzzy Bastard
Glass Tower
Golden Dream
Golden Dream
   (With Double Bumpers)
Golden Margarita
Grass Skirt
Graveyard
Greatful D.
Green Sneakers
Hairy Bitch
Hardcore
Hari Kari
Hasta La Vista, Baby
Hawaiian
Hawaiian Margarita
Hawaiian Punched
Headrest
Hit-It
Honeymoon

Huntress Cocktail
Irish Tea
Jackarita
Jackhammer
Jade
Jay Walker
Johnnie
Kabuki
Kamikaze
Kentucky Orange Blossom
Killer Whale
Kyoto
Laser Beam
Leap Year
'Lectric Lemonade
Life Line
Life-Savor
Little Devil
London Sour
Long Beach Iced Tea
Long Island Iced Tea
Long Island Lemonade
Love Potion
Lynchburg Lemonade
Maiden's Blush
Maiden's Prayer
Mainbrace
Major Tom
Malibu Wave
Margarita
Martinez
McClelland
Menage a Trois
Metropolitan
Mexican Blackjack
Millionaire
Mimosa
Mississippi Mud
Mongolian Mother
Monmarte
Morning
Mount Vesuvius
Muscle Beach
Netherland
Nuclear Meltdown
Odd McIntre
Olympic
Orange Julius
Orange Krush
Orange Margarita
Oriental
Orgasm
Orsini
Pacific Pacifier
Paint Ball
Pan Galactic Gargle Blaster
Panabraitor
Panama Red
Parisian Blonde
Pernod Flip
Petrifier
Pink Caddie
Platinum Blonde
Polly's Special
Pop-Sicle
Prison Bitch
Pterodactyl
Purple Rain
Quickie
Quiet Nun
Radioactive Iced Tea
Ramos Fizz
Rattler
Rebel Yell
Red Death
Red Devil
Roman Iced Tea
Run, Skip And Go Naked
S. O. B.
S. O. M. F.
Samari
San Sebastian
Sangria
Santiago
Scotch Bird
Sherry Twist
Sidecar
Silver Spider
Singapore Sling
Sloppy Joe
Sloppy Joe's
Southern Belle
Southern Bride
Southern Maiden
Spanish Dynamite
Spring Fling
Stevie Ray Vaughan

Strawberry Margarita
Suffering Bastard
Sunburst
Sundowner
Sunspot
Sweet Patootie
Tango
Temptation
Texas Tea
Three Mile Island
Tiger's Tail
Tijuana Titty Tickler
Top Gun
Trois Rivieres
Tropical Storm
TTT
Ulanda
Upside Down Margarita
Velvet Dress
Velvet Hammer
Venetian Coffee
Venetian Frappe
Volga Cooler
Vulcan Mind Probe
W. W. II
Waikiki Beachcomber
Wet Crotch
Whip Cocktail
White Baby
White Cadillac
White Heat
White Lady
White Lily
White Mink
White Water
White Witch
Wiki Waki Woo
Wild Thing
Will Rogers
Wind City
Wind Surf
Xango
XYZ
Zamboanga Hummer
Zaza
Zipper
Zombie
Zonker

● TUACA
Café Italia
Hot Apple Pie
Il Magnífico
Lemon Frappe
Puccini
Stuffed Toilet
Thumper
Tiger's Milk
Tijuana Titty Tickler
Tuaca Cocktail

● VANDERMINT
Black Cow
Dutch Coffee
Dutch Pirate
Trophy Room Coffee
Wooden Shoe

● VODKA
A-Bomb
Adios Mother
Agent O.
Air Gunner
Alabama Slammer
Alaskan Iced Tea
Amber Martini
American Snakebite
Anna's Banana
Anti-Freeze
Apple Pie
Apple Martini
Asian Martini
Atomic Bodyslam
Atomic Waste
B-50
Bailey's Comet
Balalaika
Bambini Aruba
Banana Cream Pie
Banana Cream Pie Martini
Banana Popsicle
Banana Split

DRINKS LISTED IN ALPHABETICAL ORDER

●VODKA (continued)

Miami Ice
Miami Melon
Mick
Midnight Dream
Midnight Martini
Midnight Sun
Mind Eraser
Mind Obliterator
Minstrel Frappe
Mint Chocolate Chip Ice Cream
Mint Condition
Mo Fo
Mongolian Mother
Monkey Wrench
Moody Blue
Mooseberry
Moscow Mimosa
Moscow Mule
Mudslide
Mudsling
Multiple Orgasm
Muscle Beach
Mutual Orgasm
Naked Lady
Nantucket Breeze
Nervous Breakdown
Ninotchka
Nuclear Kamikaze
Nuclear Meltdown
Nut and Honey
Nutcracker
Nuts and Berries
Nutty Bitch
Nutty Russian
"O" Martini
Ocean View Special
Oil Slick
Oliver Twist
Open Grave
OR-E-OH Cookie
Oral Sex On The Beach
Orange Drop
Orange Freeze
Orange Julius
Orange Krush
Orgasm
Out Of The Blue
Oyster Shooter
Ozark Mountain Punch
P. M. S.
Pan Galactic Gargle Blaster
Panty Dropper
Passion Martini
Passionate Screw
Peach Breeze
Peach Buck
Peach Bulldog
Peach Martini
Pear Martini
Pearl Diver
Pearl Harbor
Pearl Necklace
Petrifier
Pickled Brain
Pile Driver
Pineapple Martini
Pink Floyd
Pink Hotel
Pink Lemonade
Pink Missile
Pink Pussycat
Pixie Stick
Polynesian
Pond Scum
Pop-Sicle
Prince Igor
Prison Bitch
Professor And Maryann
Provincetown
Pterodactyl
Puccini
Punt E Mes Negroni
Purple Haze
Purple Hooter
Purple Passion
Purple Rain
Purple Russian
Quaker City Cooler
Quaalude
R and V
Radioactive Iced Tea
Raspberry Beret
Raspberry Cheesecake
Raspberry Gimlet
Raspberry Lime Rickey

Raspberry Sherbet
Raspberry Smash
Raspberry Soda
Raspberry Torte
Rear Entry
Red Apple
Red Death
Red Devil
Red Eye
Red Panties
Red Russian
Red Silk Panties
Red Zipper
Release Valve
Rhode Island Iced Tea
Rigor Mortis
River Berry
Roasted Toasted Almond
Rocky Mountain Rootbeer
Rosy Dawn
Roman Iced Tea
Root Beer
Root Beer Float
Roxanne
Ruby Red
Russian
Russian Banana
Russian Bear
Russian Coffee
Russian Nights
Russian Pussy
Russian Quaalude
Russian Rose
Russian Roulette
Russian Sunrise
S. O. S.
St. Petersburg Sundae
Saketini
Salty Dog
Save The Planet
Scorpion
Screaming Banshee
Screaming O.
Screaming Yellow Monkey
Screwdriver
Screw-Up
Sea Breeze
727
Sewer Rat
Sex At The Beach
Sex In A Hot Tub
Sex In The Parking Lot
Sex In The Woods
Sex Machine
Sex On The Beach
Sex On The Beach In Winter
Sex On The Pool Table
Sex On The Sidewalk
Sex With The Bartender
Siberian
Silk Panties
Silk Shorts
Silken Veil
Silver Cloud
Silver Spider
Silverado
Sinner
Sizzler
Skinny Dipping
Skip And Go Naked
Skylab Fallout
Slim Jim
SlimeBall
Sloe Ball
Sloe Comfortable Fuzzy Screw Against The Wall
Sloe Comfortable Mexican Screw Against The Wall
Sloe Comfortable Screw
Sloe Comfortable Screw Against The Wall
Sloe Dog
Sloe Screw
Smooth Driver
Sno Cap
Snowberry
Sour Apple Martini
Sour Ball
Sour Grapes
Soviet Cocktail
Spring Fling
Spring Thaw
Spy's Demise
Star Wars
Starlight
Steel Helmet

Strawberry Cheesecake
Strawberry Shortcake
Strip And Go Naked
Stump Buster
Summer Share
Summer Solstice Sunrise
Sun Stroke
Sunburst
Swedish B J
Sweet Release
Sweet Tart
Swedish Bear
T-Bird
Tampa Bay Smoothie
Tangerine
Tawny Russian
Terminal Iced Tea
Texas Mary
Texas Tea
Three Mile Island
Thug Heaven
Tidal Wave
Tie Me To The Bedpost Baby
Tiny Bowl
To Hell You Ride
Top Banana
Top Gun
Toronto Orgy
Tovarich
Toxic Shock
Traffic Light
Transfusion
Trip To the Beach
Troika
Tropical Storm
Tuaca Cocktail
Twister
Under The Covers
Universal
Vampire
Very Joll-e Rancher
Vesper
Visitor
Vodka Collins
Vodka Cooler
Vodka Gibson
Vodka Gimlet
Vodka Grand Marnier
Vodka Grasshopper
Vodka Martini
Vodka Saketini
Vodka Sling
Vodka Soda
Vodka Sonic
Vodka Sour
Vodka Stinger
Vodka Tonic
Volga Boatman
Volga Cooler
Vulcan
Vulcan Blood
Vulcan Mind Probe
W. W. II
Wadkins Glen
Wall Street Lizard
Wally Wallbanger
Waltzing Matilda
Wandering Minstrel
Warsaw
Watermelon
Watermelon Martini
Well Red Rhino
Wet Dream
Whale's Tail
White Chocolate Martini
White Death
White Elephant
White Mink
White Russian
White Spider
Wiki Waki Woo
Wild Thing
Wildebeest
Windex
Woo Woo
Y. I.
Yellow Bird
Yellow Fever
Yellow Russian
Yellow Snow
Yo Mama
Yorsh
Zhivago Standard
Zipper Head
Zonker

VODKA (PEPPERED)

(continued)

Bloody Caesar
Bloody Mary
Bullshot
Cajun Martini
Creole Martini
Fahrenheit 5
Fireball 2
Firebird
Guillotine
Holy Hail Rosemary
Hot Dog
Louisiana Shooter
Oyster Shooter
Pepper Martini
Sparks
Spicy Sword
Starbursts
Texas Mary

VODKA (PINEAPPLE)

Cheap Shades
French Martini 2
Hooter
Naked Lady 2
Pearl Harbor
Pearl Harbor (frozen)
Sex in the Woods
Sex on the Beach 2
Sweet Release
Tropical Martini
Universal
Yellow Bird (frozen)
Yellow Snow

VODKA (RASPBERRY)

French Martini
French Martini 2
Midnight Dream
Killer Whale
Mooseberry
Nervous Breakdown
Purple Haze
Purple Haze 2
Purple Russian
Raspberry Beret
Raspberry Cosmopolitan
Raspberry Gimlet
Raspberry Smash
Raspberry Torte
Sex in the Hot Tub
Sex on the Beach 3
Vampire
White Death

VODKA (STRAWBERRY)

Love Potion #9
Metropolis Martini
Nuts and Berries 2
Red Russian
Snowberry
Strawberry Shortcake

VODKA (VANILLA)

Amber Martini
Banana Split
Berline Wall
Buttafinger
Buttafinger 2
Buttershot
Cherry Pie
Climax
Cream Soda
Fallen Angel
G-String
International Incident
Kiss
Laughy Taffy Martini
Las Brisas
Love Potion #9
Ninotchka
Nutcracker
Nutcracker 2

Nutcracker (frozen)
Nutty Bitch
Oil Slick
Orange Julius (frozen)
Or-E-Oh Cookie (frozen)
Orgasm
Orgasm 2
Pearl Necklace
Quaalude
Quaker City Cooler
Russian Pussy
Russian Quaalude
Russian Quaalude 2
Russian Quaalude (floater)
Russian Quaalude (frozen)
Screaming Orgasm
Screaming Yellow Monkey
Sex Machine
Silver Cloud
Swedish Bear
Toronto Orgy
Wandering Minstrel

WHISKEY

Alabama Slammer
Algonquin
Belfast Bomber
Bend Me Over
Bent Nail
Big Daddy
Black Hawk
Blinker
Blue Valium
Boilermaker
Bop The Princess
Cablegram
California Lemonade
Canada Cocktail
Canadian Blackberry Fizz
Canadian Cider
Depth Charge
De Rigueur
Dog Sled
Dry Manhattan
Dubonnet Manhattan
Duck Fart
Eden Roc Fizz
Empire State Slammer
Firecracker
Fox River
Frisco Sour
Gaelic Coffee
Gloomlifter
Hawaiian
Heartbreak
Henry Morgan's Grog
Highball
Horse's Neck
Hot Apple Toddy
Hot Toddy
Hunter's Cocktail
Incider
Ink Street
Irish Car Bomb
Japanese Fizz
John Collins
Klondike Cooler
Ladies
Lawhill
Linstead
Los Angeles Cocktail
Madeira Cocktail
Manhasset
Manhattan
Maple Leaf
Mexican Blackjack
Monte Carlo
Mother Love
New World
New York Cocktail
New York Slammer
New York Sour
Niagara Falls
Oh, Henry
Old Fashion
Old Groaner
Old Groaner's Wife
Opening
Oriental
Perfect Manhattan
Pink Almond
Pink Snapper
Prairie Oyster
Preakness

Press
Purple Jesus
Quebec
Raspberry Lime Rickey
Rattlesnake
Royal Canadian
Salty John
Seven And Seven
Seventh Heaven
Sharkey Punch
Snake Bite
Soul Kiss
Sour Apple
Split Milk
Tarantula
Temptation
Tennessee
Tom Mix High
Trois Rivieres
Twin Hills
Vancouver
Ward Eight
Warm Creamy Bush
Whippet
Whiskey And Branch
Whiskey And Water
Whiskey Collins
Whiskey Daisy
Whiskey Fix
Whiskey Highball
Whiskey Rickey
Whiskey Sour
Whiskey Zipper
Wind City
Yashmak
Zazarac

WINE (RED)

Appetizer
Cranes Beach Punch
Drunken Waiter
Gluewein
Mountain Red Punch
New York Sour
Port In A Storm
Prince Of Wales
Red Wine Cooler
Restoration
Sangria
Scumbucket
Spritzer
Wine Cooler
Wine Spritzer
Xalapa Punch

WINE (WHITE)

Fuzzy Guppie
Hawaiian Cocktail
Hillary Wallbanger
Kir
Leslie
Quaker City Cooler
Sangria Blanca
Scorpion
Spritzer
Tear Drop
White Cargo
White Water
Wind Surf
Wine Cooler
Wine Spritzer

YUKON JACK

Canadian Coffee
Caribou Screw
Frostbite
Gandy Dancer
H. D. Rider
Mackenzie Gold
Northern Lights
Pair Of Jacks
Panama Jack
Peckerhead
Pineapple Bomber
Rattlesnake
Red Death
Rocket
Shot In The Dark
Snake Bite
Spring Thaw
Sweaty Mexican Lumberjack
Terminator
Y 2 K
Yog